The Novel of the American West

The Novel of the American West

John R. Milton

University of Nebraska Press
Lincoln and London

Library of Congress Cataloging in Publication Data

Milton, John R
 The novel of the American West.

 Includes index.
 1. American fiction—The West—History and criticism. 2. The West in literature. I. Title.
PS3563.I454N68   813'.0874   79–17713
ISBN 0–8032–0980–0

Contents

	Preface	vii
	Introduction	xi
I	The Popular or Formula Western	1
II	The Writer's West	41
III	The Evolution of the Western Novel	65
IV	Vardis Fisher: The Struggle of Rationalism	117
V	The Historical Inheritance: Guthrie and Manfred	160
VI	Walter Van Tilburg Clark: The Western Attitude	195
VII	Harvey Fergusson and the Spanish Southwest	230
VIII	Intuition and the Dance of Life: Frank Waters	264
IX	The Distant Music: Variations on Western Realism	298
	List of Works Cited	325
	Index	333

Preface

Western American literature, especially the travel narrative and the novel, has become increasingly respectable during the past twenty-five years, taking its place alongside the traditional and conventional courses in many colleges and universities in the United States and becoming a source of study for European students as well. To mention this fact is to recall that as recently as 1950 the academic struggle for equality—waged by American literature students and teachers in English departments favoring British literature—was just concluding. To go a step further at that time and ask for full recognition of the western novel was considered heresy. In addition to my reading in the more serious fiction of the West in those days, I also read—perhaps in defiance of the establishment—over five hundred popular westerns of the kind I castigate to a certain extent in Chapter I. Although most of this reading was not allowed to penetrate my graduate studies, I owe a debt of gratitude to Henry Nash Smith who was writing *Virgin Land* the year that I took a course from him called "The Literature of the Far West." My own interests have shifted somewhat to the Interior West, but I must acknowledge the influence of Smith on my early concern with the American West. The West has been subject to its own geographical distinctions for some time, and the first academic attention to its literature was regional—The Literature of the Southwest, of the Northwest, of the Far West, for example. By the late 1950s a few college courses had been established in order to examine the literature of the entire West, taking the most significant work from each of the internal regions. Meanwhile, literary quarterlies—particularly in the Southwest—were publishing articles on western writers. Further impetus came from the founding of the *South Dakota Review* in 1963 and *Western American Literature* in 1966. The latter was accompanied by the formation of the Western Literature Association, a professional organization which in just a few years had a membership of almost two hundred. It is no longer necessary for a graduate student in literature to hide his face in shame merely because he has enjoyed reading Owen Wister or Zane Grey, to say nothing of Vardis Fisher or Walter Van Tilburg Clark.

Because popular culture is now being taken seriously, in its many dimensions, the cowboy novel or western (both in print or as filmed) has joined the detective story and the science-fiction story as legitimate material for scholarly scrutiny. Although I am in sympathy with the popular culture movement, and although I have found much of interest in the many westerns I have read during the past thirty years, I find it necessary to criticize the lack of literary quality in the standard western in order to draw distinctions between this one kind of novel of the West and another kind which is a much higher form of art. It is my hope that the general reader will find names, titles, and ideas which are familiar to him in the first three chapters and will be encouraged to pursue some of the more detailed discussions of individual writers in the succeeding chapters. For the scholar, the teacher, and the serious student of the western novel, I offer interpretations and suggestions which will, it is to be hoped, lead to further discussion of the western novel.

Along the way, in my own studies, I have acquired debts which cannot be repaid, especially to the writers I have known personally. Vardis Fisher, Harvey Fergusson, Walter Van Tilburg Clark, Wallace Stegner, William Eastlake, Paul Horgan, Forrester Blake, Michael Straight, John Steinbeck, Max Evans and others have all been willing to share ideas with me over the years. To Frederick Manfred I need only mention a date—February 9, 1953. He will know the rest. To Frank Waters I owe more than can be said here, and more than he will acknowledge. He has been more responsible than anyone else in urging me to complete this book, although he cannot be held accountable for anything I have said about the western novel. My thanks, also, to 'Richard Etulain and his gentle prodding at times when my priorities were disarranged. And last, but always first, I thank my wife, Lynn, and daughter, Nanci, for their patience and understanding when I put work before pleasure.

For permission to use passages from a few of my essays published earlier in periodicals, I wish to thank the editors of *Critique, Kansas Quarterly, Midwest Quarterly, Rendezvous, Western American Literature,* and *Western Humanities Review.* Their gracious cooperation allowed me to avoid going over for the second time certain ideas which I find still tenable.

J. R. M.

Introduction

Anyone reading a standard literary history of the United States might wonder where the American West really is. Ohio is frequently referred to as the Old Northwest, Daniel Boone in Kentucky is seen as a westerner, Edward Eggleston's novels of the Indiana backwoods have been referred to as western, and the Nebraska of Willa Cather's novels has at least once been called Midwest and West on the same page. Historically, of course, the West was all the land on the other side of the frontier line as it moved from the Atlantic to the Pacific Ocean, and so, presumably, the West shrank in size as the frontier made its way across the continent. When the frontier closed (in 1890, according to Frederick Jackson Turner), that should have been the end of the West, and yet we know that it was not. What we do not always agree upon is a precise description of the twentieth-century American West which has been removed from the relatively easy definitions made possible during the two hundred years of frontier lines. For the New Yorker, Indiana may well be the West even now. (Indeed, not long ago I heard of a college course in Western American literature which, on its way west, stopped with Theodore Dreiser.) Generally, however, we have settled on a few basic regional distinctions: East, South, Midwest, West, and Pacific Coast.

Regional culturalists such as Raymond D. Gastil divide the larger areas into subregions, so that the West may consist of the Rocky Mountain Region, the Mormon Region, the Interior Southwest, the Pacific Southwest, and the Pacific Northwest. Further complications arise from attempts to locate that often elusive dividing line between the Midwest and the West. Walter Prescott Webb draws it roughly along the ninety-eighth meridian. His reasoning is that west of this line the "rainfall is insufficient for the ordinary intensive agriculture common to lands of a humid climate." The line might serve its purpose even better if it were pushed west a little to the one-hundredth meridian, which approximates the line of the Missouri River as it flows in a north-south direction through the Dakotas. Gastil uses the term *intensive agriculture* also—in this case to aid in a description of the Midwest—and so rainfall does indeed seem to be a major factor in determining the difference between Midwest and West. When other characteristics are considered, the differences may be less noticeable because people are at least somewhat the same in all regions. John Fraser Hart lists as midwest traits the following: pecuniaristic, materialistic, self-assured, functionalist, technologic, competent, simplistic, present-oriented, and xenophobic. If I were to suggest that the westerner is only the last of these (xenophobic), as I would like to, I would also be simplistic. Characteristics differ largely by degree, rather than by kind, as the rainfall also differs by degree. Midwest does not bump up against West at a particular place or through a particular person at any given time. However, there does exist a recognizable transition zone between the two regions, a zone within which rainfall is moderate and the people are not sure what to call themselves. Crossing the one-hundredth meridian, the traveler going west feels that he has also crossed the zone, although he cannot say exactly when or where the change occurred.

If we allow in our distinctions a tolerance, and do not insist upon absolutes, then we can make at least a few sugges-tions. The West is a place of aridity where the terms of the land are accepted rather than opposed. The pragmatism of the Midwest is at least partially replaced by pantheism and mysticism, signs that the West is nature-oriented. Isolation in the West, caused by wide spaces and relatively few people, leads to self-sufficiency as well as friendliness, even though the self-sufficiency may be individualistic only, frequently breaking down in the face of wide-scale group hardship which results in a call for federal aid. In literature, Roy W. Meyer, writing about the midwestern farm novel, suggests that its main function was to publicize, "to the end that social and economic conditions may be improved." The western novel is not nearly as pragmatic or propagandistic, emphasizing instead man's relation to the land and to history and relying at least as much on intuition as on reason. Desert, mountains, plains, high plateaus—a great variety of physiographic features—replace farmland. The culture and history of the Indians, as well as the Spanish, become important, often leading to a spiritual harmony between man and the land. It is this spirit as much as anything else that identifies the West of the kind of novel which I wish to discuss. It involves, usually, an almost religious response to the land and an acceptance of values which are recognized through intuition rather than reason. Therefore, it is not always possible to include the Pacific Coast states as part of the West, especially the modern Los Angeles culture which is a phenomenon of its own, or perhaps a vulgarization of the East. Steinbeck's novels of the 1930s could probably not be written in the 1970s, although the southwest fiction of Harvey Fergusson and Frank Waters could, because New Mexico has not undergone the extensive changes that California has. In Oregon and Washington, especially on the coastal side of the mountains, rainfall more nearly matches that of the Midwest, giving the relationship between man and land different emphases. (The mysticism of Pacific Northwest painter Morris Graves has not been evident in the literature of that region.) Furthermore, within the Interior West, the arid or semiarid region of great plains and mountains, not every writer has responded to the environment or the people in the same way. Willa Cather and Paul Horgan differ from Waters and Walter Van Tilburg Clark at least partly because they place less emphasis upon the land and its influence on character. And so my selection of writers for this study has been made not only on the basis of their productivity within the West, and not only on questions of artistry, but also according to their attention to man's psychological and spiritual relationship with the land.

Aside from these distinctions, it is necessary to make another, an extremely important one, between two kinds of fiction in the West. The popular, commercial, or formula novel discussed in Chapter I is a subliterary form designed to exploit the myths of the Old West, to reach a mass audience, and to provide entertainment through outdoor adventures involving heroes and villains. This is the western novel with which most people are familiar and whose chief practitioners (Max Brand, Zane Grey, Luke Short, and Louis L'Amour) are known by name, at least, to almost everyone. Here again, as with the line between Midwest and West, we cannot be as precise as we might like to be, and we must recognize a wide range of competence within the group of writers identified with what I shall call the lowercase *w* western. And, here too, there is a transition zone made up of such novelists as Jack Schaefer, Benjamin Capps, Tom Lea, Alan Le May, Dan Cushman, Oakley Hall, Elliott Arnold, and others who transcend the formula western but fall short of the high seriousness and literary quality of the best of the Western novelists. The novel which is the main subject of the present study, and which I shall call the capital *W* Western novel, is literary. It is as well written and as significant as the nonwestern novel which is given extended treatment in most American literary histories and in thematic and technical studies of "Modern American Fiction," or "American Fiction of the Forties," or "The American Novel." Yet, of the fourteen writers to whom I give most consideration following Chapter III in this study of the Western novel, only two (Cather and Steinbeck) are discussed in the most recent (1974) edition of the standard *Liter-*

ary History of the United States, another two are only mentioned by name (Fergusson and Fisher), and the other ten are not listed in the index.

One of the reasons for the critical neglect of the serious Western novelist is that his work—because it is set in the West—is carelessly thrown into the pot of the formula western. My purpose is to suggest, at least, that there are novels of the American West which rank with the best novels of any other region in the United States. Toward that end I have chastised the small *w* western a little too harshly in Chapter I, in order to set it aside from the serious literary Western novel. The first deals in stereotyped characters and stock patterns of action; it exploits the myths of the frontier; it depends upon a two-sided morality of good and evil, neglecting the many complexities of the human condition; it is characterized by sameness through hundreds of books, many of which were written by just a few people using up to twenty pseudonyms each. The second is of high literary quality (although in varying degrees, of course), is sensitive to human behavior as well as to meaningful qualities of the land, is conscious of the relationship between the historical past and the present, is engaged in defining western man (in both senses of the term *western*), and is concerned with several kinds of reality. Although the land itself is usually a powerful force in the Western novel, the realization of character remains a primary task, as it must in all significant fiction. Finally, while the Western novel is regional in its setting (as all novels are, from whatever region), its themes are in no way confined to a geographical area. Historically, spiritually, psychologically, symbolically, and archetypically, they rise above the region of their roots.

Chapter III describes the development of the Western novel and touches on a variety of writers, themes, and techniques. My choice of six novelists for lengthy discussion in Chapters IV through VIII is based upon several factors: understanding of the West, experience in the West, sensitivity to place and theme and character, and productivity within the context of the West. Much more could be written about the eight novelists who are grouped in Chapter IX, but for my purposes they are not equally representative of Western fiction. Nevertheless each makes his or her important contribution. It is not my intention to write a definitive history of the Western American novel. What I wish to do here is to shed a little light on the major writers, their insights and intuitions, their strengths and weaknesses, and their right to a place in American letters, so that their understanding of nature and human nature may be shared by more readers. The American West is often misunderstood; its literature, too often relegated to the realm of idle curiosity, not only leads to an understanding of the region from which it springs, but also adds significantly to our knowledge of the American character, of what can be learned from nonrational sources of thought, and of the importance of the land (or earth) which supports man's endeavors if treated properly.

The Novel of the American West

I
The Popular or Formula Western

The kind of novel we call the western evokes a variety of critical responses, both antagonistic and sympathetic. Acceptable as a popular and justifiable escape mechanism, designed to accommodate personal and mass fantasies, the western may be denied the status of legitimate literature on the grounds that it is better approached and studied in a cultural, historical, or psychological context than in strictly literary terms. The western seems to explain to us something about ourselves and our dreams, on both a personal and national level. And it may, in certain cases, provide an authentic portrait of the people of the Old West—cowboy, Indian, soldier, miner, rancher, explorer, railroad builder, saloon girl, outlaw, town marshal, and so on. It may be regarded as pastoral (and therefore nostalgic) or it may be a combination of the two: the peaceful and innocent natural life may be disrupted and spoiled by the violence and carelessness of man, or man's tendency toward violence may be relieved by the beauty of the land or the inherent goodness of nature.

Depending upon the viewpoint of the observer, then, standards for judging the western may be couched in cultural terms which establish relationships between the myths of the Old West and the national character, part of which has been influenced by the long-standing American Dream; or they

may be based on the question of authenticity, deeming a novel
good if it seems to portray the Old West accurately and
realistically; or the standards may be literary ones, in which
the novel is judged on its artistic merits quite apart from the
subject matter. Since we are dealing with fiction, the latter of
these approaches would seem to be the proper one, and yet it
is used least often of the three. Part of the problem here is that
there are different kinds of westerns, the differences showing
up largely in the vision (or lack of it) and competence (or in-
competence) of the writers of these novels. We need, first, to
identify a novel of the West which can be called, simply, a
western, and which differs somewhat from another kind of
novel, also of the West, which is more literary and which deserves a separate name such as the Western (capitalized) novel,
or the Western regional novel.

One way of making the distinction is by saying that the
(inferior) western is set in the West deliberately in order to exploit a romantic and adventurous situation which becomes a
commodity for sale in the mass market. In this case the West
as a place (and it is almost always the nineteenth-century
West) is chosen for its built-in appeal to the public. On the
other hand, the genuine, serious Western novel is set in the
West because its author lives there, because it is a result of his
own experience, because it represents the regional environment he knows best. Or, to put it somewhat differently, the
writer of the Western novel takes the West seriously, while
the writer of the western does not. While my chief concern in
this book is the literary Western novel which can hold its
own, artistically, with the better novels of any other region, it
may be useful to discuss first (but not exhaustively) the
phenomenon which, on the printed page or on the television
screen, is known as the western. Even within this genre it is
possible to identify different levels of competence, different
degrees of actual western experience, and different intentions
(such as to create or to sell). Occasionally a good writer believes that he can best serve his ideas through the conventional
western rather than through a more complex novel which will
be read by fewer people.

And so we turn our attention first to the popularity of the western. Why has it been read by so many people during the past three-quarters of a century, and why have western movies enjoyed the same popularity since the days of the silent screen, and why were westerns one of the stable commodities during the days of the television explosion even though many people referred to them as "horse operas"? By mentioning motion pictures and television we are already clouding the issue somewhat because many studies of the western are limited to those two media and their place in popular culture—books having become less important, apparently, in recent years—and yet the written word comes first. While the motion picture and television may linger in the background, it is the written novel, the book, to which I refer as the western. It is this kind of novel which has provided America's own romance, or romantic adventure, in the tradition of the novels of Sir Walter Scott and has at the same time supplied one or more cultural images which are recognized— if not understood—by everyone. For a time the most important of these images was the cowboy, seen as a unique figure and symbol in the context of the American West, seen, indeed, as the American hero. Conveniently forgotten were the Mexican *vaquero*, the Argentinean *gaucho*, the Venezuelan *llanero*, and the Chilean *buaso*, also Americans in the broadest geographical sense of the term but considered cultural foreigners, if considered at all. *Our* cowboy has been special in that he is associated historically with the expansion of the United States, with the American Dream, and with the need for heroes in a young country. The exploitation of the cowboy is based upon a relatively short historical period, from just after the Civil War to the great blizzards of 1886–87, and the brevity of the phenomenon may account for the continued desire to resurrect the cowboy and give him his due. He resides in the past as surely as do the medieval knights on horseback, whom he replaces in a very real sense.

The western got a boost from mass publishing which grew up alongside the cowboy and it appealed to eastern readers who wanted to share vicariously in the exploits taking place in a raw new land where men were men and the landscape took on an exotic and alluring flavor, even though it was mostly dust that the cowboy himself tasted. In this strange land, like a foreign country to most of the readers in the United States, morality plays were acted out (according to the novels), with good confronting evil and always defeating it. This was an extremely satisfying revelation to the good people of the East who had their own problems with various kinds of evil, who felt frustrated, and who could participate in the destruction of their enemies and their devils without getting involved personally, without going beyond the pages of a book. The reader could, in effect, identify with the gunslinger (whether cowboy, marshal, or maverick) and work out his own fantasies of power and skill and individualism, bypassing the repressions and restrictions of real-life society. Even in the midst of world political conflicts (1890–1920) and the national depression (1929–34) and the approach of World War II, it was possible to escape momentarily into a simpler world, a more interesting world, a more satisfying world, by reading westerns, early science fiction, and the adventures of Tarzan, all of which achieved their initial popularity shortly after the turn of the century. Unlike the complexities of real life, the patterns of behavior in the western have been fairly simple and reasonably clear-cut: romance, adventure, psychological fulfillments or expressions, a reminder of individual freedom, and the overriding allegory of good triumphing over evil. The western, therefore, was both entertaining and comforting.

In some respects it may seem that I have done (and will continue to do) an injustice to the western by oversimplifying it. Nevertheless, granting the exceptions and the occasional complications (some of them leading to a deeper level of meaning or more significant insights into the human condition), it is apparent that the normal or typical western is the result of a series of patterns and intentions which will seem to be formulaic. It is not likely that any one writer invented the complete formula or suggested the variations which might be played upon it. John G. Cawelti has said that Cooper created the western, but other candidates for this dubious honor have been proposed also: Bret Harte, Edward Ellis, or Edward Wheeler of the dime-novel era, Owen Wister, and Zane Grey, not counting the somewhat remote possibility of direct influence from the Mexican *vaquero* narrative or the South American *gaucho* novel. Because James Fenimore Cooper was the first American writer to use the frontier as a continuing theme (in the Leatherstocking Series), and because he was also a reputable writer whose influence could not go unnoticed, it was probably he who began the line of descent of which the western of the early twentieth century is the grandchild. Since Cooper also contributed to the development of the more serious and literary Western novel, we must recognize that from a literary viewpoint his Leatherstocking novels were inconsistent, with meaningful themes often partially obscured by bad writing. In general, it is the Cooper vices rather than the virtues which sired the western. And we must recognize also that much of what we condemn in Cooper was standard procedure in his time for the novel of romance and adventure, for the sentimental novel which Cooper inherited from Sir Walter Scott. For Cooper's readers the American frontier was just as remote as the medieval England of *Ivanhoe*. (For those who like coincidences which may or may not be meaningful, the publication date of *Ivanhoe*, 1820, is also the year of Daniel Boone's death—Boone being, probably, the model for Leatherstocking—and precedes the publication of Cooper's *Pioneers* by three years.) Remoteness, either in time or in distance, lends itself to the myths of romance and to the coloring, excitement, and allure of the exotic. The frontier of Western America now recedes from us in time, and that widening gap between the contemporary world and the world of the Old West serves to make the great deeds—whether actual or legendary—even more fascinating. America, in the short span of a century or two, has established its own mythical past, a set of traditions and heroes which continue to serve the needs of the nonheroic people of a settled and civilized nation. There is, of course, a certain amount of irony in "settled" and "civilized," considering the violence which persists within our society, most of it having shifted from the rural frontier to the city.

The violence in Cooper is the rather normal kind attendant to the chase-capture-escape (and sometimes further pursuit) pattern which makes up the basic plot structure of the adventure story, or the romance. In terms of myth as well, we may speak of the perilous journey, the struggle between the hero and his opposition, and finally, in either the death or the victory of the hero, an exaltation of the hero himself or of goodness or of the human spirit. The pattern is repeated many times in the Leatherstocking Tales, although the final tribute to the spirit of Natty Bumppo does not come until his peaceful death of old age in *The Prairie* (1827). Because of the frontier setting, most of the violence occurs in brief or extended warfare between whites and Indians. Cooper does not dwell upon it; frequently his narrative moves so quickly and (as in *The Last of the Mohicans*, 1826) is so full of suspense and dramatic climaxes that the reader is swept off his feet and forgets the details which may have been technically inept or wrong or bathed in sentimentality as well as in violence. Since Cooper maintained an ambivalent attitude toward his Indians, the stereotyped set of characters is more easily seen in the non-Indian cast. Such stereotypes are common in the sentimental novel and, although they are not the same characters found in most westerns, they at least indicate a part of the Cooper method which survived through Bret Harte to the later western novel. With some variations the cast of Cooper characters includes a hero who is at home in the natural world, heroines who are probably based on the author's daughters, a weak and evil guardian, a romantic lover, a comic bore, a mysterious old man, a primitive white man (these last two could both be Natty Bumppo in *The Prairie*), and an old soldier. Characterization does not run deep, although Bumppo emerges from the five novels in the series as a relatively complex person. The women are conventional and usually support the notion that almost all of Cooper's characters are "clothes upon a stick." Certainly the psychology of the characters is very simple and their actions are quite predictable. Even Cooper's attitude toward the Indians takes on a simplistic quality revealed largely in the easy division of the natives into good people and bad people, with little or nothing left for the less obvious middle ground. With a tendency to the heroic, minor variations played upon a few reoccurring terms, conventional moral standards, and a touch of humor which often approaches burlesque, the Cooper novel of the frontier provides standards that leave much to be desired in terms of significant literature. However, beneath the exaggerations of style and characterization and plot, all of which show up in the western of the early twentieth century, there is often an authenticity of person and place which also becomes a concern for later writers.

The popularity of the Leatherstocking Tales has been of two kinds. For the more serious readers, and writers, Cooper's insights into the dilemmas of the frontier have been important. For the casual reader, the one who desires to be entertained, the conventions of the sentimental novel and the Scott romance are probably convenient. The excitement of the chase helps to conceal the fact that the chase itself is one of the conventions. It may be more difficult to ignore the stereotyping of the characters, and yet the psychological simplicity of the Cooper people may be an aid in telling a story for purposes of entertainment. Cooper dealt with sexes, races, classes, and nationalities rather than with individuals. The characterization, instead of being detailed and personal, is usually vague and generalized and padded with stock phrases and abstract qualifications. With few exceptions, these people move unswervingly through the novels without acquiring any new traits or characteristics, without losing any of the attitudes they started with, and without lapsing into any of the inconsistencies or eccentricities which we associate with most real people. In this respect, Cooper has no problems—nor do his readers. His characters are not going to fool him; after he has marked them and introduced them to the reader, and sent them on their ways, they will move rather mechanically through the action, not swerving from the preset path. A

similar condition prevails as part of the western formula in the
post-Wister era and allows the reader to relax and be entertained, knowing more or less what the outcome will be. This
very fact, I think, accounts for much of the popularity of any
literary genre which is based essentially upon a formula of
some kind.

Natty Bumppo himself, although at least partially a
descendant of various heroic types throughout English literature, is a prototype of the uniquely American hero associated
with the frontier and with the opening of the West. He is a
simple child of nature, unsophisticated enough to appeal to
the child in us all and to allow us to feel superior to him if we
wish. He symbolizes the reaction against organized society,
the idea of freedom and individualism, and the utter goodness
which is presumably to be found in the primitive wilderness
yet unstained by civilization. He is natural man. His virtues
are to be found in the Boy Scout recitation, in which the scout
declares himself to be (or desires to be) trustworthy, loyal,
helpful, friendly, courteous, kind, obedient, cheerful, thrifty,
brave, clean, and reverent. This ideal need not be achieved
fully by the wilderness hero, of course, because historical
events and cultural changes in a society lead to changing demands upon the hero. Among Cooper's contemporaries,
Robert Montgomery Bird (*Nick of the Woods*, 1837) created an
Indian-hating woodsman, Nathan Slaughter, who has been
called a better-realized character than any in Cooper. James
Kirke Paulding (*Westward Ho!*, 1832) also used a woodsman—
Ambrose Bushfield—who hated Indians. *The Yemassee*, by
William Gilmore Simms (1835), includes a study of the Indian which is often considered the most influential of its time,
with the exception of Cooper's. And so the public attitude, as
revealed in the reception of these novels, was divided even in
Cooper's time over the status and worth of the American Indian. All of these early frontier writers worked in the tradition
of Walter Scott, however. One Bird novel, *The Hawks of
Hawks-Hollow* (1835), came to the attention of Poe, who said
that it was too much like Scott. Since the western is almost a

century away from these novels, it is difficult to claim any direct influence. In one respect, Cooper, Bird, Paulding, Simms, and others were simply in at the beginning of American literature's recognition of the wilderness, the frontier, the Indian, and the woodsman as parts of a legitimate American theme. In the influence of Scott, however, we find the continuing popularity of the romantic adventure story. Many of the devices and techniques of this kind of novel persisted into the twentieth century.

Bypassing nonfictional accounts of the frontier as it moved westward, although eventually they supplied grist for the fictional mill, we note a gap of slightly more than two decades between the publication of *The Deerslayer* in 1841 and four almost simultaneous phenomena which had a great deal to do with the development of the modern western. The first dime novel was published in 1860, the cattle industry began to thrive shortly after the Civil War, Bret Harte's famous stories "The Luck of Roaring Camp" and "The Outcasts of Poker Flat" were published in 1868 and 1869, and gold was officially reported in the Black Hills of South Dakota in 1874. From this series of events came an impetus toward the western novel which did not diminish for almost a century and has not yet disappeared, nor is it likely to.

Is it only a coincidence that the man who established the weekly series of "Dime Novels" grew up in the Cooper country of New York? As much as I would like to absolve Cooper of the uncounted literary sins committed in his name, it seems almost impossible to divorce him from the superficial western fiction which followed his Leatherstocking Tales. Erastus Beadle, later of the Beadle and Adams publishing company, moved to New York City and issued the first dime novel in June, 1860—*Malaeska*, by Mrs. S. Stephens. She was to write a dime novel based upon a Daniel Boone-Natty Bumppo figure in 1869, and Beadle was to commission hundreds of the short tales selling for ten cents each, devoted to adventure and thrills, and rarely exceeding thirty-thousand words in length. His intention was to create mass distribution of fiction, which he did; in order to do so, he had to find themes and techniques which would appeal to a mass audience—readers of popular rather than serious fiction—and he had to employ writers who could turn out stories quickly. The assembly-line method of writing and publication led immediately and inevitably to a formula story. Who had time to be original and literary? Not all of the dime novels were based on cowboys, of course, just as the modern western should not be defined only in terms of the cowboy; but, the frontier West with its wildness and romance, its distance from the realities of organized society, and its surface of historical incidents became the setting of most of the dime novels.

That Beadle succeeded in his enterprise is obvious. The first series of novels or tales had more than three hundred titles; over a period of thirty years there were more than thirty series. The number of titles becomes staggering. The impact upon the nation's readers, and upon writers who wished to make a living from their stories, was greater than we now care to admit as we attempt to find some redeeming grace in the modern western. And, Cooper's ghost lingered for a long time. *Seth Jones*, by Edward Ellis (No. 8 in the first Beadle series), was not set in the West but was a Vermont "frontier" story using a Leatherstocking model, and was only the first of many hunter stories produced by Ellis. As the nation moved west, the emphasis shifted to Kit Carson, then to Buffalo Bill Cody, and finally to Deadwood Dick, a completely fictional character named after the town of Deadwood in the Black Hills. The line of descent from Cooper to Edward Wheeler (the creator of Deadwood Dick) is neither direct nor clearly demonstrable, but after disallowing place and author as sequential elements it is possible to trace a reasonably legitimate line through the chief characters of popular fiction from Leatherstocking to Deadwood Dick and beyond. The hunter, scout, lawman, child of nature, savior of the oppressed— whatever he is to be called—persists in popular fiction to the present day, sometimes in contrast to, and often sharing the basic characteristics of, the heroes of other types of popular fiction such as the detective story. In fact, many of the chief characters in the dime novel—in each of the series— were Pinkerton agents or detectives.

Although Wheeler gave most of his attention to Deadwood Dick, and Prentiss Ingraham and Edward Z. C. Judson (Ned Buntline) became major dime novelists (the term is appropriate) after they chose Buffalo Bill as subject, the distinction between the invented character and the historical character was slight if it existed at all. The advantage gained by writing about Buffalo Bill was that he could be brought to the East to provide live advertising for the frontier myth. But myth it remained, because the purpose of the dime novel was not to portray the West or its people accurately and honestly but to provide the exaggeration and sensationalism which would appeal to the emotions and the sense of adventure of the mass audience. It mattered little that the dime novel fostered standard plots and characters. Indeed, these may have been a commercial virtue since the public seemed to want a formula, a mythical West which was romantic and heroic in nature and which entertained and titillated. Stories were rushed into print, and if each one sounded a little like the others it was unimportant as long as they continued to sell. Buffalo Bill stories went well past seven hundred in number. The Deadwood Dick stories of the Beadle's Half-Dime Library were so successful that a separate Deadwood Dick Library was established for more than 120 issues.

The cowboy crept into the dime novels in the late 1880s, but more as a gunman fighting outlaws and Indians, much as the hunter and scout had done earlier. Beadle retired from the Beadle and Adams publishing firm in the late 1880s also, and, as we recall that Frederick Jackson Turner set 1890 as the closing of the frontier, we might speculate that the entire western phenomenon could have—or should have—stopped right there. But the glamour and romance of the Wild West had been solidly established, and pulp magazines of the 1890s to the 1930s provided the link between the best-selling years of the dime novel and the early years of the modern western.

And, although the formula itself underwent slight changes as the western developed, the fact remains that this kind of fiction, based largely upon a West that existed for a relatively short time, owes its existence to literary conventions, to formulas, to sameness, and to a world that is more real in the imagination than it is in fact.

This is not to say that the facts were never there. One of the prime influences upon the dime novel was the cast of characters assembled in or near Deadwood, Dakota Territory, in 1876, two years after Custer dispatches mentioned the presence of gold in that area. There may be some significance in the date itself—the one hundredth birthday of the nation. Or the attention focused upon Deadwood at that time may have been the result of a realization that the frontier had almost run its course and this was the last chance to exploit it. The death of Custer that same year, not many miles away in Montana, undoubtedly stirred the public into a new interest in the Indians, the cavalry, and, by association, all the other elements of the Western atmosphere. It was not difficult to bring old stereotypes and familiar prototypes (such as Daniel Boone and Leatherstocking and Kit Carson) into a new setting, the mining camps of a gold field. Indeed, Bret Harte had already done so, with variations, in California. And so, while the stories were essentially the same, the names were new: Buffalo Bill, Wild Bill, Deadwood Dick, Captain Jack, Sam Bass, Whispering Smith, among others, and a new heroine, Calamity Jane.

It was the mining camps of California that Bret Harte mined for his own kind of gold. Harte went from New York to California in 1854 to become the editor of the *Overland Monthly*. Two of his own stories published in that magazine made him an instant success as a writer. "The Luck of Roaring Camp" and "The Outcasts of Poker Flat" were made of humor, pathos, and sentiment (like many of the stories which followed), and their creator was immediately acclaimed in the East as a Western American Charles Dickens. For a few years Harte was perhaps more popular than any American writer at

any time. Some of his success stemmed from a common nineteenth-century controversy over the nature of man. Rousseau
had suggested that primitive man was good and that civilized
man was tainted by the very society he had made for himself.
Like many other writers, Harte seems to take the paradoxical
view that man is both evil and good. However, he suggests
that goodness is inherent and that it can be revived (when
necessary) or regenerated by a life in the West, that is to say a
life away from the stifling influences of the city and the arti-
ficialities of a highly organized society. (This view is not unlike that of Frank Norris at the turn of the century.) In Harte's
stories it is not uncommon for a man to wash himself in the
pure air of the mountains and suddenly put off his inclinations
toward evil. This is the sentimental approach, and most of
Harte's techniques and routines seem designed to promote
pathos or simple wonder. His landscape, occasionally seen in
a fresh manner, is more often "singularly wild," and his characters are types rather than individuals. Harte tries to give
them the effect of realism, but he also achieves a strong sense
of the exotic—a wonderland far from the eastern cities. The
mixture proved to be just what his readers wanted, and Harte
continued to feed them his formula. How many of the stereotyped miners, soldiers, cowboys, and Indians in the dime
novel and in the modern western are attributable to Harte is
difficult to say; but Harte was probably as responsible as anyone for establishing certain patterns in western fiction which
are even yet plaguing the western writer.

Bret Harte's detractors have suggested that he did not
have enough experience in the mines or in the mountains to
describe them faithfully. It is a charge that has been leveled
against many writers who have made fiction of the West their
profession without having lived in the West. But the charge is
also an oversimplification of the problem. Before Harte returned to New York in 1871 to receive a hero's welcome, he
had at least lived in California long enough to become thoroughly acquainted with the mountains and the mining camps
if he had wanted to. It is more likely that he did indeed come

into contact with the realities of the camps but that he chose to alter that reality, or to overemphasize those aspects which he knew would service his stories better while he was aiming them at a Dickens-oriented reading public in the East. In short, he exploited his materials, giving them a sentimental background, a repeated pattern of stock situations and characters, and a strangeness of scene which appealed to his readers' romantic bent in all stories from the other end of a wide continent. It is easy to parody most of Harte's stories. Some are better than others and allow us to give the writer his due as a minor artist. But his most popular stories, such as "The Outcasts of Poker Flat," are incredibly bad by modern standards. "Outcasts" has the cool, imperturbable gambler who, after being exiled from the town, gives his life (in vain) for his fellow outcasts; the prostitute who dies in the arms of a virgin, both covered and cleansed and united by the falling snow; a young girl who is introduced to the reader as she steps from behind a pine tree and whose name turns out to be Piney Woods; and the implication that these mavericks from society are ultimately better and purer people than those who, in righteous indignation, exiled them from the town. Harte was probably correct in his assumptions, thematically, but he milked his rather sparse materials for all they were worth while remaining at a great distance, psychologically, from them. However much we may admire Bret Harte for his talent—and it was not small—we cannot ignore his primary motive of exploitation which brought him to New York and to success at the very time that Mark Twain was burlesquing him in at least one episode (the snow storm) of *Roughing It* (1872).

Exploitation is very likely the key word in any study of the popular literature of the West and in the adherence to a formula of some kind which serves as an easy reference for the mass audience of this literature. After the hunter, the scout, the Pinkerton detective, the miner, and the plainsman, the cowboy was next to be exploited.

Although stray cattle had been rounded up in Texas and along the Mexican border in the 1830s by hired hands called cowboys, the cattle industry as such, and the golden years of the cowboy, began in force at the end of the Civil War, when the West was a place where the disgruntled easterners and the dispossessed southerners could find refuge or anonymity, and when a few wet years turned the plains into a sea of grass. Many investors went west, including a large number from England and Scotland, to take advantage of the cattle boom and seek fortunes. The industry expanded recklessly as huge herds were driven north, newspapers spread the story of wealth (such as Charles Goodnight's million-acre ranch), and for a while cows took the place of gold in the American myth of Eden. During the 1870s the number of cattle in three states (Colorado, Wyoming, and Montana) jumped from one hundred thousand to one and three-quarters million. During the same period the human population multiplied many times in Texas (where the cattle originated) and Kansas (where the railroad was available for shipping). The industry peaked between 1880 and 1885 and then the boom ended rather abruptly as a result of overstocking the ranges, fencing by farmers who were also seeking land in the West, drought, and finally the great blizzards of 1886–87 during which an estimated 80 percent of the range cattle perished. By this time, however, the cowboy was already established as a romantic hero, riding the lonely range and undergoing hardships while maintaining a sense of humor and a chivalric attitude toward women. The knights of the plains, they were called. And, although that appellation did not stick for long in the general vocabulary, it called up an obvious comparison between the cowboy and the medieval knight (perhaps from King Arthur tales) which remained in many of the books written about the cowboy. This man who herded cows worked his way into the public imagination and stayed there. No single cowboy stands out in legend or fact to match Kit Carson, Daniel Boone, Hugh Glass, or Buffalo Bill among the scouts and hunters, and this may in itself account for part of the popularity of the cowboy image—he *was* mainly an image. Charles Goodnight, Nelson Story, Ike Pryor, Oliver Loving, and other cattlemen have indeed become the models for characters in some westerns, but it is not the individual cowboy who matters. It is the stereotype, and in popular fiction it is the stereotype which has the appeal. And so what remains, in fiction and in the imagination of the public, is the legendary cowboy who has in the past seventy-five years ridden through an amazing number of bad novels and a few good ones.

The phenomenon which is the cowboy story, or western, has become so deeply ingrained in our emotions, if not in our minds, that we are still arguing about the merits of the story and the characteristics of the "real" cowboy who provided the initial interest. Most readers are willing to settle for the myth or image fostered by the writers who found their own gold in the formula western story, a financial reward which has in many cases exceeded that of the cattle barons themselves. Detractors of the western, determined to get at the facts, point to Charles A. Siringo's *A Texas Cowboy* (1885), or *The Log of a Cowboy* (1903), by Andy Adams, both written from actual experience. Neither of these books has had the influence exerted by Wister's *Virginian* (1902) or Grey's *Riders of the Purple Sage* (1912). Since we are dealing with a stereotype in the western, we can even forget that there might be differences among cowboys just as their forerunners, the mountain men and hunters, had individual differences. The image destroys the depth of character, the eccentricities, the complexities, the idiosyncrasies which make one man stand apart from another. What the western formula did was to make a simple two-part division into the good and the bad. And even on this score we are at the mercy of the writer's ethics, unable to decide for ourselves what or who is good and what is bad.

Nevertheless, the image seems to take on more than one form, especially as we see it in light of two portraits of the cowboy as he *really* was. From a variety of early accounts we can piece together one portrait that is quite bland. The cowboy drank and gambled only to relieve the monotony of his drab and dull life. He was underpaid because in the early West there was not enough capital for investment. He carried a gun only to arouse the cattle and to protect himself against wild animals and rattlesnakes. He was not usually a good shot. His background was Christian and either eastern or English-Scottish. His life was all business, very hard work, with no romance whatsoever. He had a sense of honor (perhaps stemming from southern chivalry) and he felt deep regret for any deaths occurring in range wars. From other accounts, presumed to be equally reliable, we learn that the cowboy lived in the midst of daily excitement and danger, that his life (though difficult) was wild and free, that he would not exchange his job for any other, that he loved practical jokes and smutty stories, and that he loved horses, women, liquor, and tobacco, although not necessarily in that order. One theory has it that the cowboy became a romantic hero because he could be wicked and get away with it; his lonely life on the plains excused him from the blue laws of eastern society. He therefore appealed to those many readers whose behavior was restricted but who could share the cowboy's abandon vicariously through the stories of the cattle range.

Whatever the cowboy may have been in real life, he became a hero of popular fiction with the publication of Owen Wister's novel *The Virginian*, joining the ranks of the hunters, scouts, soldiers, Indians, railroad builders, town builders, miners, U.S. marshals, sheriffs, and assorted outlaws who continue to populate the Old West in the type of novel we have long since become accustomed to calling, simply, the western.

2

The Virginian has probably been talked about more than any other western, and it is often tempting to say that Wister was something more than a writer of westerns. He was a friend of President Theodore Roosevelt (who said that he would like to

write a review of *The Virginian* if he were not president) and
Henry James (who wrote him a generous letter in praise of the
novel, perhaps because of their friendship). His chief literary
influence seems to have been Mark Twain. The narrator of
The Virginian is a tenderfoot reminiscent of Twain's narrator
in *Roughing It*, even though in each case the reader is aware of
the close relationship between narrator and writer. A Phila-
delphian, Owen Wister made fifteen trips to Wyoming between 1885 and 1900, for his health. By the time *The Virginian*
was published in 1902 its author was a well man, in body and
in mind. And, just as important, he knew the Medicine Bow
area of Wyoming as well as Twain had known Carson City,
Nevada. Wister is more sentimental than Twain—although
Roughing It does not lack sentiment—and less humorous, although he occasionally plays upon the tall tale with considerable success. The question of tone—at least in certain
passages—also leads to intriguing comparisons. When a
tenderfoot in the West says that the foothills are "indefinite
and mystic," or "I wanted no speech with any one, nor to be
near human beings at all," or "I was steeped in a revery as of
the primal earth," it is difficult to determine whether he
speaks honestly for himself, sentimentally for himself,
sentimentally for the author, or in half jest. Very serious
writers were to say almost the same things later on (Mary
Austin only a year later), but the most serious statements of
this kind prior to Wister had been made by the naturalist John
Muir, who was obviously a religious mystic as well. The
quotations are, of course, from *The Virginian*, but they would
not be out of place in *Roughing It*. In spite of his celebrated
cynicism and satire, Twain was not devoid of sentimentality.
However, there is no need to associate the words *mystic* and
primal with sentimentality. It all depends on how easily the
words come to mind, on the degree of seriousness of the context and of the writer himself.

Wister moves back and forth between the kind of artistic
seriousness that James probably wished for him and the easy
response to the western landscape which has characterized

most subliterary westerns. In this respect he poses a problem to the critic who is interested in categories and in levels of achievement within the world of literature rather than within the more noticeable world of commerce. For *The Virginian* is in the tradition of western best sellers, and something made it a popular book. When Cooper was writing the Leatherstocking Tales, five Walter Scott adventure novels were on—or had just been on—the best-seller list in this country (using the formula of sales amounting to at least 1 percent of the nation's population), and eventually all five of the Leatherstocking novels also became best sellers, as did Bird's *Nick of the Woods*. In the second half of the nineteenth century the only western best seller was Bret Harte's *Luck of Roaring Camp* (1870). Then, in a period of ten years, *The Virginian* and two Zane Grey novels, *The Spirit of the Border* (1906) and *The Riders of the Purple Sage*, made the list. Popularity contests do not always establish relationships among books and authors, but it would appear that the western tradition which appealed to the public began with the Scott romances and established itself in a sequence of Cooper, Harte, Wister, and Grey. Since Wister went west for his health, we cannot insist that his emphasis on the purity of western air is attributable to Harte. Nor can his style be considered a refinement of the styles of Cooper and Harte. He is closer to Twain in this respect. But, in spite of some literary intentions and achievements, Wister established an image of the cowboy and an example of violence which contributed heavily to the stereotypes of character and action in half a century of westerns.

He might have expanded upon one of his more vivid images and given new life to the philosophical discussion—seen in Cooper and Rousseau—concerning the values of the primitive life, the way of the wilderness, as opposed to the values of civilization. Perhaps Wister did not feel strongly enough about this question even though he commuted between Philadelphia and Wyoming for fifteen years. He hits the surface of it when, in *The Virginian*, he mildly laments the tin cans—trophies of civilization—which he finds strewn about on the virgin soil of Wyoming. But only once does he locate an image capable of making a significant statement about the question: "a black pig on a white pile of buffalo bones, catching drops of water in the air as they fell from the railroad tank." The buffalo, on whose bones the pig stands, got water from a stream; the pig, domesticated, representing civilization however ironically, must stand on the bones of a former time in order to get water from a man-made tank which is there primarily to serve the railroad as it carries more and more people into a land that may have been better off without them. If the blackness of the pig represents evil and the whiteness of the bones similarly represents goodness, or purity, then Wister is not only taking a position in the wilderness-civilization controversy but he is also bordering on a mystical condition which, with its own set of ironies, appears again in Holger Cahill's *The Shadow of My Hand* (1956) when the bones of the needlessly slaughtered buffalo come back to the new people of the West, after having been used in the process of refining sugar in the East, to be stirred into their coffee. The various symbolic uses of this image are obvious and may seem farfetched to many readers, but they at least represent a serious attempt to find a thematic link between the past and the present which can illuminate a part of our experience.

Unfortunately, the legacy left by *The Virginian* is much less complicated than that and has been embraced by the writers of formula westerns to the extent that Wister has been called the father of the western. A haphazard listing of some of the ingredients of *The Virginian* will suggest, if not define, the western novel:

1. The cowboy, a drifter, unattached to normal society.
2. The cowboy as hero.
3. The cowboy as gallant in his relationships with women.
4. Emphasis on the purity of the land, the West.
5. Violence caused by evil.
6. A villain, often a shadowy figure, who is defeated by the hero.

7. A moral system based on extremes, on good and evil, on black and white, with few if any complexities in between.
8. Good always wins.
9. More talk than action (although this changed almost immediately in the writers following Wister).
10. People are intruders in the wilderness (although the cowboy is soon seen as a native, much like the Indian, and sees *other* people as the intruders).
11. An attempt at dialect supposedly unique with the cowboy.
12. Little attention given to cattle. (There are none in *The Virginian*, but exceptions can be found in the trail drive novel.)
13. Love, usually between the cowboy and a refined eastern woman.
14. The gun fight, as evil erupts and the hero must destroy it. The confrontation of two gunfighters on a dusty street became important to the western and points up that it is usually not working cowboys who people the western novel but miscellaneous gunfighters, whether they be ranchers by trade, or town marshals, or soldiers, or vague "professional" heroes like Shane.

Essentially, the four ingredients which survive as the so-called formula are the hero, violence, love, and the western landscape, and of these four it is violence that has been refined, not into an art but into a pattern of action and a condition of effect which the standard western cannot do without.

Wister arrives at violence very slowly. It is not until chapter 26 that the Virginian, incensed at Balaam, unleashes his latent power:

> The Virginian hurled him to the ground, lifted and hurled him again, lifted him and beat his face and struck his jaw. . . . [Balaam] felt blindly for his pistol. That arm was caught and wrenched backward, and crushed and doubled. He seemed to hear his own bones. . . . Then the pistol at last

came out, and together with the hand that grasped it was instantly stamped into the dust.

Even though some readers objected to this measure of violence, the stamping of the gunman's hand soon became a part of the action—a staple, one of the tricks of the trade—in many westerns that followed *The Virginian*. Who is to say, however, that Wister had betrayed either logic or the principles of justice, since his puritanic sense of right and wrong dictated some kind of punishment for Balaam and the smashing of a gun hand is effective in preventing further use of the gun. When the Virginian changes from a soft-talking, gentle man into a brutal avenger, it is only because justice demands it. Eventually, of course, it becomes difficult to distinguish between justice and an outright appeal to the sensations of the public. As the western evolved over a period of thirty years or so, practiced successfully by Charles Alden Seltzer, B. M. Bower (Bertha Sinclair), Clarence E. Mulford, W. C. Tuttle, Herbert Knibbs, Zane Grey, Max Brand (Frederick Faust), Eugene Cunningham, William McLeod Raine, and Luke Short (Frederick Glidden), violence increased in the stereotyped West, often justified by the need for survival in an untamed land, sometimes found necessary in order to mete out justice in an environment which lacked a legal system such as that found in the civilized lands to the East, but frequently included only because it had become a useful part of the formula. The major image of gunplay comes from *The Virginian* when the hero confronts Trampas on the street, is fired at, almost negligently returns the fire, and kills the villain with two shots. The ingredients for a thousand gunfights are there. Whether the gunfight means anything at all must depend upon the circumstances, the motives, the psychological attitudes of the participants, and the general seriousness of the presentation. With lesser writers, those who look for rather easy or cheap effects, the result is nothing more than melodrama. One illustration will suffice. In Zane Grey's *Heritage of the Desert* (1910), Holderness and his foreman, Snap Naab (the

name is interesting), argue over "possession" of a girl. Holderness says abruptly, "Bah!" and shoots his foreman through
the heart.

> Snap plunged upon his face. His hands beat the ground like
> the shuffling wings of a wounded partridge. His fingers
> gripped the dust, spread convulsively, straightened, and sank
> limp.

The popularity of the motion picture based on Max Brand's
1930 novel, *Destry Rides Again*, seemed to give public support
to the violence, brutality, and exaggeration of the novel. As
the western rode into the late 1930s and the 1940s, it was
accompanied by increasing doses of bullets and blood. And
when it turned from the cowboy or gunman to the wholesale
slaughters of range wars, Indian massacres, and the Custer-
like confrontations between the Indians and the cavalry, violence had already been accepted (indeed, cherished) by the
millions of readers of westerns, most of whom led dull and
peaceful lives but perhaps needed a medium through which
they could, vicariously, give vent to their inner primitive
emotions.

It seems almost contradictory that in the midst of the
shooting and the shouting of the western there lies a quiet
and chivalric politeness to women. One suggestion is that
from the western it is possible for boys (perhaps of all ages)
to learn manhood through the exposure to violence and
death—the gun fight representing the essence of life's experiences—and that perhaps they could also learn something
about women. The latter allegation seems quite farfetched
in the light of the one-dimensional woman who appears in
most westerns. (To say two-dimensional might increase the
sexual interest slightly but would not affect the shallowness
of character.) Whatever truth there may be in Freudian explanations of the western, it is a well-known fact that as the
cowboy novel has become deeply imbedded in our myths
the analysts have taken increasing interest in it. One such
viewpoint may be summarized here to serve as an example.

I refer to an article by Warren J. Barker, M.D., "The Stereotyped Western Story, Its Latent Meaning and Psychoeconomic Function," appearing in the *Psychoanalytic Quarterly*
in 1955. Dr. Barker recognizes the formula and points out the
anonymity of authorship (derived partly, I am sure, from the
frequent use of pseudonyms) which is itself characteristic of
ancient myths. The cowboy hero is the "eternal son" forever
acting out his fantasies. He is both proud and modest, bold
and shy. Courageous in righting that which is wrong, he is
nevertheless awkward with women. The villain contrasts
with the hero, although like the devil he may appear to be a
law-abiding citizen and is recognized for what he really is only
by the hero. The sheriff is often weak (as most humans are?),
so that the hero must usurp his duties for a while. The hero is
filled with guilt of one kind or another, although that guilt is
attributed to the villain. As the villain thwarts (at least temporarily) the hero in his attempts to win the heart of the
heroine, he is really the hated father of the eternal son,
keeping the son-hero from his beloved mother. From this
point, Dr. Barker develops the themes of oedipal crimes,
incest, and insurance against castration, all seen in the conflict
between hero and villain and its resolution. In a sense, one
formula yields to another, because a major part of this thesis
depends on the villain never being killed. Since the villain is
an "isomer" of the hero, his death would mean the castration
of the hero, and this would spoil the western formula. The
use of the term *isomer* does bring to mind, however, Philip
Durham's observation that the western does not have good
men and bad men but, instead, good badmen and bad
badmen. That is, the distinctions are often blurred.

Because the hero arrives from an unknown point of origin
at the beginning of the novel, we are asked to consider the
confusion and mystery felt by the average child as it wonders
about its own origins. (Do we think of Shane when we recall
the nursery rhyme? "Where did you come from, baby dear?"
"Out of the everywhere into here.") The western code
demands that no one inquire into the origins of the hero. His

loneliness at the beginning of his adventure, and again at the end (like that of Shane), runs parallel to the child's recurring wish (never fulfilled) to return to a "blissful symbiosis with mother." Like Adam, the child has been exiled from the Garden of Eden by his new knowledge of sex and hostility. The western is also like *Hamlet;* it is an elaborate account of a boy's love for his mother and the subsequent jealousy and hatred for his father. However, the healthy child will eventually outgrow the "psycho-sexual immaturity" of the western hero until his death wish (symbolized in the hero's act of shooting the villain in order to remove his competition for the woman) turns into activity which is more constructive. At this point, says Dr. Barker, the child will stop reading the stereotyped western novel. If he does not, he has serious emotional problems.

An argument such as this one is, of course, only one of the reasons for the continued popularity of the western. The historian seeks facts of the Old West, even though they may be distorted, or argues with the "mistaken facts" or with the way the writer uses them. The specialized cultural historian looks for low-level, grass-roots evidence of attitudes and characteristics of the common man on the frontier, including his legends and myths. He may also look for evidence of values that originated on the frontier and may have remained in the American character (in support of, or in opposition to, those characteristics named by Frederick Jackson Turner, for example). And the general reading public, for whatever reason, can still turn to the western to escape into a world of adventure that may or may not mean something more than the adventure itself.

What the literary critic looks for is another matter, although his concerns may include all of the others. The western represents one stage in the evolution of the serious or literary novel which emerges in the West in the 1920s. And so we can turn to it to identify some of the problems which even the more sophisticated writers have had as they attempt to wring art out of the western landscape and character, to overcome the established stereotypes, and to give the western experience a depth rarely sensed by the commercial writers who were too busy turning out carbon copies of the formula to stop and think about the philosophical and psychological implications of landscape, of primitive (Indian) religions in relation to modern science, or full character development in a sparsely settled environment. For the literary critic, perhaps, the western is ultimately important for what it is not, rather than for what it is.

Keeping in mind that we are generalizing when we characterize the western, and that it is possible to find exceptions to various elements within the formula, the best that can be said about the conventional western is that it simply portrays the violence of a new and wild land, sometimes describing that land in sensitive terms—however rarely this happens—and occasionally hinting at a significant relationship between man and the land. As John Cawelti has pointed out in *The Six-Gun Mystique* (1970), the conflicts in the western are not often the vehicles for a profound statement about life. The conflict in a conventional western is resolved very simply in terms of plot or "justice," nothing more. The best one sees is a kind of archetypal hero-villain, or the idea of good-evil, with a remote land as a backdrop for the action, partially resembling a medieval morality play but with so little variation that a dozen such novels would be quite enough. There is no need for hundreds, or thousands.

The formula is so limited that Frank Gruber, one of its practitioners who first published in the pulp magazines, could say with apparent confidence that the western exists on an extremely limited number of plots.

1. The Rustler Story. Often, the rustled cattle belong to the heroine, and it is the hero who wanders onto the ranch, discovers that the rustlers are in league with a neighbor or friend of the heroine, and after painstakingly convincing her of this fact he resolves the problem.

2. The Range War or Empire Story. A cattle baron

defends his right to graze cattle on the millions of acres of land
he wrested from the Indians, ready to kill anyone who puts up
a fence. The hero wanders in from nowhere, is shot at, resents
it, and takes up with the homesteaders or the small ranchers,
winning the war for them.

3. The "Good But Not Worthy" Story. A variation of
No. 2, the hero of this story is a gunfighter or an ex-gunfighter
who is trying to quit, who, in the course of his involvement
with a range war or a similar conflict, falls in love with the
daughter of the homesteader and, after he has defeated the opposing gunslingers, realizes that he is a killer and not worthy of
a good woman. He rides away, usually into the sunset.

4. The Marshal or Dedicated Lawman Story. The honest
peace officer stands alone against the evil elements of his town
and either wins or dies. If he wins he is often shunned by
the community as a killer. If he dies, the good people of the
town, formerly afraid to take action, rise up in indignation
and clean up the town, so that the death of the hero is not in
vain.

5. The Revenge Story. Something has been done to the
hero, or his father or mother or wife or best friend, many
years ago. He spends the years looking for the person
responsible for his misfortune and eventually catches up with
him. This story can also be a variation of the search or the
quest and can conclude with a twist of plot, or identity, which
is reminiscent of the detective story.

6. The Outlaw Story. The hero is presented sympathetically, even though he has run afoul of the law. The
story may be based upon a historical person such as Billy the
Kid or Jesse James, showing that unfortunate circumstances
turned a good boy into a bad man. Or a completely fictional
hero may be wronged in some way and retaliate by becoming
an outlaw. Unable, because of his reputation and the danger
which surrounds him, to settle down with a good woman, he
frequently seems to commit suicide by inviting death in a gun
fight—death being preferable to the alternatives.

7. The Cavalry and Indians Story. This one is usually a variation of Custer's last stand, often told from the point of view of a cavalryman but occasionally seen from the other side, perhaps through a renegade whose sympathies lie honestly with the Indians.

8. The Ranch Story. Involving the ordinary working cowboy, perhaps rustlers, perhaps two ranch owners disputing property or water rights, this story has the potential to become a portrait of the authentic cowboy, but a hero usually emerges from the ranch hands to become larger than life.

9. The Union Pacific Story. Any number of variations are possible within the framework of the building of a railroad. This story might also center on a stagecoach line or the building of a telegraph line. Obstacles arise in various forms.

Plots 7 and 9, in particular, may be subsumed under a wider category called the historical western. Here we run into the point at which the conventional western may most easily merge with a novel which is based upon one or more historical incidents in the nineteenth-century West but which is more artistic or demanding in its intentions, its complexities, its style, and its use of history. Definitions fade when A. B. Guthrie's *The Big Sky* (1947) is included in a Western Writers' list of "best westerns" and is at the same time treated as serious literature by readers and scholars who may shun the western. The question hinges at least partly on the extent to which a historical novel is original in its conception or insights or theme, or whether it follows the formula and the stereotypes of the commercial western novel. It is obvious that in the area of historical fiction of the West we will discover every shade of literary worth, from none to a great deal. The same is true to a certain extent with the more specific plot notations provided by Mr. Gruber. In the degree to which the familiar, or conventional, plot outlines are followed, and the characters within those plots behave like puppets, a novel of the West will be a part of the formula, or an attempt to get away from it, or a successful work of fiction in its own right whose label of *western* is for esthetic purposes a geographical accident or coincidence.

It is the simplified action plot that Gruber identifies, not the complex psychologically motivated or land-determined plot which avoids deliberate manipulation. For his popular audience, Gruber is willing to attach to his plot labels comments whose tone reveals a recognition or admission of the exploitive qualities of the western. For the Revenge Story: "I know he's down in that arroyo, Martha. I swore I'd git him and I will if you'll just hand me my cane and point me in the right direction." For the Empire Story: "Ah got two arrow wounds to take this land and no cotton-pickin' farmer is a-going to fence me in." For the Cavalry and Indians Story: "Did you ever see so many dadblamed Indians, general?" And so it goes. A similar tone seems to permeate the style of many of the pre-1940 writers of westerns, although we can be certain that most of these writers wanted to be taken seriously. It is a characteristic of the formula novel that its romantic ease in describing the landscape, in dealing with love, and in luring the reader into the novel and sharing a little sentiment with him at the end always sounds contrived. The western—even after 1940—frequently opens with a brief look at the landscape, intended to be exotic (though sometimes barren), or with a stilted description of the hero, or with a hint of mystery. The following first sentences may be taken as representative:

> The moon had not yet come to full when Pierce and his two companions rode down from the Sierra Diablos westward across the plain.

> The icy wind came first to the mountains.

> "Silvertip" was what men called him, since the other names he chose to wear were as shifting as the sands of the desert; but he was more like a great stag than a grizzly.

A fitful breeze played among the mesquite bushes.

The boy had spent the night at a water-hole in a little draw at the foot of the mesa.

As his goaded horse plunged into the road, Nevada looked back over his shoulder.

Goodnight crossed the river at a ford whose bottom sands were scarcely covered by water and made noon camp under the shade of a lonely willow.

Curt Thompson rode up Gurney's sandy main street through the April dusk.

Cole Sanborn sat in a tiptilted chair on the porch of the Jonesboro House, the worn heel of one boot hooked in a rung. His long, lean body was slack, apparently relaxed, but its ease was like that of a coiled spring which might be released at the touch of a trigger.

A sharp clip-clop of iron-shod hoofs deadened and died away, and clouds of yellow dust drifted from under the cottonwoods out over the sage.

These are sentences designed to catch the attention of the reader. The four which say something about the hero are entirely undistinguished and emphasize either the exaggerated physical characteristics (grizzly, stag, long and lean body, coiled spring) or the mysterious appearance (looked back, arriving at dusk). Landscape ingredients are precisely the ones we expect to find: mountain, plain, wind, mesquite, water hole, mesa, sand, a lonely tree, dust, cottonwoods, and sage. The use of "Diablos" as part of a fictional name for a mountain range is calculated to impress upon the mind of the reader the presence, or potential presence, of evil. Stylistic problems are evident in such phrases as "deadened and died." Altogether, there is nothing in these sentences to distinguish them from thousands of other formula sentences.

Although landscape also plays a part at the end of many westerns, the formula generally called for the happy ending based upon the shallow love story which is an essential ingredient of the commercial western and which leaves the reader in a romantic glow. (This often follows a series of episodes in which violence is the major element, so that the effect is of achievement in the face of adversity—a popular desire and an important basis of fantasy.) Again, the following sentences—in this case last sentences—may be taken as representative:

> With Moira beside him he knew he would never again try to turn his back on the land.

> He walked down the street without looking back.

> He set his teeth firmly and aimed his course toward the blue and crystal-white of distant mountains.

> He took her hand in his, and they rode on silently, a song in the heart of each of them.

> Afterward, Challons forever on the grass of New Mexico as well as under it—Challons with the sun-dark skins of the clean blood of the land.

> Disregarding the group at the far end of the room, she leaned forward and kissed his lips.

> "I'll have a marrying dress on in about two minutes. *If* you'll stop kissing me," she added, in a muffled voice.

> And the two cowboys wandered away in the darkness together.

> The pressure of her hands drew his head down and he met her lips again.

> Mary lifted a rapt young face to his kiss.

Here we have in succession the hero who has found his woman and can cease wandering, the hero who remains relatively anonymous and mysterious, and the hero who seems to have found determination and purpose from the events in which he has just participated. All are consistent with the stereotype. An easy and sentimentalized relationship between a people and their land is the destiny of the Challons. The rest of the story-concluding sentences are conventionally romantic, and almost silly, with the two cowboys wandering away together providing an unintentional chuckle for the modern reader and a small urge to refer to the theories of the psychoanalyst.

The apologetic scholar would like to explain away the sentimentalists of the western by viewing their novels chronologically and discovering that styles and attitudes changed between 1900 and 1960 just as they did in nonwestern fiction. To a certain degree, the western has indeed undergone a subtle modernization: dialogue is more natural, implied symbolism lends at least the suggestion of multileveled meanings, women are drawn more realistically, the landscape and weather are often a force rather than a decorative backdrop, and more writers of westerns actually live in the West and have some feeling for the place and for the people who roamed over it or settled on it during the nineteenth century. But this argument holds up largely for that rare western which rises above the formula just enough to demand attention but not enough to abandon the genre and become something else. The popular western has remained much the same for sixty years (and more, since it continues to thrive in its own way). If anyone thinks, for example, that the western improved noticeably during the forty or fifty years following publication of *The Virginian*, he need only read tables of contents, chapter titles, to see that he is wrong. From B. M. Bower's *Her Prairie Knight* (1904), "A Handsome Cowboy to the Rescue," "Beatrice's Wild Ride," and "Keith's Masterful Wooing"; from Bower's *Rowdy of the "Cross L"* (1906), "A Shot from the Dark," "Rowdy in a Tough Place," "Pink in a Threatening Mood," and "Rowdy Finds Happiness"; from Clarence Mulford's *Hopalong Cassidy* (1910), "Antonio's Scheme," "Mary Meeker Rides North," "Hopalong Asserts Himself," "Hopalong Grows Suspicious," and "Hopalong's Reward"; from Zane Grey's *Riders of the Purple Sage* (1912), "The Masked Rider," "Love," "Faith and

Unfaith," "Solitude and Storm"; from Max Brand's *The Untamed* (1919), "Pan of the Desert," "The Phantom Rider," "The Lone Riders Entertain," "Hell Starts," "Fear," and "Death"; from *Partners of Chance*, by Henry Herbert Knibbs (1921), "High Heels and Moccasins," "Pony Tracks," "More Pony Tracks," and "Two Trails Home"; from Eugene Cunningham's *Texas Sheriff* (1934), "We Need a Shooting Sheriff," "That's Going to Get You Killed," "Dead Man's Hand" (a common title in early westerns), "There Was Bush-whacking Done," and "Inside With You" (a title which becomes meaningful in Guthrie's *These Thousand Hills* [1956] two decades later); from William MacLeod Raine's *Square-Shooter* (1934), "Mary Marries a Dangerous Man," "Hotter than Hell with the Lid On," and "Self-Defense"; from L. L. Foreman's *The Renegade* (1942), "The Deserter," "The Hos-tiles," "Army Scout," and "The Last Campaign"; from Nel-son C. Nye's *The Desert Desperadoes* (1942), "A Man Drifts West," "Two Women," "Forbidden Fruit," "A Man De-cides," and "A Man Plays Tag with Hell"; and from *The Wild Bunch*, by Ernest Haycox (1943), "Voice of Hate," "Turn of the Screw" (which appears in more than one western), "Wo-men Meet," "The Taste of a Woman's Lips," and "The Last Decision." Chapter titles went out of fashion in the western in the 1940s, but book titles continued to tip off the reader as to what kind of book he was buying: *Lawman's Feud* (Steve Frazee), *The Bravados*, *Desperate Rider*, and *Warbonnet Law* (Frank O'Rourke), *The Violent Land* (Wayne Overholser), *Bold Passage* and *Blood on the Land* (Frank Bonham), *No Survivors* and *The Last Warpath* (Will Henry), *Town Tamer*, *Fighting Man*, and *Fort Starvation* (Frank Gruber), and an almost endless list of one-word titles appearing under the name of the best-sell-ing contemporary writer of westerns, Louis L'Amour. (In each case the title is the name of the chief character who is given a single name which removes some of his humanness and allows him to take on the stature of mythical superman: *Radigan*, *Taggart*, *Shalako*, *Hondo*, *Flint*, *Sackett*, and so on.)

If nothing else, chapter and book titles reveal the stasis

(stability?) of the western. It may have become slightly more
polished in recent years, but in view of its reluctance to make
essential changes from the century-old formula it may also
have become more tarnished.

3

To write a complete and definitive history of the western
novel would be a prodigious task, and it could never be
complete because the western is still being written in no small
numbers. To take the western seriously can often be difficult,
except as the cultural historian is able to see its significance
not in the novels themselves but in their audience, in the
cultural traits that allowed the novels to become popular.
Even at that, some practitioners of the formula western would
object to the implication that the western was ever intended to
be a social document. Be that as it may, there are certainly
two logical reasons for the popularity of the western story.
One is that the American experience was based so fully on the
frontier for two centuries that after it closed (presumably in
1890 at Wounded Knee) Americans continued to desire the
frontier and the partial tradition which it offered them in an
otherwise new land. America needed a heritage of its own,
fully divorced from England, and the somewhat mythical
West was all that it had. A basic need was fulfilled, then, by
the western story. As added impetus, world problems as well
as national feelings of unrest at the end of the nineteenth
century and in the years just preceding World War I
encouraged escapism and the search for national heroes. The
cowboy and all of his western likenesses (mountain man,
gunfighter, lawman, etc.) became the collective hero. And in
the post-Wister era, when the need to escape into a world of
fantasy grew stronger, Zane Grey's Lassiter disappeared into
an Eden-like valley in the American West in the same year
that Edgar Rice Burroughs's Tarzan turned up in the African
jungle. *Riders of the Purple Sage* and *Tarzan of the Apes*, both

published in 1912, became immensely popular and set trends for the romantic adventures to follow. (Curiously, each of these novels had a woman named Jane, the name itself once meaning what "broad" means in our own time.) Burroughs had served in the Seventh Cavalry and written a few westerns, but his success with the public came from the series of novels about Tarzan. (Just as Max Brand had his Dr. Kildare, and many writers of westerns had their mystery novels, often under pseudonyms.) Whether Americans needed the flood of westerns that followed in the wake of Grey and Brand is debatable, but once the popularity of the genre was established it is obvious that other writers wanted to cash in on a good thing. The West was to be a subject of interest to the mass market for a long time.

If the western is short on quality, it is long on numbers. The sheer bulk of more than seventy years of publication for the mass market is astounding. Frederick Faust, writing under nineteen pseudonyms, produced at least 179 westerns, historical romances, and Dr. Kildare novels. All, or most, of the westerns were written as Max Brand, Evan Evans, and Peter Dawson. Zane Grey, who merely dropped his first name (Pearl), wrote eighty-five books, most of them western novels. William MacLeod Raine wrote eighty, and Louis L'Amour, the most active living writer of westerns (who also continued the Hopalong Cassidy novels while writing as Tex Burns), has written more than sixty. Ernest Haycox divided his time between the novel (twenty-three) and the short story (three hundred). Most writers of westerns are prolific; the pattern, or formula, is available to them and they need not take time to be original or stylistic. It is impossible to identify all writers who have produced a western novel, but even a short additional listing can suggest the vitality of the western as well as the frequency of pseudonyms: Eugene Manlove Rhodes, Frederick Glidden (writing as Luke Short), Henry Allen (writing also as Clay Fisher and Will Henry), Harry Sinclair Drago (writing also as Will Ermine, Bliss Lomax, and Joseph Wayne), Wayne Overholser (also writing as Lee

Leighton, and, it seems, Joseph Wayne), William R. Cox, Elmer Kelton, Charles N. Hecklemann, Nelson Nye (also writing as Clem Colt), Will Cook (writing also as James Keene), Clifton Adams, Todhunter Ballard (with eleven pseudonyms), Joseph Chadwick (with ten pseudonyms), Allan Vaughan Elston, Hal Evarts, and Eugene E. Halleran. The list is by no means exhaustive.

Although any attempt at comparative evaluation would bring vigorous protests from the followers of each neglected writer, it seems to me that Zane Grey was probably the most influential in terms of establishing the formula, and that Ernest Haycox was possibly the best in terms of craftsmanship and of at least a modicum of integrity that caused him to veer away from the cowboy formula in the 1930s and turn to the historical western which could be a gateway to the literary novel. *Bugles in the Afternoon* (1944) is a good example. Whether *The Earthbreakers* in 1952 can stand equal to Guthrie's *The Way West* (1949) is a matter of opinion (DeVoto thought it could not); it did bear out the author's comment of almost a decade earlier that he doubted if he would write another "straight western." DeVoto at least paid some attention to Haycox while otherwise writing off the western as conventionalized, formularized, ritualized, lifeless, implausible, absurd, and naive in the first (1954) of two "Easy Chair" columns in *Harper's*. The second column (1955) was devoted to *The Virginian*, the Wister invention of the myth of the Old West, the novel which started the avalanche of imitators. At the time, DeVoto stirred up angry feelings among those who cared about Western literature, but with a few glaring exceptions much of what he said made sense. Unfortunately, he concluded that the "Old West myth cannot be translated into acceptable human motives" without differentiating between kinds of myth and uses of myth, limiting himself to the definition of myth which places it in opposition to reality or truth. The emphasis on authenticity and on literal reality lives on, detrimental to meaningful criticism and interpretation of western materials. DeVoto was not entirely correct, either, in assuming that the full formula of the popular western came from *The Virginian*. It is more likely that Max Brand (Faust) and Zane Grey provided the myth and the conventions to which DeVoto objects. And finally he committed a sin of omission: in contrasting the commercial western with the literary Western novel, he named only Walter Clark, Edwin Corle, H. L. Davis, Harvey Fergusson, and A. B. Guthrie as good western novelists. There were, of course, others.

An obvious reason for the subliterary quality of the western is the emphasis on mass production (as well as mass marketing). Westerns have been written too quickly, have been turned out en masse by too many writers as a livelihood rather than a careful and loving artistic endeavor. It is also likely that the westerner as a character becomes part of a serious art only when his moral code is no longer one-sided but can be seen as imperfect and can lead to a moral ambiguity. Whether such an ambiguity would also destroy the myth of the West is a question which needs clarification as much as it needs answering. To the extent that the myth is superficial, or false, or taken up with little understanding of its potential, it deserves to be destroyed. But the deep archetypal myths which rise out of man's relationship with the land, which are ancient and are rediscovered in the West rather than invented on the spot for the convenience of a myth-hungry audience, may be considerably more significant and revealing than the realistic details and the search for historical (factual) truth. It is possible also to comment upon the myth even while allowing it to be a part of the total view—commenting either obviously or with some subtlety. Three novels which are more serious than the average western, but which make use of the formulaic myth even while speculating on it, seem to represent a middle ground between the two extremes of Western fiction: Jack Schaefer's *Shane* (1949), Oakley Hall's *Warlock* (1958), and Harry Brown's *The Stars in Their Courses* (1960). Schaefer takes the mysterious avenger as hero as far as the man in black with no past and no future (except symbolically) can be taken. It is the perfection of the stereotype, and done so skillfully that there is no need to do it again. In the perfection, the myth takes on new stature. Hall does something similar but on a much wider scale. His novel, including the chapter titles, is a compendium of western stereotypes presented in such a fashion that we are forced to take them seriously (seeing before our eyes, as it were, their origins) even while we know exactly what we are looking at. *Warlock* is a *tour de force*, to be sure, but it leaves an astonishing impact upon that side of the serious reader which tends to sneer at the western. Harry Brown pulls together a cast of character types, lets them become entangled in a variety of stock situations, but manages to lift the darkened lives almost to the level of tragedy. Blood, sex, and feud are the ingredients, but they are heightened by passion and by the moral ambiguity which can indeed alter the myth but cannot destroy it altogether. With or without the myth and its consequences within serious writing, Henry Allen, Tom Lea, Elliott Arnold (especially for his sensitive though much maligned *Blood Brother*), Paul Wellman, and Benjamin Capps are among those writers who have clearly transcended the popular western but who have not, for one reason or another, achieved as much in a true literary sense as those novelists who deserve to be called major writers whether they are western or not.

Before leaving the western, with all of its uncomplimentary adjectives—popular, formula, conventional, commercial—it needs to be said that it had an effect upon the more serious fiction which began with Harvey Fergusson in the 1920s, even though the effect may have been that of reaction against the formula. The western did demonstrate to a limited extent some of the possibilities (as well as the pitfalls) of the western setting, characters, color, and history in fiction. The western cannot be written off entirely. As a popular art form it can be subjected to various kinds of criticism (archetypal, cultural, myth, Freudian, and sociohistorical) and provide at least enough interest for dis-

cussion and analysis. What the western cannot fully withstand is the application of what can be called, only, normal or
standard literary criticism. We might disagree on what this is,
but it must certainly include consideration of basic elements
of good fiction even while these elements are seen in relation
to a special (perhaps unique) environment.

1. Significance of theme. As one example, it is not enough
to show man on the land; there should be a meaningful
relationship between the character and his environment. In
the West this relationship is sometimes seen through
mysticism.

2. Plausibility. It is not necessary to be completely
faithful to the historical facts or the literal realities to produce
a worthwhile narrative, but the characters and action and
place should be believable. Rather than ruling out the
imagination, the concept of plausibility serves as a testing of
its quality.

3. Style. A literate, or fresh, or appropriate style not only
enhances the narrative and establishes tone and point of view,
but at its best it evokes in the reader those insights which have
been revealed to the writer.

4. Seriousness of intent. The writer's intentions are
important—what it is that he wishes to make of his
novel—even though the reader, or critic, must deduce those
intentions from the work. Announcements of intentions are
often false and misleading.

5. Multidimensional characterization. In E. M. Forster's
terms, the characters should be round, not flat as they usually
are in the conventional western.

6. Illumination of the human condition and its potential.
This can be done through the proper use of symbol and myth
as well as by other means.

7. Sense of place. Sensitivity is implied, and occasionally
can be found in the western. More significantly, the sense of
place should be an integral part of theme and character as well
as a feeling on the part of the writer.

Other criteria could be added to this brief list, and rather complex theories of fiction and of art in general can be useful as well as distracting. At this point I merely wish to suggest that the western, as a genre, fails to meet the qualifications for literary fiction, for that fiction which strives to become significant in both theme and form. For this reason the western remains a subliterary genre in spite of its many fascinations. What shall be called the Western novel in the course of this study is a higher form of literature, not a genre, and not to be confused (as it often is by the unknowing generalist) with the western of the lowercase *w* and its popular appeal to mass audiences.

II
The Writer's West

When Archibald MacLeish said that "West is a country in the mind, and so eternal," he was thinking of the various concepts of the West which, factually true or emotionally and mythically real in a different way, linger in the imaginations of Americans as well as readers from other cultures. In spite of attempts in recent years, by novelists as well as historians, to re-create the actualities of the frontier West, or Old West, or nineteenth-century West, it is impossible to get rid of the feelings we have inherited from the frontier movement, many of which are perpetuated in popular cultural forms such as the western novel, the western motion picture, and the western television show. Those feelings are complex. Some are based upon personal experiences of the first explorers and travelers to record their impressions of the new country. However, these early reactions to the West varied as much as the landscape did, and to put together a comprehensive collection of them would be to establish a many-sided portrait which proved only that a mind could perceive almost anything it wanted to in the immensities and extremes of the western landscape. Those feelings which are not founded upon personal experience, which are the result of hearsay, or of the mass consciousness which has been shaped by hundreds of contradictions and by commercial exploiters as well as serious and objective reporters, are more important in saying something about the national mind than about the West itself. Granted that the accumulation of myth has given everlasting life to some place which seems to exist more in the mind than in external nature, we must nevertheless recognize a physical reality which is the American West even while validating the myth for its own sake as well as ours.

We can speak of two Wests, both of them real enough, but one consisting of popular symbols, legends, myths, and even fantasies and dreams, while the other exists first as an actual place and only secondarily (or in art) as metaphor. Whatever the writer wishes to do with his material, whether give it life as realistically as possible or imbue it with his imagination until it at least *appears* to be entirely fictional, he must still begin with the place, with the history, with the objects, and with the people, all of which make up a particular geographical area. Perhaps there is indeed a West which was entirely invented, but even the popular mythmakers who manufactured thousands of commercial westerns began with some kind of fact, seen firsthand or heard by way of reports, and so the facts are important even though they cannot always be ascertained. In art, of course, they are not binding. The imagination is free to work upon them, interpreting, building, speculating, and expanding. Critics of fiction of the West have been divided in their ultimate concern for factual foundations, some insisting that the best Western novels are those which are historically most accurate, others denying the necessity of that literal reconstruction. Part of the controversy stems from the fact that much Western fiction *is* historical in nature, and so there is some insistence that the writer know his factual subject even though he may go beyond it. It might be more to the point to say that the writer should be intimate with the place, with the spirit of the place, so that even if he chooses to distort whatever historical facts he may be working with he will nevertheless remain true to them in spirit.

We may also speak of three Wests: the historical, the physical or geographical, and the mythical. All three are available to the writer, and all three offer complications. The history of the West (events, people) is available to the formula novelist as well as to the more sophisticated and literary writer, so that subject matter as such—or even the authenticity—is not a determining factor in distinguishing the historical element within the western genre novel from those Western regional novels which are based on past events. Physically, the topography and climate vary so much from one part of the West to another that it is not unusual to divide the broadly defined area into sections: the plains (northern, central, and southern), the mountains (generally the Rockies, but also the Sierra Nevadas and the Sangre de Cristos), the desert (notably Death Valley, but also on occasion the dry, high plateaus of the mountainous regions east of California), the Northwest, the Southwest, and so on. As for myth, it can take on a number of shapes, it can be commercially exploited, and it can be used (or can appear naturally out of the material of a novel) as archetypal insight into the meanings of man's destiny and potential significance. Because of unique circumstances, the three Wests are in most cases inextricably bound together, although two of them may be isolated, however superficially, for purposes of brief discussion.

2

For the novelist a curious paradox both confuses and simplifies his use of historical events. In terms of settlement by the largely Anglo-Saxon American, or in terms of his civilization or his notions of tradition, the West is a very young country. For this reason the novelist more often than not feels obligated to examine the brief history and to pull from it the things and characteristics which can accumulate gradually into the kind of tradition which will give him, as artist, a base to work from, while at the same time providing a common ground for belief and for identity among those people who have become westerners. On the other hand, the American West as a place peopled by non-Europeans is very old. The first Indian agriculturalists of the Southwest are believed to have been settled permanently at Mesa Verde as early as 500 B.C. The Cliff Dwellers absorbed or supplanted the Basket Makers at about the time of the Norman Conquest in England. Oraibi, Arizona, the oldest continuously inhabited town in the United States, was established around the year 1100. In 1300, still many years before the arrival of Columbus at the opposite end of the continent, the Pueblo culture reached its height in the Southwest. Europeans (Spanish) visited the area that is now Arizona three-quarters of a century before the establishment of the first "American" colony on the East Coast—Jamestown, Virginia. Yet, the state of Arizona was not admitted to the Union until 1912, the year of publication of Zane Grey's *Riders of the Purple Sage*. What this means to the novelist in the West is that his past and present are nearly the same time period in terms of the frontier. He is so close to his past, and his western traditions are so new, that he often tends to write what may seem to be a historical novel but which is to him almost contemporary. However, aside from historical events, he also has at his disposal, if he is so inclined and is sensitive to them, the much older traditions of the Indian, and therefore a spiritual atmosphere which can inform his writing if he allows it to do so. The historic time of society (measured by the growth of civilization) gives way in this case to the static, or timeless, condition of nature, so that the writer who is immersed in this timelessness looks at history not as a progressive series of events but as coexisting events. In normal terms there are more historical Western novels than there are contemporary, but this is a confusion of terms. When Vardis Fisher searches through centuries of man's development from a primitive savage to a modern civilized being, or when Frederick

Manfred examines two hundred years of Siouxland life, or when A. B. Guthrie works his way up from the time of the mountain man, it is to locate the various facets of self, to bring together the characteristics of contemporary man, looking into the "past" in the same way that we search "far and wide." The element of time, although it is apparently linear, is considered as concentric, and at its center is contemporary western man. In the spiritual sense (and the Western novel is ultimately concerned with the spirit in spite of shifting degrees of emphasis on the flesh) conventional chronology is unimportant, perhaps nonexistent.

Perhaps we are talking only about the timelessness of fiction as opposed to the time-consumption of history, and yet the western writer's point of view sits upon past and present in a way made possible only by the coexistence or, at the very least, the overlapping of events which in the historian's viewpoint are clearly sequential. Or, to put it another way, the western novelist bends toward, and sometimes reaches, a philosophy of oneness, of unity, whether it be of man and the land or of man and other men in a different time. The West, especially with its ancient Indian heritage, fosters mysticism.

Apart from point of view, attitude, and philosophy, however, the novelist must build his story on events and people. His formal vehicle, his narration, requires subject matter. What has there been (what is there) in the American West that is suitable as subjects for fiction?

The influx of the Spanish people into the Southwest, beginning in the sixteenth century, has provided much rich material, particularly in the broad areas of cultural, economic, and political relationships between the Spanish and the Anglos. Confrontations in Santa Fe, the Mexican War, problems of Spanish land grants, and the relations between Spaniard and Indian have all been explored, notably by Harvey Fergusson. Perhaps because of the trilingual culture of the Southwest, as well as the more favorable climate, writers have gravitated in that direction for over half a century, and more literature has come out of that area than from the central plains or the Interior Northwest. Nevertheless, the Lewis and Clark expedition of 1804–1806 continues to capture the imagination and has been re-created in fiction by Vardis Fisher (*Tale of Valor*, 1958) and a host of lesser writers. Almost any exploration of the West—mostly following Lewis and Clark—appears somewhere in fiction. The mountain man, who was explorer, trapper, trader, and scout, may well be the epic hero of America; in almost every respect he surpassed the cowboy in legendary deeds, in a life of solitude, in acts of strength as well as of courage, and in contributions to the expansion of the nation. While hundreds of novels have been based on the exploits of Kit Carson, John Colter, Jim Bridger, Jed Smith, the Sublettes, the Bent brothers, "Uncle Dick" Wootton, and others, only one of the three best mountain man novels is based upon a historical figure. Frederick Manfred's *Lord Grizzly* (1954) follows the exploits of Hugh Glass as closely as the few sources allow. Harvey Fergusson's *Wolf Song* (1927) and A. B. Guthrie's *The Big Sky*, written from intimate experience with two different parts of the West, have purely fictional protagonists who are more representative, or typical, than any actual mountain man. The same is true of Johnny Christmas in Forrester Blake's novel bearing his character's name (1948) and in a sequel, *Wilderness Passage* (1953). One of the problems in writing about the mountain man is a natural tendency toward overstatement, toward mythologizing. Guthrie solves the problem by allowing the landscape to accept the force of his enthusiasm, while the main character, Boone Caudill, is considerably less a romantic or idealized figure than he is a careless, almost despicable, selfish, real person who runs away from his problems. Manfred is more willing to let the myth take form, to permit symbols to enter the story, and to portray Glass as an epic hero; yet the style is realistic, even when rhythmic and poetic, and the hero reveals a sufficient number of human weaknesses to offset partially, at least, his uniqueness.

Much of the history of the West has been used so frequently in the exploitation of frontier images, and in the formula novel, that mere mention of events can conceal the possibilities of serious fiction. This is a chance every serious writer takes when he uses the nineteenth-century West as setting. The overland trails (Oregon, California, Mormon) offer the opportunity to a writer to set in motion a small community of characters who must learn to live together (perhaps even in a civilized manner) while they struggle against the land, the climate, the Indians, and all the obstacles which confront them on a long and tedious journey. The working out of the destinies of people forced by circumstances to undergo an ordeal together is not an uncommon procedure for writers making use of contemporary settings. In Steinbeck's *The Wayward Bus* (1947), the bus replaces the covered wagon. Several very recent novels have made use of the airplane in the same way. The significance lies not in the superficial plotting of these stories but in the relationships between people and in the revelation of character during times of stress. Other than that, all of the covered wagon, bus, and airplane stories are much the same and almost establish a formula of their own. Guthrie's *The Way West* is typical and, as such, is relatively undistinguished. It has been praised for its authenticity—Guthrie relied on a number of firsthand accounts—but authenticity is not the answer for the judgment of a book as literature. The style, structural devices, and impressionistic method of *The Land Is Bright* (1939), by Archie Binns, are a welcome relief from the typical emphasis on facts in the Oregon Trail novel. It is not only style, but vision, which will enable one treatment of a subject to rise above another. The dramatic devices are there for anyone to use: blizzards, drought, grasshoppers, plains tornadoes, heavy snow in the mountains, grass fires on the prairie and timber fires in the hills, dry arroyos suddenly flooded by a freak rain storm, cattle diseases, and human illness and death. Add to natural disasters the easy availability of stereotyped characters—settler, cowboy, mountain man, law officer, railroad builder, hunter, scout, Indian, rancher—and the western writer finds it difficult to achieve freshness, insight, and originality unless he has a particular vision of his own which can govern the story.

Many broad historical areas yield material for fiction: transportation, including stagecoach lines, the Pony Express, and railroads; mining, which offers a choice from the gold discoveries in California, Colorado, and South Dakota to the silver lodes in Colorado and Nevada; the Indian wars, seen from either of the two sides, one side opening out into U.S. military campaigns in the West, or the isolation of the military post, or problems of command, or specific officers such as Custer and Carrington; frontier law, also seen from either side, becoming a study of the peace officer or of the outlaw; the cattle industry, with a variety of conflicts; the aftereffects of the Civil War, including dispossessed or disgruntled Southerners often banded together as, for example, marauders on the plains, complicating the already confusing relationships between whites and Indians, or ranchers and townspeople, or Texans and Northerners; and a long list of specific events such as the tragedy of the Donner party, the battle at the Little Big Horn, Ashley's expedition on the Upper Missouri, the Mormon settlement at Salt Lake, the establishment of the Bozeman Road, the installation of the telegraph, the hanging of Sheriff Henry Plummer and his deputies, the Sand Creek massacre, the final slaughter of the buffalo, and Wounded Knee. It is not enough, of course, to relate as accurately as possible the events themselves or even the context for them. One kind of critic of Western American fiction will indeed conduct his evaluations on the basis of historical authenticity, on "reality." The guiding principle becomes that of mimesis. With almost unlimited wealth of historical incident in easy reach, the western novelist is hard pressed to go beyond the adventure, romance, tragedy, and popular appeal of the mere "facts." It takes an act of imagination going beyond invention, cleverness, and basic distortion to find that significance, that meaning, that illumination which will give an entirely new life to materials which already seemed old at the height of the pulp western, or else seemed fixed forever in the standard history books. Fergusson does this with the mountain man and the Spanish land grants, Fisher with the Donner party, Clark with ranch life, Waters with mining, Manfred with the range war, Stegner with the restless seeker of riches, Michael Straight with the Fetterman massacre, and Edwin Corle (among others) with the Indian. While all of these treatments are historical in the narrow sense of the word, they are more than that.

3

Achievement is all the greater because of the scope of the land, an immensity which defies the limits of even the long novel or the trilogy. The landscape is overpowering and seems to be without form. Since the land is often a character in the Western novel, as well as setting, it cannot be taken lightly. Because the land (as place) is huge in dimension and variable in all its characteristics, it invites reactions which are both outspoken and contradictory. Lewis and Clark vacillated between emotional extremes that are perhaps best identified as the sublime and the terrifying. For Joseph Nicollet, in the 1830s in the Dakotas, beauty gave way to annoying monotony. The Stephen Long expedition of 1820 across the plains to the Rockies reported that a large portion of the country was unfit for cultivation although suitable for the buffalo and other wild game. The report fostered the notion (sometimes called the myth) of the Great American Desert, serving to discourage settlement. This fact was seen as beneficial in one respect: the "desert" would serve as a barrier preventing too rapid expansion of the West. Yet when Jesse Applegate recalled his 1843 experiences along the Platte River in Wyoming, he spoke of the inadequacy of language to convey the extent, grandeur, and beauty of the landscape.

Parkman, also, even though he was to become a professional writer, lacked the vocabulary to describe the Platte Valley in Nebraska and resorted to the hackneyed term *picturesque*. Many accounts in the middle of the nineteenth century refer to the clear air and the inability to judge distance because sounds as well as visual images carried so far that distances were deceiving to people accustomed to the "murky air" of the eastern seaboard. Walt Whitman was impressed by Denver in 1879 because of the "delicious rare atmosphere" and because he could look east over the plains and prairies for "a thousand miles" while almost at his back the mountains soared to an elevation of nearly three miles.

As a region, the American West must be thought of in terms of space and contrast, or extremes. Extending from Mexico to Canada, and from the mid-continent grasslands to the Pacific coastal mountains, the area includes flat plains, towering mountains—the contrast between the horizontal and the vertical, especially when they represent very large dimensions, can be mind-boggling—deserts, forests, wildly rushing rivers as well as dry riverbeds, high plateaus (where the flat plain is at elevations of more than seven thousand feet), deep valleys (some fertile and others rocky and barren), and, everywhere, distance. Temperature ranges are indicative of the extremes encountered in the West and are impressive even as statistics, notwithstanding personal experience. From one place to another, at different times, the high temperature can be around 130 degrees Fahrenheit and the low can be 70 degrees below zero. Extremes of 120 degrees above zero and 60 below were once recorded during the same year (1936) on the Drift Prairie of North Dakota. In Browning, Montana, in 1916, the temperature plunged 100 degrees in one day. In Spearfish, South Dakota, in 1943, it rose by 49 degrees in two minutes. These are all world records, and they have been approximated more times than even the hardiest westerner cares to remember except when he is boasting of the conditions he has been able to survive. Hot and windy summers give way to harsh, cold, and windy winters in many

parts of the West, while in others the apparent moderation is
only relative. Arid conditions—characteristic of the Interior
West—are often relieved only by sporadic and violent
thunderstorms. This is a land of paradoxes, of sudden
changes, of unpredictability. A man on the open plains is
thoroughly exposed to the elements of nature; he suffers
physically from the unhindered sun and wind, and he is
affected psychologically by the isolation. Contrarily (we could
also call the West the land of contraries) he may be exhilarated
by the fresh air and a sense of freedom. He may travel
hundreds of miles without seeing appreciably different towns
or a significant change of scenery, and yet the journey itself
supports his freedom of movement. Or, where the plains meet
the mountains, he may drive from the flatland to a mountain
peak in little more than thirty to sixty minutes, completely
exchanging one world for another. Often, romantic grandeur
exists within a few miles of desolation.

The American West, then, poses a problem for the
literary imagination partly because it is the largest and most
varied region within the United States, and because it is a
land of extremities and of relatively few people, tempting the
writer to focus his attention upon the landscape and to view
the people either as pawns of nature or, if they survive well, as
heroes. Because western towns are far apart, and sudden
storms swing across the plains, and snow comes early to the
mountains, and the wind blows hard enough to be a factor in
human behavior, the writer cannot avoid the effects of the
land on its people. He may, however, as his predecessors have
done, see life as physical and spiritual ordeal, or he can view it
in terms of purity as symbolized by the clear and dry air
which, even today in most places, is undefiled by industrial
civilization. In these respects, the Western novel is likely to
stress survival *or* to be pastoral in tone, and, in keeping with
the natural paradoxes, the two emphases may stand in
juxtaposition within the same novel.

Three conditions, however, remain relatively stable—
aridity, high elevation, and sparse population. Indeed, the

West is often defined in terms of aridity. Approximately
at the ninety-ninth meridian, going west, the average rainfall drops below twenty inches. From here to the Sierra
Nevadas, with pockets of exceptions, farming is difficult or
impossible without irrigation. Estimates of average rainfall for
this entire region run from ten to fourteen inches a year; but,
since the average varies from one place to another, it is unfair
to call the entire West a desert, or to call it arid. Relatively
small portions are arid; the rest is semiarid. Nevertheless, the
fact of aridity, of abnormal dryness according to the rainfall
east of the Missouri River, is one way of establishing the
physical identity of the American West. High elevation is another. Crossing the northern or central plains, from Minnea-
polis-St. Paul or Omaha, the traveler hardly notices the
gradual rise from 750–1,300 feet to 4,000–5,000 feet at the
base of the Rockies, but as the elevation rises so does the dryness increase and the air become easier to breathe. To go west
between these two routes, across South Dakota, is to encounter the Black Hills, the 7,242-foot Harney's Peak being the
highest place in the United States east of the Rockies. Finally,
the Rocky Mountains themselves are crossed through passes
that are often at 11,000 feet, and the major peaks go over the
14,000-foot mark. On the west side of the Rockies the land
remains high, and dry, until it drops from 7,000-foot Donner
Pass to sea level, or from Flagstaff to the California desert,
7,000 feet to *below* sea level.

While the topographic and climatic conditions of the West
are conducive to good health, they are not satisfactory for the
kind of productivity which allows high-density population.
Large cities are few and far between, as are the ranches in
contrast to eastern farms. The structure of society is therefore
quite different from that in metropolitan areas crowded with
people, and loneliness in the crowd with its psychological
ramifications and dense conflicts gives way in the West to
physical isolation. Here again we run into a paradox, or a
juxtaposition of disparate images, because the physical

isolation may cause a comparable spiritual isolation or it may lead to independence of self, to a strong measure of self-sufficiency. In any case, the sparsity of people in a big land gives the writer little chance to deal with the whims and fashions of a metropolitan society—for which he has little patience anyway. The passions of the land are more primary than those of the city, and the Western novel is susceptible to irrationality not only because of the direct relationship between man (character) and land (setting), and not only because of physical isolation, but also because of the extreme characteristics of the region. And because social relationships are often subordinated to the power and influence of the land, the western novelist just as often relies on nature, on the land, for those functional rhythms which become one kind of form.

It is in these more or less permanent conditions among the many variables and extremes of the West that the novel finds its own conditions and problems. All three conditions— aridity, elevation, sparse population—are conditions of the land and cannot be manipulated. Within them the west- ern writer has a difficult legacy. He has been given the travel narrative as the only native form, and an almost uncontrollable landscape which seems to defy the use of any other kind of form. He has been given events from history which are epic in dimension and which tend to become legend and myth, leaving the serious writer in the shadow of the successful formula novelist. He struggles to be rational (unless he deliberately abandons rationalism for mysticism) in a land of violent extremes which has long been described in European and romantic terms. He is faced with a landscape which overshadows the people living on it, and he must yet create believable, convincing, and interesting characters who can show us more than a simple endurance or a heroic defeat. Especially a trial for the contemporary western writer is the task of making historical events or figures plausible and meaningful to the contemporary condition. In general, his materials are primitive in contrast to the sophistication (and artificiality) of the advanced civilization of the older sections of the country, and if he is to achieve sophistication (granting that he may not want to) he must do it through style, tone, and structural methods, all the while influenced by the harmonies and rhythms inherent in the natural world and by the ungainly scope of place, of setting.

With imagination and with acceptance of the conditions of place, he can still make a valuable contribution to the insights into the plight and hopes of mankind. The land itself yields symbols, adversaries, temptations, and serves as a sounding board against which the virtues, vices, ambitions, and quests of man can be played. The passions of the posse in Clark's *Ox-Bow Incident* (1940) fluctuate with the winds and the changes in weather. In his *Track of the Cat* (1949) the inner values of the Bridges brothers are tested against the mountain lion as well as against the forces of nature, with a particular combination of values able to achieve the proper attitude toward self as well as toward the world in which that self must live. William Eastlake makes use of depths (canyon, ravine, crevice, valley) and heights (mesa and mountain) to explore life and death, bridges to the past, continuity, the search for something that can never be found, and the sacredness of all living things. Frank Waters, with a mystical attachment to the earth, probes to the heart of a mountain for the secret of life, but does so within two contexts, one of the land's pulse and the other of man's greed. In Waters's *The Wild Earth's Nobility* (1935) as well as in Eastlake's *Portrait of an Artist with Twenty-six Horses* (1963) the protagonists are exposed to the upward tilt of the western landscape as they search for spiritual truths, so that land and spirit exist parallel to each other in actuality as well as in metaphor. Vardis Fisher's entire career—the man and his work, inseparable—was determined by the Idaho wilderness in which he first felt those fears and cruelties that sent him on one of the longest quests in literature. The land is a dominating presence in the Western novel.

4

Whether western culture will change enough to alter the directions of the Western novel is uncertain. The common view of this culture is that it is static. People whose livelihood depends upon the land—an agricultural society—tend to be conservative, although populist and socialistic movements have flourished for a time in several of the western states. The westerner is cautious when he comes to considering anything new, and yet, as Cooper recognized in himself, he has faith in progress even though he is not sure of the direction that progress will or should take. Changes which originate in the East are often so slow in reaching the West—or are accepted only after a long period of reluctance has been overcome—that by the time they are welcomed they are already outmoded. In fashions this makes little difference, but in educational theories, for example, western institutions can look ridiculous as they take up the cudgel for something that has already been replaced elsewhere. Yet the conservatism carries with it a strong measure of idealism rooted still in Manifest Destiny and frontier egalitarianism. And even here we run into a paradox, one which is perhaps American in a vague way but which is specifically western: a strong belief in individualism, on all levels, exists in close relationship with reliance upon assistance from the federal government. Again the land is probably the cause of this apparent misalliance. It nurtures individualism in the absence of a fully developed, complex, omnipresent society, but because it yields largely agricultural products and minerals which are shipped out of the region and which are subject to governmental controls or to the profits of distributors and processors outside the region, it cannot fully support itself commercially and must rely on federal aid. Without federal assistance, of course, the entire system of the establishment of frontier territories and the subsequent creation of states would have been impossible or would have taken much longer than it did. In this and in other respects, we see the continuing influence of the frontier environment, in real as well as in symbolic detail.

For the writer, however, complications and tensions hide
within the context of conservatism. Ray B. West, in introduc-
ing a collection of western writing whose title is borrowed
from MacLeish, *A Country in the Mind* (1962), suggests that
while the West may not be able to retain the youthful energy
that Whitman thought made it the most American of all regions, it will not have the difficulties of the South "in coming
to terms with the modern world" nor will it be "seduced, as
has the East, by every fancy breeze" blowing in from Europe.
Instead, the West has been, and perhaps still is, preoccupied
with its natural innocence, its closeness to the romantic innocence of nature-oriented life. If that preoccupation precedes
sophistication, and leads to it, then the western writer is cur-
rently caught between the two, wondering whether sophistication is really a worthwhile substitute for innocence. To be
caught is to be involved in a moment of tension, and that tension is in itself an important contribution to the possibility of
great art. Sophistication is both an attitude and a style, and it
is already present (though limited) in the Western novel as one
or the other, but only rarely do the two come together, and it
is still a matter of contention as to whether they should.

Conservatism is also a confusing issue in the writer's relationship with his past, both personal and regional. To continue reviving the past in order to maintain a belief that "those
were the good old days" is an act of nostalgia which is
eventually self-defeating. However, if we consider memory of
the past to be spiritual as it conquers historical time, we then
think not of a conserving memory, not of nostalgia, but of a
creatively transfiguring memory, not static but dynamic, its
purpose to keep what is alive for future generations. Because
his past is close to him, it is still a personal matter to the western novelist, and to the best of his ability he preserves it in a
reality which consists of the coexistence of those levels of time
we normally refer to as past, present, and future. Charles
Child Walcutt speaks to the other side of this attitude in discussing some Eastern novels:

There are elements of idealism in *Point of No Return, Executive Suite, The Hucksters, The Great Man,* and *The Man in the Gray Flannel Suit,* but they are carefully trimmed, represented generally in terms of nostalgic memories of childhood rather than revolt against the fundamental ills of our world, and accommodated to Exurbanite problems of keeping up with taxes, alcoholism, time-payments, and above all holding one's job. The crisis in these novels is not personal but typical; their expert reportage mixes glamour and sociology, presents the individual as obviously a product of his milieu, and accepts this world of conformity and surfaces with a bit of scorn and a great deal of complacency.

Walcutt's comments are directed toward one kind of Eastern novel which may well have its own formula and be considered commercial rather than literary, so that it would be unfair to offer a comparison between, for example, *The Man in the Gray Flannel Suit* (1955) and Steinbeck's *To a God Unknown* (1933) or Fisher's *Dark Bridwell* (1931). Nevertheless, generalizations can be instructive and suggestive as well as dangerous or, at worst, amusing, and it does not hurt to yield to temptation if the sin is not likely to be fatal. Recognizing the risks, then, I offer some tentative comparisons between Eastern fiction (in the United States) and Western fiction. Through inference it may be possible to add to the image of the place called the West as it is seen, again through inference, in contrast with the place called East.

Eastern Fiction	Western Fiction
Characters shaped directly by society—economic status, neighbors, employers. Confined to the expediencies of a metropolitan or suburban business society.	Characters are independent, although shaped by the land, and have a good deal to say about their destinies. Usually shaped morally rather than psychologically, thus allowing freedom of action.
Based on sophistication and	Based on wonder. The quest.

disillusionment. Withdrawal. The socially bound person rebels, or pulls in, compromising with society or trying to break with it.

Any surrender is usually to the land rather than to society. Characters still remain free within their society.

Concerned with a short social and psychological view, with the immediate moment and its possibilities.

Concerned with the long view, with man as member of a race or species, as part of the natural environment.

Usually Freudian, with man's behavior explained in terms of sex, childhood training within a social context, and the frustrations and guilts which can be blamed on man's condition and environment rather than on the man himself as moral being.

Usually Jungian, tapping the unconscious, aware of racial patterns which connect the past with the present, taking interest in primitivism, and embodying archetypes and natural symbols which reveal or support the collective unconscious.

Concerned with specific and temporary goods and evils, such as job, money, social position, reputation.

Concerned with good and evil as eternal qualities, as permanence within nature.

Character seeks to identify within his immediate group and social environment.

Character seeks to identify with nature, within the entire scheme of life, as representative Man.

Largely contemporary, with emphasis on current problems.

Largely historical, examining effects of past on present.

Conditioned fears.

Primitive fears.

Emphasis on the small differences in people. Attempts at

Emphasis on the sameness of people, in spite of cultural

newness in plot and characterization. Strange and abnormal people, or outrageous situations. Cleverness. Frenzy arising out of nothing.	differences. Characterization often seems close to stereotyping, and plots are often weak. Spiritual calm in the midst of fury or disaster.
Man is both caught in and protected by his society. Not necessary to win or lose—compromise is important. Confrontation with society and a search for compromise.	Man takes the test of survival alone, being naked before the universe. Escape from the confines of society; a search for Eden, or for self, or for the secrets of the natural world.
Mostly dramatic in form.	Epic, romantic, or mythic. Often lyrical.
Good and evil merge, blend, wash out.	Good and evil tend to be absolutes.
Pattern of coming to terms with hell, compromising with it, explaining it away in Freudian terms, or using it in melodramatic fantasy.	Pattern of destruction, the experience of hell, and finally rebirth. Frequent suggestion of resurrection image in terms of natural cycles.
Form is intensive. Novel begins on surface of character and plot and digs in, like peeling layers off an onion. Intensive like the crowded city.	Form is expansive. Novel opens out from character into action, consciousness, moral awareness. Expansive like the open land.
Formal traditions grounded in the immediate past—the eighteenth- and nineteenth-century British novel—and in contemporary European fiction.	Formal traditions, other than those of the British sentimental novel, jump beyond the immediate past to medieval romance, morality play, and Arthurian tales.

Relationship of characters in time. Confinement of space.	Relationship of characters in space. Often a mythic time-lessness, except for traditional type of historical novel which fixes a particular time. Even then, history often seen as flux, or as concentric.
Psychological and social ordeal.	Physical and spiritual ordeal.
Rational, or sophisticated.	Irrational, or intuitive.

William Faulkner said at Nagano in 1955 that the writers of the Mississippi Valley (presumably including himself) and of the West used the techniques of poetry in their fiction: "The Americans east of the mountains more tend to the European and they don't need to resort to lyricism. They have . . . a more precise, rational concept of the material they use, so their kinship is more to the French writers. But the so-called primitive, which would be the uncouth or middle westerner, is more prone to resort to lyricism." As with the other generalizations, this one needs to be broken down into apparent cases in point and the exceptions to them, but its main drift seems to be true. When Vardis Fisher pleads for rationality, love, and compassion—to remove fear—in his *Testament of Man*, he may or may not be thinking also of the necessity of a rational fiction of the West. He frequently stated that irrationality was the curse of Western fiction, but he did not fully manage to escape that curse in his own writing. Frederick Manfred has implied that the Western novel (he was speaking specifically of Frank Waters's work) is not complex but is profound, which seems to me a good distinction in light of the characteristics of the region and the influence of the land upon western writers. The profundity may go unrecognized by readers who are unaccustomed to the natural rhythms of theme, form, and style, and who feel lost without

the traditional imposition of the intellect upon all subject matter. But that too is relative.

5

The American West is so big, and the land itself is so indif-
ferent to the people who live on it or cross over it, that it
seems impersonal, something to be dealt with only in abstract
terms. In writing about the desert-mountain area of California, Mary Austin concluded that it was a strange mixture of
God, death, beauty, and madness—words which might be applied to the West in its entirety. It is not the words taken individually that are important, although they have their own
significance. John Muir, among others, saw the hand of God
in the mountains, and a Wordsworthian attitude is seen in a
segment of Western fiction. While death can be taken lightly
in the natural world, it can also be more tragic or poignant
than it is in the anonymity of a large city. The survivors of the
Donner party, having been exposed to cannibalism, certainly
had a special view of death. Beauty is relative, defined in
terms of personal taste more often than according to any
esthetic principle, but no one can question its presence in the
Western landscape, if not in one place then in another. Madness could easily touch the lone person lost in the desert, or,
as in Clark's *Track of the Cat*, it can attack the most practical
and self-assured person under the right circumstances. But it
is when the four concepts are combined—as they often are in
the West—that they achieve full significance and help explain
something about the land on which Western fiction is based.
The badlands and the barren plains of the north-central area
of the West possess a stark and sometimes devilish beauty
which can prey upon a man's mind, especially when he is
alone. Hugh Glass and several of his *compañeros* went nearly
mad from wandering this part of the plains, their minds filled
with ghostly visions arising from the landscape. The same
landscape, photographed by the comfortable tourist, is
weirdly but inescapably beautiful. Boone Caudill, in the

midst of a mountain paradise, was surely irrational when he killed Teal Eye in *The Big Sky*. Death and beauty coexist in Clark's cat. In the natural cycles of life, death must precede the creation of new beauty, and the event of the resurrection becomes the writer's ally when he wishes to show beauty or wisdom rising from death and ignorance. One part of the western myth makes a moment of beauty out of the brief violence and lasting death of the gunfight in the middle of a dusty street. Austin's four words taken as a totality, or, with a touch of mysticism, accepted as a single, complex attitude, reflect the variety and extremism of the West with its heights, depths, heat, cold, death, immortality, deadly storms, peace and beauty, "hell with the fires out," fresh mountain streams, alkali flats, short grass, giant cactus, loneliness, and Eden. It is no wonder that the land is respected by the people who live on it. They are temporary, but the land belongs.

The West is not cities. It is small towns, ranches, Indian reservations, Spanish villages, most of them quietly unknown. More important, it is space, unpeopled space. It is also distance, topography, and climate. The unvariable is accompanied by the variable, and the eternal is washed by the changeable. The sense of these conditions, the feeling about them, is not greatly altered by the few large cities that stand far apart from each other and whose outer edges slip easily into the immense landscape surrounding them.

The sense of place felt by the western novelists takes on different forms but is essentially the same feeling. Harvey Fergusson discounted heroics as an important element of the West but thought that if a man were lucky he would feel himself a part of the earth, and the earth would be a part of God, so that man and God became one. Fergusson was not a romantic, nor did he speak sentimentally or presumptuously about the potential union of God and man. The idea was a fact of the land. Wallace Stegner, while warning that literature cannot be made of landscape alone, has acknowledged that he likes to live where he can see a long way. It is quite likely that the long view which is often of thematic importance to the

Western novel has its literal beginnings in the western landscape. Max Evans, interested in the contemporary and non-
mythical cowboy, has insisted that the behavior of people
(and characters) is closely related to the land and its climate.
For Frank Waters, the importance of nature is obvious in the
West, where can be found the lowest deserts, the highest
mountains, the deepest canyons, the widest plateaus, and the
wildest rivers in America. It is a fabled land, and it is no wonder that nature, uncontaminated, seemed noble and brought
out the nobility of man as well. It also brought out the worst.
Everything was so big that man seemed but a speck. Everything seemed so timeless that man became concerned about
his own brief life, sometimes treating it recklessly. Spirits of
place haunted him. Invisible ghosts stalked the land. And for
all those people who fled to the West, mostly in the nineteenth
century but not all, to escape some wrong done to them, or
perhaps by them, who carried a sense of guilt into a new land,
"nature with her sublime beauty and diabolic cruelty served
as a psychiatrist's couch, as it were, to heal their wounds, or
else it offered an escape from the realities of society." Times
change. Some of the landscape has been laid waste, stripped,
raped, and scalped. Man's greed continues to attack the mountains and the prairie for minerals, timber, grass, and water. A
new madness, a new death, and perhaps a new God seem intent on destroying the original beauty of the land, and the
juxtaposition of Mary Austin's four words is jumbled and altered, but the words continue to serve as a usable definition of
the West.

In spite of change and of what civilized man refers to as
progress, the West is much the same as it has always been,
and this helps to explain the ease with which the western
novelist brings the past and present together on the same temporal plane in a given place. The western past only seems distant, because much of it became legend and myth even as its
events were taking place, but it has an immediate and pertinent reality as well, if only in the ghosts which haunt the
imagination. The landscape is still distinguished by its variety

and its size; in spite of increased irrigation it is still semiarid and therefore semiharsh. There are no heroes, but perhaps there never were. If great deeds of survival and conquest linger in the history books as well as in fiction, they should perhaps not be considered in terms of the heroic but rather in terms of the intimate and the public, or the sacred and the profane, and the western writer has been doing just that since the 1920s. The sacred places of the West have been of extreme importance to at least a few of the major novelists, just as the holy mountains of the several Indian tribal groups have nourished the spirit and the culture of the tribes for hundreds of years. The contemporary western novelist can focus temporarily on the glut of chain restaurants, motels, and drive-ins that spring up overnight at the edge of such tourist towns as Taos, New Mexico, but he cannot escape his landed heritage. The strange winds of Taos Mountain, which accept or reject the visitor to the area as well as the recent inhabitants, are still a force to be reckoned with, a vital part of the total environment and its effects upon the people within that environment. The man-made monstrosities will pass away, but the mountain and the high plains and the buttes and the river gorges will remain. The West is land. The Western novel, whatever its social implications and philosophical intentions, cannot escape from the land.

III
The Evolution of the Western Novel

Although fiction is divided into categories or types by way of a variety of critical theories, it is probably the unique historical and cultural role of the American West that must guide us in an attempt to define, explain, or describe the Western novel. Without the frontier movement of the nineteenth and immediately preceding centuries, or the several American myths and culture traits which seemed to come into existence as the result of that frontier, or the many ways in which, in the twentieth century, the materials of the historical West have become the ingredients of such popular art forms as the cowboy novel, motion pictures, and television—without these demanding circumstances there might well be less of a need, or desire, to separate a Western novel from any other kind of novel.

Yet we know that there is something we call the Western novel, that it sometimes differs in content, attitude, and emphasis from novels written in or about parts of the world other than the American West. This is not to say that the Western novel may be dismissed as a regional peculiarity lacking in universal concerns. Such an attitude is misleading both in its easy generalization and in its neglect of individual competence within either a genre or a regional literature. For example, to condemn the cowboy novel is not to condemn by association

any other kind of western fiction. The formula western must
be considered in its own terms and must not be allowed to infect the more serious regional novel. Nor can we deny objectivity or universality to a regional novel if we remember that
*Huckleberry Finn, The House of the Seven Gables, Anna Karenina,
Madame Bovary, The Sound and the Fury, Washington Square,* and
Great Expectations are all regional novels. The writer works
best and most significantly out of an ethos of a finite region;
from his own window in New York City or Oxford or Albuquerque or Twin Falls, he looks out upon the world, making observations and judgments from an established base
which is made up of his own traditions and which comprises
his rootedness. In this respect, then, the problems of the
Western regional novel are different from those of other regional novels only so far as the regions themselves differ.

The Western novel is not a maverick literary form, not an
instant mutation, and not a curiosity to be looked at only in
terms of the facts and myths of the Wild West. It has evolved
quite naturally within the historical development of long narrative, even though it has taken a turn here and there because
of its time and its place. The literature of most young countries or civilizations begins with the travel narrative or the
journal of exploration. These, in fact, were the closest literary
forms to that of the novel, and they did not evolve into what
we have long since called the novel until approximately the
first half of the eighteenth century. The American frontier
movement was in progress at that time and so it is not strange
that the travel narrative and the journal of exploration in the
West lent certain elements of form and some narrative devices
to the novel which followed. Nor is it strange that the early
novel in America should be influenced—indeed, determined—by the rapidly developing novel in England. It is
only historical coincidence, of course, but it is nevertheless
important to remember that a new fictional form in England
and a new geographical area in America were opened up at the
same time. Partly as a result of this coincidence (though not
entirely) the major literary form of the American West has

been the novel—the long narrative—rather than the poem, the short story, or the play.

It may be too obvious to say that poetry, short fiction, and drama have not flourished in the West simply because the subject (the place itself) is too big to encompass in a short work. After all, a writer may select from the whole, may choose incidents, characters, and places which are interesting in their own right, apart from the entire fabric of which they are but threads. The difficulty here is probably a psychological one in which the writer is almost forced by the immensity of the landscape to look out from himself rather than to turn inward and examine a soul in its relation to an established, manageable, clearly limited social or natural environment. Such environments are few and far between in the large reaches of the western plains and mountains, and they are, even yet, too young to have the traditions and the stability of Hardy's Wessex or even Faulkner's Yoknapatawpha. Size and space dominate the American West, making much of the short fiction appear to be sketches, the lyrical poetry sentimental and romantic in its tendency to reveal the awestruck poet, and drama almost impossible because of the containment of the stage.

We can say that the short story has flourished only if we are willing to accept sketches, anecdotes, tales (tall and short), hymns to the land dramatized lightly and often stereotypically, and character studies which lack depth unless they can be accepted as archetypes. Too often the short story has been a part of the literary exploitation of the West, serving magazine readers (especially in the nineteenth century) who wanted romance, adventure, and exotic atmosphere dished up to them in a subliterary kind of claimed or pretended history. The frontier was a provider of excitement, to be lived vicariously by people who wanted to escape from their own drab lives by flirting with cowboys, Indians, U.S. and local lawmen, and the soldiers and scouts of military campaigns. These readers did not look for literary quality, even though some of them might have done so with a different kind of story, a nonwestern story. They asked instead for the formula story with its heroes and villains, its gunfights, and its adventures in the grandeur of the mountains or the dust of the sun-baked plains. Hundreds of western stories exist, perhaps thousands, but the nagging question remains: how many of these stories are discussible in terms of style, contemporaneity, psychological depth of character, or structure, rather than for the traditional themes and landscapes and stereotyped characters of the formula story? Some, certainly, but perhaps not enough to fill one hefty volume. In any case, no such volume can be found. Western short story collections invariably include (perhaps for historical significance) a smattering of formula stories, a sampling of more sophisticated stories, and a number of excerpts from novels (usually not identified as such).

Nevertheless, some of the major western novelists have been interested enough in the short story form to give it a measure of distinction and, occasionally, high achievement: Walter Van Tilburg Clark, *The Watchful Gods and Other Stories* (1950); Vardis Fisher, *Love and Death* (1959); Paul Horgan, *The Peach Stone* (1967); Wallace Stegner, *The Women on the Wall* (1950), and *The City of the Living and Other Stories* (1956); Conrad Richter, *Early Americana and Other Stories* (1936); Oliver La Farge, *All the Young Men* (1935), *A Pause in the Desert* (1957), and *The Door in the Wall* (1965); A. B. Guthrie, Jr., *The Big It* (1960); Frederick Manfred, *Apples of Paradise* (1968); John Steinbeck, *The Long Valley* (1938). Not all of the stories in these volumes are set in the West, but of those that are, and notably in Clark, Horgan, and Stegner, many are exceptional. Frank Waters and Harvey Fergusson, although they have been almost as prolific in nonfiction as in the novel, have not been attracted to the short story. Other writers should be mentioned here, although they cannot be called equally western or equally proficient: Katherine Anne Porter, Dorothy Johnson, Jack Schaefer, Mary Austin, Bret Harte, Stephen Crane, Owen Wister, Eugene Manlove Rhodes, Zane Grey, Ernest Haycox, and Jack London. It is obvious that the West is not lacking in the short story—at least not in numbers—

but as a serious literary form the story is still developing. It has not reached the status of the novel.

Poetry has been in even less evidence, except perhaps on the fringes of the West, especially in California. Dismissing the many cowboy poets, and the storytellers in verse, we are left with a handful of poets who might be called major as well as western. Within this relatively small number there is no one poet as thoroughly devoted to the West as subject as have been novelists Walter Clark and Frank Waters, for example. Whether the poet is less likely to be satisfied with the material of one region, or whether he discovers eventually that the poem cannot absorb the enormity of the western landscape, need not be argued here. It is just as possible that, for whatever reason, poetry has been slower in developing within a region whose traditional literary concerns have been in storytelling. Even so, poetry in the West is maturing under the examples of Robinson Jeffers, Witter Bynner, Yvor Winters, Theodore Roethke, William Stafford, Winfield Townley Scott, and Thomas McGrath. In sheer numbers, at least, there are more western poets than novelists in the fourth quarter of the twentieth century. Many of them are intent on nothing more than describing the landscape, although not all in this group can be called romantic. Few California poets can be called western, and most of them do not want to be considered as such unless it means a geographical location and nothing more. With the revival of interest in the American Indian during the 1960s and 1970s many poets have taken themes, techniques, and attitudes from the Indian's oral traditions of song and chant. Too often, however, fashion and exploitation (in the manner of Bret Harte's nineteenth-century short stories) have proved to be greater motivating factors than personal experience, integrity, and objectivity. And, interestingly, the poets tend to live in cities, in spite of their apparent concern for the land, whereas the novelists have lived in relative isolation, working alone.

Isolation is not uncommon in the West and a variety of themes and attitudes—as well as methods—still lingering in the Western novel were at least foreshadowed, if not actually put to use, in the notes and reports of early nineteenth-century explorers, travelers, and adventurers. Of the American influences on the Western novel, the earliest is the travel narrative, or the journal of exploration. Some of these accounts were, of course, written by Europeans who came here to observe the wilderness. Others were written by Americans, although we must recognize that the western landscape was almost as strange to them as it was to the foreign visitors. If it can be said that one expedition opened the West, we must concede it to be that of Lewis and Clark, and their journals would seem to be of considerable importance. The difficulties and necessities which began noticeably in these reports (quite apart from such things as the abominable spelling) continued in narratives both informational and fictional through the nineteenth century and have persisted in many ways in the twentieth-century novel.

President Jefferson ordered Captain Lewis to chart all landmarks, to learn as much as he could of all Indian tribes encountered on the journey, to make notes on the "soil and face of the country," the vegetable growth, animals, minerals, characteristics of climate, seasonal variations and their influence upon plant, animal, and insect life, and dozens of other details which would serve as a useful catalogue of the newly acquired territory. The orders were extremely detailed and thorough, and with them began the westerner's habit of listing and describing "things." Part of the procedure of establishing a tradition is the naming of things in the region, the gathering of facts peculiar to the region. These serve as a basis for the building of tradition, for establishing a background from which to work, normally a slow process. One of the curses of Western fiction is that it has been forced to build a tradition and use it almost simultaneously. In this respect a novelist like A. B. Guthrie, Jr., has been perhaps more useful than literary, although I do not wish to slight his abilities as a novelist. His journalistic background has served him well in researching and then re-creating the Old West, first in *The Big*

Sky (the era of the mountain man) and then in *The Way West* (the Oregon Trail adventure), both novels making extensive use—often close to literal—of sources such as the journal of Osborne Russell, Parkman's *The Oregon Trail* (1849), and, for mountain man speech characteristics, George Ruxton and Lewis Garrard. The emphasis on western facts can take attention away from structure and plot, but if Guthrie's well-known trilogy (including *These Thousand Hills*) is taken as a single unit rather than three separate stories, then theme and structure begin to hold more significance.

It is essentially with the Lewis and Clark journals that the gathering of facts begins, accompanied by the combination of objectivity and romantic awe which, as a combination, remains in virtually all of the Western novels of the past century. Lewis and Clark were remarkably objective in their account of the Missouri River area, but they at least foreshadowed the serious problem in writing about the West—a romantic attitude in the face of grandeur and vastness never before seen by Americans or by most Europeans. In addition to a landscape which invited an emotional response, early nineteenth-century travelers in the West were somewhat under the spell of the English Romantics, especially Wordsworth who was close to them in time. It is not strange, then, to find a Wordsworthian vocabulary throughout the journals of Lewis and Clark. A scene is "singularly beautiful"; a waterfall is "wild" and "irregular" in its "sublimity"; the whole view is a "charming prospect"; and above the river lies a "delightful" plain. These terms are from the Biddle edition, and it is true that Biddle and Allen supplied some of them. However, in the original journal the language is similar. One of the most common descriptive words is "picturesque," followed closely by "magnificent," "handsome," and "beautiful." But how was one to cope with the tremendous northern plains, or the Rockies, or the flash and turmoil of mountain streams?

In spite of the evocative landscape, Lewis and Clark managed to keep a clear realization of their mission and to collect the information requested by Jefferson. However, they could not escape the ever-present ambivalence toward a land which is both beautiful and plain, rejuvenating and deadly, desolate and free, and harsh but spiritually refreshing. They described a river as "menacing" and "frowning in darkness" but also as a "sublime and extraordinary spectacle." Lewis named Maria's River in Montana after a young lady he had known, Miss Maria Wood, and in so doing he entered in his journal a feeling that was common in the early West:

> It is true that the hue of the waters of this turbulent and troubled stream but illy comport with the pure celestial virtues and amiable qualifications of that lovely fair one; but on the other hand it is a noble river . . . it passes through a rich and fertile and one of the most beautifully picturesque countries that I ever beheld . . . its borders garnished with one continued garden of roses.

The optimistic half of the view began in the eighteenth century when Jonathan Carver reached Minnesota (no longer considered a western state, of course) and saw the immense potential which led to the concept of Manifest Destiny. The West, whether in Minnesota or Kansas, would become the new seat of empire, the center of the civilized world. Carver's report was offset by those of Captain Pike and Major Long which stressed the broad and lengthy desert extending along the eastern side of the Rockies. Like Lewis and Clark, however, most explorers and visitors of the first half of the nineteenth century expressed both optimism and pessimism, sometimes alternately, and sometimes simultaneously. The West fostered ambivalence through its great variety of climate and terrain.

Some thirty years after Lewis and Clark, Joseph Nicollet led an expedition through those parts of South and North Dakota traversed by the James River. The river, to him, was a "magnificent spectacle," perhaps the most beautiful river on the continent, but the plains which extended away from the river proved to be so monotonous and dreary, so hot and fly-plagued, that Nicollet had to give his men medicine to raise their spirits and keep them going. A survey of the early nineteenth-century journals and narratives shows that every newcomer to the West reacted in much the same way. The landscape was, and still is, conducive to elation and depression almost simultaneously, because the land is diverse and beautiful on the one hand, and grim and monotonous on the other. Because the West is a land of extremes, the writer who confronts it is likely to respond in romantic terms—the romantic attitude itself being brought about by extremism in one form or another. But, because journeys into the West were also fact-finding in nature, a pattern developed which has worked its way deep into the twentieth century. The western writer is engaged objectively in the task of gathering regional details, particularly physical characteristics, and he is also subjectively affected by the overwhelming size of the land and the many contrasts in climate and topography. Western American literature, then, is almost always an unusually strong mixture of the objective and the subjective. There have been differing proportions of this mixture—as one would expect—and even a few indications that the two attitudes might be fused in the imagination (Mary Austin and Walter Clark, as two examples).

However, the earliest writers were influenced by their experiences and training in the East and in Europe, so that they tended to respond to wilderness elements in allusions and a formality which were out of place in American culture. Washington Irving was capable of spare, concise, unembellished writing such as he set down in his notebooks while on the tour of Oklahoma in 1832. He seemed to have a good eye for detail, as seen in the quick and fragmentary impressions of his journal. But later, when he wrote *A Tour on the Prairies* (1832), he "gave wings to his imagination" and did so in terms of his European experience. He described the Osage Indians as "so many bronze figures" with "fine Roman countenances"; the Indian Agency became "a little hamlet," Antoine the half-breed "an Adonis of the frontier," and an old squatter a "knight-errant of the frontier," a Lycurgus, a Draco. This is overstatement. What was needed in the West was understatement; only in this way could the already exaggerated features of the landscape become meaningful.

Two writers following Irving took large steps in the right direction. Josiah Gregg's *Commerce of the Prairies* (1844) is a quiet, factual, underplayed account of Gregg's journeys in the Southwest, mostly along the Santa Fe Trail. The writing is somewhat academic and scholarly but neither pompous nor complex. His book has been called a moral and natural history because he paid close attention to the things of the region and to social customs, especially among the Spanish speaking people. Like many other men, Gregg went west largely for his health. According to popular opinion he was consumptive (tubercular), but because of his breathing problems and his claustrophobia it is likely that he suffered from acute sinusitis and allergies. His condition improved rapidly on the plains with clean air and a measure of solitude. As an observer, he was perceptive, objective, scientific, and, perhaps most important, sympathetic enough with southwest culture to become more of an insider than either Irving or Cooper. His curiosity was boundless, but he did not allow it to romanticize the landscape or the people he encountered often enough to achieve a familiarity with them. And so he formalized the travel narrative and gave it integrity.

It was Lewis Garrard, a young man of seventeen, and Francis Parkman, only a few years older, who brought a literary quality to the travel narrative. In *Wah-to-yah and the Taos Trail* (1850) Garrard responded to his new world with the freshness and spontaneity of youth, without prejudice or preconception, but with a wisdom that allowed him to avoid the usual kind of landscape description and to focus his attention upon people and their talk and actions. The book is filled with accurate information and is useful for that alone, but it also shows flashes of modern novelistic techniques, especially in the fusion of description and action, in allowing the reader to visualize the immediate scene as the action occurs. (The normal tendency was to separate landscape description from the action of the narrative, focusing on one thing at a time.) Garrard also had a good ear for dialect, transcribing the special language of the mountain man as accurately as anyone. Neither a linguist nor an anthropologist, he nevertheless began a glossary of the Cheyenne language and gradually introduced Spanish words into his text, using them as naturally as he would have used English. He was simply eager to learn and to adapt to the country he was in for less than a year. He could be as matter-of-fact as the more scientific Josiah Gregg: "The object of the expedition was to . . . kill and scalp every Mexican to be found, and collect all the animals belonging to the Company and the United States." Later he felt compassion for the Mexicans because they were the underdogs, and so Garrard was thoroughly American, sympathetic to the conditions of the poor and the illiterate but losing his compassion in time of war. The change from gentleness and concern to a kind of hunter syndrome is a strong part of the American experience and may have been bred into us by the circumstances of the frontier. Certainly Garrard's attitudes can be traced into the modern Western novel. Similarly, he wavered between an open mind toward Indian women and the standard prejudicial reaction of his time, perhaps proving the strength of the Indian stereotype in the nineteenth century. Through his own reactions, his sensitivity to language and action along with observation of the landscape, and his ability to dramatize scenes in a fresh way, he offered hints of what was to come in Western fiction a century later.

Francis Parkman did not fare as well. A young man of twenty-three, he was on the Oregon Trail at almost the same time that Garrard was on the Santa Fe Trail (1846, 1847 for the two). Parkman's Boston Brahmin background kept him from putting his experiences into really significant terms: he could not find the language he needed to confront and convey the extent, solitude, and wildness of the West. On seeing the Platte River for the first time he registered confusion:

> At length we gained the summit, and the long-expected valley of the Platte lay before us. We all drew rein, and sat joyfully

looking down upon the prospect. It was right welcome; strange, too, and striking to the imagination, and yet it had not one picturesque or beautiful feature; nor had it any of the features of grandeur, other than its vast extent, its solitude, and its wildness.

This passage is the key to *The Oregon Trail* because even though Parkman was able to record a good deal of useful information he was always uneasy in the West. He felt that the landscape (like the Platte River valley) was indeed unusual and worth commenting upon, but it was so different from the landscapes of his previous experience that he had no words to give it life or form. Parts of the West, in fact, seemed lifeless to him: "No living thing was moving throughout the vast landscape, except the lizards." Repeatedly, Parkman was forced to use the term "picturesque" in order to state his vague and puzzled feelings about the land. Deprived of the northern "grandeur" witnessed by Lewis and Clark, he was also deprived of the term itself, except as it could be used negatively. Much of Parkman's language is, in a sense, negative— "dreary," "monotonous," "rude," "sultry," "waste," "oppressive"—but he also responded to certain scenes in a romantic way:

> Far off, beyond the black outline of the prairie, there was a ruddy light, gradually increasing, like the glow of a conflagration; until at length the broad disk of the moon, blood-red, and vastly magnified by the vapors, rose slowly upon the darkness, flecked by one or two little clouds, and as the light poured over the gloomy plain, a fierce and stern howl, close at hand, seemed to greet it as an unwelcome intruder.

At precisely this point in his trip, Parkman also felt that he and "the beasts were all that had consciousness for many a league around," suggesting perhaps a touch of Emersonianism, a consciousness with nature, that has played an important part in Western literature. The Indians, of course, attributed various kinds of power and magic to animals, carried animal totems, and left their own influence upon the relationship between man and animal in the modern Western novel. Animalism of differing kinds can be found in Bret Harte, Frank Norris, Jack London, Vardis Fisher, and many other writers. Whether Parkman felt deeply his momentary relationship with the horses, or whether he merely reflected a reading of Emerson, is difficult to say. His attitudes were generally ambivalent, partly the result of his personal conflict between progress and love of the past, or between bourgeois society and chivalric aristocracy. For a budding historian he missed out on a great many events and their initial impact upon American society. In 1846, while he was on the trail, the United States declared war on Mexico, President Polk approved the act to establish forts along the Oregon Trail (thereby giving sanction to expansion), the Mormons were on their way to Utah, the Donner party was on its way west and to a memorable winter, and many mountain men were looking for jobs—particularly as guides—because the American Fur Company had collapsed just four years earlier. The Plains Indians were still relatively peaceful, and it often seems that Parkman could have given us much more information about the people and events of a crucial period in the West than he did. Yet that may be asking too much of a young easterner, and the importance of *The Oregon Trail* to the later novel is that it pointed up problems of language and attitude that had to be resolved before Western writing could be considered mature.

Parkman's account of his trip is organized just as the trip itself was, in three parts: the journey westward on the Oregon Trail, an extended stay at Fort Laramie, and the journey back by way of Denver and the Santa Fe Trail. From the historian's point of view, Parkman's best reporting came out of his observations at Laramie. Here he notices the coming and going of the wagon trains, mountain men, and Indians and describes life at the fort with objectivity as well as color. The rest of the book is more subjective, even more so than the travel narratives preceding *The Oregon Trail*. And even though scientists went west in the last third of the nineteenth century, keeping journals and writing books just as everyone else was doing, subjectivity increased. This trend, however, must be seen as a trend, not as a strict rule. Clarence King, the geologist, had a subjective heart, perhaps, as did Mary Austin later, but he saw the land with an objective eye, with an intelligence which allowed him to analyze even as he appreciated the beauty of the mountains. His *Mountaineering in the Sierra Nevada* (1872) employed enough action to suggest that he might have been a novelist had he wished, and concern with language that indicated a feeling for poetry—all this within the framework of a geological exploration. While contemplating his theory of the catastrophic origins of the mountains, he could also look at nature passively, that is to say esthetically, and describe "the little fields of alpine grass, pale yet sunny, soft under our feet, fragrantly jeweled with flowers of fairy delicacy, holding up amid thickly clustered blades chalices of turquoise and amethyst, white stars, and fiery little globes of red."

King's book is closely linked to John Muir's *My First Summer in the Sierra* (although not published until 1911, Muir's account is based on an 1869 trip which put him in the area at about the same time as King), but while both men were natural scientists as well as possessing a theological bent, Muir was more religious and mystical than esthetic. The tone in his book is rapt and passionate even though much of the language is flat and banal. His feelings about the holiness of nature and the wickedness of man increase the subjectivity of the travel narrative almost to its highest point:

> Found a lovely lily *(Calochortus albus)* in a shady adenostoma thicket near Coulterville, in company with *Adiantum Chilense*. It is white with a faint purplish tinge inside at the base of the petals, a most impressive plant, pure as a snow crystal, one of the plant saints that all must love and be made so much the purer by it every time it is seen. It puts the roughest mountaineer on his good behavior. With this plant the whole world would seem rich though none other existed. It is not easy to keep on with the camp cloud while such plant people are standing preaching by the wayside.

It is difficult to see the plant, to get a good visual picture of it, because Muir, in his description, is more concerned with its quality of purity and with its personification into an active religious force. In Muir's mind, not only was he in the mountains, but the mountains were also in him. He felt converted, complete, immortal, purified by nature. He was certainly neither the first nor the last person to feel that way in the West.

Just as the religious awe of John Muir offset the relative objectivity of Clarence King, so did the humor (often accompanied by romantic descriptions of the landscape) of Mark Twain offset the factual journals of the westward-moving settlers. We are inclined to think of Twain as cynical, but he had his moments of romanticism:

> Toward dawn we got under way again, and presently, as we sat with raised curtains enjoying our early morning smoke and contemplating the first splendor of the rising sun as it swept down the long array of mountain peaks, flushing and gilding crag after crag and summit after summit, as if the invisible Creator reviewed his gray veterans and they saluted with a smile, we hove in sight of South Pass City.

This description from Twain's only western book *(Roughing It)* is immediately followed by a humorous anecdote of a man who is the hotelkeeper, the postmaster, the blacksmith, the mayor, the constable, the city marshal, and the principal citizen of the "city." Twain asks the reader to think of all those people crammed into one skin and then reports a comment by his traveling companion, Bemis: "If he were to die as postmaster and blacksmith both, the people might stand it; but if he were to die all over, it would be a frightful loss to the community." Here, in humor, the travel narrative reaches its peak of subjectivity.

The journal of exploration, then, was limited by the extent of the journey, was objective (often in the sense of record-keeping), with the writer-observer's personal opinions held to a minimum. The travel narrative, also limited by the extent of the journey, nevertheless admitted a measure of selection and organization, largely because it was usually rewritten after the trip ended. With the addition of human interest and drama it became increasingly subjective. The novel based on history is an extension of the journal-narrative and is subjective in that the author accepts or rejects history at will in order to make a good story, but it is objective in that the author, feeling the weight of historical events, does not often inject his own opinions. What the novel picks up is form, imagination, depth of characterization, motivations, and conflict. And yet Guthrie's *The Big Sky* ends rather inconclusively, revealing the travel narrative as a real influence. Like the travel narrative, the Western novel is never completely one-sided in tone: it is always a combination of the objective and subjective, although in differing proportions.

The fusion of the fact-gathering intellect with the feelings has been another matter, almost a rarity. The early writers reacted both to the facts as seen objectively and to the romanticism evoked by nature, and they kept the two attitudes separate. Not until Mary Austin (perhaps in *The Land of Little Rain*, 1903) do we find heart and mind coming together again. And it does not remain that way through every novel that we call Western. Some novels deal primarily in the facts of the West; others exploit the romantic possibilities, although the more serious of these go even further, into mysticism which seems philosophically more respectable and certainly more significant in the total context of the western culture as well as the landscape. But it is not often that the mind and soul become one, and when they do it is more than likely in a novel with some relationship to the American Indian's view of nature. It seems to me that Frank Waters and Walter Clark most consistently achieve or come close to this fusion, but it can be seen also in Harvey Fergusson and perhaps in Vardis Fisher, in spite of the latter's insistence on the primacy of the mind in Western writing.

2

From England the American novel imported the romance, sentimentalism, and adventure of Walter Scott's historical novels, as well as elements of the gothic novel. Even though the gothic novel has gone primarily through Poe into the South, rather than venturing out to the West, its occasional preoccupation with the wilderness, with the darkness of the forest, may be found in such diverse writers as Charles Brockden Brown (closest to the gothic in spirit and technique), Hawthorne, and Faulkner. The forest as symbol of the darkness of man, of evil, or of ignorance and mystery, may well be an early indication of one view of the wilderness later on during the frontier movement. However, since much of the West is open land, the symbols did not survive in quite the same way as they did in portions of the South or New England. Influences are dubious: it is more proper to talk about traditions which have been available. Whether these traditions had any direct bearing upon the Western novel is a matter of opinion.

It is often taken for granted that James Fenimore Cooper is either the first western novelist or that he has been the primary influence upon fiction of the West. Certainly he was the first to introduce an important—some say the *most* important—theme to American literature, that of the confrontation between civilization and the wilderness, and the resulting dilemma. In his long narratives of the frontier (the Leatherstocking saga) he more or less took an impossible philosophical or historical position: it was right for the enlightened European to bring Christianity to the Indians, to clear the land for plowing and the growing of crops, and to civilize the wilderness; but it was equally right for the wilderness to survive in its own way and to resist the efforts of man to destroy it. This is clearly the material for an American tragedy, and Cooper must be given credit for recognizing it as such. Bound to the conventions of the English sentimental novel, he was unable to find a suitable form for his material, and so the major theme is sometimes lost beneath the welter of those conventions which did indeed influence one kind of western writing. It is easy to accuse Cooper—as Mark Twain did—of faults in his writing, ranging through a variety of weaknesses which some readers will shrug off as being of no consequence. Perhaps, in Cooper, they were not, given the grand design which presumably overshadowed them. But it is necessary to rehearse them once again in order to show the pernicious effect they may have had on a later kind of frontier fiction, farther west.

We are familiar with the chase-capture-escape pattern of Cooper's Leatherstocking novels. This sense of adventure, of action for its own sake, became one of the staples of the cowboy-and-Indian western novel. Characterization of women was usually weak; language was often stilted and romantic; moralizing interfered with the pace at times; male characters, although perhaps stronger than the women, were too frequently stereotyped, cast into social, occupational, or political molds; propaganda reared its head at any given moment; and the exaggerated result of all this is the generalization that Cooper, like other sentimental novelists, dealt in stock situations peopled by stock characters. Even as a romancer he was not on a level with Walter Scott. This side of Cooper was picked up by Bret Harte. Again, whether Harte was directly influenced by Cooper, or whether the two men were simply a part of the same frontier climate, does not matter. What does matter is that a kind of formula writing developed in the nineteenth century, around the frontier, which did a great deal of damage later on. It is difficult to say who really began the western formula story, but from the three main possibilities— Cooper, Harte, and Owen Wister—it was probably Harte as much as anyone who created the basic formula. His belief in the inherent goodness of man found fertile ground in the American West where the purity of nature brought out the best in a man. His tough gold miners were soft, his gamblers were noble, his prostitutes were tender, and in the mining towns of California he hit pay dirt with his stereotypes, his stock characters (like Cooper's), his suggestions of the medieval morality plays, and his sentimentalism. These seem to be the ingredients that made him popular. With some contemporary dressing up, his stories began to appear on television almost a century later in the guise of "adult" westerns such as "Gunsmoke." (What makes them adult is the fact that every now and then the western air fails to purify one or more of the characters who manage to remain evil, at least on the surface.)

Harte—and Cooper—did, of course, establish a geo-graphical place and describe it in accurate terms part of the time. However, Harte, writing during the period of local color and early regionalism, seemed to be under the mythical spell of the West already and exploited his materials to a greater extent than did his New England counterparts, Sarah Orne Jewett and Mary Wilkins Freeman. It is difficult to for-give him for his overly romantic scenes in which the "strong man" clings to the "frail babe" ("The Luck of Roaring Camp"), or the "redwoods, burying their moccasined feet in the red soil, [stand] in Indian file along the track, trailing an uncouth benediction from their bending boughs upon the passing bier" (the funeral in "Tennessee's Partner"). Cooper could rise to higher levels of perception, especially when he was able to let the details of a scene lead to a metaphorical con-clusion:

> As they proceeded, the howls of the dogs became more shrill and plaintive. The vultures and buzzards settled so low as to flap the bushes with their heavy wings, and the wind came hoarsely sweeping along the naked prairie, as if the spirits of the air had also descended to witness the approaching develop-ment.

That passage from *The Prairie* can succeed because of Cooper's imagination, but when he wished to describe a particular landscape which he had never seen—as he had to do fre-quently in *The Prairie*—he could not be specific enough or evocative enough to allow the reader to visualize the scene:

> In the little valleys, which, in the regular formation of the land, occurred at every mile of their progress, the view was bounded on two of the sides by the gradual and low elevations which give name to the description of prairie we have men-tioned; while on the others, the meagre prospect ran off in long, narrow, barren perspectives, but slightly relieved by a pitiful show of coarse, though somewhat luxuriant vegetation.

Nothing is named. There are no details. We cannot see what Cooper wanted us to see. It is true, of course, that Washing-ton Irving and Francis Parkman, who actually visited a part of

the West, often did little better in their descriptions, not having the language for dealing with a strange landscape.

While Cooper was himself influenced by the sentimental
novel, particularly the form, he did no worse than many
modern western novelists in turning to the travel narratives
for information. In Cooper's case most of these narratives
were contemporary. He relished them as they were published
and we cannot find fault with his excitement; later writers
have been able to see the narratives more objectively and in
comparison with others. The frontier was still moving westward in Cooper's time, but it was already beyond his personal
experience and place (the area around present-day
Cooperstown, New York) when he began to write the five
wilderness novels in which Natty Bumppo is the central character. The one novel which, in its setting, went into a land
that Cooper never saw—*The Prairie*—had to depend heavily
upon information from the records and notes of someone who
had already been through the area in question. In this case,
Cooper relied on the Stephen H. Long expedition of 1819–20,
whose journals and records were compiled by Edwin James
and published in 1823, four years prior to the publication of
The Prairie. The frontier was at this time moving from the
Mississippi River to the Missouri, and so Leatherstocking
goes beyond the frontier, past the line of civilization, to die
among the Indians. He goes farther than his prototype,
Daniel Boone, did. And while the action of the story must
take place around 1820, Cooper allows us to believe that it is
1804, with his reference to Lewis and Clark traveling to the
north. Doctor Battius is modeled after Edwin James, but the
other characters are brought in, fictionally, from outside.

As a historical novelist of the West, then, Cooper was not
as concerned with accuracies as twentieth-century writers like
Guthrie have been. Nevertheless, his contributions to the
serious Western novel outweigh his shortcomings. It is true
that he could not find an American form, or a new form,
within which to house his American, or new, themes; yet the
best of the western novelists still have some problems with

form, and Cooper cannot be blamed for that. What he gave to later writers was a legacy which was uniquely American, a set of themes, any one of which could be studied and used many times without fear of distracting repetition. Europeans recognized the opportunity to observe the civilized and the primitive simultaneously by "standing on" the frontier line. Was it true that man was good in his primitive state and became corrupted by civilization? The answers were divided, but Americans (Muir, Mary Austin, Robinson Jeffers, and many others) were to carry the problem into a more advanced age of technology and increasing population and say that the wilderness was good and that it was being despoiled by man. Cooper was unable to make a clear choice between the scientific and civilized world of Doctor Battius and the wilderness of the western Indians and their friend, the old trapper. The dilemma remains, and it is still a good theme for fiction. In some ways, too, the old trapper is like the mountain men of the first half of the nineteenth century who opened the passes, discovered the trails, guided the wagon trains, and suddenly discovered that they had been pursued by civilization and that their pristine wilderness was being ravaged in the name of progress. For many Americans, that was a sad moment in their history, and they are filled with a sense of regret. Perhaps for this reason, the Western novel has more often than not dealt with the historical rather than the contemporary, and has frequently been accused of living on nostalgia. However, it is one thing to lament for the dead and for what might have been, and quite another to wish to return to the past. If history has shown us anything, it is that only surface matters change, that the essentials of human existence are the same from one era to the next. Only the forms are different. Cooper knew this. *The Deerslayer* ends with a profound statement about man and his world:

> We live in a world of transgressions and selfishness, and no pictures that represent us otherwise can be true; though, happily for human nature, gleamings of that pure spirit in whose

likeness man has been fashioned are to be seen, relieving its de-
formities, and mitigating, if not excusing, its crimes.

Although history as such may not show a great deal of progress or improvement in the general lot of man, there are those
natural revelations of the pure spirit, brief and rare though
they may be. This recognition—a kind of optimism in its own
right—is an important part of the Western novel and, on occasion, develops into a land-based or nature-centered mysticism
which is different from the romantic response to nature found
throughout Cooper's novels.

Even at the conclusion of *The Last of the Mohicans*, as
Tamenund delivers what could be mistaken for an elegy,
there is no strong tone of resentment, nostalgia, or unfair
death:

> "It is enough," he said. "Go, children of the Lenape, the
> anger of the Manitou is not done. Why should Tamenund
> stay? The pale-faces are masters of the earth, and the time of
> the redmen has not yet come again. My day has been too long.
> In the morning I saw the sons of Unamis happy and strong;
> and yet, before the night has come, have I lived to see the last
> warrior of the wise race of the Mohicans."

For a sentimentalist, Cooper shows remarkable restraint here
as he states a fact—no more. But it is an important fact, as is
the end of the mountain man era in the middle of the nineteenth century, and the end of Indian supremacy on the Great
Plains toward the end of the century. These are western
themes, and they are considerably more important than the
loss of a job, or a five-cent cigar, or an individual life, in the
various kinds of social novels which are usually given more attention by critics and scholars. Americans rest easy with
short-term problems and losses, but they are inclined to reject
the importance of the long view, and so the final scene of *The
Prairie* is viewed in terms of pathos and sentimentality almost
entirely, with little thought for the cyclical nature of life and
the beginnings which rise from endings.

I am not at all certain that Cooper had in mind the same

interpretation that I have suggested through a brief look at the endings of three novels in the Leatherstocking series, but it seems to the point that physical nature (Cooper's descriptions of it), action, and characters are all part of a large moral theme which provides a framework for the five Natty Bumppo novels. Natty may be Daniel Boone, and he may also be Kit Carson and Jedediah Smith, all legendary figures from the time of the opening of the West. As a legendary character, Natty is therefore symbolic rather than naturalistic, and when he attempts to run ahead of the advance of civilization, trying to escape from it, he is clearly making a moral judgment on civilized society. Even Hurry Harry, in *The Deerslayer*, emerges as one kind of traitor, a man who lives as a woodsman in the wilderness but who uses the wilderness as a place of business and constantly returns to his "office" in the settlements. Cooper's foresight was proven countless times when the wilderness all across the West was ravaged by exploiters. The modern Western novel makes use of the same theme, often employs the same moral indignation, frequently takes legendary people as characters and builds symbolic statements about the path of civilization, and presents ideas indirectly through symbols or feelings or the relationship between man and land (character and setting). Furthermore, the modern western novelist tends to agree with Cooper (allowing for normal complications) in placing natural law above tribal law which is in turn placed above civil law. Much of Cooper, especially from *The Deerslayer* and *The Prairie*, appears in different forms in the Western novel of the twentieth century. Whether there is a direct influence from one to the other, I doubt, but we must admit that Cooper was the first to explore areas which were later considered of extreme importance by writers dealing with the wilderness in its many western stages.

Although Hawthorne differs from Cooper in a number of ways, especially in his concern with the consequences of actions rather than in the actions themselves, he too was aware of the American restlessness and the complexities of finding a

home, or a father, or new traditions while breaking away from
the old ones, from our European background. Even while in
England *(Our Old Home,* 1863), impressed by the solidity and
permanence of buildings and traditions, his most pleasant moments were the trips, the journeys, the restlessness which
drew him from one house to another. He saw his own coun-
trymen as wanderers, vagabonds, "homeless in the widest
sense," people who had never had a country or perhaps had
lost it. The wandering is obviously both an escape from the
past and an attempt to find a new home or a spiritual father.
The ambivalence in the search for a father, a home, is at its
strongest when expressed in the love-hate ambiguity which is
archetypal. Perhaps this is a peculiarly American problem because of our special conditions in time and space, and perhaps
it can be expressed in the concept of "houselessness," the loss
of tradition being equivalent to the lack of a home. This old
and mythic theme is the story of Adam and the loss of innocence, and it is also the story of the American in a new and big
land, cut off from his European traditions. Furthermore, as in
Hawthorne, it is a dualistic search for materiality and for the
spiritual.

The theme has many facets and ramifications, but all of
them are thoroughly grounded in the American experience.
There is the escape from a confining past, and therefore the
freedom of a new land not yet bound up in social and political
restrictions; there is the quest for Eden, the last stage in the
world-wide "course of empire"; and there is mobility, both social and physical—the democratic freedom of individual enterprise, and the large open spaces of a relatively unpopulated
continent inviting the takers and the exploiters. In two senses,
then, Americans have had room to move about. This part of
the American experience—and it may be the most important
part—has reached a new significance in the Western novel;
but it has been important in American fiction since Hawthorne. In *The House of the Seven Gables* (1851) he asked: "Where
is our universe? All crumbled away from us; and we, adrift in
chaos, may hearken to the gusts of homeless wind, that go

sighing and murmuring about, in quest of what was once a world!" The physical and the spiritual are curiously mixed in this quest. In one respect the American has achieved with a vengeance what we might call physical "houseness." In the middle of the twentieth-century mass-housing developments made it possible for renters to become owners. Around each large city in the United States may be found huge areas over which legions of machines have swarmed to knock down the trees and lay waste the land in order to seed it with houses, thousands of houses set monotonously row upon row. These houses are often poorly built and subject to early decay, but they have provided any American who has a job with the opportunity to own his home. The house has become a sign of status, especially in the higher income brackets, from which the American has created the modern concept of suburbia. Particularly in the East, where many people work in the metropolitan area of New York City but live in Connecticut or along the Hudson River or in New Jersey, the house in the suburbs has become a status symbol. The phenomenon is not limited to the East, of course, but a number of Eastern regional novels have dealt with this use of home.

However, precisely because the house symbolizes status, it is temporary. In our mobile society of business and risk, fortunes rise and fall regularly; and as a man rises or falls, he moves into a better or a cheaper house. But the house is only a symbol; it does not represent family traditions as does the European house. In Henry James's *Washington Square* (1881) the women argue the advantages of the house which Arthur Townsend has taken in New York, and he replies:

> "It doesn't matter . . . it's only for three or four years. At the end of three or four years we'll move. That's the way to live in New York—to move every three or four years. Then you always get the last thing. . . . I guess we'll move up little by little; when we get tired of one street we'll go higher. So you see we'll always have a new house."

Townsend goes on to explain that with a new house one gets all the latest improvements. This is typically American, the desire for the new, for the improved gadgets of living, to the neglect of the traditional. On this physical level the putting by of the things of the past is not serious; but in its spiritual implications it becomes almost tragic.

Theodore Dreiser touches upon the spiritual and moral aspects of this kind of mobility in *Sister Carrie* (1900) and in *An American Tragedy* (1925). Carrie leaves the farm and goes to the big city in order to rise in status. In a way she does improve herself, at least financially. But she soars to the top at the expense of Hurstwood, who loses his home and family and eventually himself; and Carrie finds only loneliness at the end. Whatever advantages social mobility may have, these do not include, usually, the achievement of a spiritual home. Clyde, in the later novel, also leaves his home. His reasons for leaving may be good ones, but his search for a better home culminates in death, both spiritual and physical. Although the house is a part of our pattern of mobility, of our search, we must see as the significant characteristic of the American not physical houseness but spiritual houselessness. The American is a wanderer by nature and circumstance, an escapee from European restrictions, a chaser of dreams. One of those dreams was projected into the West.

In the literature of the West, partly because of the lingering frontier influence and partly because of the additional space, there has been less housing (Los Angeles excepted, of course) and more moving. The space is one determinant; there is room to move around in. And, just as the American in many respects escaped from Europe, so has the western American escaped from the East in his own country. Following the Civil War, for example, thousands of ex-soldiers fled west in order to get away from the effects of the war and to begin life anew. Even the social restrictions of New England and the plantation South drove men to the West, men like Natty Bumppo, Boone Caudill, and Hugh Glass.

The fact that America is a democracy has itself led to several variations of the theme of home and the road. Alexis de Tocqueville, in *Democracy in America* (1835), perceptively isolated a number of distinctions between Europe and America which find their way into our literature. In aristocratic societies, families often remained on the same location for many generations (as in England) and through the ties of a place—a house—all generations became contemporaneous. With a clear relationship between generations, a man would tend to know his ancestors almost as well as the immediate members of his family and could even think that he knew his descendants. As a result, he often sacrificed "his personal gratifications to those who went before and to those who [would] come after him." It is not so in America. Here "the track of generations is effaced." We forget those who came before us, and we are rarely concerned with those who will follow (this in spite of periodic interests in family trees and with environmental problems which affect the future). In fact, as with Jay Gatz in *The Great Gatsby* (1925) and with mountain men such as Hugh Glass in Frederick Manfred's *Lord Grizzly*, there is a deliberate attempt to cloud the personal origins, to keep the past a secret. Americans believe in the fresh start. One result of this belief is freedom and independence; but it also makes of man a lonely creature, confined "within the solitude of his own heart."

The mountain man in the Western novel is not entirely alone. What Tocqueville talks about is on the level of organized society, but the brotherhood of the mountain men goes around or beyond society as such. Hugh Glass learns that he cannot prevail alone, but what he needs, and what he finds in the West, is not social organization but a companionship on a larger and more spiritual level, something like a fellowship of the human race rather than of mere society or nationality. Democracy may throw citizens apart, as Tocqueville suggests, but it may also tighten natural ties and bring people together in heart and mind. The mountain men of Hugh Glass's time were individuals in the purely social sense; they would not put up with tyranny in any form, with restriction, or with personal meddling. But in time of danger they risked their lives willingly in order to preserve the group.

The comments of Tocqueville suggest that the questions

of tradition and home are far more complex in the American experience than they are in the European (excepting, in one sense, parts of post-World War II Europe) precisely because the American experience, like that of Adam, involves the loss of tradition and home and therefore the necessity of a search for them. The search itself gives a vitality to American fiction which is lacking in much of the literature from an older and more established social context.

The many complexities and possibilities of the "home" theme are first suggested, I think, in *The House of the Seven Gables,* although Hawthorne has not exploited his materials as well as he might have. It occurs to me that this novel would have been far more effective had it closed on the juxtaposition of the judge sitting dead and defeated in the House, and Clifford and Hepzibah escaping on the train. The house is a symbol of crime and guilt, of an unsavory past which haunts the present. Escaping from the influence of the house would be a good enough thing so that we could ignore the possible murder-guilt of Clifford. The railroad is an effective symbol of the fresh beginning: Clifford says that "this admirable invention of the railroad . . . is destined to do away with those stale ideas of home and fireside, and substitute something better." As the train bears Clifford and Hepzibah away from the house, we feel that their lives have been cleansed, that in escaping from the Judge and the house they have at last done a sensible thing. As for the Judge, we feel no sympathy for him, and so it is just as well that he remains behind, dead like the house, his influence broken. (Although the railroad is here a symbol of escape, it is worth noting that in later novels of the West the railroad brings civilization and all of its problems into the areas to which people had previously escaped. The railroad in American fiction operates, then, in two ways—a curious double symbol of escape *and* recapture.)

There is a vision in Hawthorne's chapter of the train, "The Flight of Two Owls," which is not sustained beyond that chapter; but it is a significant foreshadowing of much that comes later in American fiction. Hawthorne, through Clifford, predicts that the "facilities of locomotion are destined to bring us round again to the nomadic state." The nomadic state is considered a primitive one, as opposed to settled civilizations. Hawthorne is aware of ancient traditions, almost racial, as a matter quite different from the newer social and national traditions. These traditions from the distant past shape us also:

> While we fancy ourselves going straight forward, and attaining, at every step, an entirely new position of affairs, we do actually return to something long ago tried and abandoned, but which we now find etherealized, refined, and perfected to its ideal. The past is but a coarse and sensual prophecy of the present and the future.

This idea takes hold in Western regional fiction of the twentieth century. The particular aspect of man's development which is refinement is given full treatment in Wallace Stegner's *The Big Rock Candy Mountain* (1943). Through Bo Mason, one of the many characters in western fiction who are frontiersmen born too late, Stegner examines the influences which the rough and often cruel dreamers of the frontier West have upon their descendants. (The pattern of influences here is not unlike that suggested by Turner in his essay on the frontier.) While a man may not leave behind him a house or any other marks of a physical existence, he does leave memory, emotion, and experience. The succeeding generation absorbs its fathers, sometimes unquietly, in memory, and passes the accumulated experience on to its children. The result is a gradual refinement of the strain; but to make this strain a good one we need more than the Calvinistic goodness—we need also the recklessness of the explorer, the aspirations of the dreamer, and even some of the coarseness and wickedness which were once required in order to survive the land. In the early American West, the ancient nomadic state is repeated, so that the cycle of which Hawthorne and others spoke is seen reduced in size and played out in a shorter span of years within the boundaries of a specific nation. Nevertheless, the pattern remains ancient, racial, and universal. Although Hawthorne lived at the time when this pattern was being established in the American West, he did not recognize it as the material of fiction. Nevertheless, he had the early vision which has since been explored thoroughly by western writers.

Clifford is carried away by his vision on the train and pursues matters which do not have direct application to the theme of home and the road. His remarks on electricity, which culminate in the idea that the earth "is itself a thought, nothing but thought," predict the philosophy of Teilhard de Chardin. The relationship of this philosophy to the theme we are considering is tenuous, although demonstrable to a certain extent. What I wish to point out here is just that Clifford (and perhaps Hawthorne) is a man of vision. When the spell is broken, at the end of the chapter, he shivers, and sinks, as though he has just come out of a fever. His vision, it seems to me, is one of the important episodes in nineteenth-century fiction. The title of this chapter is suggestive—"The Flight of Two Owls." Clifford flies in the darkness of his immediate past, but with the wisdom which is attributed to the owl he sees through the darkness.

In the train scene, Hawthorne almost caught the migratory nature of the American people and the important ambivalence in the American novel: we are homeless because we have fled from our traditional home, but we immediately begin the search for a new home. In the search for the new, we are forced to turn to the past, to recreate our entire experience and through a sense of the past to find ourselves in our origins. Two of the major western novelists deal explicitly with this long and perhaps eternal search. The question, *Who are we?* becomes *Where did we come from?* Vardis Fisher goes back in time with the zeal and thoroughness of a scholar to examine in fact or in imaginative speculation the most ancient of origins. In his long series of fictionalized historical studies, *The Testament of Man*, he shows man developing almost literally from the rhythms of the cosmos, examines his primitive behavior and his psychological patterns, traces his fears and his desires, and finally finds an explanation for twentieth-century American man. He finds that many traditions, both psychological and spiritual, are based on fear and superstition. For modern man to achieve a true understanding of himself, he must recognize these old motivations for what they are (or were). Then, through an objective understanding of his entire past, he can identify himself and put down his roots in the modern world.

Frederick Manfred goes into the past less historically than Fisher, perhaps more emotionally, but for the same reason—to seek out origins upon which a man may establish identity and into which he may sink his personal roots. In *The Golden Bowl* (1944)—a smaller *Grapes of Wrath* in some respects—Maury wanders through the West during the depression years, seeking not only a job but also a place in which he can believe. Two experiences affect him deeply. The first is a somewhat mystical reaction to the dinosaur burial ground in the Badlands of South Dakota. (Manfred uses the dinosaur in several novels as a symbol of the mysterious past from which man comes.) Maury vaguely senses an origin common to all men, and the experience provides him with a positive view of the concept of "rootedness." The negative view is found in the world of the hobo with its coldness and loneliness resulting from a failure to locate spiritual roots. From these two experiences, plus a close contact with the earth, Maury learns the long view: hope is based on the roots of tradition, on brotherhood, and on the necessity of continuing the species. And so Maury settles down with a farm family, determined to be part of a home.

In *World's Wanderer* (1949–51), a long and partly autobiographical trilogy, Thurs Wraldson roams from Iowa to Michigan (Calvin College) to New York and back to Minneapolis, searching for his spiritual father as well as trying to clear up the actual complications surrounding his own birth. He wishes to identify his real father in order to bring himself an identity which can be significant to him. At the same time he is trying out three philosophies (Christianity, Marxism, and

Science) and several parts of the country so that he may settle
down both spiritually and physically. He is one of the major
examples in American fiction of the lost child looking for his
home. His father, discovered when near death, has two pieces
of advice to give his son: "Rejoice in what you are" and "Rejoice in your works." (The suggestion is that he can rely on his
own work rather than that of the past, but in order to find out
what he is, first he will have to look into the past.) As the
parents die, and the succeeding generation is left on its own
(unlike the contemporary-generations concept which Tocqueville says is characteristic of an aristocratic society), Thurs
discovers who he is and what he has been looking for. He is
one part of a long chain of generations, of a long tradition extending back to the prehistorical man who roamed the Mid-
lands, further back to the dinosaurs who left their bones in the
Badlands, and still further back to the first spark of life that
struggled out of the sea. He has the obligation of establishing
roots of his own so that he can help to continue this long tradition. For preservation (in order to endure) and for safety, man
and beast alike seek house and den. But the needy child (each
new generation) bewails his houselessness and gets no help
from his father who dies and leaves the child to his own devices. In America, then, each man must find his own home; it
is not provided for him by his ancestors or his inherited position, as is the case in many European countries.

Manfred advocates the long view (as does Faulkner, in a
slightly different way, in another part of the "West"). It is not
enough to find a house to live in: man must find the right
house, understand his place in the racial traditions, identify
himself with a particular place, and sink his roots. European
man is concerned largely with social history; American man
(at least in one major portion of American fiction) is concerned
with a larger history, almost a natural history, in which man
is part of the entire scheme of things, not just a family or national history.

This, it seems to me, is the broadest approach which any
American writer has taken to the theme of home and the road.

This is reading the theme on its mythical level, in which individual American man becomes but a realization (and perhaps a refinement) of the ancient quest for father, home, and identity. Within the theory of the archetypal pattern, it may be seen that Christianity itself was the result, and continues to be, of the search for a father.

Several other variations of the theme will show the pervasiveness and the complexity of this part of the American experience. Huck Finn is the victim of houselessness and is forced to escape to the river, where the raft becomes a temporary substitution for a home. His real home lacks traditions except for his father's traditional southern view of slavery. Huck is, in a way, escaping from a bad tradition. He is too young to be looking for a home, having little understanding of the concept of home; but he escapes from the one he has, for much the same reason that Clifford abandons his house of seven gables. It is interesting to note that the escape in American fiction is usually made by a child or a childlike man: Clifford, Huck, Hugh Glass, Natty Bumppo, and so on, each has a simple and naive side to him which stands in juxtaposition to the visionary side. But the active pursuit of tradition, the serious search for a home, is usually undertaken by a person who has at least the possibilities of sophistication and high sensitivity, or a person (like Clifford and Hugh Glass) who has an experience which blesses him momentarily with the vision to see the significance of the home. If the vision is not always available in America, it may be pursued back to Europe, back through our immediate origins. Henry James's *Portrait of a Lady* (1881) describes a fall from innocence, in which Isabel's ancient house contrasts with the Eden-like garden and exposes her to the maturity of an established culture but also to the corruption of civilization. We have here a condition of the American experience—innocence and wisdom (even through corruption)—although the wisdom has been slow in coming. We have also a European concept of "houseness," of the complex but valuable workings of a culture. We have referred to the European tradition as a confinement of the free spirit, and such it may be; but the restrictions are largely on the social level. European culture viewed as a spiritual matter is not far off from the very thing which the American wanderer searches for. There is one important exception, which I have mentioned: in much recent American fiction the search has gone back in time further than the limits of a temporal culture which is, after all, artificial in many respects. The answer may be, however, that Americans are simply bypassing an immediate past which is really not even there for them, and they are forced to go further back in time in order to find anything meaningful.

At any rate, the additional theme of innocence destroyed is also a part of the American novel. Americans have seemed to wish to retain the innocence of Isabel and to avoid the cultural-rational maturity symbolized by her house. Jay Gatsby, for example, looks for innocence, or looks from it, and the dream which he pursues is something larger than house but is part of the same problem. Gatsby has a house, but he lacks the roots (or the ability to recognize them) and the traditions which will turn his physical house into a spiritual home. He has not, unfortunately, a clear idea of what to look for, or even a sense of what he really lacks. His dream is the romantic one, the chasing after an ideal, Platonic world. Still, his experience is rooted in America. He comes from humble midwestern stock, and he reverses the westward movement to pursue his dream to the East, just as James carries his own search still farther eastward across the ocean. It is significant, though, that after Gatsby has been killed, Fitzgerald takes his point of view out onto the ocean and, once again proceeding to the West, rediscovers the new world. Through the narrator we again see the "fresh, green breast of the new world" as the Dutch sailors must have seen it. A wonderful new home. But even this home was destroyed as the trees "made way for Gatsby's house." And so the journey continues:

> Gatsby believed in the green light, the orgiastic future that year by year recedes before us. It eluded us then, but that's no

matter—tomorrow we will run faster, stretch out our arms farther. . . . And one fine morning—
    So we beat on, boats against the current, borne back cease-
lessly into the past.

Gatsby's experiences are tied to his times and the frantic search
of the 1920s is not entirely the same thing as the patient search
of Manfred's trilogy. Yet Fitzgerald rises above the 1920s in
many ways, not the least of which is his implication that the
dream can be made real only in the past. Take away the
obvious element of nostalgia from this implication (and I think
we have the right to do this), and what is left is the same thing
that Fisher and Manfred have said more recently: the clue to
what we are and what we can be is in the past. Racial man has a
home in the past, in his origins, which can be translated into a
home in the present. It is again a matter of rootedness.

    In this connection, a new fiction emerges, almost entirely
in the West; the East, in fiction, struggles along with matters
of society, of status, of physical houseness. Thus,
Hawthorne, Cooper, and even Melville (because of his theme
of search and his concern with matters which rise above
society) have stronger ties (thematically speaking) to modern
western novelists than to the eastern. One case in point will
serve to illustrate a part of this relationship—Walter Van Tilburg Clark's complex and sophisticated novel, *The Track of the
Cat*. The home in this novel is a ranch house in Nevada. Like
Hawthorne's house of seven gables, it is a scene of crime and
guilt; but unlike Hawthorne's house, its crime and guilt are
immediate rather than a holdover from previous generations.
Although some of the crime may be attributed to Mrs.
Bridges, who is a lingering puritan in the worst sense, the major guilt lies with Curt, a son, who is completely self-sufficient
and spiritually homeless. He desires the young girl who is engaged to his younger brother; and he totally rejects the wisdom of Joe Sam, an old Indian who serves as a bridge to the
primitive past. Curt pursues the black mountain lion with

confidence and intensity, and he is defeated. The house from which he goes forth is a little nest of evil; it is where the members of the family gather to infect each other through quarrels and bickering which accumulate until they can be represented by the black cat, symbol of eternal evil, or eternal mystery. One by one the brothers go from the house to hunt the cat. (Only the Calvinistic mother seems to enjoy the atmosphere of the house; the others must escape.) The cat becomes the symbol of the evil which they wish to escape from; but part of the escape must, of necessity, be an active pursuit of the symbol in an attempt to kill it. This is a story of eternal houselessness.

Hawthorne's house and Melville's search are thus combined here in the fruition of these themes. The results are seen in Hal Bridges, the youngest son in the family. He learns to respect all of the elements of his heritage—the land, the mysticism, the primitivism, and the value of the home. He will settle down, after his successful pursuit of the cat, and will attempt to live in right relationship with the land. But the search is not over: "Jeez," says Hal. "Watch it, boy. It's in you too."

3

Whereas the sentimental novel continued to affect subliterary or formula western fiction well into the twentieth century, another European influence found its way into the work of Stephen Crane, Jack London, and Frank Norris, all of whom wrote, in their own ways, about the western experience. Literary naturalism, based on determinism through heredity and environment, was ready-made for the West. Here the environment was the raw land itself, and conflict between man and the land was perhaps more noticeable than the easterly conflict between man and the city or society, at least until a slightly later time with the city-oriented novels of Farrell, Dos Passos, and Dreiser. Naturalism was relatively simple in these social novels, ranging only from the institutional determinants in Farrell to the chemism of Dreiser. The Western novel, perhaps beginning with Norris's *The Octopus* (1901), became more entangled in some of the tensions brought on by the naturalistic philosophy—the defiance of nature and the submission to it, the celebration of the natural impulses of man as well as the attempt to educate them, and the constant tension between hope and despair which controlled the impulses of the midwestern farm novel as well as those of the Western novel. One of the effects of naturalism was the change in man's attitude toward nature, first seen in the abandonment of the romantic concept of nature as a symbol of God, then in the scientific view of nature as a force which could control the will of man, and finally in the extreme reaction of terror in the face of an alien universe. The early literature of the West—from the first travel narratives—exhibited a normal ambivalence, recognizing both the terror and the presence of God in the western landscape and climate. John Williams, in *Butcher's Crossing* (1960), has dealt with Emersonianism in the context of the apparent cruelty of the West; and Vardis Fisher concentrated on the tension between man as godlike and man as animal in his 1931 novel, *Dark Bridwell*. While the tenets of literary naturalism were absorbed with ease into the Western novel, it is apparent that from the beginning they were forced into a coexistence with romanticism or with one of its offshoots, mysticism. Most of the process (not limited entirely to the West, but seen more clearly there) may be seen at its most obvious in Frank Norris.

Norris's California was closer to some of the characteristics of the West as we know it now (the Interior West) than it is at the present time—when a Californian can read Clark's *Track of the Cat* and then comment on the "disparity between the West and California." Of three books which I consider highly influential from the turn of the century, two are set in California and one in Wyoming. That these three books should have been published in consecutive years may be nothing more than coincidence, but it may be possible to date the beginning of modern Western literature from this time. Norris's *Octopus* was the first, in 1901, followed by Wister's *Virginian* in 1902 and by Mary Austin's *Land of Little Rain* in 1903. Wister set a course for the popular western novel, the cowboy novel; Austin dealt with the natural world as though it were alive with the harmonies and rhythms which the Indians considered essential and which the white civilized man had trouble recognizing and accepting; and Norris, though somewhat crudely, brought into fiction that juxtaposition of naturalism and romanticism which could be seen in somewhat different terms in several of the notable travel narratives of the nineteenth century. Whatever decadence may have befallen the end of the century in other parts of the world, if not in America, the new century got off to a rather extraordinary beginning.

The *Octopus* covers much of the ground explored in different ways by later writers. It is a seminal novel with the forgivable faults resulting from excessiveness. In its extremes or intensities of effect it is a romantic novel, and Norris confessed that he wished to write an epic—in his terms a "romance." He was aware of the great "course of empire" moving westward, from the ancient Far East to Mesopotamia to Egypt to Greece and Rome and then to northwestern Europe and finally to America, ending (presumably) on the Pacific Coast. His epic would be of the great migration across America, ending gloriously in California. The end of the migration would also mark the end of a way of life, the crown on the most spectacular part of the entire course of empire. Each of the earlier parts had produced its great literature (*Odyssey, Beowulf,* and so on), and yet no great American epic had been written to celebrate the last great achievement. Perhaps Norris was deluding himself. Perhaps there was not a great achievement to celebrate, except for the fact that Americans had spanned a continent. Steinbeck, Stegner, Fergusson, Clark—Fisher, Manfred, and more, in other ways—have since described or lamented the end of an era, the closing of the frontier, but not as an achievement, only as a fact, and often to be seen with regret. (Thus the charge of nostalgia which is made occasionally against

Western American fiction would seem to be substantiated, although I believe that in most cases the feeling is that of profound regret at the passing of an era—a feeling not uncommon to the world's greatest literature.) Certainly Norris's scheme for a course-of-empire epic bogs down, perhaps because of the collision between an industrial society and a natural world, a collision which Presley (speaking for Norris) cannot cope with in his plans for epic-romantic poems of the Far West. Presley's failure is interesting in that it drives him off the continent onto a ship headed for Asia, and we may speculate on the consequences of his departure. If he has given up, he is simply on a "slow boat to China." But he may also be completing the course of empire by going back to its origins in the Far East, and in the cycle of things we know that endings are always beginnings. Or he may have discovered the futility of trying to resolve the problem only in the terms of the Western world (as Frank Waters has sensed in his own work more recently), so that his flight is not *from* the place of his defeat but *to* a place where he might learn more about the complexities and possible solutions of his dilemma.

While the overall subject of course of empire does not develop into a theme or become schematic in the structure of *The Octopus*, a somewhat less grand theme does emerge in the schematic presentation of attitudes toward the land (or nature, or the West) in four women who represent these attitudes. Annie Derrick is a transplanted easterner, refined and educated, who is afraid of the West and is out of place in the robust and somewhat vulgar life of the wheat ranches. In the frightening vastness and brutality of the land she sees something which, to her, is almost unnatural. Having taught at a seminary in the East until she married, she is still tied to civilized culture, she likes to read "polite" literature, and she is horrified by Presley's "Song of the West," with its savage nobility, its tempestuous life, and its obscenity. She thinks of the West in such terms as "indecent," "elemental," "unconscious nakedness," and "primordial," and cannot deal with the elements represented by these terms. Sheltered by civilization, Mrs.

Derrick shrinks from the realities of the raw West and is overcome by nature.

Nature, however, is not to blame. Mrs. Derrick cannot accept the natural environment, nor can she possibly understand the child of nature, Hilma Tree. (Norris's schemata is
hard to ignore when he names his characters.) Hilma accepts
the natural environment for what it is, willingly receives its
benefits, and, apparently as a direct result of her life outdoors,
develops into a pure, simple, good woman, in love with life,
her work, and her neighbor. She possesses an inborn nobility,
a natural and intuitive refinement which is superior to the
refinement (superficially implanted) of Mrs. Derrick. Since
Hilma's life is characterized as sane, honest, and strong, the
civilized world of Mrs. Derrick is then seen (by implication)
as insane, dishonest, and weak. Hilma is also a symbol of
motherhood, exalted and fertile, like Rose of Sharon in *The
Grapes of Wrath*. Although she loses her child through a mis-
carriage, and loses her husband in a fight with the railroad,
she reaches her perfect maturity precisely by undergoing the
experiences which are the basic elements of life: love, fertility,
and death. Her simplicity is "no longer a simplicity of ignorance, but of supreme knowledge, the simplicity of the
perfect, the simplicity of greatness."

The West, according to Norris, is good to those people
who love it and adjust themselves to it. The same cannot be
said for civilization, or for the city in contrast to nature.
Minna Hooven (does her name make her a cowlike creature of
the pasture, or a disciple of the Devil once she has been exposed to the city?) does not get into trouble as long as she remains on the ranch, even though she is poor, beautiful, and
fond of young men—a dangerous combination. It is only
when she is isolated in the city, hungry and at the mercy of
the evils of civilized society, that she crosses the line between
right and wrong. The city, which treats her unkindly and
turns her into a prostitute, is represented by Mrs. Cedarquist,
wealthy, pretentious, shallow, and artificial. Unlike Mrs.
Derrick, she does not allow herself to be bothered by the vast-

ness or the rawness of the West; rather, she tries to bring eastern culture to the cities of the West, to imitate the refinement of the East and of Europe. As a result, art becomes a fad centered around literary societies, reading circles, and imposters. Her world is a fake world, and it stands shakily in contrast to the natural goodness, the natural morality, and the purity of the world of Hilma Tree. In a sense, the frontier movement failed simply because it could not escape from all that was evil in the established society that lay behind it to the East. Mrs. Cedarquist and her friends merely revert to a poor imitation of eastern culture, completely ignoring the possibilities of the new land, of the West.

The richness of *The Octopus* is tied directly to its multiplicity of concerns and its wavering tone. The ease with which Norris states his general attitudes toward nature and civilization in the interactions among the four women opens him to charges of sentimentalism and didacticism. We can agree that, as a writer, he is not subtle. But neither is he precious or timid. The railroad, a force of industrial society, brings violence to an otherwise pastoral scene, and this violence is dealt with realistically and dramatically. At the same time, wheat is seen as the salvation of the world, is symbolized as such, and the West takes on the role of saviour of mankind—the Golden Empire, the land of plenty. Although it would appear that the railroad might destroy this Garden of Eden in the name of progress and greed (both conditions of Manifest Destiny in an ironic way), the wheat as symbol of goodness swallows up S. Behrman as symbol of evil. A note of optimism therefore prevails at the end of the novel, a moral justification of the natural law which has been attacked by industrial forces. If the incident seems melodramatic—and it does—it is no more so than the mystical experience of the shepherd Vanamee as he sees the wheat spring up overnight. Yet it is probably the wheat as force rather than the railroad as force which allows *The Octopus* to be called naturalistic, since it is the wheat which has a determining influence upon several of the characters. In this sense, too, the theme of moral paradox, or purity of the West, common to much western writing, is naturalistic. Naturalism is important to Western literature even as it takes on the characteristics of mysticism in order to affirm the insights and the truths which man experiences in his relationships with the living land. Norris fails, technically, to hold all his themes together, unable to find a point of view which will encompass them; but, in his ambitious attempt to write the epic of the West, he introduces themes, attitudes, relationships, and structural problems which provide directions, if not destinations, for a wide variety of twentieth-century Western American novels.

It seems fairly clear that the serious Western novel (as distinguished from the popular western) is descended from the western travel narratives and journals of exploration, from the nonformulaic side of Cooper, and from the mixture of determinism and mysticism as found in the naturalism of Frank Norris. Of these precursors only Cooper (and only in *The Prairie)* did not write from firsthand experience, even though most nineteenth-century observers of the West were outsiders in the sense that they were visiting the frontier with formal experience, language, and attitudes acquired elsewhere. The best literature comes out of direct experience (with the few exceptions we are all familiar with, where the imagination triumphed) so that the outstanding Western regional novels are those written from within the region. We think of the work of Frank Waters, Walter Van Tilburg Clark, Harvey Fergusson, and Vardis Fisher, for example. And while some of the better writers have spent a lifetime in the West, others have lived there for a shorter time, and some have gone back and forth between different parts of the country, but all have had close contact with the land which we call the West. They write from a full knowledge of the land, from direct experience with it.

Harvey Fergusson insisted that the legitimate writer of the West had to have long-term experience and slowly acquired knowledge of the region he wrote about. It can be argued, certainly, that only a few people can be in on a thing at the beginning, that everyone coming later still has the right to contemplate and explore and use those events which transpired earlier. (This is in reference to the widespread use of history in the Western novel.) We cannot deny the validity of William Eastlake's Indian trilogy, even knowing that he spent most of his life in the East before moving to New Mexico and Arizona. Nor can we depreciate the value and authenticity of Michael Straight's two historical novels of the West (*Carrington*, 1960, and *A Very Small Remnant*, 1963), although Straight was educated in England and lives in the East—he did, however, become familiar with the physical setting of his novels. A writer may have the rapport, the intuition, to overcome the lack of lifetime regional experience. Nevertheless, most writers who have come into the West only briefly, perhaps for the explicit purpose of doing a book on what is often considered a popular subject—cowboys, Indians, a figure like Custer—have generally produced novels which were either shallow, sentimental, or parodic. Where these fictions may be called regional is in setting and subject, but Fergusson, at least, would have dismissed them as exploitive playthings.

What, then, is a regional novel? What does it do or not do? The answer lies within a complex of discriminations.

First, we must assume that there are such things as regional differences. I will not belabor this point; we all recognize the basic sameness of people, while at the same time admitting that people, life quality, and environments change somewhat from one region to another. It is on this basis that we first define, or delimit, regions. A region is a place, whatever the size, within which the behavior patterns, the speech, and the environmental influences are at least somewhat consistent, and are somewhat different from those same factors elsewhere. On this basis it is possible to identify a region, known as the Interior West, which is bounded, roughly, by the one-hundredth meridian, the Sierra Nevadas, the Canadian border, and the Mexican border. This location will suffice for our purposes although, admittedly, a number of factors will stretch the lines at certain times and in certain places.

A novel which is to be called Western regional, then, is

first of all set within the region as we have defined it. The people, the characters of the novel, will share to a certain extent
such things as ethnic backgrounds, religions, temperament,
and some physical and psychological qualities, and above all,
an attitude toward the land, toward the climate and topography of the region. This does not exclude the possibility of
variety. Nor does it eliminate the possibility of having characters from another region come into the West, reacting to it in
their own way. People may come and go, but the land remains the same, and so it must be said that the land itself is
probably the single most important element of a region. What
may seem to be a notable exception, the region which is New
York City, with little or no land as such, is simply the negative extreme of the same statement. The land must be important to the action of a Western regional novel.

What we are talking about is geographical determinism,
which helps in distinguishing one region from another and
which plays a vital role in the action of almost any novel except some novels of ideas. Vardis Fisher, in spite of his insistence on the necessity of reason, rationalism, and intellectual
thought, would have been the first to admit the overpowering
influence of the land on himself and his characters. In his own
case, the isolation and the brutality of his childhood left in-
erasable marks on him. Almost his entire literary career was
given to describing and analyzing his own childhood fears and
in attempting to explain them in broad terms. Regarding the
Testament of Man series, he was asked whether the solution
was love. He replied, "I think you lay it on pretty thick when
you say my solution is LOVE. The only thing I intended to
be implicit in the word 'orphans' is that . . . nowadays the
children of all the mammals need a measure of security until
they are ready to be pushed out of the 'nest': that more and
more of them don't get it at the 'human' level." The statement
applies to children of all regions and countries, but the experiences which led Fisher to this conclusion came directly out
of his own environment, the rugged land of Idaho.

In similar fashion, it might be argued that the lynchings of

Clark's *Ox-Bow Incident* could just as well have taken place in the South, and yet, the particular influences which led to the hangings were western—the irritating winds, the fear of storms, the power of the mountains, and the closeness of the relatively isolated people who carefully protected "their own." The lynchings themselves could well have occurred elsewhere, and the human characteristics which partially motivated them are not peculiar to the West, but the physical environment which persistently pushed the mob into action is indeed unique.

One of the difficulties in establishing behavior patterns of or for western characters lies in the great variety of weather and topographical conditions within the broad area of land we have defined. And yet there is something which brings it all together, something by which to contrast the West with the East or the South. It must be stated in relative terms, as everything must: the West is relatively dry and relatively high. In addition, it is open and it is varied. It can give a man a sense of freedom and then destroy him with its violence, either natural or man-made. Historically, it has attracted people who had the ability to take part in this freedom (and perhaps in this violence also), people willing to abandon the traditioned homes of the East, or South—the patterns of living which require little or no thought, only acquiescence to the established patterns. It has attracted people with a sense of adventure, perhaps with a touch of masculinity.

(I once said to a former southeasterner that I thought the landscape east of the Mississippi was feminine—soft hills, lush growth, protective trees—while that west of the Mississippi was masculine—hard, big, open, often dangerous, often harsh. He began to agree with me and then remembered working outdoors in the winter in Maine, and I thought of the Great Lakes fishing crews in the winter, and coal miners whose land environment is not exactly protective, and there are other obvious exceptions to my generalization. Yet, speaking in generalizations, as we sometimes must, I believe my statement to be true. It may even account for the scarcity of women novelists in the West. There have been a few, but most feminine writers have come from the coasts or the South.)

Whatever the elements of a region are, they must be portrayed with authenticity in the literature of that region. Indeed, this authenticity must extend to the nonphysical atmosphere of the region, more difficult to define. Man's most constant experience is his regional environment, but often it is subtle. It depends frequently on the rhythms of the land, the beat of its pulse, as Mary Austin often said. I do not know how to describe this beat in other regions. In the large metropolitan areas it must depend more on man-made things and on social structures than on the land itself. On the seacoasts it must have some connection also with the tides. In the West the pulse is entirely a natural one. Austin uses the basic two-beat meters of the Indian drummer to find a relationship between the primitive qualities of western art (for example, Indian chants and songs) and the biological organism of man. The pulse is the same beat as that of the drummer—one, two; one, two—and the heartbeat is similar. Man working on the land uses two arms, two hands, and works in the same beat. Actual rhythms of the land include the change of seasons, the waxing and waning of the moon, night and day, the wind, the grasses blowing, birth and growth and death, the life cycles of the many creatures on the land, and so on. Many of these are available to the eastern novel, but we see the obvious differences. It is in the West that we are more conscious of this natural environment, where it is open enough to keep the sun and moon and stars within our range of perceptions, where it is open enough for the wind to affect almost everything in its unbroken sweep, where there are fewer people and we are therefore more conscious of animals and other creatures, where we are exposed to the seasons and their changes and cannot hide behind or beneath or within tons of concrete and steel.

Perhaps I overemphasize the obvious, but it is important to remember that the Western novel, to be authentic, to be honest with the region which gives it birth, must take into account all of these factors. It must, it would seem, be a novel of the land, a novel in which the land actually becomes a character, a force to be reckoned with, part of the conflict as well as background. As a region gets older, there is less need for the landscape to be a character or agent. The landscape becomes understood and can be at least partially relegated to the subconscious. Until now, most Western fiction has accepted the landscape as a vital force in the lives of the people who traverse it, and we point to work by Clark, or Waters, or Manfred, or Fisher to illustrate landscape as character, landscape as shaping force, landscape as agent. In an earlier time, through many writers from Bret Harte to Zane Grey, roughly, the landscape was viewed in a romantic perspective: it was seen to be unbearably beautiful, or terribly harsh and violent, for its own sake or as a mere backdrop. Presumably, in a later time, the Western novel will allow the landscape its place and its influence without fussing over it so much.

Authenticity includes everything from implements, details of place, and mannerisms of speech to atmosphere, behavior, and attitude. These in themselves will not guarantee a fine literary novel, of course, but they are, at the very least, essential underpinnings. A. B. Guthrie's re-creation of the nineteenth-century West in fiction probably remains the classic example of authenticity in our region, but it is possible to find fault with the individual novels on literary and structural grounds. The novels of Harvey Fergusson come from a half-century of the author's direct experience with the land. Vardis Fisher (except for occasional exaggeration) and Frank Waters leave little to debate in the matter of accuracy. While Walter Clark's work is equally true in this respect, it begins to leave the whole question behind, to bury the authenticity, as it were, beneath other kinds of values, as does, I think, Waters's *The Man Who Killed the Deer* (1942), Fisher's *Dark Bridwell*, Fergusson's *Wolf Song*, Stegner's *Big Rock Candy Mountain*, Eastlake's *Portrait of an Artist with Twenty-six Horses*, and other novels.

Perhaps it is better to say that authenticity must come from a knowledge of the language, history, myth, and religion of the region. In the case of the western novelist this means not only the ways of his own people, whoever they may be, but also of the Indians, sometimes the Spanish, perhaps the French in the North, the Mormons in Utah and elsewhere. Whereas the Western novel will sometimes emphasize the differences among these groups, as the Eastern or Southern novel does constantly with its own diverging groups, there is a clearer tendency toward unification in the West. The western novelist is concerned more often than not with a drawing together of cultural values, which makes the historical or mythical or religious background extremely rich. I am inclined to believe that the Western American novel is unified in a cultural and textural sense to a greater degree than is the fiction of any other region.

Yet, at least at certain times, each region has its own historical curse which informs much, if not most, of its literature: slavery in the South, puritanism in New England, and rapacious exploitation in the West. These are traumas which are certainly going to appear heavily in the fiction of the several regions. The individual novels may support the slavery, the puritanism, or the exploitation, or they may reveal it or openly attack it. The tendency seems to be that the pressure against these traumas comes late, after the damage has been done, and so we expect to find the western exploitation itself being exploited in earlier and less responsible fictions, while in our current literature this historical fact and attitude is deplored. This question bears somewhat on authenticity also, since the deliberate literary exploitation of the West, perhaps in the manner of Bret Harte and the popular cowboy story writers of the 1920s and 1930s, destroys the authenticity of attitude, if not of physical detail.

Apart from the subject matter of the Western novel, and the honesty of presentation and attitude, we can, I think, look to structure and a kind of implied symbolism to help us in defining this novel. There are two ways of stating the kind of structure, or form, found in a majority of the serious, major, nonformula Western novels. One emphasizes beginnings, and the other stresses open-endedness.

The West has always been, and to a large degree still is, a place of beginnings. It is true that not everybody can be in on historical events at the beginning. But a character can have his own beginning, either actually or symbolically, as Clark suggests vividly at the end (which is not an end) of *The Ox-Bow Incident*, as the horror of the hangings begins to wear off and Art Croft looks forward to the possibility of a sunny day and of what amounts to a resurrection on the morrow. The beginnings are simply parts of, or points on, the cycle of life. The Western novel is sharply aware of these cycles, perhaps because of the closeness of the natural cycles of the environment—seasons, lives of creatures. The West is still essentially a place of hope, in spite of the harshness, the brutalities, the rapes, the destruction, the things which are a part of its history and its environment. In Waters's *The Man Who Killed the Deer*, the conclusion of Martiniano's experience within the novel is a *return* to the old ways, to the blanket, although his decision is based upon the elements of the leaving, of the rebellion. He returns to begin again. In *Pike's Peak* (1971), the important element is the search, but the search does not end in a conclusion, it ends in a beginning. Hugh Glass, in Manfred's *Lord Grizzly*, concludes his pilgrimage of revenge with forgiveness, which he does not fully understand, and his life begins anew as a part of the brotherhood he once seemed to belong to. Clark's *City of Trembling Leaves* (1945) is also a quest, part of the growing-up of the artist, and as it draws to a close it reaches a significant beginning. Stegner's *Big Rock Candy Mountain* has many beginnings within the internal structure, as the major characters move about the West looking for their rightful place. At the physical end of this novel, at the moment of refinement, there is another, larger, beginning. Although Fisher's *Dark Bridwell* comes as close as any Western (or American) novel to classical tragedy—and this means finality—Lela achieves a new freedom and a beginning.

Structure is geared to the qualities indigenous to the region. The West is open. In both Waters and Eastlake we find this openness going symbolically forever upward. In Eastlake's *Portrait*, evil is found to be most ominous and damaging below the plain, in the canyon, the draw, the gulley. The old Indian goes to the mountain top to die, as though his spirit can from that vantage point get a better jump into space. The Western novel moves out and up, in contrast to the rather typical nonwestern novel which moves down and in. It may be, again, that we are saying only that the Western novel is dominated by its landscape, while the nonwestern novel is dominated by the tightness and closeness of masses of people squirming together in a hell of their own making.

Another look at Guthrie will illustrate both the open-endedness and the cyclical movement of the Western novel. Taken individually, his three major novels—*The Big Sky*, *The Way West*, and *These Thousand Hills*—seem to be formless. In particular, the concluding lines of the first two are unsatisfactory in terms of fulfillment, of tightness of structure. They are open. They leave a sense of being unfinished, except as Boone returns home for a while and the members of the wagon train reach the West Coast. They are novels of wandering, and at best they terminate at a physical place. In *The Way West*, this place was the goal which was sought after by the people. But when they reach the place, the reader shrugs "So what?" Boone, in *The Big Sky*, has not had a tangible goal, and so he has reached nothing. What the reader can reach at the end of the entire narrative sequence, however, is an insight into the archetypical condition of the rise of civilizations. An almost unnoticeable frame has been established in the simple phrase "was coming in" from the first sentence of *The Big Sky* and "Then he went in" at the conclusion of *These Thousand Hills*. In the many hundreds of pages between, everyone has been going out. The significance of the possibly unintentional frame is that it points up that man flees from the established society, goes out on his own or with others who are doing the same, and eventually returns to established society, this time one which his own people have made. Or, to put it another way, it is the process of refinement, as seen vividly in *Big Rock Candy Mountain*. The structure is both open and cyclical; beginnings conclude in further beginnings.

Form is a restraint; it keeps the material from becoming loose and chaotic. Form and/or structure are geared to the region. Many Western novels appear to be formless, or entirely open-ended, until viewed within the context of the region. The literary context includes at least the following suggestions:

Characters are often less memorable than they might be because of the overpowering presence of the landscape. They tend to exist more in space than in time (excluding the peculiarities presented by historical novels), and they usually look outward, into that space, as much as they look inward into themselves—perhaps more. Plot construction, point of view, and theme often are derived from the medieval romance, from Malory, from the morality plays, as well as from the early Western American travel narrative and journal. When there is a looking inward, either on the part of the characters or by the novelist himself, it is less psychological than it is mystical in a land-oriented sense. Characters are more or less free to shape their own destinies, except as they are controlled and formed by the land. Thus, we find a constant and emphatic duality between the freedom of the social West and the dictates of the physical West. In treatment, the Western novel is extensive, constantly engaged in an opening out, from character to action to landscape to a concern with racial consciousness (rather than individual), which is Jungian and which allows significant acceptance of the myths and rituals of the American Indian. Archetypal patterns are common—hell and rebirth, or destruction and resurrection, for example, or the hero figure in some cases. There is an important reliance on the number three in structural patterns as well as in symbolism. This is not the beginning-middle-end of Aristotle but rather the death-descent-into-hell-resurrection motif which has at least one natural counterpart in the seasons. The easy use of this pattern may be seen in *Shane*, where the mysterious figure rides into a town that is figuratively dead, participates in its hell, and gives it a new chance, a new birth, before riding away. Stylistically, the pattern is emphatic in *Lord Grizzly*, taking on structural significance in smaller sections as well as overall. Religiously, and showing the cleansing power of nature over man's psychological evil, it may be seen in *The Ox-Bow Incident* as the mob descends into hell and then (part of it) wakes the next morning to the coming of spring and a fresh new day.

It might be said also that the Western novel is essentially pastoral, although it is frequently shaken by violence and by man's rape of the land. In any case, the land looms large in Western fiction, and man is small unless raised to heroic stature through the employment of the devices of myth, symbol, and archetype. However, the pastoral element, properly defined, contains an attitude which runs through thoughtful western artists like a spiritual bond—the recognition that the land is sacred. The men and women who people it, who perhaps destroy it or exploit it or misunderstand it, may be profane in their ignorance or arrogance, but the land itself is the source of life, the holder of secrets, the means by which the intuitive or open-souled observer may achieve a spiritual harmony, an earth-rooted salvation. Perhaps this is what we mean by "the Western attitude." Perhaps this is what lies at the center of the highest level of the Western novel.

IV
Vardis Fisher:
The Struggle of Rationalism

It is customary to think of Harvey Fergusson (born 1890) as the first of the major novelists of the twentieth-century West. His *Blood of the Conquerors* (1921) preceded Vardis Fisher's first novel, *Toilers of the Hills,* by seven years. Before Fisher's second novel was published, Fergusson had completed his Santa Fe Trail trilogy as well as three other novels. Yet Fisher (born 1895) was often called during his lifetime the dean of western novelists. A reason for this distinction is the obvious one of volume. Fisher produced twenty-six novels in thirty-seven years, while Fergusson published only ten in thirty-three years. (Both men wrote nonfiction as well, but these books do not change the statistics appreciably.) A case could be made for greater care on Fergusson's part, and for a strange kind of recklessness in Fisher's career, which could account for the difference in productivity. Or one might say somewhat facetiously that the siesta culture of the Southwest could not match the brisk energy of the Northwest where work keeps a man warm. Either way, it is fitting and plausible that the earliest fiction of literary stature in the modern American West should come out of New Mexico with its old cultural traditions of the Spanish and the Pueblo Indians. And it is fitting, too, that it should be in the cold wilderness of Idaho that the tortured soul of Vridar Hunter (and

117

his creator, Vardis Fisher) should search desperately for
warmth, or, lacking that, for the reasons behind the coldness
and cruelty of both land and people.

Although they were far apart geographically, and their
styles were dissimilar, Fergusson and Fisher insisted that the
West be approached realistically, and also shared a cynical
attitude at times. Fergusson deplored the mythical West and
the many traps that he felt some of his fellow writers fell into.
He thoroughly condemned inaccuracy, believing that good
fiction could be written only out of personal—intimate—experience with the land: "I have had my feet on all the country
I have written about." This attitude led him to make caustic
remarks about those writers who, in his opinion, did not look
carefully enough at the flora and fauna of the West, or who
merely visited the region without getting to know it. His comments about Willa Cather *(Death Comes for the Archbishop)* may
have been unfair—"She had the most singular ignorance of
the West, you know. She didn't know the country at all"—but
his opinion was shared by Mary Austin, who also believed
that "outsiders" could not interpret the region properly. Fisher's argument, often presented more vociferously, took a
slightly different direction. He expressed a belief in intelligence, in people who did not think with their emotions. He
too could be caustic, levelling his anger and irony against
writers (as well as politicians, critics, and other people of similar bent) who lacked integrity. Both Fisher and Fergusson
were so utterly honest that they frequently antagonized
critics, writers, readers, and even friends. Of the two, Fisher
was perhaps more vehement, and he allowed his opinions to
show in more than a few of his novels.

Fergusson's last novel was published seventeen years before he died in 1971 at the age of eighty-one after a lingering
illness. Fisher's last novel was published only three years before his death at the age of seventy-three, and he was apparently still writing with enthusiasm just before he committed
the act that resulted in his death: the action was careless (and
therefore nonintelligent) and thus seemed to symbolize his

paradoxical condition of rationality and excessiveness. His major ally, vocally, in asking western writers to embrace rationalism (indeed, he said that Western literature would not survive under any other conditions) was Alan Swallow, the publisher who took on those Fisher novels which eastern houses were reluctant to accept. The argument for rationalism may well have been valid, but as it was carried to its extremes it became emotional—perhaps the final irony.

2

There are at least two sides to Vardis Fisher's preoccupations with the American West. After a series of Idaho novels, based upon personal experience, he embarked upon a study of the nineteenth-century West in six historical novels. In spite of events that were often less than pleasant, and apart from frequent attempts to shock the reader through graphic descriptions of primitive behavior and barbarous actions, it is apparent that at this stage of his writing Fisher loved the West. Mingling with the historical atrocities are tender passages in which he reveals a compassionate and a harmonious relationship with nature that seems appropriate for poetry and that touches sensitively on an unspoiled consciousness. However, in his eight earlier novels, those which reveal his feelings while growing up in the Idaho wilderness, he emphasizes the inability of the unspoiled consciousness to withstand the cruelties, the harshness, the insensitivity, and the fear which were all part of the environment. Vardis, the boy, was caught between a father who loved the wilderness life and a mother who was puritanical and envisoned her boy becoming a Mormon bishop or apostle. Emotionally, the boy was an orphan, searching for a parent and trying to forget the wolves, cougars, and loneliness of the frontier. Much later, when he began the remarkable twelve-volume *Testament of Man* series of historical novels, he was the rationalist, seeking to dispel superstition and fear, striving to find his identity in a world which, though he loved at times, he found filled with ignorance. Throughout these three phases of his writing career (the Idaho novels, the historical novels, and the *Testament of Man*) Fisher lived and practiced two extremes: his chief fault was an excessive reliance upon the use of scholarly sources, an almost irrational passion for what he considered historical and psychological truth; his chief virtue was an underlying tenderness and humanity that often went unnoticed beneath the crust of rationalism.

It is in one of his excursions into the nineteenth century *(Tale of Valor,* 1958) that Fisher comes closest to stating outright the major theme of most of his fiction. As Lewis and Clark are proceeding through the mountains, perhaps in Idaho, Lewis says, "The longer I live the more I realize that hunger is a more powerful force than fear." Whether the statement carries the weight of objective truth is not important; the two conditions are relative and one often leads to the other. In the historical novels hunger is probably a stronger force than fear, but in the Idaho novels it is fear that prevails in spite of the occasional presence of hunger, and the same is generally true throughout the *Testament of Man*, especially if we keep in mind that man hungers for more than food and can be fearful even though he is neither cowardly nor weak. Fear and hunger are basic, elemental, subsocial, and Fisher's concern with them indicates his intimacy with the primitive or animal world. The basis for this concern is probably a belief that in spite of centuries of development (or the opportunity for development) man is still essentially primitive, still an animal in his desires and his nonintelligent behavior. With thematic emphasis on fear and hunger, a realistic approach is indicated if not demanded. Fisher's brand of realism takes several directions. When he has source materials such as the journals of the Lewis and Clark expedition he follows them closely in an attempt to be as historically accurate as possible, even telling the reader that he is doing so by inserting parenthetically, as Lewis or Clark thinks of something deemed important, "what this evening he was to enter in his Journal." Yet, many pas-

sages designed to be thoroughly realistic pose a problem in
tone:

> It made some of them gag to see the way Indians cut out a buf-
> falo or elk stomach, filled it with water and tipped it up and
> drank; or ate animal guts without turning them inside out to
> wash them; or gulped down a hunk of liver with the gall blad-
> der attached.

> A little buffler calf . . . only a little while ago it was so warm
> and full of living, so eager, so friendly to all things; and now it
> was only a smear on the earth, a few bones, a skull with the
> eyes sucked out, its flesh and most of its blood digesting in
> wolf bellies.

Through these thoughts, coming from the point of view of
Lewis, we are at once aware of a selection of details which
seems designed to shock, and, on the other hand, a feeling of
sympathy and regret, so that we waver between what is gory
for its own sake and what is merely the balance of nature. At
some point, however, the barbarisms seem to become exaggerated:

> He had seen famished wolves at a carcass, and jackals, but they
> had not been so savage in their blood- and hunger-lust as these
> creatures before him, tearing the spleen apart with their two
> filthy hands, the liver, kidneys, the lungs, and guts, while
> blood gushed from the corners of their mouths and their eyes
> rolled in rapture as, choking and gasping, they wolfed it down.
> The one who fascinated Lewis most was a scrawny bowlegged
> brave who had managed to possess nine or ten feet of the small
> intestine and now fed it into his mouth and down his throat,
> his cheeks and tongue sucking it in, his throat muscles rising
> in blood-filled rolls, as his two hands squeezed down the tube,
> forcing the contents out at the other end. In what seemed to
> Lewis only a few moments the long piece of gut disappeared.

This long passage may serve as a typical example of the way
in which Fisher deals with barbarisms or primitive behavior.
What we are to make of such descriptions is not entirely clear

to me. To say that Lewis is fascinated when he might well feel repulsion does not explain sufficiently the particular kind of detail Fisher dwells upon—detail presumably intended to aid in the characterization of the observer. Nor can we with full justification read any element of racism into the passage. The fascination seems to belong to Fisher. His intention may be to shock us, or it may be to illustrate man's barbaric qualities and suggest that civilized man has the ability to rise above the behavior of savages, or it may be to draw an analogy between the frontier West and the condition of man very early in his development. The frontier West brings us dramatically close to those conditions which we should now be able to avoid, having traveled the long road of refinement. It is possible, too, that Fisher merely regards these incidents as facts—nothing more. This would be the attitude of the realist. What complicates the tone is a touch of irony or humor, sometimes hardly noticeable, as though Fisher were having fun as he assaults the senses with brutalities, horrors, or subhuman actions.

Humor, of course, is a normal part of the exaggeration which is itself a frequent extension of realism, a relief from the total objectivity presumably desired by the rationalist. But, again, tone as perceived by the reader may differ slightly from tone as intended by the writer. Do we call the following passage realistic? Or is it grimly humorous? Perhaps it is both:

> Will Bratton was the sickest man of all: he just fell over to his back and heaved straight up, letting the boiled duck of his noon meal spill over him like the incessant and accursed rain.

But when Reuben Fields is beset with fleas, and complains, it is clear that his comments are true to character, and so there is no corresponding problem of tone as in the Bratton passage:

> "From here on I'm going to ask every minister I meet why God made fleas: If he can't answer me I'll leave the church."

These problems, it would seem, stem from the enthusiasm which almost constantly plays against Fisher's avowed rationalism. He writes with such energy that he does not always

pay attention to subtleties of phrasing, and within his mass of
wordage through twenty-six novels he is bound to be guilty
(though perhaps excusably) of verbal inelegancies such as
"looked cooked" and "numb his gums," and of weak sentences: "Some of the weaker men were getting weaker."

Nevertheless, Fisher's historical novels are powerful,
often vivid, and usually convey an authenticity which supports the narrative and characterization. In spite of stylistic
defects, *Children of God* (1939) and *The Mothers* (1943) are as
successful in dealing with their events as any other novels
which have been written about the Mormons and the Donner
party. To achieve both objectivity and drama, Fisher divides
each of these novels into three parts as far as point of view is
concerned. The effect of the method is almost judicial, im-
parting a sense of fairness to controversial events in American
history by viewing them from several sides. In *Children of God*
the founder of Mormonism, Joseph Smith, is responsible for
the first third of the narrative; Brigham Young, the first great
leader of the Mormons, is the focus of the middle third; and in
the final section our attention is largely on a minor character
who is in disagreement with the Mormon leadership. Although the historical characters do not quite come to life as
fully as we might like, the idea of Mormonism does. Fisher
was born in a Mormon community but abandoned the Mormon beliefs early in his life. He neither attacks nor approves
the Mormonism which he saw firsthand or that which he
learned about from careful research. He is sympathetic to the
Mormons and yet he portrays them exactly as, in his opinion,
they are—deluded but sincere. With the same objectivity he
treats the few cases of cannibalism in *The Mothers* with appropriate horror mixed with a sense of the ultimate necessity in
the eating of human flesh. Here the first two parts of the narrative come to us through men in the party—Charles Stanton
and William Eddy—but the third part, and clearly the most
important part, is conveyed through one of the mothers,
Tamsen Donner. Morally speaking—and Fisher is ultimately
a moralist—the most intense feelings and the most difficult

decisions must come from the mothers whose children, weak as they are and subject to early death from hardship, must be protected at all cost because they represent the survival of the race as well as of the family. Artistically, however, both novels suffer from the changing focus and from the episodic construction of the narrative, concentrating on flurries of action and often playing down both characterization and description of scene. Yet the novels are important for their fictional and dramatic treatment of historical events and for the objectivity which is frequently tempered by the sensitivity of the author but never lost. Fisher is usually inconsistent in one way or another, but he never departs from his serious attempt to get at the truth of Western American man and his environment.

Characterization becomes more significant in *City of Illusion* (1941), the story of the Comstock silver lode. Eilley (Mrs. Alison Orrum Hunter Cowan Bowers) and her husband Sandy are on the scene when silver is first discovered and they soon become wealthy. Eilley has married Sandy primarily because she needs a husband in order to appear respectable and does not have much choice at that time and place. She is shrewd, but her greed makes her naive and her desire to be Queen of the Comstock blinds her to her basic flaw. Sandy, the simple and uneducated man who is fond of mules and rough but good friends, is finally responsible for Eilley's downfall. Unwittingly, a kind and elemental man causes the ruin of a scheming and greedy woman. Perhaps this is an oversimplified piece of poetic justice, and yet the context supports it in this case. The Bowers's success comes at the expense of the mine workers who labor under dangerous conditions; the descriptions of some of the deaths resulting from mine accidents make the cannibalism in *The Mothers* seem tame. Furthermore, the life of violence in Virginia City is juxtaposed with Eilley's attempts to rule and reform the city. She believes that she can determine each person's behavior, but the people remain themselves, individuals, clearly delineated although often exaggerated, and basically humane, even though each character has at least one serious flaw. In a perversion of values, Eilley tries to stop the killing, the drinking, the carousing and whoring, even while she allows men to be killed in her own mine so that she can accumulate more money to be used in changing and reforming her world. The moral lesson, such as it is, is not belabored and does not take attention away from representative characters who provide a summary of western types and therefore a portrayal of early western society. (Walter Clark does a similar representative portrait, although more nearly archetypal, in *Track of the Cat*; like Fisher, he avoids mere stereotyping.) Eilley is, of course, symbolic of the greed which played an important role in settling the West, seen first in the fur company trapper. As much as Americans dislike admitting it, greed is one of their major characteristics. Even so, Sandy, who wants to be left alone with his friends, and who does not desire riches, is not an anachronism. Nor is Steve Gilpin of the local newspaper, who is cynical about the entire community but who keeps a level head and a sense of humor. He might be considered a Mark Twain type except that Twain enters the story on one or two occasions as a separate character. Julia Bulette, the prostitute who acts from compassion and serves as a voluntary nurse, bears at least that much resemblance to Calamity Jane of the Black Hills.

Although *City of Illusion* is cumbersome and suffers from a large cast of characters, and although the theme of illusion is philosophically superficial, the final chapter but one (Chapter 40) suddenly focuses on a minor character who undergoes an experience that touches in its simple way on a kind of mysticism, or, at the least, an example of Emersonian oneness. The chapter was later printed with slight alterations as a short story, "Fellowship," in Fisher's collected stories, *Love and Death* (1959). Luff McCoy, one of the mine stock owners who lost everything in the collapse of the market, drinks himself into a stupor and falls into an abandoned mine shaft. While contemplating death, which seems inevitable, he discovers that he is not alone. That the other creature in the shaft is a goat matters not at all; Luff is overcome with emotion and the knowledge that he will not die alone. The goat represents friendship, warmth, not just something to milk or eat but "something that he could die with." Resting his head on the goat he is conscious of two heartbeats, much more satisfactory than one. Yet, the two come together:

> For both of them now there was the same uselessness of mind, of wealth and position, of pretense and purpose and power. They needed only a spot to lie on and come together in the ultimate fellowship of death.

No mystic, Fisher allows the potentially mystical moment to carry the thematic weight of the novel, to point up the futility of wealth and power and greed. Nevertheless, the overtones are there for the reader to ponder, as they are in Francis Parkman's "for I and the beasts were all that had consciousness for many a league around." Whereas Walter Clark and Frederick Manfred exploit through symbolism certain implied relationships between man and animal, Fisher touches on them briefly, tantalizingly, and then moves on, as though mindful that he is an avowed rationalist. One such episode, striking in its potential, occurs in *Tale of Valor* as Lewis is pursued by a gigantic bear. Chased into the river, Lewis turns and raises his hand and shouts, whereupon the grizzly runs away and Lewis is left with the mixed emotions of a man who has encountered the unexpected. Frightened, Lewis is also astonished that the bear keeps looking back, as though to see whether he will be pursued. We want to ask if there is any significance in this episode, or if we are to take it at face value, no questions asked. Lewis then proceeds up the river and encounters a cougar, or mountain lion, a creature with which he is not familiar. A shot from his gun scares the cat away and Lewis reflects that "today for some mysterious reason the whole animal-world seemed bent on his death." Fisher, however, continues to shy away from the implications of his mystery and, instead, confronts his character with yet another incident of a similar kind. When three buffalo bulls charge at Lewis he advances toward them, knowing that he is foolish to do so, and the bulls stop their charge and turn and run away. Lewis comments to himself, "I'll be damned!" Before reaching camp he has seen or imagined shadowy forms and has heard the rattles of rattle-snakes. The conclusion to Lewis's foray into the wilderness, alone, is simply that it is a wild world through which he passes. One of the weaknesses of the rationalistic method is seen here in that the events are merely described, presumably in order to point out that the wilderness is (or was) unlike the civilized world of the cities. Fisher's method is to pile it on, have three incidents do the work of one, rather than to explore the significance of the action. A mystic potential hangs over Lewis's experiences, but Fisher will not touch it. We remember Emerson's words about finding faith in the woods, about being secure in the wilderness because there we are a part of God; but there is no indication that Fisher may intend to say such a thing. Nor can we be sure that he wishes to express the superiority of man over animal, or to make any statement whatsoever about the relationship between man and nature. (Nevertheless, I am reminded of the title of an article on Emerson—"Nature: Meek Ass or White Whale"—and am dismayed at the possibility of Fisher illustrating in Lewis's experiences the first of those two choices.)

Fisher could not avoid an ambivalent attitude toward nature, toward the wilderness, toward the land. Never able to shake off the fear, cruelty, and violence which he lived with closely during his Idaho boyhood, he still recognized—and occasionally probed with great sensitivity—the beautiful, the pristine, and the awesome in nature. The juxtaposition of love and fear in his own character finds a parallel in many of the novels as Fisher stresses the extremes of the natural world and its landscape. A red-blooded, he-man approach is often qualified by hesitant tenderness. In this respect he is not unlike other western writers who find it impossible to locate a middle ground between beauty and death, or between God and madness, and quite deliberately exploit the easily available extremes. I do not use the word *exploit* unkindly here, because it is difficult to draw a line between the normal exaggeration which attends the events and places of the West and a pre-meditated stretching of the truth for either literary or commercial purposes. Fisher's two mountain man novels *(Pemmican*, 1956, and *Mountain Man*, 1965) are interesting ex-amples of this problem.

Pemmican was the victim of one of the most venomous and uninformed reviews ever written *(Time*, June 25, 1956). Ig-noring the historical background (less obvious than in the other historical novels), the reviewer concentrated on the sub-ject of pemmican and the character of David, a trader for the Hudson's Bay Company in the early part of the nineteenth century. The novel is identified as the definitive book on pemmican, and David as a dimwit who does not know whe-ther he is a man or a moose, whose chief interests are pemmi-can and women's thimbleberried bosoms, and who stupidly gets himself into various laughable difficulties before he heads farther west, "perhaps to Hollywood." Fisher himself is re-ferred to as a "saga-gaga" novelist (with reference to the *Testa-ment of Man* series), and his literary exaggerations are confused with the literal truth—cold which can split a tree seen as the same kind of outrageous "claim" as "mosquitoes as big as owls." Hyperbole and fact go hand in hand without distinc-tion. Because the land itself is the real center of interest in *Pemmican*, related closely to characterization and to relation-ships between men and women, anyone unfamiliar with the land (in this case central Canada) is liable to miss the point:

> . . . and he was thinking that this kind of country did things to a man and to a woman—it gave them the wariness of forest things and the aloofness of high-mountain things and the si-lences of deep-river and lake things, so that you found it diffi-cult to take off your mask and submit to a thing as defenseless as love.

The land is the dominating force of *Pemmican;* the people who live in the wild north country are a strange breed, acting out of a combination of animal passion and cold aloofness, a com-bination which can lead to irrationality if not madness. To

survive, however—and most of them do—the people of the
northern wilderness need only to accept the paradox of nature, the juxtaposition of the beauties and the cruelties. As
Fisher speaks of the sensuousness of nature, of the hazards of
living in the wilderness, of violence and ugliness, his tone
changes from a mellow, tender, sympathetic sensitivity—often much like that of nature poetry—to a shocking "delight"
in the ugliness of suffering, and then to a quiet humor which
seems to put everything into its proper perspective. His overall intention is to be realistic, and at least part of his excessiveness may be attributed to the desire (shared by other western writers) to enumerate the "things" of the land—trees,
birds, animals, lore, customs, climate—in order to give an
epic quality to a region which is epic in physical proportions,
and to provide the basis of a tradition in a new land. The love
of "things" then stands in contrast to the question of survival,
to the harshness of the elements of nature as well as the cruelties which man frequently inflicts upon other men. When a
description of Marguerite shortly after she has been scalped is
set beside a description of Princess Sunday butchering a buffalo and looking adorable with "blood smeared over face and
even on her eyelashes," we realize that the north country is
dark enough to demand occasional impishness or outright humor as welcome relief to the reader as well as an internal
necessity to the people of the land, the characters. A phrase
such as "impudent gesture of mockery" belongs to Fisher as
much as it does to the Indian girl who makes the gesture.
And, given the context, both Fisher and his readers must
share David's reaction to a scene capable of evoking nausea:

> David walked back and forth in the gore, smelling the tons of
> raw flesh, the guts, the dung, the bones and hair in fires;
> watching the squaws handle the meat with filthy hands, seeing
> them blow their noses without turning their heads, smiling to
> observe how many things went into pemmican merely because
> they got in a woman's way.

In spite of some apparently outrageous elements of plot
and characterization, easily satirized (as in *Time*), *Pemmican* is

in some ways Fisher's most significant historical novel. It is rich in the lore, the "things," the darkness, "the vast obscenity of the north country" where a man must learn "to respect the silences" and where he stands near and sometimes within a dark and primitive life, a life which can be "as ruthless as death." In characterization, Fisher's tendency is to attribute ruthlessness and cruelty to primitive people, which usually means the Indians in his novels of the American West. In the *Testament of Man* he places such emphasis on the primitive qualities of Man as species that the distinctions between race or sex are relatively unimportant—it is intelligence that Fisher looks for, and he rarely finds it. Intelligence as such is not a primary issue in Fisher's American historical novels, although his attitude toward the Indians occasionally seems racist because he allows them to represent primitivism in contrast to the relative enlightenment or civilized qualities of the white man. One incident in *Pemmican* is so vitriolic that it might be misinterpreted as an attack on women as well as on Indians. For interfering in a domestic affair between an Indian woman and her husband, David is tied to a tree and, while the woman holds a knife against his stomach, a piece of his thumb is cut off by a young boy. David has already been dismayed by the animal lust and the cruelty of the Indians, and his feelings toward the woman are bitter:

> This was no buck, no warrior, for whom courage was the greatest thing in life, but a damned nasty bitch of a female whose vanity had just been outraged and who in her perverted mother's heart was twice as savage as any man on earth. . . . So this was a woman! This was a wife, a mother, this thing!

Princess Sunday, on the other hand, is loving, helpful, and a good mate. It does not matter much that she is also white, because she has been depicted as living with the Indians and has become accustomed to their ways. It is more likely that Fisher sees in women the same beauty and harshness, the same cruelty and tenderness, the same fickleness and stability that he sees in nature. In this respect, he may equate the female of the species with the natural world, thereby allowing the male some superiority in his relationships with the female just as he maintains (at least philosophically—theoretically) superiority over nature.

And yet the women in Fisher's fiction, taken as a group, appear as a rather normal cross-section of women everywhere, with no permanent attitude emerging from the novelist unless we read into the characterizations a sense of guilt left over from Fisher's first marriage and frustration from the second. Otherwise, his female characters are consistent with their historical situations and with the environmental contexts. Subservience is normal under polygamy; the mothers' fight for the survival of their children at Donner Pass is instinctive; Eilley's greed, ambition, and hunger for power in Virginia City is just like that of a man under the same conditions; and whether Jane Morgan's insanity after losing her family *(Mountain Man)* makes her weaker than a man is debatable. I doubt that Fisher considered women less able than men to survive in the western wilderness or anywhere else.

What prompts these generalizations is that most of the characters are based on historical figures, and Fisher is therefore concerned with objectivity, so that many of the characters are somewhat superficial. Fisher is reluctant to invent, to imagine, to plumb the depths of their souls. The novelist who takes extreme liberties with the facts of history can breathe life into historical characters even though the fictional life may be untrue to the historical life. The novelist who is determined to stay close to his historical sources, to be (how shall we say it?) honest, objective, faithful to the known facts, rational rather than imaginative—and so on—performs a service in dramatizing historical people and events, but he often avoids those devices and liberties which might be called literary tools. The result can be a feeling of distance between reader and character. While the characters are based on real people, on records of them, on history, the novelist does not probe as he would with an invented character, and so in his objectivity he establishes a more rigid distance than the "psychical distance" defined by Edward Bullough in his esthetic theory. *Pemmican*, of Fisher's Western Americana, makes the fewest claims to actual events and people, and we feel closer to David, the invented character, even though he is sometimes exaggerated and slightly implausible. It would seem, then, that the historical novel which stays close to the information of its sources and tries hard to achieve historical accuracy is likely to be less satisfactory as fiction, as art, than the novel which allows freer use of the imagination. History, no matter how extensive its documents, does not provide the entire record of any given experience or event. The novelist must therefore fill in gaps even while he is simultaneously selecting from the available information. Fisher's method, as avowed rationalist, is to provide several points of view in an attempt to reach objective conclusions which could otherwise disappear beneath the normal subjectivity of a single point of view. He is most successful in this respect in *Tale of Valor* as he plays off Lewis and Clark against each other, as well as combining the two viewpoints when necessary. When several points of view remain completely separate, as in *Children of God*, the result is an episodic narrative which does not have the virtue of suggestiveness but which may appeal to the realist who is aware that although history is continuous no one ever sees it that way.

Although Fisher allows the narration of the historical novels to emerge from a variety of characters, it should be noted that he always maintains his own authorial omniscience; only in this way can he keep control of his scholarship and of his insistence upon a faithful rendering of the events of the nineteenth-century West. Unfortunately, the method can backfire, as it does in his last historical novel, *Mountain Man*. Subtitled—and therefore advertised—as "A novel of Male and Female in the Early American West," the novel is really a portrait of the mountain man archetype, the superman of the western wilderness. Loosely based on the ex-

ploits of John Johnston, otherwise known as Liver-Eating
Johnson, the narrative owes most of its validity to the 1958
book by Raymond W. Thorp and Robert Bunker, *Crow Killer*
(another designation applied to Johnston). Fisher does not
acknowledge this source although his prefatory "To the
Reader" cites other sources which are intended to prove that
there were such people as the mountain men, that there really
was a wilderness of beauty and grandeur, and (because Sam
Minard is musically inclined) that the "eloquent art of music
has long been the handmaid of the Nature-lover." We are involved here with what Richard M. Dorson has called "pristine
oral legend." Chapter 3 in Thorp and Bunker is titled "The
Making of a Legend," and part three of the book is called "A
Man Among Men." Fisher did not, of course, uncover the
legend; but in taking it for his own use he has turned John
Johnston into the ultimate stereotype of the mountain man,
the exaggerated essence of both the fact and the myth of the
breed of men who trapped the early West, discovered passes
through the mountains, established trails, both fought and
lived with the Indians, and shunned civilization for the wild
and beautiful world of nature.

Mountain Man is Vardis Fisher's hymn to the wilderness,
to its beauty and grandeur, to its privacy, and to the qualities
in man that allow him to love it as well as to survive in it. The
tone is both optimistic and nostalgic, although the echoes of
death ring between the music of Beethoven and the melodies
of Mozart: "This was not a country for persons dedicated to
the prevention of cruelty by the living on the living." Fisher
has not forgotten the many years and the many novels devoted to lamenting and explaining this cruelty, but here in his
last novel he juxtaposes the cruelties with an almost ungov-
erned enthusiasm for the Old West, especially the mountains:
"God, how he loved it all!" In an attempt to deal with his subject completely, to say the last word about it, Fisher overplays
his hand. Descriptions of action are brief but violent; scenes
are often melodramatic, as though to pull at the emotions; ex-

pository information is worked into the narrative to make certain that everything is said that can be said about the West and the mountain man; and Sam Minard is too full-blown, too heroic, too sensitive, too knowledgeable, too perfect in his way to be plausible. It is as though Fisher wrote the novel as an exercise in dealing with his favorite subject. *Mountain Man* is neither realistic (except in scattered passages) nor mythic (except as we allow it to be). It is "representative," an amalgamation of the major characteristics and lore found in Fergusson's *Wolf Song*, Guthrie's *Big Sky*, Blake's *Johnny Christmas*, and Manfred's *Lord Grizzly*. It is, in short, a summing up, not an individually realized work of fiction. But it is also a work of love, a final tribute to the men and women of the mountain wilderness, with images from music and art enhancing the romantic response to the beauties of nature and softening (or at least explaining in a different way) the harshness of winter, madness, and death.

Whatever can be said of the individual historical novels—and I think each one is successful in its own way—as a group they make an imposing portrait of the nineteenth-century West. Fisher glorifies the course of empire even as he exposes the foolishness, greed, horror, starvation, exploitation, human cruelty and madness that accompanied it. His romantic nostalgia for the wilderness (in spite of its realities) and his equally strong desire to be rational and objective often clash, but he more often exaggerates than understates and we can only conclude that his feelings for the West (divided though they were) had a strength that could not be matched consistently by his scholarship and rational thought. If it is true that one of our strongest myths is the notion of finding salvation in a return to primitivism, and that part of the western story is that very myth, then we can understand the conflict in Fisher, the man and the writer, who scoffed at many of the forms and consequences of primitivism even while he was working his way back in time to locate some explanation of who and what he was.

3

Before Fisher's first historical novel was published in 1939 *(Children of God)* and he was suddenly hailed as an objective writer, he had written eight Idaho novels which the critics called frank, naturalistic, introverted, and autobiographical— excursions into the subconscious. Because of his personal association with Thomas Wolfe, and because of comments in the Vridar Hunter tetralogy, Fisher was thought of as another rambling, egotistic, disorganized pursuer of the self. It is true that these early novels established his pattern of thought and self-investigation that was to last through the final huge volume (partly a rewriting of the tetralogy) of the *Testament of Man*. It is equally true that he pursued intelligence and scholarship with such passion that it was usually impossible for him to become entirely objective and that Fisher the man is present in varying degrees in all the novels. This is particu- larly true, however, in the Idaho narratives, leading to some interesting speculations. Had Fisher not been so adamant in his growing concern for intelligence (as opposed to intuition, for example), had he continued to write about his Antelope Hills in Idaho, had he tempered his obsession with personal fears, desires, and failures through the application of psychi- cal distance in the tetralogy, he might well have established a fictional region comparable to Faulkner's Yoknapatawpha. *Sartoris* (1929), the first of Faulkner's county novels, was pub- lished one year later than Fisher's first novel, *Toilers of the Hills*, which established a branch of the Hunter (Fisher) fam- ily in the Antelope Hills of southeastern Idaho. Whereas fifteen of Faulkner's nineteen novels were set in Yoknapa- tawpha, only nine of Fisher's twenty-six were set in Ante- lope. With critics making periodic attacks on regionalism (granted that they do not always define it properly), we may wonder why Faulkner achieved literary fame—including the Nobel Prize—while Fisher remained relatively unknown during his lifetime except to students of the American West.

Aside from such considerations as style, originality, and complexity, several answers might be suggested. Fisher abandoned his Antelope country for a long time, but perhaps there was nothing more to say about it. His people were new to the region, settling in a traditionless wilderness, occupying themselves in coping with nature, the land, as much as with other people—perhaps more. Faulkner's county had an additional century of traditions and family relationships, so that as industry invaded the South a complex set of themes became available, the decaying family traditions and the conflict between industrialization and the values of the wilderness being among them. Additionally, the conflict between the whites and the blacks was of considerably more social importance than the rather shallow relationships between whites and Indians on the frontier. Yet, perhaps the telling difference between Faulkner's treatment of Mississippi and Fisher's handling of his Idaho materials is that Faulkner remained the artist while Fisher became the protagonist. His themes, at least in the Idaho novels, were personal, and his emphases often turned to ideas, to the didactic presentation of these ideas, rather than to narrative techniques and to dramatizations.

I do not offer these distinctions as criticism of Fisher's Idaho novels as a group. The novels are uneven in conception, structure, style, and impact, and it may well be that one of them (*Dark Bridwell*) is Fisher's best novel and that another (*No Villain Need Be*, 1936) is his worst.

Three families comprise the essential part of Fisher's fictional community: the Hunters (Fishers), the Brantons (Thorntons), and the Bridwells.

Joe Hunter:	in Wyoming in 1869, on way west from Missouri.
	marries Rose O'Rourke, 1870, in Ogden.
	first child born, Joe (Vridar's father), March 12, 1871.
	seven other children, youngest is Dock of *Toilers of the Hills*, probably born about 1879.
Samuel Branton:	youngest child, Prudence, born 1870.

Joe Hunter:	the younger, meets Prudence Branton in Annis, Idaho, 1894.
	marries Prudence, 1894.
	first child, Vridar Baroledt (Vardis Alvero), 1895.
	second child, Mertyl (Vivian Ezra), 1897.
	third child, Diana (Viola Irene), 1901.
Dock Hunter:	with wife Opal settles near Antelope creek, 1906.
	Dick born October 15, 1906.
	Bill and Emerald born September 21, 1907.
	Ruby born December 24, 1908.
	Garnet born April 6, 1910.
	Jack born August 17, 1911.
	Amethyst born October 7, 1912.
	Jim born June 26, 1914.
Charley Bridwell:	marries Lela, 1891.
	Beth born, 1892.
	Thiel born, 1893.
	Jed born, 1894.
	Bridwells move to Antelope Hills, 1897, across the river from Hunters.
	Hetty born, 1908.
	Ham (Hamlin) born, 1912.

These and other less important families appear—occasionally with a change in name—in five of the Idaho novels. Because the population of the area is sparse, and social relationships are limited, the community's potential for fiction is less dense, less complex, than Yoknapatawpha is for Faulkner. And because Fisher disliked his environment (whereas Faulkner remained more detached), the vein ran out as he finally lost interest and turned to other material in other places. However, some of Fisher's best writing (including style, tone, and form) can be found in these early novels before he began to search out the intellectual as well as the irrational and to preach for the one and against the other through his fictional self, Vridar Hunter.

The Antelope Hills region, as seen in *Toilers of the Hills*, is a country of loneliness, indifference, and silence given a treat-

ment which prompted most critics to use the term *harsh*, but
which is also extremely sensitive. The mystery and madness
of the land and its people are conveyed quietly and evoca-
tively. As in several of Fisher's novels, the male (in this case
Dock Hunter, one of Vridar's uncles) comes to the wilderness
eagerly, and the female (Dock's second wife, Opal) comes reluctantly. Dock believes in the promise, half-myth and half-
truth, that everything will work out "next year." He concen-
trates all of his energies on conquering the land, making it
yield its bounty up to him; he works hard and cheerfully
while his wife bears children and gradually decays, spiritually
as well as physically. For Dock there is hope because he seems
to have overcome the arid land with his formula for dry farming; but Opal becomes old at the age of thirty-one.

    Not surprisingly, the land gets as much attention as the
people. Within the western juxtaposition of the harsh and the
beautiful, the ugly and the tender, Fisher locates the area of
life's mysteries, and he is at his best in describing—not defining—this area of emotional and spiritual response. His descriptions are frequently magnificent when he is dealing with
the landscape and its implications. The people, on the other
hand, appear weak and flawed. The lucky ones survive their
environment with a measure of grace, but most are seen as
part of a vanishing species. They are a people without a tradition, without a legitimate place on the frontier; they have
brought little with them, and it is already too late to carve out
an empire from a frontier which is disappearing and leaving in
its wake only a vague tradition of hope and courage. Yet as
Opal senses the isolation, as she sees nothing but dust and
sky, as she feels the silence of the place, an aura of mystery
and perverse beauty hangs over her:

> And everywhere were silences, strangely apart and alone: the
> small green silences in coves along their way, the round silence
> of each hill or the flat silence of each plain, great solitudes that
> filled the sky and lay over the mountains and beyond.

This is the very characteristic of the land that attracted the
mountain men, that lured them out of the noisy towns and

drew them deeper into the wilderness. The difference is one
of time and circumstance. Opal knows, at least
subconsciously, that there is no longer a rainbow with a pot of
gold at the end. That search, that part of the American
Dream, has ended, leaving only the backwash, the poor farmers struggling to make a living on reluctant soil. It has been
suggested that Fisher in his early novels shows a kinship with
Erskine Caldwell, although he lacks Caldwell's grotesque humor. But Fisher, in the midst of portraits of squalor and futile
perspiration, responds to the land in a way that is perhaps
possible only in the West:

> [Dock's] mind groped for words that would make her under-
> stand the mystery of these [mountains], the deep living power
> of them, almost the intelligence of them. Between all these and
> himself, he admitted, there existed a kinship, something for
> which he could find no words, a feeling of love sometimes, or
> of fear and wonder.

Throughout Fisher's fiction it is usually the male trying to
convey his love of the land to the female, but I believe that
Fisher is not so much making a statement about the strengths,
weaknesses, and complexities of the male-female relationship
as he is trying to convince himself, to force his masculine side
to overcome the childhood fears of the wilderness and of
many of the ways of nature, fears which he subconsciously attributed to a feminine side which represented (or nourished)
his extreme sensitivity. The fact that there are no words
through which to understand the mystery of life, of nature, is
not a shameful limitation for either Dock or for Fisher; the
verbal affliction is common to all writers, and it is especially
noticeable in Western fiction because of the importance of the
land and its mysteries. Fisher at his best—when he responds
to his sensitivity without becoming too subjective—evokes the
feelings of place, of the natural life, of the spiritual overtones
in the physical environment, as well as anyone. But he does it
largely in the earlier novels, before he began to turn research
and scholarship into fiction. In *Toilers of the Hills*, as might be
expected, it is the cyclical drama of nature which commands

our attention, first as a "ruthless power, unseen and beyond control," and then as an awakening in the spring, endowing the farmers with new hope. At the last, Opal becomes reconciled to the land and to her house. She and Dock, uncomplex but durable, discover the sense of place, houseness in a new and traditionless land of limited opportunity.

Toilers is a simple and satisfying novel, playing off the hopelessness against the hope, and written with sensitivity and objectivity. The novel which follows *(Dark Bridwell)*, although set in the same Antelope country, is more excessive in mood, richer and more exuberant in style, darker in its social and philosophical implications, and much closer to genuine tragedy. It is quite possible that *Bridwell* (reprinted in softcover as *The Wild Ones* in 1958) is not only Fisher's best novel—although only his second in a long career—but also one of the major accomplishments in modern American fiction. It is a true symbolic tragedy of the end of the frontier; it achieves the status of myth, although it is anchored firmly in Idaho soil; and Charley Bridwell, through his˙ peculiar strengths and weaknesses, may be the closest American relative of King Lear. Fisher's own weaknesses as a writer are held in check more successfully in *Bridwell* than anywhere else, and, although the people and the incidents are similar (in many cases the same) to those in the early part of the Vridar Hunter story, they take on a deeper significance in *Bridwell* and are shaped more artistically and more powerfully. The narrative is related through, or around, three characters, Charley Bridwell first, then his son Jed, and finally Charley's wife Lela. Overlapping of a number of incidents, because of the three views of essentially the same story, does not cause the narrative to falter or seem repetitive; instead, events seem to proceed inexorably, pulled along by fate, by a destiny which cannot be controlled by any of the characters. Brooding over the entire tale is the author, in a limited omniscience, unobtrusive. Once again a reference to Faulkner may be enlightening. In *The Sound and the Fury* (1929), published two years before *Dark Bridwell*, a series of events is presented four

times, as told by four different characters. There is no reason
to believe that Fisher was influenced by Faulkner; the two
writers were mapping out their fictional-real regions simultaneously, and it is likely that neither was even aware of the
other at this time. However, their technique of going over the
same material several times from different points of view
serves to establish the reader's own point of view at the correct
distance between himself and the material. We are drawn into
the story by its immediacy and reality, but we are also aware
that we are confronting a work of art and we can disengage
ourselves from the narrative experience and make a judgment
upon it. Stated in theory, this ideal point occupied by the
reader was identified by Edward Bullough in 1912: "the *utmost decrease of Distance without its disappearance.*" That is, the
reader is allowed to come close to empathy but is nudged back
before he loses himself in the story. On the writer's side, the
task is to produce a work which neither fully repels the reader
nor lures him all the way into the experiences of the narrative
so that he forgets that he is confronting a work of art. In *Dark
Bridwell*, letting either element get out of hand, the cruelties of
life in the wilderness could repel the reader, while the beauties of the virgin land could attract him. Too much emphasis
on the one would create a gulf between book and reader; too
much emphasis on the other could lead to loss of objective
judgment. As far as I know, neither Fisher nor Faulkner knew
of Bullough's theory. The control of esthetic distance is partly
a refinement (even though also an expansion) of the central intelligence of Henry James and is, I believe, one of the major
technical achievements of twentieth-century fiction. Although
its origins may well be in *Madame Bovary* (1857), it seems to be
found more in American fiction than in European, and more
often in Western American fiction than Eastern, although not
always in the same form. Frederick Manfred's *Lord Grizzly*
and F. Scott Fitzgerald's *The Great Gatsby* show psychical distance operating successfully but in different ways. The
technique may be a reaction against turn-of-the-century
naturalism and realism which limited the reader's response by

limiting the means of art. In any case, John Peale Bishop's comparison of Fisher, Caldwell, Faulkner, and Wolfe—made in 1937—does a disservice to Faulkner's *The Sound and the Fury* and to Fisher's *Dark Bridwell*. These are not simply regional or naturalistic or autobiographical novels.

Bridwell may indeed be identified as a naturalistic novel: the destinies of the characters seem determined by their environment, life is harsh and the forces of nature are unremitting, and existence seems to be set apart from any notion of a supreme deity. But Fisher, not ordinarily interested in symbols, goes beyond the restrictions of naturalism and suggests, or implies, through parallels between his individual characters and a much broader portrait of mankind, a symbolic or archetypal image of life that goes far beyond his Antelope Hills.

Charley Bridwell is a child of nature. He drinks a great deal and indulges in "unpitying devilries," but he is also likable. He takes what he can get and gives what he has. He is completely at one with nature, fearing nothing, daring everything, but content to let things take their natural course. He is not ambitious, and he is not without tenderness; yet, like an animal with a short memory, he will disregard his own family unless they are in physical danger. He is deeply affected by his natural environment, although his reaction to it is a primitive one. When he watches the forces at work in the swift rapids of the river, similar forces well up in him:

> And as Charley watched, there came upon him that strange and deep emotion that always took him by the throat when he saw life wrenched into blind violence. It was a lust to kill, as if through murder he would have to seek his way to peace. It was a black power that gripped him and made him do brutal or reckless deeds. He had little strength against it; and if he did not abuse man or beast, drawing from savagery an aftermath of calm, he had to give himself to some fierce experience.

In this particular instance, he dives recklessly from a high bank into the boiling river, disappears from sight until Lela faints from fear, and then appears with a devilish grin on his face, "triumphant . . . a river demon." Charley is a man with a place but without a time; he is a mountain man born too late. The frontier, the life of the wilderness, is gone forever, and Charley cannot adjust to even the meager society of rural Idaho.

Neither is Charley able to adjust to his natural environment entirely. He does not fear a dangerous and busy life, but neither does he want it. He prefers peace and solitude and serenity, and thus appears lazy to his family and his few friends. Like an animal, he would reconcile himself to nature, but instinctively, to a mystical aspect of it, not to all the realistic particulars. On the other hand, Lela hungers for a dangerous and busy life of a kind which is not available to her, but is afraid of it. And so the two people are at cross-purposes with each other and, importantly, also within themselves. The river becomes a symbol of these differences:

> Charley hated it. He hated the river's senseless going to an unknown and futile end, the loud tongue of its monologue, its grotesque buffoonery, its crazed barn-storming on its way to the sea. And its stage-struck gestures, its steady infernal booming, awakened a cruel hunger that had stood unused in his being. He stepped out of long indolence, feeling the great surging of life, yet despising it. How, he wondered, could a man rest in peace, when Nature dramatized even the melting of snows?

The description of the river is significant, because it is also the description of Charley. In a way, he is nature, or natural man, and when he hates the river he hates himself. He senses that he is possessed by some kind of dark and primitive evil (perhaps ignorance), but he can do nothing about it. He even breeds another like himself, his son Jed, who can with fascination study a snake:

> Though they were enemies, the spirit of this snake was his spirit; their two souls reached back anciently to the same dark source. Their ancestry was the same wilderness of desire.

And so Charley and after him Jed symbolize not just wilderness man but the dark origins of man, the primitive spirit, evil in its ancient sources of ignorance, base desires, and lack of intelligent control. Yet Charley is capable of tenderness, and Jed is capable of turning against his father. The ambiguities overrun any simple explanations.

Lela finds something else in the river:

> It was a tireless hunger, ancient but forever young, baffled but forever seeking, as if under the earth's calm surface there was a great unrest, out of which it came eternally, speaking the language of life. Night and day . . . she heard the sound of its travel . . . until life spun within her like an eddy of feeling isolated from all meaning, condemned to a timeless fever of striving, but exiled from all change.

She never finds what she is looking for, because Charley is always there to frustrate and thwart her desires, but the river remains a "symbol of the up-reaching life, and its going [gives] her strength." Like the white whale in *Moby Dick*, the river is whatever man makes of it; it is a mirror in which each person sees himself. Like Ahab, Charley Bridwell hates what he sees, even while fascinated by it. But, like King Lear, Charley is blind to the dangers around him, blind through vanity, and this blindness leads to his defeat.

Two people hate Charley. One is his son Jed, named after a man whose teeth Charley once kicked out. The other is a sheepherder named Adolph Buck. Adolph runs off with Charley's daughter, and Jed takes away Charley's wife. Charley, the man for whom truth lay in "the lurking sunlit vision, standing in all the accidents of ill luck and chance," finally becomes the object of a hatred which rises to a superhuman level, to myth, and destroys him.

Jed has inherited both the Bridwell lust for devilment and the deep brooding intensity of his mother. The latter gives him the sensitivity to see that his father is cruel (though perhaps innocently) to Lela; the former charges him with the desire to excel his father's "cunning ingenuities." The mixture makes Jed into a strange boy, intensely cruel, yet often likable, shaped not only by his blood inheritance but also by his environment:

> Everything around him . . . invited him to solitude or to reckless deeds. The great mountains, the untamed headstrong river, the wild animal life and the lonely blockade of winter months—he felt the power of all these, and their ruthlessness, and their savage ways.

Jed leaves home when he is fourteen. During the next nine years Charley becomes lazier and more cruel, neglecting Lela while she bears more children and is slowly and spiritually starved. She is isolated in the wilderness with a man who is little more than the wilderness himself. Then, in an archetypal pattern, Jed returns to take his mother away. The final scene in the novel is large in scope, wild, and significant. (It may be one of the most effective scenes in American fiction.) Charley, in an animal rage, turns on Jed and almost kills him, but Lela beats Charley senseless with a club and goes off with Jed. Another son waits for Charley, thinking that he too will leave with them, but Charley remains, and in madness he drinks and raves, curses and laughs like a devil, and tries to come to terms with his grief. He cannot change, and in the morning he walks away, never to be seen again. Yet his ghost remains with us, just as the ghosts of primitive men still walk beside us and ride in us whenever we succumb to the dark forests and the strange madnesses of our savage origins.

The major tension of the novel, aside from actual family incidents operating on a lower level, is at the point where conflicting views of primitivism and civilization touch each other in a tangle of potential meanings, "the dark tangle of the good and the bad," unresolved by Charley's conclusion that "his world had been pitched on the rocks, by whatever it was in human beings that drove them to seek that which they would never find." Fisher was to continue the search himself, through psychology and the examination of man's origins in history, anthropology, religion, and speculation; but, in *Bridwell* the significance lies in the ambiguities and mysteries of life, not in answers. This, in part, is what maintains the high artistic level—no interference from scholarship or didacticism. In the conflicts between Charley and Lela, and between Charley and Jed, the thematic similarities to Cooper's *Prairie* (the dilemma of wilderness and civilization) are obvious but are also more complex. In the Rousseauan sense, primitivism as represented by Charley is good, and it is society which sees it as—or turns it into—evil. (One of the lovely little ironies of life comes to mind here: *rousseau* with the lowercase *r* is a Canadian term meaning fried pemmican. Did Fisher know this when pemmican came close to being a symbol in his "natural man" novel by that name?) But primitivism must also be bad because it is nonintellectual. Charley is therefore both good and bad and Lela finds him an enigma. Yet Lela, as woman, is "the darkest riddle of all," and, in a sense, so is nature. We then approach a paradox: what is wrong with society is that it is not intelligent enough but also that it has lost its intuitive touch with nature.

When Charley disappears, so does a way of life; the American frontier is gone forever, for better or for worse. On the less abstract level of the human condition—the family, man-woman relationships—it is a case of two people unable to live in harmony, each finding it impossible to adapt to the other person's mode of living and quality of desires. The children, caught between their father's "big wholesome laziness" and their mother's "restlessness and the covetous hunger of her heart," tend to grow into the latter condition, leaving Charley isolated from his family. The river he loves becomes a symbol of the going away of the family, an escape route. Unable to comprehend the difference of attitudes, Charley bursts into a rage at the end of the novel and seems quite mad as he finally moves off "into the empire of solitude." Having thought that he was all-powerful, that he was doing the right things, he loses at every turn. The implications are social, national, philosophical, psychological, and archetypal, and because the unanswered questions are in the realm of ethics, the individual man, and the dichotomy of good-evil, the novel—powerfully written—comes close to being a genuine American tragedy, something we have thought impossible because of the continuing belief in the American Dream. *Dark Bridwell* is an essential Western novel in which the dilemma raised by Cooper is dramatized and given new complexities through symbolic naturalism.

As far as characters and environment are concerned, *Toilers of the Hills, Dark Bridwell,* and *In Tragic Life* (1932) are all of a piece. What is different about the third of these novels is that the Idaho experiences become highly personal and Fisher himself becomes the protagonist. As Vridar Hunter he stands at the center (and fills most of the edges) of a tetralogy which continues with *Passions Spin the Plot* (1934), *We Are Betrayed* (1935), and *No Villain Need Be* (1936). The four titles are taken from the last three lines of sonnet number 43 of George Meredith's 50-sonnet sequence, *Modern Love:*

> In tragic life, God wot,
> No villain need be! Passions spin the plot.
> We are betrayed by what is false within.

Much of Fisher's intellectual biography is found, not altogether cryptically, in these lines. Other lines from Meredith's poem yield phrases which could have served almost as well: "and raged deep inward," "the tender fool," "the sting is dire," "the mad Past," and "they shall suffer." A passage in the thirtieth sonnet is pertinent to Fisher's lifetime concerns:

> What are we first? First, animals; and next
> Intelligences at a leap.

From the tetralogy through the twelve volumes of *The Testament of Man,* Fisher examines the primitive qualities of man, his animalism, his superstitions and fears, and his slow move (in spite of Meredith's "leap") toward rationalism. Through the fictional process of these sixteen novels, artistic taste and form give way to exposition, scholarship, preaching, and footnotes. Even with these noticeable weaknesses, the autobiographical novels and their historical-becoming-personal sequence are powerful and intense in their overall impact. Fisher is above all else moral in purpose and hon-

est in presentation. In the first volume of the tetralogy he
is still more or less the powerful novelist of *Dark Bridwell*, producing effective action, characterization, and scene, as well as
a strong sense of conflict. Then, gradually, through the next
three volumes, fiction gives way to a kind of loosely dramatized exposition of ideas.

Vridar (unquestionably Vardis) is the oldest son of Joe
Hunter, an early settler in the Idaho benchland, a simple but
hardworking man who is married to a puritanical woman.
Vridar is caught between the rigidity of his mother's beliefs
and the easy lack of belief of his father. Because his father ignores him and allows him to run loose while his mother frightens him with her strict code of behavior, Vridar grows up
confused. Adding to his uncertainties, the brutal and wild life
of the Idaho wilderness wounds his psychological and emotional sensitivity, and although he goes to the city
eventually—Salt Lake City and Chicago—he never learns
from the experience and retains his self-pity after he grows
up. Whatever social themes are available in the tetralogy are
negated by Vridar's self-complacency.

In Tragic Life contains the best-written part of Vridar's
story; although it is episodic, it is extremely realistic in its descriptions of the crude Idaho environment, and it establishes
the force of this environment on Vridar's life. His childhood
is tragic in that he is beset by every fear that it is possible for a
child to know. The rest of his life seems to be governed by the
first eighteen years. Whenever Vridar seems prepared to face
life without fears, and with love, something turns up in his
non-Idaho world which has direct correspondence with the
pressures and cruelties of his childhood environment. In *Passions Spin the Plot*, Vridar takes his grief and fear with him to
college in Salt Lake City. His life at college is both pathetic
and humorous; Vridar is the victim of his extreme shyness,
his sensitivity, his deep concern with morality, and his fear of
the fierce competitions and dishonesties of life. This is a dark
book. Vridar is, by most standards, mentally unbalanced. He
sees all life as evil and purposeless. Read out of context, this

novel is hopelessly grim; but it helps to establish Fisher's thesis that man is constantly under the control of senseless fears, whether in the Idaho wilds or in the city. Vridar is the product not only of his Idaho environment, but also of his entire culture and of his race. Although he is an exaggerated character, he is true to his role as representative of the men who are victims of their cultural history. This includes almost everyone.

The love story of Vridar and Neloa Doole is one of the wildest and most frustrating in American fiction. Neloa makes love indiscriminately to other men, acting from a natural and animal-like impulse. She ignores Vridar for years after he has fallen in love with her and finally marries him for what seems to be a matter of convenience more than anything else. Vridar the idealist, the romantic, is tortured by Neloa's lack of concern for him, but he must marry her anyway. Like Philip, in Somerset Maugham's *Of Human Bondage*, who felt compelled to return again and again to Mildred, the "vulgar slut," so Vridar must have Neloa although he loathes her and can find no reasonable purpose in loving her. In a symbolic sense, Neloa is dark and mysterious Woman, an archetypal figure out of the primitive mists, and her power over Vridar is simply that of woman over man. Taken by itself, the relationship between Vridar and Neloa makes a powerful story, one of the most fascinating episodes in Fisher's work; but the conflict is never resolved, and the relationship ends rather meaninglessly (Neloa commits suicide) except for the sense of guilt which it gives to Vridar.

We Are Betrayed, the third volume in this series, finishes Vridar's years at college in Utah. His motto at this time is that "Honesty has to pay its price. It used to pay in hemlock or hanging. Now it pays in isolation." Vridar thinks that he is learning to be completely honest, and thus different from the people around him; but he is little more than a youthful idealist trying to play the role of the realist. The closer he comes to what he considers realism, the more absurd he becomes. He has several, indeed many, honest characteristics, but they are exaggerated to ridiculousness. In typical youthful fashion he addresses himself to the exhortation, "To thyself be true," and then proceeds to destroy (in his own mind) everything that has been built up in the past two or three thousand years. Much that is in our traditions may deserve to be destroyed, or relegated carefully to its historical place, but to have the cultural and religious structure of the world annihilated in one novel is, I think, going beyond the bounds of plausibility.

Vridar now, in rapid succession, serves time in the army, becomes a bootlegger and a friend of whores and pimps, becomes a father, and begins graduate study in English at the University of Chicago. While in Chicago, he spiritually deserts his unfathomable part-Indian wife and falls in love (intellectually) with Athene Marvell, an educated girl who is completely different from Neloa. Neloa drinks poison and Vridar goes to pieces in the hospital and in the morgue, and a little later vomits as her body is put into the furnace at the crematorium. But first he has vowed, in her name, to finish his work and to be honest with himself and others. Unfortunately, honesty by itself is not literature, not even realistic literature, and the force of Neloa's death and of the heightened writing in the passage which tells of her death is lost in Vridar's foolishness and in Fisher's determination to make literature out of what he considers truth. Truth figures prominently in this novel and in the one which follows, but it is abstract and never given life. It is the truth of the scholar's facts, not the truth of humanity. Fisher often tended to think that the two were the same.

No Villain Need Be concludes the tetralogy with a noticeable lack of action. Through endless conversations, Fisher presents all of his ideas in encyclopedic fashion, thinking them through as he goes along. The novel is tedious and resolves nothing. Fisher later was aware of this, although he occasionally pointed to an anonymous reviewer or two who thought this volume was the best of the four. At the end of the novel, he pleads for "thorough exploration first, and then a tradition leading to, and finally resting upon, the inviolable responsibility of leadership." He indicates that Freudianism and Marxism have something to contribute, but does not make clear what that is or to what, exactly, they are to contribute. Fisher was not a politician; he might have liked to be a psychologist; he probably was more than anything else a moralist. But he too was dissatisfied with the conclusion of Vridar's story, and he wrote the entire *Testament* series in an effort to resolve Vridar's problems.

First, however, came a brief and curious interlude during which Fisher wrote what he later called his favorite among his own novels, *April* (1937), as well as *Forgive Us Our Virtues* (1938), the novel Fisher most wanted to forget. Although *April* is a part of the Antelope sequence, with some of the same characters that peopled the earlier novels, it is a different kind of story in tone and emphasis. One might speculate that Fisher had tired momentarily of the tetralogy nightmare and allowed himself to indulge in a daydream of escape. Kitty Weeg and her daughter June are removed from the real world by their interest in the romantic world of cheap novels. Of Kitty it is said that she knew nothing of "the mad and terrible and beautiful world," and she remains fat and serene until she is ultimately forgotten, having come to nothing. June, tainted by the atmosphere of the romantic novels she has read, tries to ignore her suitor because he is in reality as homely and lonely as she is, and instead courts the attention of more interesting people. One is a hired hand who thinks he is a poet and with whom June pretends to be another girl named April—an identity taken from some of the girls June has read about. Another is an old maid, Susan Hemp, with whom June feels a rapport even though she is continually thrown out of Susan's house. (Symbolically, we are to understand that June must find her own house.) The third is Virgin Hill, the most beautiful girl in town, and very popular, to whose house June goes one day in order to look, observe, admire, and finally kiss Virgin to find out what it is like to kiss a beautiful girl. The unreal atmosphere suggests that Fisher is creating a fable set within the very real Idaho landscape, using the romantic or poetic imagination of June to see the environment more kindly and more mysteriously than Vridar was able to see it. June is one of the many "little" people, hardly the material for tragedy, and so the novel becomes a successful comedy, cheerful in spite of the many human weaknesses that are revealed, and in some ways as haunting as the house of June's suitor is to her:

> In the course of time he fell upon the subject of his empty house and this became for her a symbol of his need: something empty and unused, a loneliness waiting for a woman, for gentle ways to smooth it into beauty and repose. The house haunted her.

The irony of this passage is apparent in the context of the western experience of houselessness, of wandering, looking for a place to settle. June has such a place—or at least it is available to her—but its reality conflicts with her romantic notions of life, with, perhaps, a variation of the American Dream which lured so many people into the West. Finally, however, June accepts the house by conquering it, cleaning it, cooking a meal for Sol Incham—its owner and her suitor—and thereby achieving a little victory which is consistent with her character as a little heroine. The commonplace and the poetic in this fable stand apart from the exaggerations and heightened realism of the other Idaho novels.

Forgive Us Our Virtues is obviously an exercise in psychological self-examination that does little but clear the air while Fisher gets himself prepared for the mammoth *Testament* as well as the historical novels of the American West. Made up of several shorter novels which had been rejected by publishers, it lacks psychological significance and acts only as a buffer between the Idaho novels and the new concentration on history as the material for fiction. Within four years (1939–43) Fisher was to publish three novels of the American West as well as the first volume of the *Testament*.

4

Only the final volume of *The Testament of Man* is set for the most part in the American West. The first eleven volumes run a wide gamut from prehistoric times to ancient history to the Middle Ages, all of it necessarily set outside our own relatively new continent whose history is recent and short within the broader context of the development of man, his society, his religions, and his characteristics. What makes the *Testament* pertinent to a study of the Western American novel is not only the fact that it was written by a Western American novelist but that its explorations and theses have their impetus from Fisher's dissatisfaction with life on the American frontier. Furthermore, Fisher felt that his self-analysis in the Idaho tetralogy was incomplete and that only an extended study of a much earlier history could offer the explanations he was looking for. In one sense, then, the *Testament* is the supreme act of the rationalist, a scholarly search for the origins of intelligence or for those factors which have prevented man from becoming a creature devoted to reason rather than emotion. Ironically, Fisher's monumental work, while interesting in itself, does not add much to what he has already said in the story of Vridar Hunter. What it does provide (in addition to provocative treatments of primitivism and religion) is a rationale for the weaknesses and the childishness of modern man. It is, in effect, an exposé of our distressing past as well as an attempt to—in Fisher's words—"understand why [he] made a fool of [himself] in the fourth volume of the tetralogy."

Notwithstanding these personal motivations, Fisher begins his task with a vocabulary familiar to Western American themes and concerns. In an opening hymn to the origins of life, "prairies of the infinite" and "vast prairies of . . . light" are part of the "geography of space," and the search for roots which occupied a stage of the American frontier movement is seen as an essential element of the first life of the soil on the planet Earth:

> A withdrawing tide stranded a sprig of seaweed in a sheltered
> cove where winds had laid a thin soil, and it clung there, not
> with roots, but with the simple wish to feel itself rooted and an-
> chored.

During the course of *Darkness and the Deep* (1943), man appears,
still without speech but already caught up in such elemental aspects of life as food, sex, egoism, and the survival of the fittest.
Personal hungers are foremost, although the female of the
species shows some concern for her offspring. And in an echo
of the short story "Fellowship," Fisher proclaims that "out of
dread, out of anxious loneliness in self, has come such fellowship as we have."

As the species proliferates in *The Golden Rooms* (1944), and
fire is discovered, one tribe feels that it is handsomer and more
intelligent than another tribe and decides to hunt out and ex-
terminate the lesser creatures in order to "make the world conform to their notions of what it should be." Racial prejudice
and war are recognized as the products of self-love. Since the
victims resemble the conquerors, however, the "superior" people suffer from man's very first twinge of conscience (represented in part by ghosts) and try to propitiate the forces of
thunder and lightning which bring the ghosts. In primitive terror the people cry and perhaps utter the first human prayer. As
though these actions had nothing to do with notions of good
and evil, with superstition or magic, Fisher then states in *Intimations of Eve* (1946) that "only in that time, have human beings been free" because they knew only the physical world and
with its concrete facts sought to "determine the logical relationships of cause and effect." His claim seems to be vaguely assumed and based more on wish than on fact; but, the claim is
used to set up the next several novels which deal with superstition, magic, and cruelties in the name of a subjective cause. In
the ascendency of woman, through the ability to give birth and
the prerogative of refusing sexual relations with man, man is
frustrated and turns often to war or to what has since become
art. *Adam and the Serpent* (1947) introduces the concept of sin,

foretells of a male deity to replace the Moon Goddess, and suggests an analogy between the snake and the human penis and a further analogy between the genitals and the symbol of the cross. As men become priests in *The Divine Passion* (1948), replacing women as the conductors of religious rites, sex continues to receive the emphasis. Fisher suggests that later symbols of religion and art came from primitive sex worship. These first few novels in the series attempt to show, in historical terms, that sex is one of the major frustrations of modern man. While this may indeed be true, a hermit coming out of the wilderness to cut off his penis as a sacrifice is hardly a satisfactory image of that frustration, and the inferior writing throughout *Adam* and *Passion* indicates a carelessness of theme as well.

The Valley of Vision (1951) takes the narrative somewhat past the speculative primitive times to King Solomon and his conflict with the Maccabeeans, in which the king loses. Fisher finds this loss highly significant in that a rigid desert psychology was imposed on an agricultural people, thus shaping the modern world more than any other event. It is impossible to say whether the rigidity was associated in Fisher's mind with the puritanism of his mother (or Vridar's mother), but the closing sentence of *Vision* seems to support the possibility: "So let's drink to love, and say that love is both the Father *and* the Mother, who together are God." The separate elements of this proclamation appear again at the end of the *Testament*, arranged somewhat differently, and seem of the utmost importance to Fisher. The same is true of the themes of the next three volumes—*The Island of the Innocent* (1952), *Jesus Came Again* (1956), and *A Goat for Azazel* (1956)—in which the differences between Greek and Jew are examined from two centuries before Christ to the formation of the Christian Church. Despite many contradictions and confusions, with Fisher trying harder than before to avoid taking sides, ideas emerge which can be carried over to the twentieth-century American West. The rationality of the Greeks is brought into conflict with the emotionalism of the Jews, just as transience (the Greeks' belief in mutability and change) differs from the Jewish belief in permanence, in that which is stable and deep-rooted. Although Fisher must support the rationality of the Greeks, he reveals a deep sympathy for the Jewish faculty for poetry, parable, metaphor, and symbol, and is certainly aware of the irony in the modern homelessness of the Jew, a homelessness which cannot be completely different from that of Vridar Hunter or other dwellers in the American wilderness. As Fisher passes quickly over the dangers of ignorance, the barbaric rituals of the Christian church, and the detrimental effect of priests and theologians, the quest for an answer to the major conflicts seems to come to an end in the wish that a fusion of Greek and Jewish beliefs might be possible (or might have been possible twenty centuries ago) in order to combine reason with poetry. Presumably this is precisely what Western American writers should do, what Fisher himself tried to do, what Yvor Winters may have accomplished in his poetry. Philosophically, then, God would not be the vindictive Jehovah of the Old Testament but would be the "divine intelligence; the power that contains all powers; the idea that embraces all ideas . . . and love."

The "intellectual" dialogues between Greek and Jew give way in *Peace Like a River* (1957) to the Christian asceticism of about 330 A.D., to the search for sainthood through the rejection of things of the flesh. The many horrors are described with gusto, reminiscent of descriptions of primitive behavior in *Tale of Valor* and *Pemmican*, which bracket *Peace Like a River* in the Fisher chronology. But even as human degradation continues in *My Holy Satan* (1958), through the feudal system and the inquisition of the Middle Ages, it is unable to defeat the human spirit. A comment on Richard, the young serf who searches for truth, sounds very much like a comment on Fisher himself:

> There he stood, deeply afraid of the world and its people, yet fired with a will to raise himself above the level of his origins, to enrich his mind with learning, to open his soul to the light.

Here too the lonely fellowship of which Vardis-Vridar speaks so often appears in a familiar image: Richard, in a cell and waiting for guards to take him away, clutches and fondles a rat which is as dear to him as Luff McCoy's goat.

At this point the *Testament* narrative takes a big jump from the thirteenth century to the twentieth. Having pursued truth through two thousand "authoritative" books in order to dramatize it in eleven novels, Fisher returns to Vridar Hunter in the tetralogy and begins again the story of the sensitive and terrified boy in the Idaho wilderness. *Orphans in Gethsemane* (1960) includes the tetralogy, revised, rewritten, and cut, and then adds a fictional account of the writing of *The Testament of Man*, of which it is a part. In a "Word to the Reader" at the beginning of *Orphans*, Fisher writes of the *Testament* series:

> I stand on this, that if mankind is ever to build a civilization worthy of that devotion which it seems richly endowed to give, it will first have to accept in the full light of its mind and soul the historical facts of its past, and the mutilations and perversions which its hostility to those facts has made upon its spirit. Only in the forces, ideas, and traditions that produced it, and are the essence of its being, can mankind find its sanctions and powers; but we must hope that it need not forever cherish, because of fear and ignorance, the atavism in these forces, ideas, and traditions, or continue to be so much an expression of their will, once the necessity in their origins is understood and respected.

Such a creed of intelligence, the understanding of history, and the respect for origins can apply to the American West as well as to the world at large. Whether Fisher intended to resolve his own spiritual and intellectual identity, or whether he took Vridar Hunter only as fictional character and pursued his problems, or whether he needed to satisfy an insatiable thirst for knowledge (Fisher almost went blind from reading while in graduate school) does not matter. What does matter is that Vardis Fisher represents a point of view in western writing, one that asks for a sound historical basis and a rational response to all things western. While the theory itself may be debated, the unfortunate consequences of Fisher's determination leave us without a clear example of the theory. His scholarship and research need not be questioned; but, since we are dealing with fiction, we must ask whether his insistence on rationalism led to significant art. Speaking to this question, Fisher admitted that there was a lot of the preacher in him, perhaps too much, but wondered whether art was as important as helping people toward enlightenment and making their lives more livable and more pleasant. It is perhaps possible to be artist as well as preacher, but Fisher's preaching becomes excessive and promotes the kind of emotion associated not with art but with sentimentalism, argumentation, and prejudice, qualities which detract from clear-headed rationalism.

Orphans in Gethsemane, though not a small book, is Fisher's world and work in miniature. In most of the scenes which describe Vridar outdoors, or which evoke the elements of the natural world, the writing is swift, sensitive, masculine, dramatic, and clean. The rewritten tetralogy is an improvement over the original, but some of the faults of the expository and dead fourth volume remain. What is worse is that these faults are multiplied to embarrassment in the new material, in the additional matter of *Orphans*. No one denies the validity and necessity of honest writing, of integrity. Fisher often confused honesty with totality, completeness, the willingness to lay out the full set of facts. As a result, *Orphans* disintegrates into an extended dialogue between Vridar and his wife who discuss the problems of writing the *Testament* in what is obvious and painful autobiography. Perhaps this is the pain of truth, and we are being taught a lesson. Nevertheless, there is little art in the *Testament*, and we are left with ideas only. We look to see what it is that Vridar has learned through his twenty-one-year excursion into the deep past. Aside from a host of valuable insights into primitivism and the rise of religions, the major thesis is that we are children, still fettered by chains of ignorance and superstition, and that as children we need love and compassion, especially from our parents as we are attempting to mature. Implicit in the word *orphans* is that too many children lack the security they need before they are pushed out of the nest. They are unloved, as Vridar was, and as Vardis

Fisher was. Whether this condition can be attributed entirely to Christianity is perhaps open to discussion; as a middle-aged man, presumably wise, Vridar finds that the Romans gave to civilization the idea of an orderly society, that the Greeks insisted on the freedom to express their creative powers, that the Jews taught dignity and moral responsibility, but that Christianity (at least the apostle Paul) "left us the monstrous notions of moral depravity and original sin, which produced unspeakable brutalities and horrors, and the schizoid Western world." *Orphans* ends strangely and inconclusively, which may prove that the Western American materials which gave birth to this personal search are not suited to the rationalistic treatment Fisher proposed. For full significance, and to keep art in harmony with the western landscape and the people who are influenced by it, perhaps we need poetry, evocation, suggestion, mystery; if not alone, then in and around the raw facts.

Vardis Fisher's work is impressive, and most western writers must be measured against him, but his lifelong quest ends (the last page of *Orphans*) with Vridar disclaiming adulthood, amused by the grown persons who *think* they are adults, and then referring to himself as "this child," which is exactly the term early nineteenth-century Western American mountain men used for themselves. After an unbelievably long trip through history via fiction, we are back where we began. Beginnings. Perhaps that is just as it should be.

V
The Historical Inheritance:
Guthrie and Manfred

The frequency with which novelists turn to the recent past (the nineteenth-century West) for their subject matter is not really surprising, although it has led to accusations of escapism, nostalgia, and evasion of contemporary problems. The period during which the West was explored, opened, and settled is rich in incidents—large and small—which not only capture the imagination but also provide what heritage there is for a relatively new land. Tempting as it may be to think of the West only in terms of space, the passing of time cannot be ignored. Nor can we forget that modern man is at best a refinement of his ancestors, those who lived a century ago as well as those in the dim past explored by Vardis Fisher. To understand the children, study the parents. Yet the past is attractive for other reasons as well. A. B. Guthrie, Jr., one of the more popular of the serious western novelists, has indicated that the past might be easier to deal with than the "confusing present" because the past is documented. The implication here is that truth is more readily available from a historical period which, having ended, can be studied from the perspective of a later time. Thus truth, at the very least, offers the enrichment of experience through the study of sources and their re-creation in fiction with the aid of the imagination. Whether the degree of objectivity applied by the novelist to history makes an important difference in his use of history is another matter. Guthrie and Frederick Manfred are alike in that they share a love affair with the vanished wilderness of the American West. Guthrie is often charged with succumbing to nostalgia, with attempting to bring back times and places which seem—at a distance—to be more attractive than the contemporary world. Manfred, on the other hand, has been criticized for his worshipful naiveté in relation to the wilderness or the primitive life, even though he (like Guthrie) is more often than not a down-to-earth realist. Yet Manfred is finally more subjective than Guthrie, taking his themes well beyond their factual origins and attempting to do a great deal more than turn history into fiction.

What allows us to bring these two writers together conveniently is the fact that each has written five historical novels of the West, that each began with the mountain man as subject, and that in each group of five novels the first three are the best. Guthrie's were written in the order of their internal chronology. *The Big Sky* (1947) takes place in the western wilderness of 1830–43, the last decade or so of the fur companies' major activities. Three mountain men of differing experiences and ages are the center of attention, although they share it with the landscape itself. Dick Summers, the oldest of the three, appears again in *The Way West* (1949), a story of the Oregon Trail of 1845. In the organization and daily functions of the wagon train Guthrie emphasizes the crude beginnings of a society, moving away from the more primitive life and the isolation of the mountain man. Settlement, with ranching and the establishment of a town, follows in *These Thousand Hills* (1956), whose action occurs from 1880 to 1887 and whose characters include Brownie Evans and his son Lat, members of the wagon train in the preceding novel. These three volumes stood for fifteen years as a self-contained sequence, a loosely structured trilogy, and must still be considered as such, even though two more novels appeared later in an obvious attempt to bring the portrayal of the West up to present times. From internal evidence it seems that Guthrie began his work with three volumes in mind, so that the fourth and fifth, written considerably later, seem to be set apart from the trilogy. When *Arfive* was published in 1971, its dust jacket announced that "With *Arfive* A. B. Guthrie, Jr., completes his four-novel series about the West." The historical time is 1910–17 and the environment is a western town which has grown enough to acquire respectable elements and to foster a conflict between Victorian (or eastern) values and the looser behavior of a western society as yet unrefined. With this novel, however, Guthrie shifts from history to personal experience, from the objectivity of research with documented facts to the subjectivity of autobiography and memory. Born in 1901, Guthrie was taken to a small ranch town in Montana before he was a year old. His father, the first principal of a newly established public school, could well be the model for Collingsworth in *Arfive*. For whatever reason, the loss of detachment (the condition existing in the trilogy) and the addition of autobiographical elements prove detrimental to the contemporary extension of the trilogy. *The Last Valley* (1975), which brings the town of Arfive and some of its old-timers up to the year 1946, is unquestionably a dull novel. Full of dialogue, short on action, almost forgetful of the land, it lacks a sense of history and tries too hard to be modern in its language and its handling of sex. What is real and within the personal observation of the author does not, somehow, seem nearly as real as the reconstructed events and people of *The Big Sky*.

Whereas the historical span of the five Guthrie novels is 1830 to 1946, that in Manfred's five *Buckskin Man Tales* is approximately 1800 to 1892. When Manfred confronts his own time and, like Guthrie in his contemporary novels, makes extensive use of personal experience, he retreats from the historical West to his own region of Minnesota and Iowa in the Midwest. While environmental determinism may prove to be a slippery explanation of the essential differences between Manfred and Guthrie, there is at least one point at which Guthrie's long residence in the West may seem important: throughout his historical sequence he bemoans the passing of the wilderness, not in a loud voice but insistently. In contrast (although it may seem a weak contrast) Manfred makes love to the wilderness as though it will last forever. Guthrie re-creates the Old West as accurately as he can, often working material from journals and reports directly into his narrative. He is concerned with a sequence of events containing a cause-to-effect inevitability over a century's time, and his three premodern novels may well work best (at least architecturally) as a series rather than as individual narratives. To a degree, at least, his experience as a newspaperman limits his personal opinions, keeps the tone objective, and restrains the language. Manfred is more exuberant and is more personally involved in his fictional treatment of five historical eras or events. Furthermore, his overall intentions are different from Guthrie's, leading to a less sequential portrayal of the nineteenth-century West.

Because of the grouping of five novels under a single title—*Buckskin Man Tales*—it has been tempting to make a comparison between Manfred's Buckskin Man and Cooper's Leatherstocking. The implication is that Manfred has created a wilderness man who embodies the same characteristics, more or less, as those of Natty Bumppo. It is true that Manfred is looking through history for the type of man—albeit a composite—who can act as prototype, or forefather, for modern western man. However, it is ultimately more satisfying to accept *Buckskin Man* merely as a term of convenience, an easy identification of a group of novels, than it is to assume the existence of a new Leatherstocking. Manfred's novels work best individually; despite frequent eccentricities of style (especially language) and a romantic attitude which penetrates the realistic details, Manfred achieves a structural completeness in each novel and places more importance on the building of theme than he does on the adherence to a careful historical sequence of events or character continuity. He explores the sources of our own characteristics, illuminating the places and people of our not-too-distant past to find out how we have been affected by that past. *Conquering Horse* (1959) speculates on the Indian values and virtues in the prewhite Interior West of the year 1800 or thereabouts. *Lord Grizzly* (1954) is based on the life of mountain man Hugh Glass, concentrating on a segment from 1823. Departing somewhat from a strict sense of place, *Scarlet Plume* (1964) is set in Minnesota during the Sioux uprising of 1862. The action of *King of Spades* (1966) moves from Sioux City, Iowa, to the Black Hills of South Dakota in 1876. Last, according to narrative chronology, is *Riders of Judgment* (1957), based upon the Johnson County wars in Wyoming in 1892. In a curious similarity to Guthrie, Manfred was unable to carry the artistry of his first three novels *(Grizzly, Judgment,* and *Horse)* into the last two.

2

The mountain man as subject of fiction is more scarce than one might imagine. As a minor or miscellaneous character he appears frequently, but as the protagonist of a novel with more than passing significance he is still available for further examination. What has been done with him thus far is seen largely in three novels of the Northern Range (those by Fisher, Guthrie, and Manfred), three novels of the Southern Range (Harvey Fergusson's *Wolf Song,* and Forrester Blake's *Johnny Christmas* and *Wilderness Passage),* two novels by Don Berry *(Trask,* 1960, and *Moontrap,* 1962) set in Oregon at the end of the mountain-man era, and a novella set in California—Bill Gulick's "Conquest" (in *White Men, Red Men and Mountain Men.)* For many years, it must be admitted, facts about the mountain men were hard to come by. Restless, nomadic, adventuresome, these men crossed the continent far in advance of civilization, and crossed it so fast that they left little impression except in the legends which grew by word of mouth, perhaps finding their way into a newspaper long after the claims could be verified. Many of the legends were nearer to the literal truth than they were to myth, but myth they became, providing Americans with their own heroes, their own knights roaming the wilderness, slaying Western American dragons, conquering the Indians (or living with them), and leading a life of quest and adventure not unlike that of King Arthur's knights. The mountain man was the real pathfinder of the West and, beholden to no man except as he hired out to large trapping and trading expeditions, he became a symbol of the freedom which is thought of as uniquely American. Whether he was entirely heroic is open to question. Adapting to the ways of the Indian, the mountain man nevertheless brought guns and whiskey into the wilderness along with the white man's diseases, so that he may have made it easier for others to follow (by weakening the Indian) and also more difficult (by providing the Indians with guns). Perhaps a more complex person than he was given credit for being, the mountain man nevertheless referred to himself as "this here child" and maintained an attitude of innocence throughout his paradoxically violent and idyllic life. Names are familiar: Jim Bridger, Hugh Glass, James Beckwourth, Joe Meek, Jed Smith, Kit Carson, John Johnson, Joe Walker, Tom Fitzpatrick, Old Bill Williams, Bill and Milton Sublette. These men and almost three hundred others of their kind, some identified only in recent years, have provided statistics which can give one kind of composite picture of the mountain man. On the average, he was born in 1805 and died in 1869. He was probably born in Canada, Missouri, Kentucky, or Virginia, and departed for the mountains from Missouri between 1825 and 1830. He was married once, probably to a white woman, although there was a 30 percent chance that he would marry an Indian girl; and, if he married more than once, his chances of marrying an Indian increased. He left the mountains in 1845 and died peacefully somewhere west of the Mississippi.

To be known only through legend or through statistics, however, is to be trapped in a limbo which does not yield the full complexity, vitality, or meaning of the man. Guthrie has, in a sense, taken at least part of the composite picture for his characterizations of Boone Caudill, Dick Summers, and Jim Deakins in *The Big Sky*, while Manfred has focused on one particular mountain man, Hugh Glass. Each choice has its advantages. More important, the choices lead to quite different approaches to the subject. Guthrie's mountain men are entirely fictional, and because there are three of them interacting with each other as well as with the wilderness it is possible for Guthrie to include all of the characteristics which, taken together, could make up the typical or representative mountain man, "that mixture of hardihood, dissipation, heroism, brute action, innocence and sin." Guthrie shuns romanticism, preferring a kind of dramatic reportage told in language which is clean, informal, and direct. His mountain man is not Leatherstocking, but "the engaging, rude, admirable, odious, thoughtless, resourceful, loyal, sinful, smart, stupid, courageous character that he was and had to be." Although some of the adjectives would seem to indicate that Guthrie was opinionated, and although he is not above eulogizing the land occasionally, *The Big Sky* is a remarkably objective novel with a judicious mixture of imagination and historical souces (Parkman, Garrard, Ruxton, Osborne Russell, and others).

Not unlike many of the same breed, Boone becomes a mountain man by running away from the confinements and social problems of an "eastern" settlement. Feeling needlessly persecuted, he becomes a loner; individualism is at least partly the result of rejection. The flight from civilization is reinforced by the notion that civilization (in this case industrial Louisville) is impure and that the wilderness out ahead is the only antidote. As members of a riverboat party going up the Missouri River, Boone, Dick, and Jim survive an Indian attack and find themselves alone, cut off from civilization. This timely attack (which stands out as a plotting device) allows Boone and Jim to learn the ways of the wilderness and join the veteran Dick Summers as real mountain men. At first their life in the mountains is almost idyllic, the land perhaps an American Eden echoing oldtimer Zeb's remark that "God, she was purty onc't. Purty and new, and not a man track, savin' Injuns', on the whole scoop of her." Even as Boone discovers this paradise it is changing, but Guthrie first attempts to suggest the pristine beauty of the mountains—shining grass, newborn earth, a high and fine singing, the pines talking, time humming, more sky than a man could think—even as he recognizes another side of the land:

> A raw, vast, lonesome land, too big, too empty. It made the mind small and the heart tight and the belly drawn, lying wild and lost under such a reach of sky as put a man in fear of heaven.

In this environment it is "the little things that made one at home in the world," and so Guthrie, like most writers who confront the vast spaces of the West, pays attention to those little things, either observing on his own or borrowing passages from Parkman's *Oregon Trail* and other sources and altering them very little. As Boone and Jim are drawn into the wilderness they begin to see the realities which already lie behind the attractive landscape: man has brought into the natural beauty of the land his own characteristics and weaknesses, including greed, violence, jealousy and cannibalism. Worse even than those primitive qualities is the attitude of those civilized men who are beginning to traverse the wilderness, to invade Eden, in order to take advantage of political and economic opportunities. One such man, Elisha Peabody, insists that it is the American's right to put aside the British, the Spanish, and the Indians in order to take what is rightfully his "by geography, contiguity, natural expansion." Indeed, it is destiny, inevitable.

Whether Boone is finally driven from the wilderness by the expansion of civilization or by his own weaknesses may not be important in the long view. Within the immediacy of the narrative, however, the relationship between Boone and his friend Jim plays a larger part than does manifest destiny. Guthrie is certainly concerned with the broader outlook, with the changes made in the West by people like Peabody and the travelers to Oregon and the settlers. But his primary interest (and ours also) is in his characters. Even though they can be understood through observations of their actions, short but direct sketches are provided of Boone and Jim after Dick Summers has left them to return east:

> Where Caudill was silent, Deakins talked; where Caudill flared
> out, Deakins fashioned a joke; where there was in Caudill the
> suggestion of quick ferocity, there was in Deakins the indication
> of considered action. . . . The two constituted a good if godless
> pair, the one balancing and conditioning the other.

If Boone and Jim begin to sound like Cain and Abel, it may
seem necessary to extend the comparison to Boone's killing of
Jim and to his subsequent expulsion from the garden. This is a
dangerous course to take, even more risky than viewing Boone
as Adam unable to cope with his new-found knowledge.
Guthrie's intention is not to suggest archetypal patterns but to
follow the normal reactions to the wilderness as seen in any
number of nineteenth-century journals beginning with those of
Lewis and Clark, to re-create the primitive West as he has been
able to discover it through historical sources, and to dramatize
some of the conflicts apparently common to men in the wilderness. Speaking momentarily through Peabody, a character
with whom he would not otherwise be in sympathy, Guthrie
summarizes very nicely what early travelers felt about the
West and themselves: it was an enormous world that almost defied the imagination, proportion run wild, everything in extremes (including the human soul as well as the landscape), alternations between a wild freedom and a depressing sense of
darkness or between unbounded optimism and oppressing
fear. The same contrasts are embodied in the persons of Boone
and Jim, so that psychologically they represent the characteristics of the wilderness. The fact that it is Boone who survives
may indeed suggest that the attractive aspects of the wilderness
will in time be destroyed, as Jim is himself destroyed. But,
aside from the attention paid to the wilderness, and a feeling of
nostalgia for it as it is about to be invaded and raped, the emphasis in *The Big Sky* is on Boone Caudill as an exaggeration of
the American who has never fully understood the wilderness
or the necessity of discipline in achieving freedom. In spite of
this apparent exaggeration, Guthrie remains a realist and
Boone may be accepted fully as a particular kind of person,
with or without mythic overtones. Philosophically, perhaps it

is in the wilderness, attractive as it is, that man learns the futility of chasing after paradise and so returns disappointed, not knowing where to search next for the elusive truth of his life. Such an illumination may indeed come to us through Adamic or Edenic analogies; but, Guthrie does not play it that way, preferring to be matter-of-fact in his presentation of a way of life which lasted for a short time and is now gone forever.

In the going-out and coming-back there is little satisfaction for the wanderers and no one returns a hero. The best that Dick Summers can do is admit that what happened to them was of their own doing—perhaps an oversimplification of the fate of the mountain man. Boone Caudill has one belated regret for Jim's death, and then feels nothing more. Artistically, *The Big Sky* fails to come to a conclusion; there is no rounding out, no lesson for the chief character, only an end to the story. However, there are several ways of explaining this inconclusiveness. Because we are dealing with a trilogy of sorts, we can accept the fact that Guthrie holds the ultimate conclusion in abeyance until the final pages of the third volume. If we believe that fiction imitates an action or a place, we can see in the open-endedness of the novel the limitless landscape. If we believe that the wilderness as subject (as well as place) is socially, psychologically, morally, philosophically, and spiritually limited, then we can understand Boone's failure to learn anything there. And, finally, if we accept Boone for what he is (and was, before going to the mountains), and remember that more than one mountain man was immature according to the standards of civilization, we need not wonder that he is still a child, emotionally and intellectually. Then we need not expect anything from him in the way of insights or self-discovery. He is what he is, perhaps not a true representative of the mountain man, certainly not a hero, but a real and believable person whose tragedy is known to us but not understood by him.

Lord Grizzly is a different kind of book altogether except for the realistic details and a similar measure of confusion on the part of the protagonist at the end of the novel. Manfred's choice of Hugh Glass for the dominant character in a historical novel of the Old West was inspired. Enough is known about Glass to provide a basic story of considerable interest, and yet the verifiable facts are not so voluminous that they are able to stifle the imagination. Indeed, the legendary nature of the Hugh Glass story invites mythmaking or the attempt to create an American epic. Rather than concentrating upon moral and historical truths, as Guthrie does, Manfred wrings every conceivable meaning out of his material. Focusing on the year 1823, when Glass, a hunter with General Ashley's expedition up the Missouri River, left his comrades to escape the "tyranny" of the General only to be mauled by a grizzly bear and left for dead, Manfred builds his narrative around Hugh's survival and his crawl back to civilization. The usual western elements are present—Indian fights, the lore of the mountain men, a pretty Indian girl, an act of cannibalism, a search for revenge, and a solid base of realistic incidents—but if the story is read entirely on this level it inevitably disappoints those readers who feel that Hugh's forgiveness of the men who deserted him is not plausible, or, at least, not satisfying.

On the structural level it is possible to show that Manfred probes character and establishes themes which extend beyond the confines of the West. The novel is organized in three parts. In "The Wrestle" Hugh is a member of a group, albeit a group of individuals. As some of his companions died during a battle with Indians, "They looked inward, then outward at the red dawn and their comrades, then inward again, and died." Introspection and isolation mark two of the three stages of dying. Conversely, Hugh is alone in only one of the three parts of the novel, "The Crawl," and then returns to the group in part three, "The Showdown," reversing the process and thereby allowing the important question of the individual in relation to society to remain unanswered, although the complexities and ambiguities of the problem have been fully suggested. If there is indeed an answer to the question, it is probably that while man is able to perform great deeds alone in his desire to survive, his ultimate meaning lies in a relationship to other men. The individualism of the Old West was a good and necessary quality, but, as in the modern world, it cannot be enough. As Hugh looks for the men who abandoned him after the encounter with the grizzly—presumably Bridger and Fitzpatrick—his mind plays tricks on him, memories overtake him, and he is gradually prepared to forego the revenge he has vowed. It is the desire for revenge, however, which motivates him most strongly in his will to live, in his stubborn refusal to give up as he recovers slowly from the terrible injuries inflicted upon him by the grizzly and as he crawls laboriously toward the river leading to Fort Kiowa. At first he cannot believe that he has been deserted. His moral code, which is presumably that of his comrades as well, states that he cannot scalp a live Indian, cannot desert a friend, cannot take orders from a tyrant, and cannot harm Indian women. But once he decides that he has indeed been deserted, it is his need for revenge that keeps him alive; and, as his condition improves, and he is favored by several elements of nature, he begins to feel that the Lord is protecting him until he can fulfill his vow of revenge. The revenge is therefore justified, and Hugh begins to think of himself as a special person, protected and nurtured by divine guidance. This feeling may be the pride that goes before the fall, but Hugh's nemesis is not the gods and not a man with the strength to oppose him. It is, rather, a subtle alteration of his way of thinking, a psychological change caused by a smattering of past and present incidents, memory reinforced by new experiences.

The first is a dim memory of an act of cannibalism, and even though Hugh had not known at the time that he was eating human flesh he nevertheless realizes that he too is a sinner. Furthermore, even though Hugh's desertion of his family years before was understandably provoked, it was still a running away from responsibility, so that he is perhaps no better than the two who ran away from him. As these events work on his mind, he is aware of being followed by a bear. It is not clear whether the bear is real or a ghost in Hugh's conscience, perhaps stalking him in the same way that he is stalking Jim and Fitz. Not yet convinced that he should forgive his deserters, and feeling like the angry avenging Jehovah of the Old Testament (Biblical patterns run throughout the novel), Hugh is then asked by General Ashley to be aware of men's weaknesses, to recognize imperfection and forgive it in the attitude of the New Testament. At this point three other mountain men—Dutton, Jim Clyman, and Fitz—walk in from the wilderness, one at a time, gaunt as skeletons, and Hugh realizes that he is not the only one to suffer great hardship. Like the saints or martyrs of the early church coming off the desert, the remarkable mountain men gather together and Hugh begins to think back, to remember "his boys"; although some of them are only ghosts in his memory they are very real to him, and he softens enough to say, "First thing you know I'll be thinkin' on Fitz as one of my boys." Which he soon does. The idea of revenge evaporates, leaving Hugh Glass a trifle confused but a part of the brotherhood once again.

Another structural pattern, in part two during the crawl, introduces still another thematic level. Glass survives the wrestle with the grizzly by becoming an animal for a while (before the notion of revenge sets in), eating snakes and ants and drinking the blood of a wild dog. He crawls on his belly, like a snake, before he is able to rise to hands and knees (like a four-legged) and then to stand upright like a man. This part of the novel is divided into eight sections, which begin as follows:

1. A cold nose woke him.
2. A cold nose woke him.
3. A cold touch woke him.
4. A cold nose woke him.
5. A cool evening breeze woke him.
6. Hugh never did remember . . . .
7. Hugh climbed steadily.
8. Wild geese were flying south . . . .

Although this pattern was not provided consciously by Manfred (according to him he was completely unaware of it until it was pointed out), it evokes the progression of man from the animal level to the human level and on to the edge of some kind of spiritual recognition. In the evolutionary process, the life which became man was animal for the greater portion of its existence; thus, half of the sections are devoted to the simple struggle of the animal to survive, almost entirely by instinct. ("Touch" instead of "nose" is only a stylistic variation.) To be awakened by a breeze requires more sensitivity than to be disturbed by a cold nose, and so section five is the transition point at which the animal begins to emerge as a higher creature. The possibility of remembrance is a suggestion of the existence of the mind, unique in man. Steady climbing suggests the relatively rapid progress made by man with the use of his mind. Finally, we look up at the geese in a simple image of the spiritual life which may evolve next.

Hugh Glass forgives the deserters reluctantly, not understanding precisely why he allows them to live although a number of motivations have been provided throughout the story. He vaguely senses something spiritual at work, but he is not yet a spiritual being except in the primitive act of breathing his spirit into his horse's nostrils. Manfred suggests that Hugh is representative of the human race, and that where he stands at the end of the novel—in an uneasy spiritual act—is where the race also stands in its development. Perhaps this is the major theme of the novel, but, if so, it does not encompass the total significance. In addition to the symbolic evolution of man, *Lord Grizzly* can also be read for its historical base—the Ashley expedition—for the revenge motif, for the conflict between the individual and the group, for man's relationship to the natural world and its creatures, for the religious analogy to the passion of Christ, for the love story of a white hunter and an Indian girl, for pure adventure, and for the patterns of escape and pursuit reminiscent of Cooper. Any one of these elements would lead to a reasonably satisfying story. However, as they and their internal details come together, rhythms are established which insinuate themselves into the subconscious and provide a less obvious but more meaningful form.

In some ways the good Western novels are poems. Traditionally, the novel has been devoted to social themes and the delineation of men in direct relation to the group-forms which men have created for themselves, willingly or not. Also traditionally, the poem has been a vehicle through which the poet could respond to nature in a personal way and could, as it were, sing to his universe. (There are, obviously, many alternatives to this easy distinction.) Because of man's awareness of natural elements in the West, and because of his own relative insignificance in the face of this wide and often cruel world, it is not strange that he should respond in two ways—in realistic portrayals of his struggles with the land, and in lyrics to its beauties and wonders. Usually the two approaches exist side by side, so that the Western regional novel is constantly in a state of rhythm, an ebb and flow between the brutal and the beautiful, between the painfully real and the ideal.

In *Lord Grizzly* and many other Western novels, the alternations of significance lead to a regular and almost musical pattern. Hugh's experiences must be understood and appreciated on three levels—the animal or naturalistic, the psychological and moral, and the symbolic and universal. As the reader goes back and forth among these levels (and he cannot avoid it), he is involved in one of the rhythms of the novel. Furthermore, everything that occurs in the novel has a counterpart, a parallel. In the establishment of repetitions, Manfred, like others, has been influenced by the King James Old Testament style. As these parallelisms and repetitions play upon each other they merge into a kind of musical pattern and become a complex rhythm. This formal rhythm is made up of several minor rhythms, just as rhythm in poetry is the result of its metrical patterns:

The rhythm of looking inward, outward, and inward just before death, and the similar rhythm—although reversed conceptually—of Hugh's being a part of the social group, then outside it, and finally back in.

The physical rhythm of Hugh's crawl for survival as seen in three stages—on the belly, on all-fours, and upright. When Hugh is crawling, the reader is aware of man's normal upright position; and when Hugh rises the reader still remembers his former position. Thus, with each stage of the process we are painfully aware of the other stages.

A natural rhythm as the arrangement of threes in the other rhythms is supported by the waxing and waning of the moon three times during Hugh's crawl and raft trip to Fort Kiowa.

A psychological rhythm as the three mountain men stagger in from the plains, one at a time, impressing upon Hugh's mind the fact that he is not superhuman. There is an interesting similarity between this device and the crowing of the cock, three times, for Peter, who had also removed himself from his immediate group in the New Testament.

A symbolic progression as rhythm in that the novel has three grizzlies. First, Glass himself is referred to as a grizzly among the mountain men, and he is given the name "White Grizzly" by the people of his Indian wife. Second, there is the real (actual) bear which almost kills him. Third, the phantom bear which follows him during the first stages of his search for revenge may be real or may be a function of Hugh's conscience or former self, so that we are again involved in movement— from Hugh-the-Bear to the actual bear and back again to a symbolic or psychological Bear-in-Hugh.

Stylistic rhythms are prevalent throughout the novel:

> He slept. The wind soughed up from the south and tossed the heavy cattail cobs back and forth.
> He slept. The November sun shone gently and revived the green grass in the low sloughs.
> He slept. The wind soothed softly and rustled the ocher leaves in the rushes.

This unit, like some others, is divided into three parts, parallelism maintained by the repetition of "He slept," and further movement implied in the cattails tossing back and forth in their own rhythm, the grass dying and growing in cycles, and the leaves rustling in the rushes. The style is kept from seeming affected or mannered by its integral part in the large scheme of rhythms.

The point of view through which Manfred tells the story
has three positions, or degrees of variation, so that even in the
point of perception through which we see the action we are involved in a rhythmic movement. Essentially, the action is seen
through the chief character, Hugh Glass. Part of the time the
view is from Hugh's mind in a modified stream-of-conscious-
ness technique. More often the view is from Hugh's eyes, so
that narrator and reader are perceptually identified.

> When nothing happened, he cautiously and noiselessly
> wormed his way to the edge of the canebrake and parted the last
> few stalks and looked out from a spot low near the ground.
> A tepee all right. And the wild dog too.
> But it was only one tepee, and an odd one at that. It looked
> Sioux but it wasn't Sioux exactly.

The reader and Hugh see the tepee simultaneously, from
the same vantage point. The reader is in the scene; but then
Hugh, back in his mind, makes an observation about the tepee
which the reader could not make. The reader slips in and out of
his identification with the character.

The third position of the point of view is slightly outside
Hugh, at a short distance away from his eyes. It is from this
point that Manfred is able to say some things about his character which the character would not likely say about himself.
This limited omniscience is important to the Western regional
novel, especially those novels which are based upon historical
incidents and characters. A mountain man such as Hugh
Glass, although fairly intelligent, is not the kind of man to dig
out the meanings of his experience for us. He cannot operate as
a central intelligence because he is, in a very real sense, cut
off from society, from education, from intellectual companionship, and is at the same time so emotionally involved with the land and nature that his judgments cannot
avoid being colored by his immediate experience. Therefore,
the esthetic distance which is necessary for impartial judgment
in correct proportion to reader-identification—the two
together leading to recognition of meaning—must come from a

deliberate manipulation of point of view on the part of the author. By the treatment of detail, the vividness of the experience, and the point of view, the reader is forced into an identification with Hugh Glass. However, Hugh acquires no definite meaning from his own experience, and so the significance of the man and his actions must be supplied through the rhythms and structures within which Hugh's experiences are confined, but which are ultimately the means of defining the experiences. The form of the novel is an extension of the author's style, then, and the rhythmic overlay provides the meaning.

The separate elements or themes of *Lord Grizzly*, when taken out of the full context, are merely parts of a skeleton, of a structural framework upon which a texture is built. Form lies in the combination of these elements, or in the rhythms established within them. The search for revenge or the relationship between man and animal are themes, but they do not become meaning (which is quite different from theme) until they have been combined and ordered within the texture and rhythms of the novel. The conclusion seems to be that rhythm and form are identical.

Yet rhythm is essentially emotional while form is intellectual. Rhythm is biological in its source, but form is supplied by the creative mind of man in his attempt to make the universe palatable, or less frightening. Part of the difficulty in the traditional western novel has been the surplus of emotion in the reaction of man to the terrors and glories of the land. He is overwhelmed by the landscape before he can give it any form. He is taken in by the superhuman deeds (such as the Hugh Glass wrestle and crawl) before he has a chance to achieve objectivity. The mark of the mature Western novel seems to be the very tensions which exist between the emotions of rhythm and the meaning of them. Here we find the basis of whatever form is actually to be called a western form. It cannot be said to be unique, because similar conditions have existed elsewhere in other times. But it does seem to set the Western novel apart from the Eastern or British or European novel of the twentieth century.

Form involves both emotional texture and artistic control, the balance controlled largely by psychical distance. The elements of structure, when submerged in the context, texture, and details of the novel, supply a feeling for form which helps the reader to understand and evaluate the experience of the novel. The meaning, finally, is the novel itself, not the stated themes, the psychological conflicts, the plot, the social concern or other elements of structure. The meaning is the form, the sum of the rhythms of the novel, which must be *felt*, however intellectually. In *Lord Grizzly*, as in other mature Western novels, form, meaning, and rhythm are very nearly synonymous. Neither social problem nor psychological conflict nor philosophical argumentation explains this fiction. It is characterized, rather, by an elemental and sometimes mystic or mythic fusion of man and land, animal and spirit, the rational and the irrational. Western fiction does not often attempt to probe and resolve contemporary problems except in the indirect way of trying to establish and clarify myth which can serve as the foundations of the contemporary search for meaning. The mountain man, freed from at least some of the restrictions of his factual biography, can be a valuable part of these foundations.

3

From a common interest in the mountain man, Guthrie and Manfred have gone their separate ways, Manfred to explore the legendary use of history and Guthrie to continue his chronological re-creation of the premodern West. Guthrie moves logically into the 1840s when thousands of people traveled overland in wagon trains to Oregon or to California. In his novel of the Oregon Trail, Guthrie again makes use of many historical sources, incuding fragmentary journals kept by some of the travelers. The emotional impact of the land upon these people is keyed to a passage in Parkman's *Oregon Trail* as it is restated for Lije Evans in *The Way West*. Lije, a farmer, eventually becomes captain of the wagon train guided by Dick

Summers, now forty-eight and the only character retained from *The Big Sky*. As the party approaches the Platte River in Nebraska, Evans is expectant just as Parkman had been. Whereas Parkman registered some confusion because the scene struck his imagination and yet lacked "any of the features of grandeur, other than its vast extent, its solitude, and its wildness," Evans registers incomprehension:

> He couldn't believe that flat could be so flat or that distance ran so far or that the sky lifted so dizzy deep or that the world stood so empty. He saw old Rock chase a badger into a hole, saw a bunch of antelope drifting, saw the river sluiced and the woods rising on its islands and the sand in a great grey waste, but it was something that he couldn't put a name to that held him.

Parkman's reaction had been stated in similar terms, but with less emotion:

> For league after league, a plain as level as a lake was spread beneath us; here and there the Platte, divided into a dozen threadlike sluices, was traversing it, and an occasional clump of wood, rising in the midst like a shadowy island, relieved the monotony of the waste. No living thing was moving throughout the vast landscape, except the lizards that darted over the sand and through the rank grass and prickly pears at our feet.

Yet whereas Parkman was unable to find the appropriate words for the scene, saying only that "it had not one picturesque or beautiful feature," Lije Evans responds first in an emotional outburst to Dick Summers—"By God, Dick! By God!"—and then thinks, "Great was the name for it, the only name he could find in his mind."

While reactions to the landscape and the things of the natural environment have their importance in the wagon train experience, Guthrie emphasizes the social conflicts within the organization of the train, although some of these conflicts arise from the natural obstacles of the journey in that the obstacles test the courage, endurance, and overall character of the people. Because these people are ordinary and are required to get along somewhat amicably, to cooperate for the good of the group and its common goal, their normal rivalries and jealousies are magnified by the smallness and closeness of the group. The leaders do not take kindly to independence during a situation which requires group effort. Before Tadlock is replaced by Evans as the train leader, he condemns Summers's lack of respect for authority, feeling that it will contaminate the company. He acknowledges the scout's expertness in hunting and following the trail, but he is disturbed because Summers is "hard to manage or impress." The freedom expected and enjoyed by the mountain man does not sit easily with the restrictions of society; crude as the wagon train's social structure may be, it is nevertheless a structure. And so the typical Oregon Trail novel, such as Guthrie's, begins to take on the traditional methods and themes of fiction—increased use of dialogue, more attention to characterization, and interest in social history—even while the contrast between eras, or between the agricultural pioneer and the mountain man, leads to equally important themes.

The land remains influential to human behavior but less so than in the true wilderness novel. For a wagon-train company to reach its destination successfully, assuming its ability to overcome natural barriers, it must function as a cohesive social unit, each member working for the good of the whole. It is the group that provides whatever unity there may be in *The Way West*. Otherwise the novel is merely a detailed, episodic, impressionistic story of a number of people, told through a number of points of view, and stressing the atmosphere of experience rather than a formal presentation of plot and theme. Perhaps the ultimate problem of *The Way West* is that it is *too* typical a representation of the Oregon Trail and the people who traveled over it in the 1840s and later. Competently written, sensitive, authentic, it nevertheless suffers from its intentions—to re-create a historical period rather than to create a work of art. The characters act more or less as they would anywhere, in any environment (which may, of course, indicate a kind of truth in itself), not responding to the influence of the land except on brief and apparently insignificant occasions. "It seems so far" is not an impressive statement coming from a farmer's wife who has never before been exposed to "the awesome face of distance." Nor does a quick reference to identity compensate for the significance given to pathmaking by Stegner (as one example) in *Wolf Willow* (1962), although Guthrie seems to feel obligated to work it into the story, however briefly:

> Thought lighted his narrowed eyes. "This here country puts its mark on a man, and the mark is that he ain't sure who he is, being littled by the size of it."
> "I don't see—"
> "So he puts his mark on the country, like they're doin' on that rock, and then he can say to hisself, 'By Godfrey, this is me, all right. There's my name writ right there in the stone.' "

Somehow, the incident is merely melodramatic. Guthrie does not explore in depth to the extent that he does in *The Big Sky* and *These Thousand Hills*, perhaps proving that the closer he adheres to historical facts and circumstances the more difficult it is for him to think in terms of artistry. Although *The Way West* has generally been accepted as the be-all and end-all of Oregon Trail fiction, other possible contenders to the throne should not be ignored—*The Land Is Bright* (1939) by Archie Binns, for instance, or even *The Covered Wagon* (1922) by Emerson Hough, which is often dismissed as a juvenile novel because of its romantic plot.

The trail itself provides Guthrie with a measure of unity, although the unity is literarily superficial. History, as dramatized, is Guthrie's primary concern, and one looks hard for a theme that is individualized as well as social, or personal as well as universal. Toward the end of the trek, after several people have died, one more death affects Lije Evans more than anything has done on the entire journey, and a single shocking image suddenly emerges, suggesting a meaning larger than that of the trail and its destination: "Mrs. Byrd opened her eyes, opened them dead into those of Evans." Death, at last, opens the eyes of Evans, and in a moment of insight he recognizes the

kinship of all the members of the train. They are more than
units of a crude but developing social structure; they are comrades in much the same way that the mountain men were before them. Furthermore, they are not heroes, for all their stub-
bornness and endurance in crossing the plains and mountains;
they are "humble, hurtful, anxious, hoping." Lije is still able to
think of the cost, measured partly by the deaths, and can
speculate in rather trite terms about nothing worthwhile
coming easily, and then slip into the easy generalization that a
"nation couldn't grow unless somebody dared." The novel
ends on this patriotic note, mixed with sentiment, as Lije cries
out, "Becky . . . hurrah for Oregon!" This Oregon Trail
novel merely trails off at the end with no real sense of theme or
fate or art. The many details, the many points of view, the
many little incidents simply come to an end.

The Way West was written in six months and was awarded
the Pulitzer Prize. Neither of those facts can say anything
meaningful about the book, but they may have prompted
Guthrie to continue writing the story of the West. Although he
had not planned a trilogy before he finished the first two
volumes of what did indeed become a trilogy, it is the third volume, *These Thousand Hills*, never as highly thought of as its
predecessors, which rounds out the entire narrative and gives
it the thematic force necessary to warrant Walter Clark's comment that it is "something like a spiritual epic of the Northwest." In speaking of a fictional purpose, in the trilogy, that is
equal to the historical purpose, it is necessary to give the proper
recognition to *These Thousand Hills*. Guthrie has referred to this
novel as his most difficult to write and as his least successful of
the Old West trilogy. (I do not know whether he meant least
successful personally, or financially and critically. It is true
that the critics have been less than kind to *Hills*.) Because he
was dealing with cowpunchers, he knew that he had to avoid
the western myth, the stylized and formulaic cowboy story.
With one exception, he is successful—his "green as grass,"
twenty-year-old cowpuncher, Lat Evans, does everything well
right from the beginning, suggesting a stereotype of the ideal

cowboy. But that problem readily dissolves. *These Thousand Hills* provides the necessary conclusion to Guthrie's "epic" and is, in its own right, a better novel than *The Way West*.

Lat Evans is the grandson of Lije and the son of Brownie, both from the Oregon Trail portion of the trilogy. His position in the overall story is crucial. Boone Caudill was rough-hewn, partially bad because he was escaping from a problem rather than confronting it, and partially irrational because of his inherent characteristics and the way in which they were affected by the wilderness. Lije Evans, a step along, still somewhat crude, was at least honest and well meaning in his beliefs and actions. Lat is the last step before refinement and, as such, he is the most tragic of the figures involved in the process because he is on the line between the old and the new, between two ways of life, both of them necessary in their own times. He is the one who is caught in the change, knowing that the choice is not between right and wrong but between two sides equally right. The conflict originates in the ranch country of eastern Oregon, a region settled (as were others even farther east) by the backwash from the greener coastal areas, and is staged in Montana. Lat leaves his Methodist family to move out on his own as a cowpuncher, quickly learning the cattle business and striking up strong and lasting friendships with nomadic cowboys, with miscreant Tom Ping (in spite of their different moral systems), and with the prostitute Callie (who becomes a madam and assists Lat both financially and emotionally). Reflecting Guthrie's own feelings about the land, Lat is attracted to the "things" of Montana:

> The Tansy. The Sun. The Missouri, better called the Smoky Water, as the Indians called it. The Goose Neck. The Knees. The Judith. The Musselshell. The Dry Forks. The Marias. The Crocondunez near Fort Benton. The Freezeout. The Two Medicine. Names strange to Ma [Lat has just received a letter from his mother] but wild and sweet on the tongue. . . .
>
> Names and places, and things no words could tell. Spring in Montana. Summer. Fall. The look of ranges, bench on bench. The month of the wild rose. The time that cactus flowered.

> Everywhere the grasses straight or blowing. Cows and calves,
> and all the fat earth for a pasture. The chinook, out of its mother
> cloud over the mountains. The feel of winds. Winter, even, and
> the tonic feel of cold. The sky. Always the sky.

The style here is much like that of the journals of Washington
Irving, Francis Parkman, and other sources of a later period—
many of them used extensively by Guthrie—before those journals were revised, rewritten, and refined for book publication;
that is, before they were made "literary" for public consump-
tion. Guthrie knows the value of the first impression, of the
honest and personal reaction untainted by artifice. The naming
of names and the listing of things may not be intellectual but
these stylistic techniques are true to the land. They lead, at
times, to the subtlety and suggestiveness of poetry, so that the
total view of the land ranges from cataloguing to near-mystical
vision: "And yet, and yet, at the edge of hearing, the singing
rustle, like a low chant from the land or like the flurry of far
wings." Lat is fully at home in this natural environment, and
his associations with Tom Ping and Callie are an important
part of his natural sentiments and of the freedom to be found in
the life of the open range.

Unlike Boone Caudill, however, Lat recognizes both the
necessity and the inevitability of a developing society and he
gradually moves into a position of respectability in the community centered around Tansytown. The motives behind his
ambitions and his willingness to be a part of the community are
as complex as they should be under the circumstances. Lat is
not an opportunist, nor does he try deliberately to maintain a
balance between a way of life he likes and another kind of life
that will allow him to achieve status, position and wealth
within a society which he might otherwise condemn. When
forced to choose between his two worlds, he goes through one
agonizing dilemma after another, giving reality to Fenimore
Cooper's theory. As restated from *The Way West*, Lije Evans's
words now make sense to Lat: "A man likes to grow up with the
country. And when he gets growed up, he likes the country

growed up, too." The question of public benefit, absent in *The Big Sky*, hinted at in *The Way West*, now becomes a central issue in the growing societies of the late nineteenth-century West. Lat's background has prepared him to face this issue, but it has also tied him to the ways of the past. Crudity and refinement clash inside this man, just as they do on a wider scale in his western environment. On the one side are the open land, the somewhat primitive and irresponsible life of the cowhand, the friendships with Tom Ping and Callie, and the reluctant but unavoidable relationship to disreputable Hank McBee. On the other side are social respectability, financial success, church and school activities which support the community, a wife and family, and a nomination to the territorial senate. To Guthrie's credit, he does not allow the internal conflict of his chief character to become anything less than understandable and vital. Lat cannot be viewed as a humble cowpuncher renouncing his socially unacceptable friends in order to take advantage of the opportunities offered him by polite society, nor can he be dismissed as a "sinner with a heart of gold" who suddenly sees the light and actively takes the side of goodness.

Although the growth of the town serves as a broad base for the narrative, and the moral uncertainties of civilization pose the chief problems, Guthrie turns to images of the natural world in his crucial scenes. Ironically, we are prepared for Lat's major decision by his wife's reaction to their ranch:

> But there were the wind and the cold there and the punishing sun and the wind and the great loneliness and the wind, and Lat coming out of them and desiring her beyond her desire. She had tried to keep her crying to herself, to cry alone, and the wind would cry.

When Callie, Lat's former mistress and a part of his precivilized life, is accused of murder, it appears that the only thing which will save her is character testimony given by Lat, testimony which will reveal his relationship to Callie. As Lat rises to declare that he will testify, risking his reputation and his marriage, Guthrie returns to the imagery of the natural elements: "Lat got out of his chair slowly and by degrees straightened up and stood like a man daring the weather." He is, in fact, daring society, but he has not shaken off the life of the past, the attachment to the land, and he makes a decision which lays bare the fullness of his life, which stands him out on a naked hill for all to see—an act not only of courage, but also of commitment to the inevitable.

It is, finally, the inevitability of the action that holds the trilogy together and brings it around full circle. Lat is pulled into civilization at great expense to himself, admitting a relationship with Callie, refusing to face Tom Ping in a shoot-out, and thereby damaging his potential for a political future. But his public recognition of Callie is the only way he can let her go, and although Ping calls him a coward it is obvious that the time of honorable gunplay is past and that cowardice is not a factor in the refusal to participate. When Lat's political friends seem to disown him, Ping quickly comes to his defense: "You cheap chippies, he's a better man than all of you." Lat's wife needs a little time to understand his friendship with Callie, but Guthrie does not sentimentalize, and as the novel (and the trilogy) ends, Joyce calls to Lat:

> Her voice cried to him, "Come in! Come in out of the wind!"
> For just an instant he waited. The wind whipped him, the warm wind, the sweet wind, the wind with the bone of winter in it unnoticed till now.
> Then he went in.

Back at the beginning of *The Big Sky*, the first sentence expressed the same idea of "going in": "Serena Caudill heard a step outside and then the squeak of the cabin door and knew that John was coming in." The controlling factor, the means to form, of Guthrie's sprawling and fact-filled dramatization of the history of the Old West is this metaphor of the woman waiting inside for the man to come in out of the "sweet wind." It is the woman who finally represents society, civilization, stability, home, and moral structure. Adventuring man is reluctant to give up his dreams of freedom and of conquest, rel-

ishing the wind even when it turns bitterly cold. Boone Caudill leaves home to go into the wilderness, but his act is only the
beginning of a cycle of life which is eventually concluded when
the wilderness becomes secondary once again to civilization
and Lat Evans goes in to his wife. In the long view, this is the
real significance of the frontier experience, of the expansion
across the continent in the nineteenth century, and of Guthrie's
recreation of the experience. The Old West was, in a sense, an
interlude, a time of desperate freedom, adventure, and mythmaking, a last fling in the wilderness.

Perhaps civilization is not the ultimate answer to man's
needs. *Arfive* and *The Last Valley* do little more than make that
very suggestion. Society, too, has within it the seeds of its own
destruction. And while the wilderness has slowly retreated before the advances of man's technology, the land nevertheless
seems to be the only thing that will endure. "Injuns come later
and die off, buffalo go, but toad stays," says the Indian,
Smoky, in *Arfive*. This toad, under an ancient rock, gives Collingsworth assurance that something can endure. If all else
dies, the toad will remain. But suddenly, in our own age of environmental destruction, we see the irony of it all. The toad
may die also.

4

Frederick Manfred has not proceeded chronologically or se-
quentially in his *Buckskin Man Tales*, nor has he tied his narratives neatly together, choosing rather to let five separate tales—
each considered as an individual artistic endeavor—be linked
only by the implication that the characters form a composite
picture of our Western American ancestors, a picture which
may reveal to us something about ourselves in the twentieth
century. Formally, at least, each of these novels works better as
a self-contained work of fiction than do Guthrie's historical
novels. Manfred offers the potential for more kinds of significance, more interpretations, and more complexities of theme
and style than Guthrie does. The question is whether his fertile

imagination has bitten off more than it can chew, whether—to
change the metaphor—he has scattered his shots too widely
and missed whatever unity he may have been aiming at in the
Buckskin Man Tales. These tales fit together only in a loose
way—atmosphere, a broad setting, a base of assorted Western
American historical events, and elements of style. Manfred's
intention may have been to examine facets of the search for
western identity, or to show nineteenth-century man growing
toward maturity in the West, or to illustrate a statement by D.
H. Lawrence in *Studies in Classic American Literature* (1923):
"The very common sense of . . . Americans has a tinge of
helplessness in it, and deep fear of what might be if they were
not common-sensical." It may even have been, much more
simply, to evoke love, or a relationship between man and
nature; or, to complicate it again with Lawrence, to show
American man before and during the process of having his
"blood-consciousness sapped by a parasitic mental or ideal
consciousness." However, no one of these intentions—if such
they are—clearly subordinates the others. Perhaps it is style
and tone rather than theme which holds these novels together—mannerisms, poetry, exuberance, excesses, details,
and a mixture of the romantic and the realistic.

We recognize a variety of themes: values of the nature-
oriented Indians, endurance, the uneasy struggle toward love
and forgiveness, natural love in opposition to puritanical
mores, self-fulfillment, the search for identity, the attempt to
throw off European influences, heroism in varying degrees, the
sacrifices necessary to obtain justice, and so on. The themes are
placed in historical settings so that to a certain extent Manfred
too is re-creating the Old West with its intrinsic interest and its
susceptibility to mythmaking. Because Manfred is an enthu-
siastic storyteller, his novels exude energy and promise. *Lord
Grizzly* fulfills its promise, but I am not sure that the others do.
For all their wealth of information (Manfred does not slight his
research) they appear somewhat contrived, as though personal
ideas, emotions, and feelings have been *inserted* into a historical context. Aside from *Grizzly*, this intrusion is least notice-

able in *Conquering Horse* and *Riders of Judgment*, the novels which
open and close the series. Perhaps it is because the act of re-
creation is stronger and more important in these two novels.
To the extent that the historical context is less important, especially in *King of Spades*, ideas of the writer from his own character and experience are clothed in historical incidents but not
really affected by them.

Wallace Stegner has spoken of Manfred as a "natural force"
for whom "reality is too small, language is sometimes too
arthritic for his needs," and whose "efforts to loosen and en-
large them are not uniformly successful." This does not mean
that Manfred is an innovator in technical forms or in language.
It does suggest, however, that he continually moves beyond
realism toward myth and romance, and in doing so employs
the grotesque, the symbolic, the bizarre, the outrageous, and
the exaggerated, all of whose effects will strike readers differently. It is not possible to avoid at least a suspicion of symbolic
intent when "Cain came riding down through a cloud" opens
Riders of Judgment. The symbol seems to be reinforced at the
end, at Cain's funeral, even though Manfred is careful to explain that the puff of steam which spurts out of the coffin and
vanishes over the clouds is caused by the contrast between the
warm air inside the coffin and the wintry cold outside—a phenomenon said to have occurred at the burial of Sinclair Lewis's
ashes, on which occasion Manfred delivered a eulogy. It is difficult to accept the cutting off of Scarlet Plume's plume (penis)
almost twenty-four hours before he is hanged; he does not seem
to suffer from the grotesque mutilation, and we are asked to accept its significance in terms of social commentary and to ignore the improbable physical circumstances. In a bizarre
episode in *King of Spades*, Magnus shoots his wife in the toe,
foot, hairline, nipple, and eye in succession. Similar examples
from throughout the *Buckskin Man* series would indicate that
Manfred is a teller of tall tales, a frontiersman reincarnated,
reaching for the heroic and the mythic at the expense of plausibility.

There is no question about the visual presentation of place, the vivid portrait of Siouxland, or the sensitivity to "things" in the various stages of the American wilderness, whether this wilderness be physical, psychological, or moral—and it is all three to Manfred. Nor can there be doubt concerning strength of narrative or applicability of "wilderness events" to modern life. Much of the value of *Conquering Horse* lies in its accurate portrayal of ritual and the analogy between No Name's vision quest and the less clearly defined process of maturation for a white young man of the twentieth century. In sharply delineating, through ritual, the stages of life which constitute the achievement of manhood, the Indians show an understanding of life cycles and of the cost of manhood which in modern times is confused and clouded by the trappings of a technological society. To be disoriented from the natural environment is to miss the significance of the pain, beauty, pride, tragedy, and humility of taking one's place in the world. No Name learns the lesson of generations—the pain of growing up, the difficulty of the vision quest, the disappointment and then the gratification of achievement, and finally the pain of manhood (as well as the responsibility) as his father dies and he becomes the generation next to death. Within this universal experience—made more poignant and meaningful through ritual—death can be seen as satisfying the demands of the life cycle. No Name, told in a vision that he will be given his rightful name after he has conquered the white stallion, successfully locates and rides the stallion. However, before he can feel any sense of triumph he must jump off the horse just before it soars off a cliff rather than be dominated by a human:

> Then, descending like a statue, Dancing Sun passed from view. A moment later there was a shrill scream, triumphant, derisive, and then came the crash of bulk and bones on rock.

The triumph belongs, instead, to the stallion. The dead animal is the victor. No Name, weeping and lamenting, cuts out the heart and drinks the blood. The language at this point leaves no doubt of the relationship between primitive and Christian beliefs: "It was still filled with blood and he drank therefrom.

Then he cut a few slices off the heart and ate them." And, as in Christian communion, No Name then says, "This I do to bring our spirits together." The implication is clear enough, but it is pursued still further as No Name talks to the dead animal lying on the rocks below the cliff:

> It was from all these that you were formed and it is to all these that you must return. Life is a circle. The power of the world works always in circles. All things try to be round. Life is all one. It begins in one place, it flows for a time, it returns to one place. The earth is all that lasts.

While the commentary by No Name (and Manfred) seems a little obvious—almost didactic—the death of the horse is nevertheless tragic and artistically satisfying.

According to the vision, the second death must be that of No Name's father. After finding a newborn white colt (son of the dead stallion) and nursing it to sufficient strength for the journey home, No Name confronts the second part of his vision, unable to understand why he must kill his father, and unable to see the full consequences of the cycle of life. But Redbird has had the same vision; he knows that he is old, is no longer needed in the tribe, and that at his death No Name—now called Conquering Horse—will assume the leadership of his people. It is an ancient pattern, unbreakable, inevitable, and this is what Conquering Horse learns. He is spared from killing his father directly, but the death occurs as the vision said it would. Conquering Horse cuts off a part of his own finger and throws it into the sky after his father's spirit, to be retrieved when he comes for it in the afterlife. The honor and idealism of these primitive people stands as a model of courage, spirituality, and faith for the supposedly sophisticated society which has replaced the Indian way of life.

Such irony is not confined to *Conquering Horse*, although it operates differently in the succeeding tales. In *Lord Grizzly* it is seen in the forgiveness which ends Hugh's quest for revenge. In *Scarlet Plume* it shows in the finding of love in an unexpected circumstance and place. More contrived and less effective,

Ransom's discovery in *King of Spades* that he has mistakenly
slept with his mother, and that his father, presumed dead, is
the one who has figured out the infamy, leads to his suicide in a
rather mawkish scene that almost destroys the double irony of
the situation. Finally, in *Riders of Judgment* the ultimate irony is
that of the achievement of victory only through death.

While an ironic view of life may serve to hold the five novels
together, it does not guarantee an equality of thematic significance or technical skill. *Scarlet Plume* (to a lesser degree) and
King of Spades are inferior to the other tales in both respects. The
historical context works well in *Scarlet Plume* because the account of the Sioux uprising in Minnesota in 1862 is grimly
realistic, providing an effective base for tragedy. The incident
is tragic because the white victims are individually innocent in
the political sense but their government has neglected to provide food for the Indians, and so hunger provokes the massacre
and part of our sympathies must be with the Indians. Yet beneath the surface of the white community lies an insidious
racism which appears occasionally throughout the story. The
dramatization of the historical event is excellent—concise and
accurate. But it is used—used to provide Judith Raveling with
a chance to experience true love. Although her own daughter
has been raped and killed during the massacre, she finds a love
that her husband could never give her, and finds it with an Indian, albeit a peaceful one. She is liberated from the restrictions of a polite society and discovers freedom in the natural life
of the Indian. In one respect she is an early liberated woman;
but the significance of this liberation lies mainly in Manfred's
concept of the male as stallion. (In a bad pun, with irony intended, one of the ineffectual husbands in the community is
named Codman.) What liberates woman is not so much her
freedom to choose as it is domination by a superior male who
loves freely, without inhibitions. The phallus becomes a symbol of all that is natural, right, and free. Civilization (represented by the woman who mutilates Scarlet Plume) tries to put
blinders on people, to restrict sex; civilization thereby dis-
courages the growth of honest, fresh, meaningful relation-

ships. Manfred's position is not entirely unjustifiable, but it takes on more importance in the story than it would seem to warrant. Indeed, the most effective scene in the novel is one in which Judith is alone and frightened in a deserted town. She is more believable while alone with her thoughts than she is with her Indian lover.

For Manfred, the role of the stallion in the animal world (protector, father, procreator) carries over to the human world. Even though there is little in *King of Spades* to support the idea, the final two words of this novel (which was the last of the five to be written) are "The stallions." It might seem that these are the words Manfred wants us to remember most clearly, but they will not suffice. Because of its mixture of English background, oedipal theme, pastoral paradise, gold rush in the Black Hills, suicide, and assorted characters who may be present only for atmosphere, *King of Spades* invites the playing of guessing games—superficial speculations on its meaning and its contribution to the western tales as a group. The novel begins with promise in Sioux City of the 1860s, appearing ready to explore the question of identity—not just that of two individuals, Magnus and his son Roddy, but also of America in relation to England. (The potential, as seen in D. H. Lawrence's *Studies*, is of considerable magnitude.) However, plot machinations and the rather dubious Black Hills setting later in the novel diffuse the original intentions. Unfortunately, *King of Spades* is too fanciful, contrived, and formless to hold its own in the series. It is the weak link because it is unable to focus on a historical truth or to reverse the normal process and turn myth, already established, back into the wishes, aspirations, or fears which led to its formation. Western myths, like others, spring from their own sources.

By internal chronology *Riders of Judgment* is the real conclusion to the tales. It is an interesting, unconventional cowboy story if read only on that level, but it also serves to comment upon the early maturity achieved by Conquering Horse. Cain Hammett, lacking the simple yet visionary ritual of the Yankton Sioux, becomes entangled in an elaborate Freudian complex of relationships which he cannot resolve. (From one end of the tales to the other we are made aware of the distinction between progress and fulfillment, an important difference often lost to Europeanized white society.) Unheroic as Cain may seem, he is able to give his life in order to bring peace to the cattle country. The vision of the more primitive society has been lost, and the new society has not yet replaced that visionary quality with intelligence and understanding, but remnants of courage and selflessness from a former time can still be nurtured. The western heritage which Manfred has examined in five areas of historical experience is available to those who will recognize it and learn from it. This, I take it, is the substance of the *Buckskin Man Tales*—not an exemplary figure held up for our emulation (there is no Buckskin Man) but a selection of deeds and lessons from the past which can serve men and women in modern times.

Guthrie's method is linear. Manfred's is circular. Yet Guthrie's line returns to its beginning and Manfred's circle remains unfinished. That is because Guthrie stays closer to his historical sources and Manfred allows his imagination to take him where it will. The first method is neat and clean—though not barren—and fosters realistic characterization. The second method is chancy, sometimes leading to brilliance of style and meaningful insight, and at other times going astray, but always leaving room for writer, reader, and critic to argue, speculate, think, and imagine in a continuing dialogue. Each method has its place and makes its contributions to an understanding of Western American man through examination of his development prior to the contemporary period.

VI
Walter Van Tilburg Clark:
The Western Attitude

Although it is not my purpose to revive the smoldering argument about western writers and eastern critics-reviewers, a few brief comments on the subject may be of some relevance in approaching the work of Walter Clark. With a few exceptions, the reviewers have given favorable treatment to A. B. Guthrie and Harvey Fergusson, have been unkind to Frederick Manfred and Vardis Fisher, and have been more than a little nonplussed by Frank Waters and Clark. Presumably, Waters and Clark have entered that world of the intuition, the nonrational, or the mystical, that the intellect-oriented critics cannot understand. When the major values of a novel—in this case the Western novel—spring from such concepts as unity, harmony with the land, intuitional response to primal energies, or the "magic" of the circle, the city-dwelling critics can do no better than cry "Foul!" and retreat quickly from a physical, spiritual, moral, and philosophical environment which does not lend itself to their ready-made terminology.

In this context of critical uncertainty, Clark's own life must seem confusing. During his first forty years—up to the publication of his last novel—he spent an equal time in the East and in the West, prompting at least one commentator to say that he was an adopted westerner rather than a native and therefore

195

had the advantage of a degree of detachment from the region to which he belonged. There is truth to the statement; Clark's detachment was at least enough to stop him short of Waters's more complete reliance on intuition and his willingness to accept the mystical. Furthermore, Clark's father (president of the University of Nevada) provided the kind of academic environment which encouraged respect for the intellect, so that Clark eventually attempted (successfully, I think) to bring the rational and the irrational together in a single mode of thought. To him this was an "effort to personalize the land and put the human tragedy back into its natural setting," to renew the old unity between man and the land.

In another respect, Clark created his own unity between the East and the West, not by reconciling the two but by living in the East while doing most of his writing about the West he loved. Born in Maine in 1909, he spent his early childhood in West Nyack, New York, before moving to Reno in 1917. Fifteen years later he returned to the East to attend the University of Vermont, earning his second Master of Arts degree there. It was during this time that he wrote the 446-line narrative poem which was the germ of what was to be his last published novel, *The Track of the Cat* (1949). During the first winter of his ten-year stay in Cazenovia, New York, he expanded the poem into what may have been a short novel but which Clark referred to as a prose-poem after he burned it. With the exception of a year spent back in Nevada, Clark remained in Cazenovia, teaching high school English and coaching basketball and tennis, until 1946. While there he wrote *The Ox-Bow Incident* (published 1940) as an exercise, trying to rid himself of the clichés, stereotypes, and formulas attached to the popular western. It was immediately hailed as a new kind of Western novel, and for years its reputation rested largely on that fact, with little or no attention paid to the essentially western way of perceiving life through the subconscious as well as the conscious mind. Clark's second novel, *The City of Trembling Leaves* (1945), also written in Cazenovia, made use of his growing-up experiences in Reno. It was easily labeled "autobiographical" and dismissed by reviewers as sprawling, uncontrolled, easy-going, and romantic, and so Clark was compared to Thomas Wolfe by those critics who then lamented his departure from the "fine and precise objectivity" of *The Ox-Bow Incident*. In the fall of 1945 Clark moved to Rye, New York, to teach, but by the spring of 1946 *The City of Trembling Leaves* was bringing in enough money to enable him to return to the West (Taos, and then Nevada) to recuperate from his years of teaching and to begin writing *The Track of the Cat*. (To get the reviewers out of the way, let it be said that many of them objected to what one called the "obtrusive" symbolism of *Cat* and also claimed that the novel was too self-consciously organized.)

Clark was to stay in the West for the remainder of his life; but he published no more novels, although he wrote at least one and refused to submit it for publication. It was as though he knew that the critics were unable to understand what he was doing. Nevertheless, in spite of his residence in the East, where he wrote or conceived all of his major work, Walter Clark has come to be known through the years as the essential western novelist, the one who did perhaps more than anyone else to define (in his fiction) the mode of perception, the acquisition of knowledge, and the style which we tend to call western. Clark wrote a good deal of poetry, although little of it was published; his prose style is imagistic, symbolic (or metaphoric), and direct, tapping the subconscious but staying in touch with the real world. (His style is not unlike that of Harvey Fergusson, but it is more forceful and more frequently evocative, probably because of his stronger concern with a sacred as well as a profane world.) His perception of reality rests heavily on dualities and contrasts, in imagery as well as in characterization, and he assumes that knowledge acquired through the intellect or the conscious mind is, at best, incomplete. He searches for unity, and while the distinctions or contrasts of experience are not resolved openly—as they might be for a mystic—they are joined by implication. Through intuitive recognition of the relationships between the two sides of dualities, there is also recognition of likeness (perhaps sameness) of the real, observable, personal world and the mythic or unconscious world of origins—this latter world at least approximating the primal world.

Not a pantheist, Clark nevertheless sees "likeness through all creation" and an alliance between man and nature as well as with the eternal. But these likenesses are often seen as, and stated as, opposites. Whatever fusion of elements is possible must often be implied, must be seen in the point of tension between the opposites, as though between the intellectual and the intuitive means of perception. In one sense, *The City of Trembling Leaves* acts as a relief of the tension by circling around it in a manner which is sometimes almost playful. (Thus allowing the novel to be called easygoing or uncontrolled or romantic.) Consider the piling up of images and thematic suggestions in a few passages and chapter titles: trinity of heroes, kisses and prayers, divine and pagan, aspen as intermediary, nuclear, the eternal and the moribund, the magic wilderness of the spirit, the eternal and reproductive old, the deep [and] sad kinship of everything, a wild and gentle god, wise and silent watchers, gay sprites, malicious demons, junction of roads, The Tracks of the Turtle, The Well, In the Time of Mountains, In Which the Circle Closes. In a way, of course, *The City of Trembling Leaves* is preparation for *The Track of the Cat*, the novel which had been in Clark's mind longer than the others and which required a mulling over of ideas, a sorting out of images which would reflect, or point the way back to, primal images. In particular, Clark is interested in unity—of things, of past and present, of man and nature—and in the circle of life, whose image is the symbol of unity or completeness. Yet on the surface—considering structure superficially—it does not appear that Clark's novels arrive at a point of definite completion. *The Ox-Bow Incident* opens and closes with the somewhat hopeful song of the meadowlark and with the presence of two characters—Art Croft and Gil Carter—who are spectators to the action of the novel more than they are participants in it. Theoretically, this kind of circular structure does not prohibit development along the way. It does not destroy the linear. It simply turns the line back on itself, to a new beginning as it were. Questions and beginnings are more important to the Western novel than are answers and conclusions, as may be seen in all of Clark's work, in Fergusson's *The Conquest of Don Pedro*, (1954) Manfred's *Lord Grizzly*, Waters's *The Man Who Killed the Deer* and the Colorado mining trilogy, and even in some of Fisher's novels.

Quite apart from philosophical considerations, *The Ox-Bow Incident* expresses unity in its construction. Clark was knowledgeable in the area of classical literature and it is not surprising to find the Aristotelian unities of time, place, and action in *The Ox-Bow Incident*. Everything centers around the hanging and takes place in two days within a few miles of the Ox-Bow and the town of Bridger's Wells. Thematically, the unity is not as obvious, relying on suggestion and implication, whereas in *The City of Trembling Leaves* it is more apparent in the theme than in the structure, and in *The Track of the Cat* these two approaches are modified and brought together in what Clark must have considered the most meaningful way of getting at his truest statement of life. What I am suggesting is that the intuitional (supported by the reasonable) motivation toward ultimate unity as expressed by the circle is not superficially neat but is built into structure, texture, symbol, action, and characterization in different degrees and at different times. When "the circle closes" it does not cut off all further discussion; it brings a cycle to the conclusion which is then another beginning. Despite an increasing emphasis upon intuitional beliefs in the unity of life, the major Western novels are open-ended. Furthermore, although some of them point to a link between the images of our world and the images of an ancient, even primordial, world, this is not the romanticism of Plato's ideal world. It is the reality of the unconscious linked to the reality of origins. It is archetypal and Jungian. And yet, each novel has a consciously real, human, and dramatic base, so that it can be read on several levels: (1) as a story which can be accepted literally, (2) as a representation of common types of people and actions, and (3) as a symbolic or mythic or archetypal recognition of the deeper significance of the unconscious and its ability to reveal a link between man and the universe. A diagram of the symbolic structure of *The Track of the Cat* will show one such link. The elements of the diagram will be discussed later, but I wish to point out the relationship of two levels of meaning and make the observation that when these levels come together with a third, and possibly a fourth, the result should be a single full realization, an insight that cannot be stated in any other way.

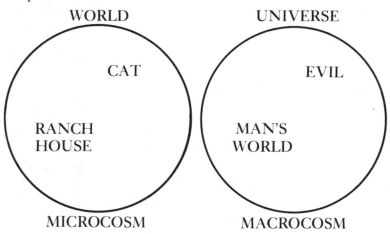

In his reliance on the intuitive search for truth, Clark is most closely related to Frank Waters. It is interesting to note, also, that in establishing historical time for their fiction these two writers have not gone much further than the immediate past, contrary to the practice of Guthrie, Manfred, Fergusson, Horgan in one novel, and, most noticeably, Fisher. The use of the immediate past (1895 and 1900) in *The Ox-Bow Incident* and *The Track of the Cat* enables Clark to isolate the action, to keep it pure, untainted by the machines and the growing population of the twentieth century. Furthermore, he has used no specific historical incidents. No such hangings as those in *The Ox-Bow Incident* have been recorded in Nevada. And while western ranchers have indeed tracked mountain lions, *The Track of the Cat* is not based on any particular incident of that kind. The places, too, are imaginary to the extent that they are fictional combinations of existing locations. Only *The City of Trembling Leaves* is set in an actual place, identifiable, and it is also more contemporary. Perhaps the two novels set just a little before Clark's own lifetime are more successful precisely because they are not bound by historical or experienced facts, allowing the imagination to dictate all of the terms. A remark in *The City of Trembling Leaves* may have some bearing upon this matter: "The air grew sad and experienced around him, thick with history rather than thin and clear with life." If Clark's novels are "mirrors to the unconscious," we may conclude that the elements of those mirrors are not old historical events—perhaps cannot be—but are rather the images we see all around us, the obvious things that we do not know about ourselves, or will not admit knowing.

2

On the surface, at least, *The Ox-Bow Incident* appears to be quite different from the two longer novels which were written later. It can be argued immediately, of course, that the simplicity of the plot belies the richness of the total experience, and that although texture and characterization are handled deftly and concretely they also suggest a good deal more than the surface reality. Nevertheless, the novel is a model of economy, even though the action proceeds slowly throughout many portions; and it merely implies man's dualities (which may be why it has been more popular than the later novels), whereas *The City of Trembling Leaves* discusses the dualities and *The Track of the Cat* illustrates them. Clark has said that he wrote his first novel as an exercise in which he could come to grips with the stereotypes of the typical "horse opera," using all the ingredients of the formula western novel in order to rid himself of any inclination to use them as they had been used already. At the same time, Clark was aware of the dangers of Nazism and Communism in the late 1930s, had read Sinclair Lewis's *It Can't Happen Here* (1935), and felt that in the United States "we had a good deal more to worry about in a Nazi tendency than we did in the Communist tendency." Readers responded to these surface realities, some accepting *The Ox-Bow Incident* as another

popular western—although perhaps better written—others
pointing out the Tetley-Hitler similarities and finding the
novel topical, and still others rejoicing that the western stereotypes had been broken and that 1940 (the year of publication)
marked, at last, the emergence of the mature or adult or myth-
stripped cowboy novel. On a somewhat less literary level, people from almost every state in the West wrote to Clark to say
that they knew which lynching episode he was referring to and
which Nevada town was the model for Bridger's Wells. (Clark
could find no evidence in the records of a lynching in Nevada
for rustling or horse stealing. The town he had in mind was
Bridgeport, California.) The point of all this is that, right or
wrong, reader-identification came more easily with *The
Ox-Bow Incident* than with the later novels, and so it has remained the most popular of Clark's work.

Serious Western novels had been written before 1940, but
it was *The Ox-Bow Incident* that brought dramatically to the
public's attention the nonromantic cowboy and the unresolved
western conflict that boldly defied the conventional patterns of
the shoot-out and the clear-cut victory of good over evil. Contrary to the comforting predictability of the mass-produced
western novel, the situation in *Ox-Bow* is discouragingly real.
After three innocent men have been lynched by a posse of assorted cowhands and townspeople, Davies, an elderly man beset with the ghosts of conscience, judges himself harshly in
terms that apply not only to the necessary violence of the traditional western story but also to the world's political conditions
at the time the novel was written:

> "I knew Tetley could be stopped then. I knew you could all
> be turned by one man who would face Tetley with a gun.
> Maybe he wouldn't even have needed a gun, but I told myself he
> would. I told myself he would to face Tetley, because Tetley
> couldn't bear to be put down, and because Tetley was mad to
> see those three men hang, and to see Gerald made to hang one of
> them. I told myself you'd have to stop him with fear, like any
> animal from a kill."

Aside from the undertones of Nazism, leadership by force, and the domineering military father who cannot abide a weak (thoughtful) son, the major focus is on that western convention in which a man appears with a gun and halts the mob in the name of goodness and justice, pitting his gun or his bluff against the mob and getting away with it because he represents the common anger against evil. The psychology of this act is defensible, certainly, because a loosely organized group of men may be turned easily by a strong will or personality. What characterizes *The Ox-Bow Incident,* however, is the lack of the strong will and the fast gun. No one comes forward to accept the role of hero and savior, even though it might have been done rather easily. Davies confesses further that he was glad he did not have a gun, implying that without it he was at least partly excused from attempting to stop Tetley and the crowd. Davies is not alone. There are no "superior" characters in this crowd; even Tetley, the leader, is ultimately shamed into suicide, although his shame centers on his son rather than on the lynching which he ordered. These are real people, exasperating in their plausibility. While Art Croft, the narrator, serves technically as the central intelligence as well as chief character, he is not intelligent enough to understand fully what is happening, nor is he strong enough to risk the disapprobation of the people of Bridger's Wells. Although he basically condemns the indiscriminate judging and hanging of the three men accused of theft and murder, he is not willing to do anything about it. His companion, Gil Carter, is a strong man, capable with his fists and his gun, but he is unmindful of consequences (one of the shortcomings of the nonintuitive man?) and therefore easily swayed by the mob. Davies, with the strongest moral repulsion to the act of violence, tries to preach to the crowd but is finally too weak a man to take charge of the situation. Osgood, a clergyman, is indignant at the men's behavior, but he lacks the emotional and spiritual strength to cope with it. Only Sparks reveals enough courage to deal with the madness of the crowd, but because he is a Negro in a white society he is ineffectual. And so the circumstances lead to a lynching by a group of average men, first aroused by the notion that one

of their friends has been murdered, then spurred on by the talk-
ers in the crowd, later hesitant to act but equally hesitant to
back out, and finally chagrined and perhaps shamed by the
knowledge of the victims' innocence.

If this were all, however, the novel would be unusual for its
time but not necessarily significant. Several things keep it from
being "the exercise" Clark said it was. As in other wide-view
Western novels, man is shown here in the intermediate stage of
his development. A primitive, almost savage, instinct is perva-
sive in the animal-like thirsting for blood. We are reminded
that western regionalism occupies a unique place among the re-
gionalisms of America, dealing with a broad area of change extending from the primitive, mysterious, elemental world of our
ancient ancestors to the threats of artificial, mechanical,
modern society. Man has for centuries been moving westward
on at least two continents, doing away with those races of people standing in the way of materialistic expansion at the expense of those spiritual truths and cultural values found among
the primitives who derived their way of life from the earth and
the world of nature. This is the dilemma to which Fenimore
Cooper directed his attention in the Leatherstocking novels. At
every step of the way there has been a frontier line at which the
oncoming civilization confronted the concepts of a savage and
primitive people who sought personal harmony with the land
and who did not understand materialism. Today the western
United States is geographically and spiritually the last remaining area with conditions similar to those of every frontier at one
time or another, or with a strong memory of those conditions
because they occurred in a recent past. Because the area is still
young, its writers have the opportunity of taking a position between the Indian and the white man, between primitivism and
civilization, between the land and the city, and so examining
within a unique time-space complex the essential spiritual
problems of a godlike animal who within the short span of seventy-five years has exchanged his oxcart for a rocket ship. This
is the broadest context, historically, within which Clark
writes, and the fact that *The Ox-Bow Incident* takes place in (ap-

proximately) 1890—the year Turner identified as the last of the frontier—indicates that Clark wanted to get back far enough to find a West that was "real enough to be used in the imagination" and also real enough to use in spite of the clichés of the Max Brands and the Zane Greys. To touch the immediate past and make it real for himself—this was apparently the effort required of Clark before he could go on to more complex rendering of the western experience.

Low passions take control of the community of Bridger's Wells, and the concept of legal justice as developed by a civilized society stirs ineffectually. Yet it remains always on the edge of the action, and it is given a measure of moral force through the stricken conscience of Davies and through the willingness of narrator Art Croft to listen to all sides of the argument, including the lengthy but somewhat confusing ramblings of Gerald Tetley. Neither the animal forces nor the moral causes of justice prevail strongly and clearly. The world of the Ox-Bow and Bridger's Wells is full of contrasts and paradoxes—good and evil, moral strength and weakness, physical strength and weakness, deep concern and casual curiosity—and the problem is not resolved except by implications which prove unsatisfactory to the reader who requires definite possibilities if not outright solutions. Even the parallel between the lynchings and the crucifixion of Christ is perhaps more tantalizing than real. Of the three victims, two—though innocent of the crime for which they are hanged—are not altogether guiltless in a broader sense. Martin, however, appears to be spotless, pure, childishly innocent in every way. Just before the hanging, "even the bitterness was gone from his face. He had a melancholy expression, such as goes with thinking of an old sorrow." It is as though young Martin is grieving (as Christ did) for the entire human race as represented by the foolish men who are taking his life. Yet, he was careless about a bill of sale—part of the machinery of civilization—and is, in a sense, hanged because of an unnatural technicality. (This in itself has implications which might be pursued into the general theme of innocent natural man corrupted by, or ruined by, society.) The world has turned dark for two days, but a kind of catharsis works on some of the participants of the lynching, and even stubborn Gil Carter tries to atone in a small way for an unkindness which he had done earlier. An era seems to end with a brief promise of tomorrow's resurrection. Tomorrow, of course, will be far in the future, because man still has too much animal left in him. The spiritual promise remains, but the evidence is skimpy. The action concludes at sunset of the second day, with the sky clear again after a snowstorm, meadowlarks singing, and Gil—thinking of the recent events—saying that he will be glad to leave.

Although the action is based almost entirely upon momentary psychological relationships, all of which have a plausible basis, there is a compelling undercurrent of nature symbolism, so that the novel proceeds on two levels, both completely believable. This is Clark's general method, and in one respect this method is a western one, making use of the awareness of natural elements. The Western novel is often taken to task for its reliance on landscape, on nature, on weather, to the neglect of characterization. The strong winds, for example, are a constant influence upon the momentary behavior of man. An unceasing wind makes a man restless and strips away some of the control from his emotions, exposing him to other elemental influences. The wide and open plains enforce an isolation which can make man independent and resourceful but can also drive him into himself so that he becomes ornery and antisocial. These characteristics are illustrated in a Clark story, "Why Don't You Look Where You're Going?" (1941), in which a man in a small boat is almost hit by a huge ocean liner, frantically veers out of the way, shakes his fist at the passengers on the liner, and then cheerfully and independently proceeds on his own way. The broad expanse of the sea is not unlike the prairie, and the tall waves are a reminder that Clark is essentially attracted to mountains, which can act as an uplifting force or can as easily overwhelm a man. It has been suggested often that *The Ox-Bow Incident* is not really a western novel, that the lynching could have occurred anywhere. (Attesting, perhaps, to the fact that *Ox-Bow*, like any good regional novel, transcends its locale.) Yet, it is not the lynching itself that is important but the motives and pressures—the specific human behavior—which lead to the lynching or allow it to happen. What causes injustice? The answer to that question seems to stand as an indictment of man and is reminiscent of the charges against man made by Fisher in *The Testament of Man:* irrationality, prejudice, racism, emotionalism, ambition, passion, lust, bestiality, latent primitive desires, lack of love and consideration and compassion, frustration and compensation, perverted love (as for the "victim"), and groupism (as opposed to individuality). As Manfred implied in *Lord Grizzly*, man has not yet reached a spiritual stage in the evolutionary process, even though he occasionally seems to be moving toward it. Clark, however, is also aware of circumstances of place and of weather which cannot be put down easily by logical thought, which insinuate themselves into the characters of *The Ox-Bow Incident* and determine their behavior at crucial points of the action.

Very early in the novel a brief descriptive passage makes us aware of the bending and straightening of long grass in the wind, and of the alternation of shine and shadow which later becomes an important image relating human behavior to natural conditions of wind and weather in the mountains. Man, like the blade of grass, is two-sided, and whether he thinks rationally or acts emotionally can depend on the same wind which sways the grass. The wind also motivates in two ways: it becomes so irritating that it drives the posse on to an act of supreme irritation, but it also proves discouraging and prompts a wish to retreat. The contrasts of the environment are repeated in contrasts in the behavior of the characters. Furthermore, the total environment in this case—wind, darkness, mountains that look higher than they are, the threat of snow—leaves some of the men "thick with the . . . feeling of mortality." What brings Amigo back to normal is getting out of the wind so that he can roll a cigarette and "make his hands feel natural again." Man is buffeted about in his sensory perceptions of the land: black shadows, patches of white snow, purple

and gold violets, chill—loveliness and loneliness. It is not only
the arguments and the prodding of Tetley, Davies, Mapes, and
the others which keep the men unsettled emotionally, it is also
the natural conditions around them. The land plays an
important part in determining action, and its images also lead
to a progression of thought encompassing more than the single
act of the lynching. Prominent among these images is the
black-white contrast:

> I could see the white towel he still had in his hand.

> Through the trees, black in shadow, showed patches of
> snow which hadn't melted yet.

> . . . scrambling in the snow of the clearing in the black
> woods, with the pack in the shadows behind them.

> "I set myself up as the light to oppose Tetley's darkness."

Black and white imagery (memorable in Conrad's *Heart of
Darkness*, 1899) seems to be an important element in all three of
Clark's novels, and the easiest way of dispensing with it is to
equate black with evil and white with good and arrive at the
same kind of allegorical patterns found in the subliterary western novel. Certainly Davies's statement of his light opposing
Tetley's darkness resembles at least a part of Marlowe's attitude toward Kurtz in the Conrad story, and the apparent victory of evil over good destroys the easy stereotype of the conventional cowboy novel. But Clark's use of the white towel
(and Lawrence's white shirt in *The City of Trembling Leaves*) is
more subtle than outright symbolism and allows us to absorb a
feeling from nature which can then, at the right time, suggest
something more than the object in the image. The "pack in the
shadows" is a case in point. Almost exactly in the center of the
novel, in the shadow under the mountain, Gerald Tetley, considered weak and effeminate by his father as well as by the
group, babbles to narrator Art Croft about "the pack." (Clark
uses the verb "babbled" twice within this passage, as though to
throw us off the track of any reasonable significance; yet this
may be the most significant section of the novel.) The pack is

first of all literally real, i.e., the posse, the mob which begins to act collectively and will not tolerate weakness, fear, or internal disagreement. The individual who fears the pack is stifled. But the pack exists in dreams also: "We've all had those dreams. In our hearts we know they're true, truer than anything we ever tell; truer than anything we ever do, even." This is the only mention of dreams in *The Ox-Bow Incident*, but they are used extensively in *The Track of the Cat* to show the vital relationship between the unconscious and what we tend to call "real life." In dreams the pack is everywhere:

> They're behind the trees in the black woods we dream about; they're behind the boulders on the mountains we dream we're climbing, behind the windows on the square of every empty dream city we wander in. We've all heard them breathing; we've all run screaming with fear from the pack that's coming somewhere. We've all waked up in the night and lain there trembling and sweating and staring at the dark for fear they'll come again.

The question is whether these are, in effect, the same "watchful gods" that lurk behind the trees in several of Clark's short stories. In "The Buck in the Hills" (1943) they seem to be the protectors of the natural world, or perhaps an extension of man's conscience when he knows or suspects that he has violated a natural law. They can as easily be images projected by the deep-seated fears in man, either the individual's fear of the group, or collective man's fears of what he does not understand and cannot control. The first is essentially psychological, but the second goes even deeper than that, into the unconscious, allowing the image of the pack to represent primitive forces which man does not understand because he is unwilling or unable to establish contact with primordial sources. When the unconscious or the collective unconscious or the primal are spelled out in Jungian terms, many readers are still left with the uneasy feeling that they do not understand—any more than Clark does—precisely how dualities are to be unified, or what man must do in order to establish contact with the primal sources, or how he can learn to achieve harmony with nature. These are big questions and Clark does not provide definite and

consistent answers. The significant characteristic of narrator
Art Croft is his normality, his commonness, his closeness—
perhaps—to the reader, and we recognize his rightness as narrator in a story intended to suggest but not discuss areas of intuitive ideas and primal qualities. Gerald Tetley may seem
crazy to the rest of the men, but his apparent irrationality is the
very thing that allows him to see—at least partially—those
deep-seated fears harbored by men who are unable to come to
terms with that primordial source just hinted at by Croft when
he compares Davies to Gerald Tetley:

> And yet both of them gave you that feeling of thinking outside
> yourself, in a big place; the kid gave me that feeling even more, if
> anything, though he was disgusting. You could feel what he
> meant; you could only think what Davies meant.

Only think. Reason, logic, rationality are not enough. They
cannot dispel the ambiguities and mysteries that lurk in the unconscious and that provide man with a felt relationship to the
earth, to the primitive that is deep within us, and beyond that
to the almost unspeakable primal source with its indefinable
energy and unity. This is, admittedly, pretty heavy stuff, but
Clark keeps it tucked away within the narrative and does not
insist that it be isolated, pulled out for inspection, or totally understood (especially on the rational level).

How far one can go in identifying symbols and archetypes
is debatable. The passages under discussion here are immediately preceded by conversation concerning Frena Hundel, a
mysterious woman who seems to play only a momentary part
in the story and is easily forgotten. She does, however, provide
us with a clue to Clark's method. On the surface she is merely a
frustrated woman who would like to get married, is shunned
by men, and therefore in retaliation wishes all men dead. In his
analysis of her, Gerald Tetley goes beyond the idea of revenge
and insists that Frena's real desire is for power. (With men out
of the way she could make women her slaves.) The argument
soon falters and we must wonder whether Clark himself fal-
tered at this point or whether the argument is superficial and
serves largely as a device to keep the reader occupied while his

unconscious absorbs—again—some kind of insight barely suggested or planted, as it were, subliminally. An earlier assessment of Kinkaid's character had attributed to him "a gentle, permanent reality that was in him like his bones or his heart, that made him seem like an everlasting part of things." While he is presumed dead, Art Croft assumes that Frena's wildness over his "death" is the result of her liking him, even being "sweet on him." It is then that Gerald says she is sweet on Kinkaid only because he is dead and that she wants all men to die. Croft makes no sense of Gerald's statement. No one seems to know what Frena Hundel is really like; she sits on the page like a spectre, inviting attention and also discouraging it. Out of curiosity rather than a wish to belabor archetypes and symbols, let us take a brief look at the name *Frena*. It is not far off from Freya, the goddess of love in Norse mythology. Does Frena hate men because they have forgotten—or never learned—how to love? Or perhaps Frena is the feminine form of *frenum*, a small fold of membrane or skin which restrains the motion of the organ to which it is attached, or retains eggs until they are hatched. The image may be suggestive of the male-female relationship or of the deeper man-nature (man-cosmos, man-primal source) relationship which is violated, misunderstood, or unrecognized by man in his intermediary stage of development from source to animal to man to spirit and back to source.

I do not wish to call Clark a purveyor of exotic and private symbols. It is reasonably clear, however, that beneath his skillful handling of the psychological realities of his characters and the dramatization of landscape as character or force lies a dark and mysterious level of meaning that is available only through intuitional perception or feeling. In various ways in *The City of Trembling Leaves* and *The Track of the Cat* he attempts to bring these perceptions a little closer to the surface.

3

To most readers of Clark, *The City of Trembling Leaves* is the least successful, or interesting, or original of the three novels.

On the surface, at least, it is different, and differences within a writer's work tend to bother us. We want consistency. Reactions to *Leaves* have stressed the autobiographical emphasis, the shifting point of view, the use of "Walt Clark" as narrator, the profuseness (translated into lack of organization), and the variety of styles. The novel has also been dismissed as just another initiation story. It is true that Clark thought more fondly of this novel than he did of the other two because it came closest to his personal experiences; however, rather than identifying himself with the chief character, Tim Hazard (whose very name may indicate, among other things, the dangers of such an identification), he appears as "Walt Clark," the narrator. This device, perhaps old-fashioned, serves both the narrative and the author in several ways. It helps to throw off the charges that the novel is fully autobiographical. It provides esthetic distance to a contemporary time, allowing the archetypal images and themes to work more acceptably. Almost paradoxically, "Walt" the narrator can at the appropriate moments *remove* distance, creating a sense of immediacy by linking the writer to the experience. Structurally, the narrator gives the novel its epistolary effect, quieting the archetypal emphases and the stronger rhythms and structures of the other two novels. And finally, on a more personal level, because *Leaves* was written in New York it is possible that "Walt" the narrator firmly establishes Clark's western identity. I find any or all of these possibilities quite satisfactory. The western novelist is not bound to fashionable forms or styles, and the literary independence of *The City of Trembling Leaves* is a refreshing case in point.

The sense of innocent wonder pervading this novel perhaps offends the intellectuals and the sophisticates, but the capacity for wonder is an integral part of Clark's view of the world and the renewal of this wonder is essential to Western literature in general. Renewal itself is the major characteristic of the natural world, and recognition of this fact is vital to anyone who thinks in cyclical rather than linear terms, who seeks unity rather than diffusion, and who accepts death as a part of the cycle rather than fearing it because it marks the termination of the individual linear lifeline. Even so, Tim Hazard's capacity for wonder is not entirely naive. Many of the actions and feelings deemed important in the growth of an adolescent are treated ironically. "Walt Clark" can see the ironies in the standard ingredients of the growing-up story and can protect his chief character from the smothering effects of sentimentalism. Yet irony is not the only attitude in the novel. To the consternation of the critics, *Leaves* admits of a variety of tones, attitudes, and styles. Clark, however, is neither careless nor confused. Courageously, he establishes as much variation as he can in his pursuit of unity, this being the honest and realistic way of conducting the pursuit. Furthermore, if there is a style which can be called western, it is not one limited to a single voice. It is generally lyrical, but it is laced with irony, concrete realism, metaphor, straightforward narration, and natural symbols. It may seem pastoral because the images are usually taken from the natural world rather than from a man-made world, but it is not governed by nostalgia. It is strong in rhythms, corresponding in varying degrees with the rhythms of the land. To the extent that there may be a western style, its origins are in the land, in the natural cycles, in the primitive two-handed beat stressed by Mary Austin, and in the search for and recognition of an underlying unity in the natural life. Individual styles are, of course, affected by the degree of sophistication and intellectualism each writer brings to his work. Nevertheless, key passages from Fisher, Waters, Clark, Manfred, Fergusson, Eastlake, and Steinbeck (to name only the obvious examples) have much in common.

Timothy Hazard reflects the western style in *The City of Trembling Leaves* as he reacts directly to nature and its elements. He is mindful, although subconsciously at times, of numerous black-white contrasts, of colors, lights, shadows, and of motion. The "shivering and twinkling" of aspen leaves in the wind make him feel that he is "in the presence of some vast, benevolent and very gentle force" which he is unable to perceive. But he opens himself, emotionally at first, to the images around

him, feeling and being filled with the "motion and light of the
little aspen," and gradually he senses and almost understands a
nonrational importance in nature and in ancient things.
Eventually he is able to pray:

> "Great spirit, Thou Who are all things, and in all things, give
> me to remember that I have beheld Thy eternal waters, that I
> have stood before the rock of time and numbered my little years,
> that I have seen the cities of men, and lo, their lights died in the
> darkness, and the stars were no older and shone. Grant me the
> peace of this understanding. Make me the well of this silence."

Timothy Hazard takes the motion, the waters, the rocks, the
trees, and the stars and makes of them the material for the
music he is by this time striving to compose, and so Clark's
ideas about the city, about nature, about multiplicity and
unity, about adolescence and the search for maturity are bound
up with his concept of the serious artist. The cities have grown
old quickly and have decayed, offering no more hope for the
understanding of the essential meanings of life, and the artist
must go to more enduring sources. Clark's western city of
Reno, Nevada, is still young, still growing, and can symbolize
the adolescent stage, still close to the mountains and trees, and
still cognizant of the natural world which surrounds it.

> In the late afternoon it was always easy to understand that the
> sacred Truckee Meadows contained the city of adolescence as
> easily in time as they did in space, that they would never check
> the trembling of leaves.

At some time these conditions of the city will cease, because
what man makes and what man thinks tend to be linear in form
and in reach, and what is linear must end. The end of man himself is death. Only the landscape, permanent as the mountains
or renewable as the meadows—if man does not tamper with
them—can provide clues to the origins of things and their cycles. Here, then, the artist can work, reminded of the method
of his task by Mount Peavine, "dark and brooding . . . earth
god, the lover of multiplicity," and Mount Rose, "the lover of

sky, the one who reached for unity." The artist, like any man, must of necessity be grounded in the earth, in the multiple confusion of the literal or physical aspects of life; but his job is to unify, to seek the organizing priniciple, to reach for the sky—or the primal sources of life. His work must have roots in the land first of all, and this characteristic is strong in Western regional literature. However, out of the earthly context must spring an awareness of and a search for the ultimate unity which transcends the multiple object. Bound up in this process is what I call "the Western attitude," an attitude which Walter Van Tilburg Clark exemplifies perhaps better than anyone else.

The struggle toward this attitude is difficult, as may be seen in the story of Tim Hazard and his poignant encounters with realism, intellectualism, idealism, purity, and perfection. To this extent, at the very least, the Western novel has moral complexity and ambiguity—deemed necessary to reality—even though it often seems to arrive at nature-based solutions which appear too easily gained. Tim's journey toward marriage with his childhood sweetheart, Mary, is complicated by his attraction to Rachel, whom he sees idealistically rather than within the realities of his own life and ambitions. Tim's major struggle may be toward realism, toward balance, belying the notion that the unity for which he searches (as does Clark) is ethereal, mystical, perfect, or in any way unrealistic. Tim confronts obstacles of misguided desires in the people he associates with, either briefly or at some length. Lawrence Black (whose name may or may not be significant) seeks perfection and, unable to find it or achieve it, is unable to make use of his artistic talents; Teddy Quest (ironically named) is too concerned with techniques; Knute Fenderson is a fanatic in the name of purity. In one way or another, Tim's friends are either too analytical or not reasonable enough. It would seem, then, that Tim's answers would lie within a compromise, on a middle ground, and that his own work might then be in danger of losing its focus, its direction, its vision. Here we must remember that Clark has never posed questions which he could answer fully; he does not pretend to resolve the mysteries of life. What is important is the question, the suggestion, the touching of the mystery, the indication of a path, a glimpse into the sameness of past and future. Tim Hazard (and now he seems to be Clark, along with the narrator, "Walt Clark") learns the value of questions and the necessity of letting his work come out of him without either the stifling intellectualism or the disembodied mysticism which we hold up too often as the only choices.

The story of Tim Hazard and Reno takes on a larger significance than that of an immediate time and place, and yet it is through the time, and often particularly the place, that the artist achieves his awareness of the larger meanings. Tim looks deeply into many people and undergoes many experiences before he finds his own meaning in a deep-rooted love for a woman who represents all people and in a place which represents all places. From these roots the artist sends out his music, "whole, circular, complete," and in the end there is no other answer, the important thing being that the question is still alive. The Western novel is frequently called a form of the quest. Man goes back constantly to his sources, looking for the answer, and after each attempt the cycle begins again. "Upon the east the slow, white dance begins." And, "Upon the west the splendid peaks behold it." *The City of Trembling Leaves* is a necessary statement of the experience which we call variously "Western," "Jungian," "irrational," or "intuitional." Grounded in the kind of reality which everyone can understand, it nevertheless allows the pursuit of primal unity to take place in a contemporary setting, bringing together the twentieth century and that ancient time, shrouded in mystery, in which lie our origins.

4

The Track of the Cat, Clark's major novel, reveals his philosophy most clearly and makes the most effective use of his western materials. It has the fullness, and almost the length, of *The City of Trembling Leaves,* and maintains much of the unity and clarity of *The Ox-Bow Incident*. (Critics who have objected to what they call the "dense symbolism" of *Cat* will disagree with this last statement.) It is carefully grounded upon a western ranch with all of its literal details, and yet it operates consistently upon a symbolic level. The natural symbols are this time an organic part of each consciousness, and each character serves as a facet of Clark's view of the world. A shifting point of view enables Clark to make the most of his situation and his group of characters. Yet strict unities of time, place, and purpose give the entire work the impact of immediacy and emotional reality.

The time is a brief period of two or three days, approximately in the year 1900; the place is a ranch house and the valleys and mountains immediately surrounding it in Nevada. Of the eight characters involved, six are members of the Bridges family. In addition, Gwen Williams is at the ranch as the house guest of her future husband, young Harold Bridges; and Joe Sam, a Piute Indian about seventy years old, does a few odd jobs such as caring for the horses. On the surface this is a relatively normal family situation on an isolated western ranch. But it soon becomes apparent that all of these characters are invested with symbolic significance and that Clark has worked out a careful scheme to illustrate what may be Ideal Western American Man. A second major theme revolves around the concept of evil and man's relationship to it and to nature. Here again the theme itself and the accompanying images in contrasts of black and white suggest Conrad's *Heart of Darkness*.

Old Mr. Bridges is a cantankerous leftover from the earlier frontier days, from the winning of the West. Unlike Steinbeck's Grandpa Joad, however, he has been tainted by the civilization of San Francisco and so also represents Clark's warnings against the decadence of the city. Mrs. Bridges represents doctrinal, strict, Bible-reading religion in all its propriety, sobriety, and lack of flexibility. She may or may not be Clark's own symbol of the religious attitude, but it is at least significant that she contributes little toward an understanding of evil or toward an ideal behavior. Arthur, the eldest son, is a dreamer, a mystic. He seems to be at peace with life, having arrived at some kind of understanding of nature which is impractical but wholly satisfying. He is also the first to be destroyed by the cat. Curt, at thirty-seven a few years younger than Arthur, is completely practical, earthy, self-confident, physically strong, respectful of almost nothing. He has the utmost faith in himself, little faith in anything else, and he is the second to be destroyed by the cat. (It should be mentioned, perhaps, that the elder Bridgeses are also destroyed by the cat, although spiritually rather than physically.) The one girl in the family, Grace, possibly thirty-five, is sympathetic to Arthur, but she is ineffectual in taking his place after he has been killed. Gwen Williams, a subtly complex character, seems to absorb from the Bridges family those qualities which will be most needed in her later contributions as a wife to Hal. Joe Sam obviously represents primitive man, savage and superstitious, close to nature in a mysterious and also mystical way. Finally, Young Hal, in a striking similarity to Shakespeare's Prince Hal (although this point must not be belabored), learns from all of these people and retains those traits and beliefs which seem to be valuable and sensible. Hal is a composite character, made up of respect, thoughtfulness, action, practicality, the ability to get along in a natural world, and the insight necessary to penetrate the literal details and at least partially understand the broader significance of life. He is man as yet relatively undeveloped because he is very young, and once more we find the suggestion that mankind is in the stage of adolescence. Clark, then, is attempting to set up a series of stages through which man may achieve maturity.

The theme may also be stated as one of survival, a theme common to Western regional fiction. Arthur is typical of the early settlers who were dreamers, who came from many places to the western land of their hopes only to be defeated because they could not cope with the harshness of the land. In this respect Curt is then representative of other settlers, who were ruthless in their conquest of the land, who never felt a spiritual tie with it, and who therefore died also. Hal, really from the next generation, is a mixture of these two types and therefore

one who learns and who survives. The lesson of the land is both
spiritual and physical. Hal learns to respect Joe Sam's superstition and Arthur's mysticism just as much as he learns from
Curt how to hunt and to get along in the wilderness. Hal respects animals and he respects the love of a woman. Like Mar-
low in *Heart of Darkness*, Hal for a time walks the thin line between good and evil, and he is aware of his position and is able
to draw back.

Clark deals with the problem of evil on three different levels, or through three different relationships which we might
call the human, the natural, and the supernatural attitudes. On
the first level, evil is seen to be a part of the human character,
revealed through petty bickering, misunderstanding, and
selfishness. Mr. Bridges, for example, spends most of his time
drinking, playing cards, and making nasty remarks. In one ex-
plosive scene he accuses his wife of being a whore who has
chosen religion over honesty:

> "You got a good enough price yourself, old woman," he said,
> grinning. "The best of them would have settled for clothes and a
> carriage, but what did you charge me, huh? I'll tell you what
> you charged me. My life, that's what you charged me, my
> whole damn life. And no fun for my money either."

Presumably, Mr. Bridges drinks in order to compensate for a
wife who is the "most expensive whore in the whole damn
world," and "a clothes-pin in bed, a goddam, 'normous,
wooden clothes-pin." Mrs. Bridges, in turn, rages at Gwen
Williams, whom she suspects of being a loose woman because
she has seen Gwen and Hal close together several times; and
she orders Gwen out of the house. In the background of this
rotten situation is Curt's desire to have Gwen even though she
is betrothed to his brother. Only Hal seems to be immune to
the infection which breaks out again and again in the ranch
house group until it finally becomes an apparently incurable
sickness of the mind.

Whereas the human level is dealt with literally, the natural
level appears both in a literal and a symbolic sense. Regional in-

fluences such as isolation, confinement during cold weather, the constant blowing of the wind, the deep snow in the valleys, the lack of shelter on the ridges—these things combine to discourage and even defeat man so regularly that they seem to have a corporate will or determination whose sole purpose is to destroy the human being. Curt, however, is the only one who comes to believe this, and it is primarily for his belief that he is destroyed. Once a strong, competent, and practical man, he is overcome as his mind shatters under the unceasing pressures of natural forces. Ironically, his weakness lies in his certainty that he can defeat nature through physical strength and through careful reasoning. Thus, the literally understood pressures of the natural environment (an important aspect of Western regional fiction) function symbolically as well. Man has been separated from nature and has forgotten his right relationship to the natural elements. Clark's method of illustrating this break is his usual method of expanding the naturalistic details of his region into images which are striking without being violent. It is the ease with which the image is formed that is impressive in Clark's writing:

> Harold stopped too, to stare down. It made him uneasy to see the print of a naked human foot in snow. It wasn't right there. The split-heart print of a deer, the dots and dashes of rabbits, the fine tail line and tiny forget-me-nots of wood mice, or even the big, broken flower of a panther or a bobcat, these were all as right in snow as black letters on paper. But this complicated, unique print, not even a little like any of them, was all wrong. There was too much time forgotten between.

Man has drawn too far away from nature; in fact, he has ravished nature and, in turn, himself. The gods of nature are aware of the man-creature and stand ready to destroy him. Yet Clark does not seem to believe that nature is necessarily malign. In one of his stories, "The Buck in the Hills," Chet McKenny is guilty of the evil of "being out of tune" with nature, and his companions feel the guilt by association: "There was something listening behind each tree and rock we passed, and something waiting among the taller trees down slope, blue through the falling snow. They wouldn't stop us, but they didn't like us either. The snow was their ally." On this level, then, man is free to make his choice within the context of nature. His victory or defeat depends upon his personal relationship to nature. This is why Clark continually stresses the move toward maturity and toward unity.

The focus of the symbolic level of *The Track of the Cat* is the cat itself. Through the cat the chief characters view nature in such a way as to reveal their personal philosophies. Arthur, whose quest in search of the meaning of life has driven him inward, has arrived at a calm acceptance of things as they are. For him the cat is merely a cat, a part of the natural context, to be accepted for its face value. Yet he is sympathetic toward Joe Sam's view and carves animal charms for him. Curt sneers at the Indian's superstitions and yet is killed by the cat just as surely as though the cat were indeed supernatural, because Curt pits himself against external nature instead of absorbing it internally as Arthur does. For Joe Sam the cat is a personal nemesis. Joe Sam lost his wife and oldest daughter to an animal which he identified as a big black cat; other misfortunes followed until Joe Sam began to think of the cat as a symbol of the gods who had allowed the Indian to be destroyed by the white man. Later, when Joe Sam sees in Curt the representative of the rapacious white race which has violated both nature and the Indian, nature's true people, he subtly alters his attitude toward the cat symbol to make of it a god of vengeance which he can then turn against the white man in Curt.

Joe Sam's first attitude has a counterpart in "The Indian Well" (1943), a short story in which a white man comes to an oasis in the American desert, loses his burro to a cougar, and then maintains a winterlong vigil until he finally kills the cougar. Jim Suttler takes it as a personal affront that nature has claimed his burro, and through endurance he is able to change the natural patterns of the Indian-well region for a time. However, when he moves on, in the spring, the patterns resume and it is as though man had never been there. This is a prelude to the suggestion in *The Track of the Cat* that nature and certain values such as evil remain eternal while men come and go; man conquers briefly and indecisively and then moves on.

The second attitude leads into the historical and spiritual problem of the relationships between the white man and the Indian. This problem occupies a central position in a large number of western novels, including second-rate ones, because of its double appeal. First, the problem is that of westward expansion with its paradox, as stated by Cooper, of the economic and historical necessity of expansion at the expense of the primitive peoples who stand in the way as opposed to the moral necessity of treating the Indian according to the established Christian ethical system. Second, since the Indian is a barbarian according to the social standards of the civilized white man, he becomes the symbol of a natural and unfettered way of life which may be opposed, philosophically and spiritually, to the artificial and soon decadent civilized life as represented by the city.

Clark introduces the negative aspects of the cultural significance of these problems in "The Anonymous" (1941), a story of a young Navajo man who is "culturally adopted" by a wealthy white woman, Mrs. Varney. The great tragedy of this story is that Peter Carr (his English name) has been removed from all his landed culture, from his own heritage, in order to be a plaything for a woman who possesses the common romantic attitude of the sentimentalist. Peter is forced to deny his Navajo heritage and become an eastern or European type of gentleman. He has lost the character and feeling of his own people. He is exploited in a new way, highly romantic in motivation and completely degrading in execution, by the white race which had earlier taken most of his land: now the very soul is taken also. Peter wears Indian clothing because his white benefactress does not want him to forget his heritage, but the retention is obviously artificial and foolish, except to Peter. He is a man without a country, and he does not realize it. "The sap," says Mrs. Farney's chauffeur. "He don't even know he's nothing but a toy."

In contrast to Peter Carr, Joe Sam carries within him a deep feeling toward his heritage and a great hatred for the white man who has thoughtlessly destroyed the Indian. Through his belief in the supernatural (which is, more properly, an inclination toward superstition) he assigns to the cat a value which is felt by Curt, so that Curt is opposed by Joe Sam as well as by the cat, or by racial vengeance as well as by nature or evil or death. For the cat symbolizes all of these things, and when it is finally killed by Hal and Joe Sam it is only an ordinary cat, not The Black Cat. The cat's death, like Christ's (after three days of hell culminating in resurrection) results in a knowledge of evil and of death and of a way in which Hal and all men can face these realities; but evil and death and nature remain, and each man must face them continually and by himself. This is the lesson learned by Hal, the focal character.

Although Hal matures within a fairly complex situation involving other characters who represent various facets of his own consciousness, Clark has also dealt with the maturation process in a simpler story which pits a young boy directly against the forces operating within him. "The Watchful Gods" (1950), a novelette, emphasizes the new power which is given to Buck in the form of a twenty-two rifle on his twelfth birthday, and the resulting choice which Buck must make between the forces of darkness and the forces of light. Here again is the wider implication of man achieving distinction in technological skills and being forced suddenly to re-examine his relationship to nature in the crucial moment of a moral choice. The novelette is a kind of Western American *Pilgrim's Progress*, with Buck beset by temptations on every hand, the temptations appearing in the forms of natural objects and living creatures which are more or less divided into two camps under the leadership of the fog god and the sun god. Buck is sent out with the right to choose between good and evil. The choice itself (and both sides of the choice) is represented by the gun, which is also the gateway from the world of the boy to the world of the man. Buck is, in a very real sense, an Indian youth sent out to find his own particular place in the general scheme of life. In form, then, the story is an interesting combination of Christian pilgrimage and Indian ritual.

Again the significant imagery is presented in terms of color, usually light in contrast to dark. And again the gods of nature lurk everywhere, passively waiting to see what man will do. Buck is sensitive to these gods, just as the narrator was in "The Buck in the Hills." And he is torn between the desire to ravish or destroy nature with his man-made power (the gun) and the equally strong desire to achieve a kind of union with nature. The tense immediacy and drama of the natural scene suggests a comparison with another of Clark's stories, "Hook" (1940), which is a masterpiece of nature-writing. (Clark's powerful ability to dramatize animal life may also be seen in the first part of "The Indian Well.") In point of view, however, there is an important difference. Hook the hawk is governed entirely by the basic natural drives of hunger, sex, and survival. Buck has little concern for any of these drives, except that his encounter with the rattlesnake admits the possibility of death and survival on the literal level. Buck is part of an allegory. He is tainted by evil (ignorance) and the Pacific beach is dark when he arrives there at the end of his journey. However, he has repented, and the sun begins to shine as he is once more confronted by his inner devil. "You aren't going home without spoils, without a rabbit or some game, without something dead to show your sister and family as a result of your newly acquired power, are you?" Buck cuts off the temptation. He has made his choice, and the confusing battle between the sun god and the fog god is ended, at least for the time being.

Clark, then, is concerned with universal themes—good and evil, adolescence and maturity, man and nature—which he objectifies with the materials of the American West. He cannot, as do eastern and southern writers, probe into family relationships and traditions over many generations. The West is young and does not have lengthy family or social traditions, and so the Western regional writer must concentrate on man in nature to a large extent. In addition, of course, nature is more directly important in a practical way in an area devoted to ranching and farming than it is in a metropolitan or industrial area. The traditions which the western writer has to work with are first directly in nature itself, then in the cultural and spiritual history of the American Indian, and only finally in the more recent traditions of the western white man. As these traditions come together in *The Track of the Cat*, Clark does not try to cement them intellectually. Again, there are more questions than answers, not only in relation to theme but also concerning method, or techniques. To what extent is the cat—and the entire narrative—symbolic? Does Clark rely too heavily on symbolism? What is the function of the dream sequences? Is the black-and-white imagery as obvious a device as it seems? And can Clark be accused of stereotyping all of his characters? The very presence of these questions partially explains the richness of the novel as well as exemplifying the open-endedness of Clark's method.

Clark's characters do not have the faddish or curious eccentricities that some novelists (especially nonwestern) give their characters in order to make them appear original, startling, or real. Without these artificial quirks, Clark's characters often seem to be either thematic or typical—not stereotypes (although a few come close), not always archetypes (although some are), but representatives of not uncommon kinds of people. To the extent to which they are representative, they foster the idea of unity. As individuals, however, they interact with each other and with the environment with full psychological and emotional plausibility, so that Clark is a psychological realist even while he is also an intuitionist and very nearly a visionary. A mystic he is not, because his quest for oneness is firmly rooted in the earth and in people who are not in the least disembodied. Particularly in *The Track of the Cat*, the characters seem to belong to a deliberate scheme, with each person playing a role within discussions of good and evil, of man and the cosmos, of attitudes toward the land, and of archetypal meanings which do not yield to examination in terms of reason, science, or the so-called rational Freudian psychology. Clark, like Jung, is willing to tap the ancient mysteries, to find archetypal meanings in the unconscious. Freudians, presumably more empirical, look into the unconscious for repressions which have been forced from the conscious mind and which must be dealt with in order to make the conscious mind

healthy. The Freudian theory is, in a sense, comforting because it claims to deal in facts and because it gets at repressions
through terms which seem understandable—sexuality and infantile impulse, for example. The study of archetypes takes a
different kind of thought, and it relies on such things as myth,
intuition, nonlogical perception, wonder, acceptance, the long
view. Perhaps even such a simple matter as the need for, and
the wonder of, renewal is more compatible to Jungian thought
than to the less spiritual approach of Freud. What makes
Clark's novels—and especially *The Track of the Cat*—seem
either confusing or overly symbolic to many critics and readers
is that the novels may be examined from the Freudian viewpoint as well as from the Jungian. All this proves, I think, is
that the characters are so true to life that they are susceptible to
routine Freudian analysis. Yet they are much more than that.
In time, perhaps, Clark will be cherished for his psychological
perceptions and his skill at creating characters, while his theme
of unity will be accepted as an undercurrent (and a vital one)
rather than as the surface significance.

   I have said earlier that the Western novel seems to lie within
the sphere of Jungian influence. However difficult it may be to
offer indisputable proof, there is certainly a tendency (seen
perhaps most strongly in Clark and in *The Track of the Cat*) to
avoid intellectual judgment and to engage in the experience of
the unconscious. Because Jung said that it was extremely difficult for the occidental to have this kind of experience, it has
often been assumed that at least some Western novels have
been influenced by oriental thought. (Waters, for one, has actively studied oriental philosophy.) Yet, the connection is not
obvious, and it is more likely that American Indian religion and
the special relationship which the westerner has with his land
have been the major influences. The westerner uses the word
primitive in relation to earth-based belief and behavior, and also
in terms of prehistory, the role of the collective unconscious,
and the importance of the connection between the
contemporary and the primal, the personal unconscious and
the ancient or prehistoric unconscious. The Freudian, on the

other hand, tends to equate primitive with infantile, indicating a linear development of the rationality of man. For the Jungian westerner, development is cyclical, with a "return journey" to origins an integral part of that development.

None of this is so obvious in *The Track of the Cat* that it endangers either characterization or narrative. Reference to Freud and Jung might even be unnecessary were it not for the dream sequences, and there is a strong possibility that the dreams were included precisely to draw attention to the Jungian attitudes underlying the narrative, for these dreams are not the kind to be studied for repressions and guilt complexes—they are projections, not signals of repression barriers. They are revelations of inner truths and realities; they point to inner and outer dangers and may even suggest the solutions. Therefore, a relationship exists between the individual's dreams and his waking state, or between his unconscious and conscious minds, or, to push it further, between his own unconscious experiences and those of archetypal figures from the dawn of time to the present. Curiously, these dreams are saturated with color imagery, the dominating colors being black and white (one of which is devoid of color, and the other a dense mixture of all colors), imagery which appears in almost all of Clark's writing but which is used more profusely in *The Track of the Cat*. The obvious symbolism of black and white is the religious one of evil and good, and it is this use of the image which is dominant in the hundreds of formula westerns. Although it is possible to make the same application to *Cat*, it is more likely that Clark is concerned with all dualities, not just one: good and evil, the sacred and the profane, intellect and intuition, lightness (enlightenment) and darkness (ignorance), and so on. He then implies the ultimate necessity of a fusion in each case. He does not bring the black and the white together, but he lets them stand in juxtaposition. The unconscious mind brings them together, just as the conscious mind (mistakenly) maintains their separation. (An interesting analogy may be seen in the inability of the piano—an achievement of the technical mind—to produce a blues note with one key. The note lies in the crack between two keys and both must be struck, simultaneously, to produce the note. This in turn brings to mind the poet who cannot find the exact metaphor or image he is looking for and, instead, uses two images in juxtaposition, with the real meaning lying, unseen, between them. Understanding comes through something other than the conscious intellect.)

Something similar must be done with the cat, because there is not just one cat but several: the real, tawny cat which has killed Bridges cattle, the black cat in the minds of Joe Sam and Curt, the cat fetishes carved by Arthur for Joe Sam (and himself?), and another black cat which is eternal, mysterious, and both similar to and different from the cat Joe Sam seeks and Curt runs from after his powers of reasoning have failed. Whatever other interpretations might be applied to this multiplicity of cats, or to the black one in particular, we know that "things" are not always as they appear to be—especially to the "rational" mind—and that the problem of the Bridges family is one which each of us encounters and tries to resolve more than once in our lives. We are dealing here with the eternal, with origins, with the primal, and with ourselves. The problem, however it is stated, will not go away under Freudian analysis.

In dealing with the primitive in its Jungian sense, Clark is aware of the more popular use of the term and, ironically, of the contemporary disappearance of what it represents in both senses. In a short story, "The Rapids" (1940), Clark tells of a city businessman who temporarily rebels against the restrictions and conventions of his life and seeks a brief respite in primitive activity, in outdoor physical adventure by a river. This is the best he can do. Our meaningful primitive tendencies are dying out; what we have left of them is relegated to the status of a game, a vacation in the wilderness. In another complaint, in *The City of Trembling Leaves*, Clark speaks of the method of *The Education of Henry Adams* (1918): "Why, all through the two great books, is there nothing about a mountain, a river, a tree, a flower, a bird, fish, snake, animal, star, unless they're in stained glass?" The objects and creatures of the natural world may certainly take their place in man's art, but direct experience with them enhances and clarifies our understanding of the unity of nature and of man's vital relationship to the harmonies, rhythms, and cycles of life. At least this much is necessary to the Western attitude.

VII
Harvey Fergusson and the Spanish Southwest

Labels are made to be broken, like promises, but if Walter Clark is to be called a psychological or archetypal or Jungian novelist (the terms themselves carrying a special interest), it may seem appropriate to find an equally exciting term or general description of Harvey Fergusson's approach to western materials. This is difficult to do because Fergusson appears to be a historical novelist, concentrating on the Spanish Southwest, avoiding myth and legend, and using conventional novelistic methods. Those critics who admire his work have been hard pressed to explain why Fergusson does not get the same attention given to Clark, Waters, Manfred, Fisher, Guthrie, Stegner, and Horgan. One easy explanation is that Fergusson seems to belong to an older generation, an earlier era. Even though he lived until 1971, his work was concentrated between 1921 and 1937, with two novels published in the 1950s. Whatever the reason for neglect may be, I am inclined to agree with Frank Waters's assessment that the critics do not know how to discuss Fergusson's novels because "he is too damn simple and profound." In his way, he is a rationalist, but unlike Vardis Fisher he does not allow autobiography to interfere with his views of the West. He condemns myth and

faithfully follows the truth of the western experience, both historically and spiritually. Yet his love of the land is as strong as
anyone's, and he is aware of the harmonies and rhythms of the
natural world and can write about them in a kind of poetry
while avoiding sentimentalism and false optimism. Above all
he believed that knowledge of the land is of prime importance
to a writer:

> I know that I couldn't write about people if I had never seen the
> land they lived on. I couldn't, for instance, write a book about
> people in Spain or England, two places I have never been. I
> would have to know the land. I think of the land as being basic.

Of his ten novels, two are set in Washington, D.C., where
he was a newspaper reporter for a time, three more between
New Mexico and New York, reflecting his residence in New
York City and frequent trips back to his native Southwest, and
five are set in New Mexico, the place of his birth and the place
he knew the best. Even though his last two novels (and possibly
his best) were written during his long stay in California, Fergusson's heart and mind were always tied most closely to New
Mexico. As historical novelist, he writes from what might be
called a limited personal experience in that some of his information (including incidents which he later used in his fiction)
came from his maternal grandfather's memoirs. Franz Huning
came from Germany to America in 1848, went to St. Louis, got
a job with a Santa Fe Trail freight caravan, and after reaching
New Mexico in 1850 remained there for the rest of his life. His
business in Albuquerque flourished, although he was less a
businessman than a trail-type merchant and adventurer. Several of his grandson's novels can be related to the influence or
the actual experiences of Huning. Beyond these family experiences, Fergusson acquired a broad view of the entire American West; his grasp of the total western experience exceeds
that of most of his contemporaries and lends special significance to his more particularized treatments of Anglo-Spanish
relations in New Mexico. (The western writer must have
some notion of the complete West, of course, not just his own
locale. The larger view is necessary even though the immedi-

ate story centers on a relatively small area. This may be why—for one example—Larry McMurtry among the younger writers usually labeled western does not seem to be a western writer, but Edward Abbey does. McMurtry's *Horseman, Pass By* [1961] and especially *The Last Picture Show* [1966] are provincial. They are case studies of isolated areas in Texas that seem to have no awareness of any country beyond them and no interest in history or traditions. The incidents could occur in any backward, crude, and dismal small town. Sex and bravado are the main ingredients, not *place*.)

Of his particular place, however, Fergusson knew the intimate details. He wandered and hunted in the mountain-desert wilderness, learning the ways of the land through personal experience and keen observation. In later years he severely criticized any western writer who did not know the facts about his region. I do not know precisely at what point in his life Fergusson achieved the objective point of view which he made his trademark (his friend Mencken may have had something to do with it), but he went through the more normal phase of naive romanticism concerning the land, the pioneers, and the past before he detached himself from the so-called romance of westering and looked with some skepticism at the characteristics attributed to the pioneer experience by writers of adventure and nostalgia. From worshiping the past he moved to a position from which he could look forward, or, as a realist, could deal with the "inescapable present." The transition can be seen in his novels, but not markedly—Fergusson was never overwhelmed by romanticism. What is more noticeable is the consistency of style and tone; the variations are slight. It is the consistency of attitude that maintains the style. From the first, Fergusson recognized that history—the past—had two parts. One is idealistic, stemming from our inability to know everything that happened, so that the writer selects those fragments which correspond with his own needs. To this extent the past is a dream. It is, however, also a reality which (whether we know it or not) influences the present. The result is a conflict between mythmaking and the desire for literal truth, and Fergusson, knowing that "reality forever eludes," nevertheless turned his back on mythmaking. The romantic impulse may still be seen in *Wolf Song* (1927), his second fully Western novel, but it is tempered satisfactorily by realistic characterization of mountain man, Indian, and Spaniard. In succeeding novels, the "hero" continues to lose his dominance and to be shaped by his natural and social environments. To Fergusson's credit, his increasing detachment from the dreams of the West, from the myths and the melodrama, did not decrease the intensity, the pace, or the rhythms of his style, a style perhaps best described as a happy union of exposition and poetry.

The historical period which is Fergusson's domain is that part of the nineteenth century which can be called the formative years of Anglo civilization in the Spanish Southwest, beginning with the mountain man in Taos and Santa Fe, continuing with increased trading and commerce by way of the Santa Fe Trail, the influx of settlers from the East, the building of the railroad, and finally the growth of cities and the breaking up of the Spanish land grants. While the Southwest Indians play a part in this overall story, Fergusson's major interest is in Anglo-Spanish relations. The novels are solidly based on the facts, images, and details of the land, but they are also structured around the domestic life of the Mexicans in what was later to be New Mexico, harboring an ever-growing number of white American Anglos, but maintaining an uneasy balance of power in the racial contact which provides theme and drama for most of Fergusson's work. The Southwest differs from other parts of the West because the Spanish were not subjugated as the Indians were. And so the confrontation between American and Mexican, between northerner and southerner, is not one-sided. At the present time, Spanish culture is still strong and in some parts of the Southwest is dominant. Therefore, compromise rather than conquest is central to Fergusson's novels, and social conflicts that are more subtle than conflicts of physical force provide much of the drama. Harvey Fergusson's fiction, then, if we are to apply a label in spite of ourselves, is sociohistorical.

2

Because five of Fergusson's novels of the Anglo-Spanish Southwest are all of a piece, it is not strange that three of them *(Wolf Song, In Those Days,* 1929, and *The Blood of the Conquerors,* 1921) were gathered together and published in one volume as *Followers of the Sun* in 1936, although Fergusson himself had not visualized the three novels as a trilogy while he was writing them. The stories, taken as a logical progression, cover almost one hundred years, from the mountain man's wilderness life to the decay of an old Spanish family in Albuquerque. The historical delineation of a broad and important era is excellent. Dramatic conflicts between individuals as well as groups are dealt with efficiently and dramatically, but underlying the entire trilogy is the confrontation between the Anglo-Americans of the North and the Mexicans or Spanish-Americans of the South. Fergusson felt that this conflict and its resolution (such as that resolution was), producing a unique culture, was one of two consistent factors in our national past—the other being the westward movement in its entirety.

Wolf Song invites comparison with Guthrie's *Big Sky* and Manfred's *Lord Grizzly,* these three novels being the best fictional treatment of the mountain men. Guthrie is probably the most realistic about his subject in the area of details and action, Manfred the most romantic in that he retains the mythical quality of the Hugh Glass story and becomes almost excessive in language and rhythms, and Fergusson is the most lyrical and evocative even while getting at the ironies of the mountain man's condition more successfully. Although general distinctions can be misleading, I would at least suggest that *Wolf Song* is essence, *The Big Sky* is drama, and *Lord Grizzly* is legend. However, Fergusson is not above melodrama in his early work. *Wolf Song* opens with "Up from the edge of the prairie and over the range rode three." The tone is that of hundreds of opening sentences among the popular western novels of the day. It is repeated halfway through the novel: "Three squatted on their heels in the plaza and held pow-wow." The romanticism surrounding the popular image of the mountain man is used as a

tonal frame, quite deliberately, and much of the narrative concerns a romance between mountain man Sam Lash and Spanish aristocrat Lola Salazar; but the texture is clean and inci-
sively evocative, the factual details are brief and significant,
and the dilemma of Sam Lash is presented both sympathetically and ironically.

The story is that of a mountain man being tamed by a woman and by civilized traditions even though his heart lies in the
wilderness. Informal narrative—much of it summary—and description take precedence over detailed scene, with the first two
chapters serving as perhaps the best available summary of the
life and land of the mountain man. (This section has been reprinted as a short story, much to Fergusson's dismay, but the
temptation to lift it from the novel is understandable.) Distances in this land are broad enough to make even a wide-
traveling mountain man feel as though he "moved against a
space too great to conquer," so that particular places of rendezvous, like the Taos of *Wolf Song*, become oases even though
they also prove confining to the restless trappers. Because of
the special characteristics of the mountain man, an established
town or village provides the opportunity to set up conflicting
feelings and values and to squeeze drama from them, as Fergusson does. First, of course, the town is a place of pleasure:

> Taos was a place where Indians and Mexicans had lived
> since God knows when . . . a place where corn grew and
> women lived.
>
> Soon or late every man in the mountains came to Taos.
> They came to it from as far north as the Red and as far south as
> the Gila. They came to it like buffalo to a salt lick across thou-
> sands of dangerous miles. Taos whiskey and Taos women were
> known and talked about on every beaver stream in the Rockies.
> More than any other place Taos was the heart of the mountains.
>
> When they saw Taos they rose in their stirrups and let a yell.

It is also a place of contradictions: dust and music, sweat and
wine, sensuousness and squalor, laziness and violence, friendliness and hostility. The contradictions of the place parallel the
conflict in Sam Lash once he has fallen in love with a Spanish

woman who threatens his equally strong love of the wilderness. Although the mountain men are portrayed as
conquerors, "gathering wealth [in] a country soft and fat where
nothing stood against their hard-bitten hazard-loving
strength," they do not really conquer the Spanish as they have
conquered the Indians. Sam Lash, "a man nourished on wildness," cannot fully penetrate the old Spanish civilities and customs and must at last choose between the woman and the wilderness. The strength which is pitted against him is not that of
the woman alone (she rides away with him willingly) but also
the force of the Catholic church and the traditions of the Salazar family. Having taken Lola to Bent's Fort, farther north, he
goes back into the wilderness with a party of trappers, expect-
ing her to wait for him. While he is gone, the girl's family takes
her back to Taos. Eventually he too returns to Taos, eager to
marry the girl, and discovers that he must join the church in
order to do so. While discussing this problem with the padre,
Sam remembers everything that he has always disliked about
church, since he was a boy, but images of the girl crowd into
his mind as well: "All of these things were church. . . . And
her breasts were white and round and once incredibly a long
time ago they had pillowed him." Earlier he had tried to shake
off the desire for Lola by riding away from Fort Bent, putting
miles between him and the witch-woman:

> The country took him back to itself seizing him by every
> sense. Wind heavy with earth smell washed the memory of her
> hair out of his nose and the steady beat of hoof on sod soothed
> away the sting of the curses.

The church frightens him with its airlessness, darkness, and its
life-sized wooden Christ painted with blood and crowned with
thorns. The padre urges him to give in; it is his knees that do so,
and he closes his eyes to the wooden Christ which then changes
in his imagination to the soft body of a woman. The scene of
capitulation is almost humorous in its irony.

> The image of his desire ousted Christ from his cross and walked
> smiling to meet him.
> He got to his feet in a daze and met the padre's look with a

smile of bewildered peace. The padre seized his hand, looked
long into his eyes—then with a sudden grip almost crushed his
fingers.

"My son, my son!" His suavity was gone. His voice almost
broke. "You have come to your God!"

Marriage brings with it a huge land grant as dowry from the
Salazars, and it would appear on the surface that Sam Lash is
far better off than he was in the wilderness and that from the
point of view of his trapper friends he has simply sold out. To
Fergusson's credit, again, he keeps the dramatic conflict
plausible. Of the three mountain men who rode into Taos to
drink whiskey and have fun, only Old Rube wants to leave early,
accusing Sam and Gullion of going soft—a "woman-loving
softness." This is, clearly, the beginning of Sam's compromise,
but what is important to remember is that the compromise is
probably more realistic and true than the absolute refusal to
leave the wilderness, a refusal which has been a part of so many
western novels that it has taken on the aspect of myth.

Wolf Song is, in effect, a pair of love stories—man in love
with the land, and man in love with a woman. It involves a
choice which is not really a choice but a human necessity, an
act of the body over the spirit, an act which removes Sam from
the legendary or stereotyped company of heroes and makes
him mortal. The suggestion seems to be that life in the wilderness is deceptive, that it is less than the myths of the West
would have it be, and that Fergusson is looking at these myths
with a skeptical eye and dismissing them from his more objective viewpoint. Even the two chapters in which Black Wolf appears point in this direction, but with the subtle complications
which are almost a trademark of Fergusson's fiction. Black
Wolf, a member of the Southern Cheyenne tribe, is
twenty-one and is going on the warpath alone for the first time.
To please the father of the girl he wishes to marry, he must return with many horses. He is determined to have love and
power or to die. There are no other alternatives, and he is
therefore distinguished from Sam who is given power and love
without having to think of death as an alternate solution. Per-

haps this makes Sam Lash less noble than the Indian, but it also makes him more human within a non-Indian context. Black Wolf is primitive and he is superstitious. Fergusson deals with him briefly and explosively in contrast to the slower and more detailed treatment of the Spanish, and we understand that on the more general level of western expansion the same kind of distinction holds true. That is, the white man was able to subjugate (almost annihilate) the primitive Indians but he could not, or would not, do the same to the Spanish with their more highly developed civilized ways and their long European traditions. The Anglos and the Spanish join forces, even though the union is tenuous even at the present time. And as much appeal as the wilderness may have, or once had, it is a dead end; change is inevitable and the merging of cultures is inevitable. In this respect, Fergusson is a realist in attitude in spite of some romantic plotting and a few faulty notions about women. He knows the land and its history, and he rides with change, if not as compromise (as in the case of Sam Lash), then as acceptance. He is not guilty of nostalgia. Nor does he allow Sam to show any remorse after he has killed Black Wolf: "Weak he stood, but proud, alone and little but sufficient to his fate—a blood-stained atom of unconquerable life." The tone is somewhat melodramatic until, again, the irony becomes visible. The "conquering hero" returns to Taos, "dirty and half starved, his buckskin stained with blood," and finds peace in the house of the padre who is trying to bring him into the church he dislikes. The house is "rooted in permanence," and Sam, without realizing it, is being prepared for his capitulation to the demands of the padre and the Salazars. The Black Wolf episode has served several purposes just as the occasional romanticism and melodrama in *Wolf Song* serve the cause of truth through irony.

Two things, then, are particularly refreshing and significant in *Wolf Song*, aside from the portrayal of an important time and place in American history. The first is the subtle complexity which underlies what seems to be nothing more than a simple love story, a story with the right ingredients for a popular motion picture starring Gary Cooper and Lupe Velez. The second is a style which is unobtrusively rhythmic and poetic, with simple but effective images, nothing startling or particularly quaint, just a quiet gracefulness and frankness.

In Those Days, longer and covering a half-century of New Mexican history, is of necessity structured differently (more loosely or episodically) and perhaps suffers a little from expository methods, but it is nevertheless a striking portrait of the changes brought about by commerce, the railroad, and the automobile in the Anglo-Spanish Southwest. Of the four parts into which the novel is divided ("Wagons," "Indians," "Railroad," and "Gas") two begin with the title phrase, "In those days," and the third with "Those were the days," as though announcing a nostalgia which is not really there. (Missing, of course, are the words "good old," and Fergusson does not want them, even by implication, except as they become an expression of the people he is writing about—"Once more the good old days were gone"—and even then one senses Fergusson's own attitude of ironic amusement in "Once more.") It is difficult to say which he criticized more frequently in the writers of his day, their use of easy myth or their tone of nostalgia—if the two can be separated at all. His own intention was always to tell the truth about the West, and if he indulged occasionally in romantic melodrama it was either a beginner's mistake (which he admitted) or a foil for the play of irony. In any case, "In those days" is a simple statement of fact, and the sentence goes on to identify the time as just following the Civil War. Fergusson gets through a half-century panorama in a relatively short time because of the judicious use of summary narrative and detailed scenes. Much information is picked up through flashbacks, memories of what had gone before: the narrative movement is first slow and then fast, as detailed scenes, exposition of manners and customs, summaries of historical periods are frequently broken up by a backward look at what happened in between times. The advantage of this method is that the so-called looking back is done through the character's memory which picks up only those details which remain important at a later time. The novel is like a mosaic, appearing to stand still part of the time, to remain fixed, and yet the pieces of action move the narrative forward as inexorably as history itself moves.

In order to treat effectively a historical period of fifty years in a relatively short novel, it is not only necessary to make use of exposition and summary narrative but it is extremely important to create immediacy whenever possible through imagery that brings specific feelings into the general flow of action.

> Many a night Robert Jayson lay between wagon wheels, wrapped in scanty blankets, listening to wind in the grass or to the cold steady voice of spring rain and thinking miserably.
>
> Often he lay thinking until wheel spokes barred a paling dawn sky.

Time progresses with "Many" in the first paragraph and "Often" in the second, and yet we are stopped to listen to the wind blowing through the grasses, to hear the voice of rain, to feel the cold, to sense the misery of Jayson. The visual image, joining the aural, reinforces the sensory reality of a given moment, even though within these two short paragraphs there are in effect many such moments marking the passing of time. Similarly, in point of view, the limited omniscience allows a broad portrait of the area and of a span of time while maintaining a more specific focus on Robert Jayson, a newcomer to the West who must learn his way around, must adjust to the conditions of the land and the Spanish people, and who is called "old man Jayson" by the end of the novel, an old codger who was there before the railroad came through. Fergusson is extremely good at covering ground, so to speak, without being cumbersome.

Robert regrets, at first, that he has left his beloved Elizabeth in the East. Like so many men in the West he drags "a load of memory and regret as heavy as a wagon." His past is painful and his future leaves him in despair, a more realistic attitude than the mythical one which promises immediate success in a new land. But he grows accustomed to the land, giving in to the old-timers' advice to get himself a "sleeping dictionary" in order to learn the Spanish language, and through a mistake acquiring a strong friend in Diego who gets him into Don Aragon's house and Spanish society. Soon he feels alien to himself, having done things which leave him full of shame and remorse, although by the newly discovered standards in his new land they also make him feel full of life. By the time he has made a trading trip to the land of the Apaches and returned safely in spite of terrible weather and other obstacles, he feels that he belongs in the Southwest. Although the woman he admired in town married someone else while he was gone, he makes love to her just before he opens the mail and (in a second irony) finds a letter from Elizabeth. The letter is a strong link to the past, and although the plot becomes slightly superficial (Robert brings Elizabeth to the West, she is captured by Indians and never seen again, while Robert goes on to relationships with other women) the point is well made that the West is not the Garden of Eden, it does not solve all problems, and regret and longing for one's own past are a natural part of moving into the future. To offset the loss of Elizabeth, a curiously ambiguous passage purports to give the point of view of the Indians who took her:

> In those days a world was being destroyed—an old and savage world, rich in Gods and rituals, a world of cruel happy children living in a fairyland of imagined monsters. . . . A wild and beautiful world was being destroyed.

The passage is interesting—and unusual—because it juxtaposes the arguments made in defense of the primitive life of the Indian with the arguments made in support of eliminating this life. There is sympathy in "a world was being destroyed," "old," "rich," the capital *G* in "Gods," "happy," and "beautiful." But there is condemnation in "savage," "cruel," and perhaps even, in a strange way, in "fairyland of imagined monsters." The passage is one of the most tantalizing I have read anywhere in Western literature. It is followed by a brief but vivid description of the actions of the Indians in defense of their land, the torturing of white people appearing as justice as well as horror.

The section in which Indians participate in the action is

short, as it was in *Wolf Song*, and Fergusson, having made his statement about them, hurries back to the Anglo-Spanish world with which he is more familiar. In some ways, however, the brevity of the Indian episodes brings forth sharp insights, whereas the longer examination into the history and manners of Spanish culture, and the confrontation of Mexican and Anglo, can at times be detrimental to plot and characterization. As the new town of the whites rises next to the old town of the Spanish, Robert Jayson is rich from silver discovered by an old prospector whom he helped stake, and his position in the community is now governed by social rules, many of them adopted from the old Spanish families. People move in and out of Robert's life, minor characters who are colorful and well drawn but relatively unimportant, and major characters who are real but not very memorable. It is the time that is most important, coupled with the place, and the entire West seems to be living out an era and getting ready to embark upon a new one, so that Taos, Santa Fe, and Albuquerque take on a symbolic significance. The old leisurely life of the Spanish, like the freedom of the Indians, is being replaced by "the sting of moneylust." A man is weakened by thoughts of the past, by "soft reminiscent sensuality, mixed with regret and longing." Robert's marriage to the daughter of his landlady, a girl he had watched grow up and had sent to school, is not only a culmination of his love for her, but is also a shoring up against old age and change. "The world he had lived in was dying all around him and it became his duty to bury the dead." Respect for the land is gone, the old Mexican families have lost their fortunes ("Mexicans . . . no good at business"), and the growing town has no adventures for the old-timers. When his wife dies of cancer, Robert reflects once again upon Elizabeth as he might reflect upon the Old West; they were both a dream except for "one burning moment" of realization, and yet in them he had discovered something of himself. The discovery is not explained, nor does it need to be stated in terms other than those which apply to the entire experience of the West—adventure, dreams, the creation of a destiny, the expansion of horizons, and the necessity and pain of change. As though he were aware of the cyclical nature of all life and had escaped from the linear view of the non-landed intellectual, Robert is unafraid of death because he has lived.

The tragedy of change is not so much his, however, as it is the Mexicans'. Fergusson's first novel, appearing as the third in the trilogy, follows the decay of traditional Spanish life after the influx into the Southwest of the new high-powered methods of commerce. The Dons are replaced by the modern businessmen. Thematically, then, Fergusson is doing for the Spanish aristocracy in the Southwest what Faulkner did for the plantation owners of the South whose way of life was changed by industrialism. Fergusson does not give his own approval to change, because he recognizes that change does not necessarily mean progress or improvement, but he accepts change as inevitable, with no obvious regrets. His characters, however, find it difficult to arrive at a compromise between the old and the new, the mythical and the real, the individual self-reliance and a dependence upon society. The primary function of the new way of life seems to be that of acquiring wealth, and the man who has lived with a different value system is lost in the world of money. Morgan Riley, in a later novel, *The Life of Riley* (1937), returns to his New Mexico home after World War I to take over his father's saloon but finds that he cannot make a successful business with his father's now outmoded methods, yet is reluctant to change because the mere act of making money is foreign to him. Even after he manages to compromise his principals (if they be such) a few times, he is ultimately a failure. Whether Ramon Delcasar of *Blood of the Conquerors* is the same kind of failure may be a matter of opinion; the final impression of him is couched in terms of retreat to the past, and although his action seems to be one of defeat, or inability to adjust to change, it is not altogether impossible to believe that the past of Ramon is in some ways better than the present of the growing Anglo society around him. Fergusson, as usual, does not take sides. He chronicles the changes, accepts them, but does not pass judgment on the people whose values come from the past

unless they are utterly false values, romanticized and sentimentalized and used entirely for escape from reality. The line
between the struggle to retain old values and the inability to accept new ones is often thin. This means that the tone of Fergusson's fiction is of utmost importance and must be handled with
great skill, avoiding sentimentality and the expression of regret
for a lost past but also resisting the temptations of cynicism and
satire. Fergusson accomplishes his purpose as a sympathetic
realist by maintaining a dispassionate attitude most of the time,
with occasional—and apparently deliberate—lapses into either
the romantic or the cynical responses to his material.

Because *The Blood of the Conquerors* is Fergusson's first novel,
and because it takes place in the Albuquerque where he grew
up—in the early part of this century—it has more personal
opinion of the region and the types of people who inhabit it,
and more information about Spanish traditions and such local
phenomena as the penitentes, than his other novels. In almost
every way it is an informative novel, a re-creation of time and
place, with a love story and a plot involving land deals and
values to hold it together. Ramon, although probably not an
archetypal figure, is representative or typical of the young
Mexican who tries to shore up the fortunes of his family in the
face of continued threats from the new Yankee commercialism.
Tied to the old Spanish values, attempting to survive through
the new methods of acquiring money (as opposed to merely
having it), he becomes a man trapped between two systems, belonging to neither. His solution is to withdraw from the conflict, selling the family land in order to buy an old adobe house
away from the town, a sheltered place in which he can settle
down to a leisurely life of contemplation and dreams.

The Southwest at the turn of the century is appropriate to
the theme because it remained unchanged longer than did New
York, New England, and the Middle West. Not until the railroad reached Albuquerque did the new town spring up near
the old Spanish town.

> It was ugly, noisy and raw. It was populated largely by real
> estate agents, lawyers, politicians and barkeepers. It cared little

for joy, leisure, beauty or tradition. Its God was money and its occupation was business.

Implicit in the tone of this description of the new town is a condemnation of the arrival of a way of life which destroys such things as joy and tradition, but Fergusson's handling of the limited-omniscience point of view is so skillful that he can rarely be accused of inserting his own opinions into the narrative. Rather, as here, it is the opinion of a character or group of characters—in this case the Delcasars and the other Dons. It is not true, however, that Fergusson lacked feeling for the situation, for the displacement of leisure and beauty by ugliness and noise, for the apparent destruction of the civilized Spanish way of life; he was simply aware of the inevitability of change, and whether something akin to progress was the result of each change could not matter to the realist. Furthermore, even at a time when only the destruction was visible, Fergusson was able to keep in mind the new development which would follow in due time. As a southwesterner he could quietly lament the changes, but from his broader viewpoint as thinker and artist he saw the movement of history as a fact as well as a challenge and an adventure. Not at all inconsistent with this view, I think, is his idea of the land as a base of belief, a permanence in the midst of change. It may be true that an individual person is incomplete without social interaction, that a life alone on the land is not enough, perhaps even crippling. Yet, without the land there is nothing but artificiality and pseudointellectualism. Typical of Fergusson's images used symbolically is the union of land and woman in the mind of the chief male character. In *Blood of the Conquerors*, Ramon Delcasar is the first of his family to "face life with his bare hands," and the last to battle against the gringos. Living no longer in a solidified Spanish society but mingling with Jews and gringos, he falls in love with Julia Roth, an eastern girl who bears a Jewish name but is not identified as Jewish. At the same time he is involved in business deals foreign to his background and life style. The only peace he finds is out on the open plains, away

from the city, and here the earth and sky combine with
thoughts of the woman and eventually with her presence:

> At the crest of a rise he stopped the car and stood up, looking
> all about at the vast quiet wilderness, filling his lungs with air.
> He liked that serene emptiness. He had always felt at peace with
> these still desolate lands that had been the background of most
> of his life. Now, with the consciousness of the woman beside
> him, they filled him with a sort of rapture, an ecstasy of rever-
> ence that had come down to him perhaps from savage forebears
> who had worshipped the Earth Mother with love and
> awe.

It is easy to attribute these feelings to Delcasar alone, and just
as easy to see in them the romantic response of a young writer
who is still so enamored of his land that he cannot yet find the
detachment of his later and more mature work. It by no means
discredits Fergusson to insist that he was indeed close to the
earth and that he too struggled with the duality of primitivism
and civilization, of earth and the world of men. "Each of them
in turn filled his mind with images and emotions." This
thought comes from within the point of view of Ramon, but it
is certainly not contrary to Fergusson's own thinking or artistic
methods—his images throughout his work are taken from both
sides of the coin. Where he differs from his characters is in the
disposition of the duality; he allows each part of it to have its
proper place, whereas many of his characters, like Ramon, attempt to judge between them, to make a firm choice, and, unable to do so, feel impotent.

Ramon's problem is that in the face of the new kind of
society which is overtaking him, he seems primitive. As primitive man, he enjoys "sensuous indolence," has also the "capacity for brief but violent action, quickened by the "vast and
barren land," and, in spite of his intelligence, he is superstitious. For him, fortune is a deliberate force in the affairs of all
men, and when he runs afoul of bad luck his depression robs
him of the intelligence which might show him a course of action. He does not make love to Julia until after she has married

and moved to New York. Although the ten days he spends with her are considerably more than satisfactory, they must end when her husband returns from a trip. The stay in New York has exhausted his funds, he comes home to a severe drought, and although he has urged all Mexicans to refuse to sell their lands to the gringos, he now sells his. As he retires to a kind of re-creation of his past, he cannot even become interested in Julia's last letter to him. Ironically, she is dissatisfied with her life but can do nothing about it, while Ramon finds a measure of satisfaction in not doing anything.

3

The trilogy, as assembled, is an impressive piece of work despite its occasional Germanic inverted constructions and haphazard piecing together of narrative sections, and notwithstanding its tendencies toward exposition when the author attempts to characterize the time and place in relation to a broader context. None of these minor lapses is disturbing, and the trilogy remains one of the major works of Western American fiction.

Only two other Fergusson novels appeared during the twenty-one years between the trilogy and his next panoramic novel. *Footloose McGarnigal* (1930) stresses the differences between the sentimentalized West and the real West as a young man who has heard tales of the wilderness from his New York great-uncle uses his inheritance to seek in the West the same kind of adventure he has been told about. Needless to say, he finds that the stories were not true and eventually he follows a girl back to New York. *The Life of Riley* deals with sentimentality in a somewhat different way, but the result is the same— failure to measure up to the realistic routine of life in a region which still suffers from its mythical image. By 1950, with the publication of *Grant of Kingdom* (followed by *The Conquest of Don Pedro* in 1954, his last novel), Fergusson had matured into an exceptionally good novelist, not changing his locales or his themes but handling them with impeccable craftsmanship. As with his previous novels, much of the material comes from his personal experience with the land and the Spanish people, but now he has it well under control. Only three or four Western novels might be called better in some way than *Grant of Kingdom* and *The Conquest of Don Pedro*.

Irwin Blacker's edited collection, *The Old West in Fiction* (1961), includes short stories and a few excerpts from novels by such writers as Guthrie, Clark, Steinbeck, Conrad Richter, H. L. Davis, Stephen Crane, Jack London. What seems surprising at first is that Blacker also includes *Grant of Kingdom* in its entirety, certainly a recognition of the quiet genius of Harvey Fergusson. In his brief introduction to the novel, Blacker says that "probably no novel covers the whole wide sweep of Western history better than does *Grant of Kingdom*, and few novels have been written about the West by men who have known it better than Harvey Fergusson. . . . [who] has told not only of those who possessed the land and those who wanted it, but also of the land itself." I mention this tribute only because such praise and consideration were relatively rare during Fergusson's lifetime, and those writers who are beginning to evaluate his place in Western (and American) letters wonder why he was neglected for so long. To use the vernacular, no one could get a handle on him. At his best, in the last two novels and possibly in *Wolf Song*, he handled style, structure, imagery, tone, and symbolism so quietly, simply, and capably that his virtues were hidden in his craftsmanship. There was nothing eccentric or startling or faddish for the critics and reviewers to pull out and examine.

Grant of Kingdom is a formal novel, divided into four parts: "The Conqueror," with Jean Ballard, who might be an extension of Sam Lash from *Wolf Song*; "The Autocrat," whose James Lane Morgan may speak for the author and who returns to narrate an epilogue; "The Usurpers," with Major Arnold Newton Blore; and "The Prophet," with Daniel Laird at the center of attention. In his foreword to the novel, Fergusson addresses himself to three of these characters in addition to a

gunfighter employed by Major Blore: "Here were the benevolent autocrat creating order, the power-hungry egoist destroying it, the warrior tragically bound to his weapon, the idealist
always in conflict with an irrational world." Jean Ballard is not
referred to here, but it is certain that he is the one Fergusson
felt closest to. In the epilogue, Consuelo Coronel Ballard tells
Morgan, "He was a great man. No one else could ever take his
place. It was never the same after he died." And Morgan, after
making other inquiries, agrees that Ballard's widow has told
the truth. This may be as close as Fergusson ever comes to
nostalgia, to regret that men such as Ballard no longer live, and
yet the effect of these statements is on character, not on tone.
Ballard is also given a special place early in the novel, in the
scene which results in his attraction for Consuelo. Fergusson
spoke of this scene late in his life, when memory for many other
things had dimmed, and indicated that it was the kind of scene
he always tried to write, not always succeeding. Because his
comments dwell upon method, they are worth quoting in full:

> I don't know exactly where the characters come from, and
> that's the truth. There is quite a mystery to the working of the
> imagination, but imagination is, in the very nature of the word,
> a making of images. The central unit of composition is not the
> word but the image. This is something I have long thought
> without ever quite formulating it.
>
> The opening scenes of *Grant of Kingdom*, where the women
> are bathing in the hot springs, is a procession of images. I was
> not in Hot Springs, but I did see a woman do this act (showing
> him all she had) in a beautiful, clear-running stream in Mexico.
> The women didn't swim, they just bathed in those long white
> gowns. One of the women made this sweeping gesture with her
> robe. Maybe it was accidental. Maybe she was about to lose it in
> the rushing water. But she did it. The woman in the opening
> scene of my book never says a word, but there are three images
> of her. In the first place, when she smiled at the man, she looked
> at him for a while, seemed to decide that he was the man, and
> then smiled at him. And the third image was this gesture of the
> robe. It was directed at the man too. And although she never
> said a word, you knew what she was thinking. Everything about

her was a procession of images. And these certainly are the essentials of composition. There is always movement. It is perfectly futile to describe a person as being about five feet ten inches with red hair and so forth. You've got to show him making
a gesture of some kind. A moving image is really the unit, and
the image always moving to a tune. I think it is just as true of
poetry as it is of prose, and to me there is no dividing line between them. My feelings of poetry are in my novels. They are
all poems to me.

It is the "procession of images" which was important to Fergusson, which at least partly explains why structure in his novels is usually less organic than it is formal, expository, or
merely natural in the sense of obvious divisions according to
time sequences, changes of place, or changes in point of view
(meaning only a shift of attention from one character to
another). Indeed, *Grant of Kingdom* may not be as poetic as *The
Conquest of Don Pedro* simply because it takes in a broader span
of time and place, telescoping time through the use (once again)
of summary narrative, placing somewhat less emphasis on the
spiritual reactions of man to the land. *Don Pedro,* on the other
hand, is more carefully limited to one protagonist, one specific
situation, and a narrower chronology, allowing for a more sensitive and imagistic treatment of the relation between the chief
character and the evocatory aspects of the land. Fergusson's
normal method, then, is to alternate between the panoramic
and the detailed scene, between the larger view and the
smaller, always keeping his characters and images enclosed
within a framework of the history of the West, and letting the
action proceed according to the procession of images.

Jean Ballard of *Grant of Kingdom* may be seen as an extension
of Sam Lash from *Wolf Song*—it is not unusual for Fergusson to
go over the same kind of material several times. As a mountain
man, with a family background from Virginia and Kentucky,
Ballard has good instincts, a fondness for women, and experience in trapping, leading wagon trains, and trading with Indians. In Taos he falls in love with Consuelo Coronel and runs
into those obstacles erected by established Spanish families to

keep out the gringos. Persisting, he is able to make love to Consuelo in a rare moment of privacy, after which she tells him to
return to Taos in three months. Not knowing why he should
do so, Ballard waits out the specified time, during which interlude Fergusson pauses also to explain Mexican customs and
manners. (In one sense he might well be called a novelist of
manners, although his brevity distinguishes him from nineteenth-century English novelists.) When Ballard is called to
meet with the abogado representing the Coronel family, he discovers that Consuelo is pregnant and that he will therefore be
taken into the family. What could be melodrama is handled
with a sophistication that contrasts with the raw enthusiasm of
the somewhat similar circumstances in *Wolf Song*. As a dowry,
Ballard is given a huge land grant (known in later times as the
Maxwell Land Grant, lying between Taos and Cimmaron in
New Mexico, and subject to extensive litigations). The land
has been unused because of habitation by the Indians, because
(as Fergusson generalizes) the Mexicans do not like mountains,
and because Don Coronel dislikes anything new and unfamiliar. Ballard, however, has the gringo-American characteristics
of restlessness, curiosity, and the "need of action and conquest," and is delighted to get the land. Going immediately
into the mountains, he meets with the Utes, negotiates with
them, and, in one of the common ironies of the West, the Indians become Ballard's wards in exchange for a limited freedom.
Since the world of the Indian is dying in the midst of a wave of
change in the Southwest, the Utes feel that the best they can do
is have the protection of a man from the "new" world. Ballard,
in turn, feels a sense of power, which he enjoys, but he does not
recognize that change continues and that one day his own
world will die.

Part two of the novel—"The Recollections of James Lane
Morgan"—is narrated in the first person, an extremely rare occurrence in Fergusson's work. The device works well, however, in getting at Ballard from the vantage point of an observer
who can be somewhat objective, and also in giving Fergusson a
chance to comment on the action and characters without the

distance of omniscience. Since Morgan is a lawyer, we appreciate the detachment and fairness of his observations, and yet because he tells of his experiences from a personal point of view he can express himself emotionally, sometimes with exaggeration, to catch an immediacy that is often found only in strong feelings. Morgan arrives in New Mexico in 1878, having come west to alleviate his tuberculosis as well as to apply for a job with Ballard. At this time Ballard has been in his big house for almost twenty years, is about fifty-four, and is ill and threatened with bankruptcy. As Morgan gradually learns the history of the Southwest, of New Mexico, of land grants, the reader is exposed once again to material found in other Fergusson novels. And, again, times are changing, so that now Morgan is excited about *his* possible opportunities in a world different from that in which Ballard established his power. Part of Ballard's problem is that he remains true to the older style of life, refusing to break promises he has made to the Utes and the Mexicans. Over the years he has been consumed with power but has also remained faithful to the people entrusted to his care, the one exception perhaps being his wife who has been neglected— not quite sacrificed to the building of an empire. She can forgive him because of her deep understanding of the times and the society in which they live. As Morgan also becomes part of this country, grows healthier, and enjoys the "rare combination of society and solitude" in which he lives, he recognizes the changes which are imminent in the new world of money, mortgages, and fences, this world represented by Major Arnold Blore, agent for a Denver syndicate which wishes to purchase the land grant. As Ballard dies, his power goes over to Blore.

That portion of the novel which is ostensibly given to Blore and his own pursuit of further power is in reality a miniature of the building of the West in the second half of the nineteenth century. A variety of characters emerge as Blore's company builds a town and establishes a conflict with those ranchers who feel they are on free land and do not need to buy from the company. Through legal maneuvers, the company has extended the boundaries of the original land grant, thirsting for more power, more money, more control over the old-timers who had either lived under Ballard's protection or had been considered independent ranchers outside the limits of the grant. A philosophical conflict is also implied in the contrast between the older Spanish society of patronage, with peons subjugated to ricos but accepting their status with traditional stoicism and a strange kind of understanding, and the new gringo society offering the appearance of democratic opportunity but creating another kind of subjugation through the power of money and the legal loopholes of land transactions. On the surface the differences may appear to be slight. There are those with money and power, and there are those without. However, the class distinctions of Spanish society were understood and more or less accepted, with the church offering consolation to the poor, while the newer Anglo society was presumably founded upon the principle of equal opportunity for all but was in fact based upon greed. It is not easy to say that one system is better than the other in the context of the moment of confrontation between the two. Yet the myths of equal opportunity, of free land, of something for all in a land of unlimited wealth must certainly be disposed of in the face of the overpowering greed which played an important part in the settling of the American West.

Blore tasted power as a Confederate officer in the Civil War and eventually went to St. Louis—the funnel to the West—with the idea of maintaining that power. In a place and time of "easy come and easy go" money, Blore hangs onto his tightly and becomes a respectable gentleman even as he turns into a schemer, a student of land grants determined to gain control over the Ballard property. That he succeeds is no surprise. Nor are the details of his methods different, except in scope, from those surrounding the establishment of many western towns. A madam is imported from Dodge City to manage the hotel, and a gunfighter (ex-peace officer, also from Dodge) is brought in to enforce the regulations of the company. Betty Weiss and Clay Tighe are much like their counterparts in hundreds of western novels, and in their characterizations it is soon evident that Fergusson has assembled most of the major types of the late nineteenth-century West—the free rancher of the prerailroad or prefence era, Mexicans and Indians in various roles, the power-hungry businessman, the prostitute who does well financially and then wants a decent life, and the gunman who does not like the false morality of his job but remains faithful to his employer. All of them know the end is in sight, and all seem to be playing roles; but they are treated with such dignity by the author that they become real people, explained carefully and accurately in the historical context which lends authenticity to the representations and allows for sufficient documentation of personal idiosyncracies. Historical background is presented briefly enough so that it does not interfere with the dramatic action. Curiously, Tighe's story is told more closely to his own point of view, and with more immediacy, than the stories of Ballard, Blore, and Betty Weiss, as though Fergusson is particularly anxious to overcome the stereotyping of the gunman, to get behind the myth. Tighe is forced into killing, against his will, by circumstances and by his professionalism. His portrait is dangerously close to the standard characterization of the western gunfighter, and because of our familiarity with this type of person from the popular western novels we are not likely to feel that Fergusson has made an original contribution at this point. While this portion of *Grant of Kingdom* may be the weakest in that respect, it is nevertheless a remarkably succinct summary of a phenomenon which was of the utmost importance in the expansion of the American West.

Daniel Laird, the prophet in part four, does not come through as an idealist nearly as well as Davies in Clark's *The Ox-Bow Incident*, despite James Morgan's assessment in the epilogue: "Daniel Laird was the most enigmatic of the four who had exercised some kind of power in the Dark River Valley," a man who "had never found the means of his own development, but had nevertheless evolved his own set of values and remained faithful to it." Laird is then seen as a typical idealist whose only victory was a moral one—refusing to compromise. In his own right he is an interesting figure although he too represents one aspect of the frontier. Son of a Tennessee woodsman, exposed to camp meetings—revival meetings at which emotions rise to a pitch and are satisfied largely through sexual release—Daniel indulges in alcohol and a woman at one of these meetings, awakens the next morning strangely purified of the experience, and heads west. As Ballard's chief builder he enjoys status and a measure of power, but he also preaches on occasion and fiddles at dances, so that he achieves importance among the lower classes of people as well. Full of personal conflicts, attracted to Betty Weiss, he is accused of playing a part in the deaths of the two men killed by Tighe and flees to the mountains. At peace for the moment, he decides to be a mountain man and live alone; but he has loved Betty Weiss and begins to think about her, first with desire, then with resentment. Unable to endure the solitude of the mountains, he descends to a village, surviving a snowstorm and feeling that he can conquer his problems. The two weeks in isolation have made him less angry, more detached, yet wild-looking, a fugitive needing human company again. To his amazement and disappointment (he does not want to be singled out for special attention) he is greeted enthusiastically by the Mexican women and hailed as a messiah. After helping the people of the village by hunting for food (they have no guns) and becoming a friend of the Alcalde who considers him a fellow outlaw, Laird decides to turn himself in to the Taos deputy sheriff. He finds out that he is not wanted for any crime but that Betty Weiss has been looking for him. She has left Blore. She and Laird find what they are seeking in each other.

The actual plotting is simple. But *Grant of Kingdom* is really the story of the land grant and its influence upon a number of people; the grant shapes their destinies, whether for good or for evil. The land is therefore a character also, but passive in a strange way, and it is how men react to it that makes the drama and reveals the human personalities, the desires, the strengths, and the weaknesses. The epilogue of the novel brings James Morgan back to the Taos area in 1906. Of the participants in the land grant development, only Daniel Laird and his wife

Betty are still living, "both of them . . . rebels and individual-
ists." Fergusson seems to have a special interest in Laird, not, I
think, because he is an idealist but because he is human, stubborn, honest, and somewhat at odds with both the past and the
present. Morgan, on the other hand, has prospected, practiced
law in the East, collected Western Americana, and at last made
a visit to Taos because he has been haunted by the memory of
his life on the frontier: "Certainly the modern world, whatever
its merits, seems a bit tight-fisted and calculating by comparison with that reckless and ample day." At the end, Morgan
seems to speak for Fergusson, perhaps; echoing the feelings
that Fergusson had when he returned to New Mexico from
California to gather more material for this novel:

> To me the droning tales of these old-timers had the quality
> of elegy. I felt as though I were witnessing the process by
> which the past becomes a beloved myth, simplified in memory
> so that one may see the meanings that are always obscured by
> the noise and dust of the present. The sleepy inertia of the little
> town made its past seem truly heroic.

This is not nostalgia but rather Fergusson's observation of a
process and therefore his answer to the nostalgia and the myths
of popular American consciousness of the West. He refers to
the nostalgia and the myths but does not indulge in them. In a
minor way his characters partake of a myth of their own, and
some of them appear at first glance to be heroic; but, heroism is
often moral rather than physical, so that people achieve their
own kind of courage and motivation, not with guns or force (although these are also present) but with the spirit. Fergusson's
people are caught in sweeping changes in history. As far as action is concerned, the characters have little choice but to sweep
along toward their destinies. They do not lament their fate.
What energy they may have in shaping their lives is spiritual,
and since the spirit is tied to the land it may be said that the land
is the major force in all respects. The compromise of Sam Lash
turns into the inevitability of Robert Payson, Ballard, Blore,
Tighe, and even Leo Mendes in Fergusson's last novel. Look-

ing back, perhaps we must recognize Lash's compromise as having a kind of inevitability of its own.

As a historical novelist, Fergusson is most interested in change and in the acceptance of change—from the Old West to the New West, from a life of freedom in the wilderness to civilization or society, from the Spanish landed aristocracy to the gringo businessman, and from inherited fortunes to the making of money. In the nineteenth-century West it was largely the railroad that brought change and shaped conditions. As the railroad altered the destinies of the gringos, they in turn brought change to the Mexicans and settlement brought it to the wilderness. Fergusson's approach to these changes is seen through a variety of characters from slightly different time periods as they react in their own ways to the passage of history. Although he does not stress the cyclical nature of man's events and therefore of history, Fergusson had the insight to know that events can indeed circle back upon themselves. And, within his otherwise consistent detachment from the events he describes, we can see a sympathy for the Spanish people as well as for the land itself. The Alcalde's wish that Daniel Laird might go to Santa Fe as an emissary for the mountain people has been fulfilled in actuality in modern times. The question of the land grants is not yet fully settled. Spanish-speaking people still try to reclaim the property of the old Mexican and Spanish grants, hiring lawyers to appeal their cases in court. Leaders come to the fore, as land-grant patriarchs, to focus attention upon the struggle for the one thing the Spanish-Americans respect almost as much as they respect God—land. The conviction of these people is that if they got their land back they could maintain a decent and successful way of life because their culture is based upon the land. Northern New Mexico, especially, has not changed a great deal since the time of which Fergusson writes in *Grant of Kingdom*; the importance of the land is spiritual, to the Spanish and to the Indians alike, because it represents their ties to ancestors and traditions. The problem is regional, but it persists with the timelessness of the land it in-

volves, and its insistence upon the importance of the land is indicative of a broadly Western characteristic.

Although *Grant of Kingdom* may be Fergusson's most personal novel in terms of utilizing familiar events and places, with
the action concluding in his own time, it is probably Leo
Mendes of *The Conquest of Don Pedro* who most clearly embodies
his philosophy of man's relation to the land and to the changing
ways of life. History in this novel is subordinated to the Jewish
peddler's spiritual quest which is, ironically, related to his social and economic conquest of the village of Don Pedro. The interplay between quest and conquest establishes a tension
which can be resolved only by near-tragedy that turns apparent
defeat into moral or spiritual victory. The story of Mendes is
told from within his frame of reference, but, as almost always
in Fergusson, it is a third-person objective view that is the same
as limited omniscience. Fergusson can then tell us what he
needs to from outside Leo's consciousness and can also identify
with his character to present his own views:

> He believed a man's destiny is a thing he discovers, a mystery
> that unfolds, and he pursued his ends always in the spirit of in-
> quiry rather than of heroic determination.

For Fergusson, striving to get behind the myths, it was curiosity more than heroism which was responsible for much of
the settling of the West. Leo is a brave man in his way and he
possesses the determination to set up business in a town
where he is not welcome, but when the crucial moment of his
life arrives he chooses understanding and self-sacrifice rather
than attempted heroism.

Leo's presence in the West is explained plausibly. He is ill
with tuberculosis, the disease that sent many young men west
in the nineteenth century, and he is following in the steps of a
number of his forebears when he takes up peddling as a means
of establishing a career. What is most unnatural to him at first is
the land, which he fears as only "a child of crowd and pave-
ment" can. Gradually the Southwest casts a spell over him, as
the Padre said it did with most people who came "to regain

their health or make their fortunes." Even as the empty distances continue to appall him, he experiences an intimacy with
"sand and water, bird and beast." Lying beside a river he is
caressed by sun and water and feels at home for the first time in
his life. The change takes place slowly and fears remain with
him throughout the ten years of his stay in southern New
Mexico.

To make his way within the Mexican population of the
Santa Fe area he serves as the bearer of news as well as peddler
among the lower classes. As his health improves, Leo Mendes
wishes to settle down in a business of his own in the town of
Don Pedro (Doña Ana, between Las Cruces, and the Mexican
border), a town governed by Augustin Vierra, a powerful
Rico. To ensure some measure of success, he makes an arrangement with Aurelio Beltran, himself a descendent of an old
Spanish family, who has nothing left but a house. It is this
house which becomes Leo's store and trading post. The success
of the business makes Leo the richest man in town, and yet he is
socially isolated until the Padre introduces him to Doña Lupe
Vierra and he is invited to attend the afternoon ritual of choco-
late drink. From this point, with Mendes in a position of
power, the plot branches out into the patterns created by Leo's
relationships with the important people of the town. The first
is with Doña Lupe, a hostile romance in that she wants Leo to
be the aggressor but he is afraid of the consequences even
though he desires her. Fergusson describes their "affair" in a
series of images which move the action quickly and without
embellishment. Leo first notices that Lupe's arms, while
pretty, are "so thin that her delicate olive skin [is] shadowed
along the line of her collar bone." Later, as they dance, their
"bellies [are] tensely intimate" for just a moment. When she
comes to his house it is for the Rico game of sex in which sin is a
thrill and the woman pretends to resist so that the man will
overwhelm her, a game which Leo cannot play because he has
"neither the spirit nor the technique." The scene is quietly
comical until the moment of passion when the two people of
differing traditions and moral systems make love furiously,

without tenderness, as though they are taking revenge on each other. They meet again many times, "creatures . . . born of different worlds" who "would never think or feel alike," joined in a world of common humanity when they have shed their clothes and their social roles, and their love-making is a part of the natural world in which crickets make "a small nearby court-ing music" and a dog howls "his feelings at the moon." The scene is typical of Fergusson's handling of male-female rela-tionships in that sexuality is not Victorian and yet is subdued so that it is not exploited.

Leo's full acceptance into Spanish Rico society comes after he has married the niece of the Vierras, a young girl of six-teen—Leo is forty. The marriage is arranged only because Padre Orlando intervenes, he and Leo being the two most im-portant men in the town, but the Padre cautions Leo: "You have not the believing mind. I think you have no faith in any-thing but life itself." (The comment could be applied, just as sympathetically, to Harvey Fergusson, and one must wonder how closely he became identified with his character, Mendes.) Because of Magdalena's youth and beauty, she is pursued by younger men, a problem to Leo because he lacks one important quality which he should have as head of a Mexican family and as a Mexican gentleman—the gift of command, an autocratic authority. He begins to wonder if he really *possesses* his wife. When he discovers that he does not, that she has been with his friend Robert Coppinger, he has long thoughts about what he had learned from Lupe about Spanish marriages and adultery and knows once again that he is really an outsider.

Two ethical questions form the dramatic conclusion to the plot. Coppinger, a Texan with a sense of Anglo opportunism, fences in the salt lake which has been visited and used by Mexi-cans for many generations. He wishes to charge a fee for the salt. According to the customs of the country, Coppinger's ac-tion is a violation of common rights. Paradoxically, his deter-mination to stand alone against the Mexicans is heroic. Leo is placed in a difficult situation. Because Coppinger has been his friend, he feels that it is his responsibility to deal with him, even if it means killing his friend in order to preserve the ways of the land. However, everyone knows that if a gringo is killed it is the Mexicans who will be blamed. To extricate himself from this moral dilemma and to submit himself to the will of destiny, Leo ordains that Coppinger may have Magdalena if she loves him and if he loves her enough to give up the salt lake. Stated baldly in this fashion the situation seems melodramatic, and Fergusson does indeed move so quickly that the moral and ethical questions are almost lost in the action. What is important, of course, is the implication once again of the necessity of change and of the further necessity of acceptance of change. As Leo prepares for it, certain of the outcome of his challenge to Coppinger, he becomes momentarily symbolic for the first time in the narrative. (I have resisted the temptation to see Leo as a western "Wandering Jew," and I am quite certain that Fergusson intended no such comparison. Leo's Jewishness serves mainly to set him apart from the Spanish aristocracy and make his "conquest" all the more difficult.) Earlier, however, Leo's store, Tienda Mendes, is seen as a kind of clearing house for many types of historical figures, including actual personalities such as Billy the Kid, and affording Fergusson the chance to summarize (once again) the notable historical events and people of the West. This use of the store brings disparate characters together (as John Steinbeck did in *The Wayward Bus*) so that they may be observed in relation to each other within physical proximity. The store as a symbolic center of the late nineteenth-century West is a useful device.

Eventually, as Fergusson knew, the store must be left behind, actually as well as symbolically. It is good to put down roots, to grow and mature and become attached to the land; but the past cannot live forever and a man must discard it—except in memory and in knowledge—and move on, as everything moves onward. The recurring theme in Fergusson's work is seen in Leo's acceptance of the conflicts between new and old, mobility and tradition, and past and present. Mendes promises the Padre that he will return for a visit, but he departs with the words, "I long for new work." His journey across the Jornada ten years earlier was itself symbolic of the westward movement across the continent—a journey of death and a journey of desire. He has survived by outliving his fears, by becoming intimate with wilderness, solitude, and space. He has learned much from the land, and if he has a religion it is the faith in life of which the Padre spoke—derived from faith in the land. This emphasis upon the land calls for two comments. It is not landscape as such that dominates the Western American novel, as Fergusson illustrates. A novel as effective as *The Conquest of Don Pedro* succeeds because of the right combination of land *and* people. Fergusson is so eager to portray the kinds of people who inhabited the West that he often draws them as representative, as types; yet he understands human nature and allows his characters to be individuals. That a character can be himself as well as a symbol is seen clearly in the person of Leo Mendes. And that the land remains as the one relatively unchangeable element in man's destiny, while historical events come and go, may be seen in the images and rhythms employed by Fergusson. Finally, it must be noted that "land" as respected and loved by Fergusson is somewhat different from the "earth" which evokes a mystical response from another southwestern writer, Frank Waters. "Land" is historical, traditional, to be respected but also to be possessed. "Earth" is primal, sacred, to be experienced and absorbed through intuition and, ultimately, mystical oneness. The distinction is often difficult to make, and the two words are used interchangeably as often as not.

Harvey Fergusson is aware of the mysteries of the earth, of the religious response to certain kinds of natural environment, but his chief contribution to Western literature lies within the history of the land—people and places. He has demythologized the West, not by attacking or denying the myths, but by explaining them and giving careful attention to their historical origins. In Leo Mendes we may well see our national character, our ambivalence in the matter of roots and mobility, our destiny determined by the nature and characteristics of the landscape and what it has to offer. In contrast to the American desire to get ahead, to progress, to improve, the traditional Spanish culture—representing old Europe—is ordered, stable, based upon a class system within which each person has his place. Fergusson makes few, if any, judgments in these matters, portraying both sides, old and new, with objectivity as well as sympathy. The controlled tone of his writing is exceptional; it allows us to trust his narratives to an extent that is unusual in a literature based upon the frequently myth-clouded events and places of the American West. His fiction is rich in historical facts and in spiritual truths, but perhaps his genius is seen most clearly in the rhythms of the movement among four strata or levels of presentation: the individual people who are caught in a period of change, the special qualities and traditions of New Mexico, the broader portrait of western expansion and settlement, and the application of the western experience to our national character. No other writer has succeeded as well in such a grand design.

Specifically, *The Conquest of Don Pedro* is an example of craftsmanship and style so deceptively simple in its rational prose, imagery, and rhythms that it seems to belie its greatness. It is ironic that upon publication in 1954, this novel was neglected in the wake of the more distinctive styles of Faulkner in *A Fable* and Manfred in *Lord Grizzly*, while Hemingway was receiving the Nobel Prize that same year with a presentation reference to *The Old Man and the Sea*.

VIII
Intuition and the Dance of Life: Frank Waters

It is no coincidence that the literary reputation of Frank Waters has grown markedly since the beginning in the late 1960s of a parallel growth of interest in the literature and culture of the American Indian. His two nonfiction works on southwestern Indian life and religious ritual *(Masked Gods,* 1950, and *Book of the Hopi,* 1963) were reprinted in paperback editions in 1970 and 1969 respectively, enjoying an immediate popularity not given to the earlier original editions. His Indian novel *(The Man Who Killed the Deer,* 1942), although kept alive by publisher Alan Swallow in this country and reprinted several times in Europe, did not reach the mass market in an inexpensive paperback edition until 1971. Before the advent of recent and sudden exploitation of all things Indian, Waters was relatively unknown except to a small and faithful group of readers, most of them Europeans or scholars of Western American literature. What kept him from a wider acceptance during the 1930s and 1940s was a disinclination on the part of the general reader and most critics to accept his almost mystical view of life. Waters, of course, is not a mystic in the strictest sense of the term because he does not abandon the physical world in which he lives. His reaching out toward something which may well be indefinable is done from a firm rootedness in the earth.

A southwesterner like Harvey Fergusson, Waters was born under the influence of Pike's Peak, in Colorado Springs, and this area furnished him with the materials for what is usually called his mining trilogy—*The Wild Earth's Nobility* (1935), *Below Grass Roots* (1937), and *The Dust Within the Rock* (1940). However, his association with New Mexico goes back to the mid-thirties, and he purchased the adobe house in which he now lives in 1947, on the edge of the Pueblo land of which he had written five years earlier. This is the general area of Taos, that sleepy Spanish village of the mountain-man era which has attracted artists from all over the world and writers such as Mary Austin, Robinson Jeffers, Aldous Huxley, Walter Van Tilburg Clark, and D. H. Lawrence. Despite an almost continuous influx of tourists in modern times, Taos has retained the spiritual aura that invites thoughts and feelings of permanence, continuity, the cyclical pattern of all life, the Indian's harmonious relationship to the earth (especially to Taos Mountain), and the truths of intuitive recognition, often expressed in archetypal images. The place has a spirit of its own, and that spirit coincides nicely with Waters's spirit as man and writer. Furthermore, the attitudes toward this place, and the beliefs of the Indians, lend themselves to the formulations of Carl Gustav Jung concerning the unconscious, the psyche, the archetype, the primordial image, individuation, and racial memory. It is not strange, then, that Waters with his part-Indian heritage should have an affinity to Jung.

Nor is it strange that Jung should be fascinated by the Pueblos. When he visited the Taos pueblo on his 1924–25 trip to New Mexico, he was told that the white man was mad because he thought only with his head, while the Indians thought with their hearts. (The heart in this case stands for intuition rather than emotion.) The mysteries of the Pueblo religion gave the people their unity and cohesion, and although they would not reveal those mysteries to Jung they became excited and almost emotional when speaking of the things which pertained to the mysteries. Their religious conceptions were to them not theories "but facts, as important and moving as the corresponding external realities." When asked by an Indian, "Do you not think that all life comes from the mountain?", Jung recognized the river rushing down from the mountain as the outward image of the truth of the question, for water is the bringer of life. Explanations of the importance of the sun were not as obvious to the perception of the outsider, although Jung drew a characteristic conclusion to the Indians' assumption that their religion benefited the entire world. After listening to the story of the Pueblos' life on the roof of the world, children of Father Sun, helping the father go across the sky each day because if they did not do so the sun would no longer rise, Jung wrote: "Knowledge does not enrich us; it removes us more and more from the mythic world in which we were once at home by right of birth." The rationalism of our European heritage pales before the Indian's intuition which allows him to be immediately convinced of his place in the world and of the "unprovable" facts of his necessary relationship to the things and processes of the world. Through his intuitive knowledge, his ancient and primitive beliefs, and his rituals celebrating those beliefs, the Pueblo Indian is in harmony with himself and his place. He is, in the terms of the white man's psychology, a whole man. The secret lies in the blending of the practical and the esthetic, the mundane and the mystical, and can be seen even in the architecture of the buildings in which the Pueblos live, stepped five-storied buildings, like pyramids on two sides, firmly based on the earth but pointing (flowing) upward, symbolizing a life which is led as naturally among the necessities of the earth as it is among the mysteries of the sky and mountaintop. Among the Indians, then, Jung seemed to find the illustration of the collective unconscious and its archetypes of wholeness, of primordial images become conscious, of the instinctual nature of the psyche, and of the power of the inner world.

Waters has not set out to be consciously Indian or deliberately Jungian, although his work is increasingly discussed in those terms. He is aware of the conflict between the two worlds represented by the Indians and the European whites, as he must be in light of his own mixed heritage; but he does not establish this conflict as a thesis, to be explained or debated. His method is to describe it, and the conflict is perhaps not so much between white and Indian ways of life as it is between the rational and the instinctual. The emphasis, then, is on a kind of perception, and the white-Indian dichotomy is illustrative rather than autobiographical. What Waters is attempting to get at is primal apperception, which goes beyond normal conceptual words but which must nevertheless be stated as well as possible in normal language. Of necessity, this means a use of stylistic devices which may be misunderstood: not wordiness, but repetitions which allow the idea or feeling to acquire a proximity to what cannot be stated precisely; images which are based on environmental realities but which point to psychic realities; and a purity of language which admits of the crudities and grossness of the objective world of the body while suggesting spiritual conditions whose nature at least borders on the mystical. Waters's style, then, reflects both worlds, sometimes unevenly but often with a clarity that belies the complexities of the relationship. When the latter occurs, polarities or dualities dissolve momentarily and even the uninitiated get a rare glimpse of the ultimate unity of things. Whereas Harvey Fergusson's strength lies in the broadly spiritual relationship of man to the land, and Walter Clark's emphasis is on the psychological effects of the land on man, Waters's concern is with the harmony between psyche and earth (not land, or nature, although the three words are frequently used synonymously). If such a concern borders on mysticism, we must keep in mind that Waters has insisted that characterization comes first, and if the characters seem to recognize an "ineffable nature," or if they have what seems to be a mystical experience, they do so as characters, as people, not as contrived reflections of the author's personal point of view. The distinction is between novelistic methods and the novelist's persuasions.

Of these three writers—whom I consider to be the most important Western American novelists—Frank Waters is the most involved in form as space, or space as form. Fergusson relies most heavily upon temporal form, and Clark is somewhere between the two. In Western literature we are perhaps more accustomed to the linear development of events than to a logical or intuitive imposition of form upon the material. The early literature consisted mainly of travel narratives, journals, and diaries in which the action proceeded from day to day and time was often an important factor in the movement from place to place on the journey. Since it was Fergusson's desire to depict the Old West truthfully, stripped of its myth, he went to nineteenth-century themes and types of people which allowed him to make use of historical sequences, to recognize individual or family chronicles over a period of time, to see the changes in the people and in the land, and to construct a perspective for the twentieth-century West. Along with his perceptions and his poetry, he remained true to sequences of events, to a kind of chronological inevitability. His imagery illuminated the moment; it did not strive for structural or broadly symbolic meaning.

Clark, on the other hand, while also leading the past into the present, gave more attention to the niceties of logical, or imposed, structure leading to a more conscious sense of form. Although his two novels which might be called historical allow us to feel that we are in a time past, they do not specifically or necessarily rest on identifiable events in western history. They are closer to being archetypical than they are to being either historical or unique. Yet, the element of time passing—the chronology—is essential to Clark while he is rounding out his large themes. And, in spite of implications of continuance as each novel draws to a close, the themes and their supporting narratives are sufficiently rounded off to leave the impression of completeness in each case. In *The Ox-Bow Incident*, the specifically guilty man (Tetley) is dead at the end, along with his victims, even though the other men, temporarily cleansed through violence and remorse, may well repeat their behavior at another time. In *The Track of the Cat*, the real cat is dead, along with its victims, even though the symbolic cat lives on in the fears of man. Structurally, there are so many patterns of threes in Clark's novels, emerging in various ways, that we are at least aware of the possibility of Aristotelean form with a clear beginning, middle, and end—a linear movement. Even Clark's major images of color (usually black and white) and space work within a time sequence—in *Ox-Bow* a going-out and a coming-back, and in *Track of the Cat* a repetition of that pattern as the isolated ranch house serves as a focal point and the brothers and Joe Sam go out from there and return, even though the homeward journey may be in death.

I cite these few facts about Fergusson and Clark because they were the western novelists whom Waters has respected the most. And while Waters's work has some similarities to theirs, it is the differences that allow Waters to stand apart, to have special significance, and to be relatively ignored or misunderstood outside the area in which he lives.

Writing entirely about his native Southwest, Waters is unabashedly a regionalist. This label, however, should not prevent anyone from seeing that Waters is concerned with no less than the universe itself, and man's place in it. The Southwest is a fitting stage for such a cosmic pursuit, because in the mountains and on the desert man comes into direct contact with the natural forces and elements which existed long before man emerged and which played a full role in the ancient religious systems. (While most of Waters's fiction has been "contemporary," he has been going further back in his nonfiction studies, as to the Mayas in *Mexico Mystique*, 1975.) Furthermore, the interplay of three cultures, the intuitive knowledge of the old Indian tribes, and the kind of isolation which not only allows but forces a man to think about himself and his relation to beginnings and endings—these are immediate presences in New Mexico. Waters's journey has taken him back into time, into primitive and nonrational philosophies and religions, and into Jungian racial consciousness. His ultimate concern is not with a selected portion of the historical past but with *all* of the past as it reveals eternal verities. The end of the journey, should it ever be reached, will be a fusion of Oriental thought and perception with European rationalism and linear time. How far Waters himself (as seen in his novels) has come on this journey is a moot question, but one indication is apparent in a comparison of the opening of the first volume of the mining trilogy (1935) and the conclusion of his last novel, *The Woman at Otowi Crossing* (1966). These two passages provide a tentative frame for Waters's fiction.

> "Hee-yah!"
> The sharp guttural cry roused Rogier from his reverie in the shadows of the porch where his heavy square-built body lounged motionless in a chair, his gaze enmeshed in the vast web of twilight translucent between the row of cottonwoods before him and the imponderable barrier of mountains rising farther west to cut off his world of thought.

The sentence is heavy, ponderous, and completely lacking in the sudden discovery, the insight, and the penetration of the intuitionist. It is, of course, an introductory sentence, offering information. Rogier is cut off from the revelations he will have later by the very mountains that will provide the near-mystical experience. Motionless, he has not yet begun his search for whatever fulfillment awaits him. The opening cry is momentarily ambiguous and therefore serves a dual function. Not unlike the cry of a teamster or stage driver wheeling his horses into town, it suggests linear movement and the excitement attending the building of a new place where strangers to the land will seek their fortunes. In contrast, the major image of the last page of *The Woman at Otowi Crossing* is circular—the "spherical geometry of the complete rounded moment"—and the novel ends with its own cry:

> Be glad! It's our greatest experience, our mysterious voyage of discovery into the last unknown, man's only true adventure . . .

The reference for the "it" of this sentence is "awareness," "awakening," or the Indian "Emergence." And so it would seem that during the voyage of seven novels Waters has journeyed from a cry of haste, human rush, the transportation of goods, people moving in quickly on new economic opportunities—the white man's "progress"—to a cry of celebration at the achievement of psychic awareness. This is true, but it is not all. In reality, "Hee-yah!" has been uttered not by a stage driver but by an Arapaho Indian passing with his people on the way to a multitribal encampment where the annual dance will reaffirm their oneness with their earth. In this respect the beginning and ending of the journey are the same, and we have come in a full circle. Placing the linear and the circular side by side underscores the dualities which are very real and the unity which is attainable but remains a potential rather than an actuality in most men.

"Be glad!" may be taken as a translation of "Hee-yah!" so that Waters's voyage ends where it began. Furthermore, the end is but a new beginning, as all endings are in the cycle of life. After the cry, the first passage is explicit and physically detailed, whereas the second (or last) is almost vague in its implications and is cut short as though words will not suffice to communicate the fullness of the experience. The considerable distance between the two passages (both physical and spiritual distance as well as chronological) is indicative of the difficulty in recognizing and accepting the new awareness. Yet, the tailing off into space (a function of the ellipsis points) signals not an end but an expansion, or an exploding outward, which is characteristic of Waters's thought and also of the structure of many Western novels. The juxtaposition of atomic study at Los Alamos with the spiritual concept of oneness held by the Indians nearby may seem to indicate a conclusion, but it is more likely a sign pointing out the direction of the journey to final awareness.

Waters has been called a visonary and a mystic. This is all right as long as we do not limit those terms to a condition which presupposes a lack of close relationship to the physical world. Waters is not a dreamer, disconnected from the world around him. His mysticism is earth-based, object-based. His visions spring from nature and from those people whose ancestry is traceable to nonwestern origins. The mixture of cultures in his work reveals the similarities in them. In other similarities too, between primitive myths and modern thought, or between such things as creation stories in several major religions, Waters is concerned with common denominators, with the sources which prove essentially the same for all cultures and times. In dealing with sameness, oneness, and the eternal, Waters is therefore deemphasizing the chronology of time, the clocks of the modern western world, and seeking a timelessness and perhaps even an essential form which can ultimately be called formless.

Granted that the Mayas (with whom Waters is involved in *Mexico Mystique)* developed an elaborate system of timekeeping, and that the narrative in the mining trilogy proceeds from one generation to another in sequential order, still the drumbeat in *The Wild Earth's Nobility* serves as an image of blood relationships, not of linear sequences in a form of music. As Rogier listens, the rhythms of the drums hypnotize him, stop him in time, enter his blood stream in a way that is neither gentle nor smooth. The "timeless rhythm" grows in his blood and soon he believes "with his blood more than the capacity of his mind could ever admit." For all this emphasis on blood consciousness, Waters is much closer to Mary Austin than he is to D. H. Lawrence. In "The Woman Who Rode Away" (1928) and in *Apocalypse* (1931), Lawrence leaps past the land and its immediate images directly into human sacrifice and the cosmos itself. Austin, on the other hand, is intimate with the land, its creatures, and the natural rituals of people living close to the land; her attention is therefore focused on rhythms (the same two-handed beat that is basic to the Indian drumming in Waters) and on the achievement of harmony with the earth. The point may seem labored, but it is important. Lawrence jumps irrationally across the reaches of western thought to find a blood relationship with the undefinable cosmos; Waters and Austin keep their feet on the ground, exploring images which can convey a relationship between intuitive man and the mysteries of nature and, therefore, of life. Blood need not be let, or spilled; its rhythms, or pulse, within the body are akin to the eternal pulse, and the heartbeat, like the drumbeat, is not considered as evidence of the passing of time but as a source, an energy, a vital link between man and nature. Rogier goes into the heart of the mountain in search of this pulse, the secret of life. The Mayas and Aztecs sought this secret in the sun, and it was only in death that they were placed deep inside their mountainlike pyramids, hidden from the sun. The place of death parallels the place of life, yet both are out of the sun which is an obvious source of life, an ancient deity. This is one of the many ambiguities which the intuitive mind recognizes and accepts without subjecting the conflicting parts to rational scrutiny. In this sense, then, Waters is a mystic.

As such, he might well be less concerned with structure or superficial form than were Fergusson, Clark, or a number of other western novelists. As he notes in *Below Grass Roots*, "not the sorry form, but the splendid substance" in which "the subtle truths" are not known but felt. Waters applies this thought to all of American history: the tales and legends of the West, especially, "stand there, close and touchable, [moving] truthfully with all their faults and without form." And in *The Man Who Killed the Deer* Palemon speaks (in the poetic and italicized words of the language Waters gives to the Indians in the novel) of form as a body. Man is imprisoned in the form which is his physical body but he must have faith in it nevertheless, as well as in the form of life which is his greater body. If he can find this faith he may then be released from his bonds: "That will free your spirit into a formless life without bounds, which will overflow and taste of all life."

This spiritual form may or may not be comparable to a kind of artistic form in the books themselves. Perhaps we are again involved in an ambiguity, saying that faith in form leads to a wholesome formlessness. It occurs to me that Waters is searching for nothing less than the perfect form, the circle, the traditional symbol of unity. In each of his novels he makes progress around the circle but never quite completes it. The circle encompasses space, and the physical space of the American West is difficult to contain, or to frame. Furthermore, it is likely that Waters believes, with others, that the important thing is the journey, not the destination. In the Colorado mining trilogy, in

many ways the longest of the Waters journeys, March, out of
Boné and Rogier, travels a long distance, searching for himself,
and the conclusion is as open-ended as the land. *The Man Who
Killed the Deer* opens with Martiniano in trouble near Blue
Lake and closes with an image of a pebble on water, suggesting the completion of a circle (the lake and the rings sent out
by the impact are themselves circles). Yet the mass of images
throughout the novel and the widening circle of ripples in the
metaphorical lake spread to "unguessed shores." And they do
so "in the timeless skies of night."

   With his interest in Jung and oriental religions, and in
American Indian ceremonialism, it is not difficult to believe
that Waters equates sand paintings with mandalas, the symbols
of psychic wholeness, and that his entire work is an effort to reconstruct the circle of unity. In this respect his work is timeless
and spatial. He reaches further than Clark and Fergusson, and
in doing so he perhaps sacrifices some of the more mechanical
possibilities of artistic form to the largeness of the vision and to
the intuitive processes necessary in achieving that vision. The
sounds of the drum echo throughout an immense space.

   Within this space, landscape also plays an important part in
the form of the Western novel, not only for Indian-oriented
writers like Frank Waters but also for a witty, ironic, and frequently irreverent writer like William Eastlake whose Indian
novels are technically more suited to urbane readers. The
topography of the land is the same for the two men: the plains
are high and arid, cut by deep canyons, and dotted with mesas
which look like steps to the higher mountains. The view, then,
is mostly out and up, the direction of man's spirit in this land.
To defy this natural movement is to suffer or die. Evil lurks in
the lowest places.

   When Waters's Rogier goes inside, and down into, the
mountain to search for his meaning, he is defeated. And when
Ring (in Eastlake's *Portrait of an Artist with Twenty-six Horses*)
lies dying he has sunk "into eternity at the bottom of the
arroyo . . . looking up at the soft gray-green slopes that led
away to the world." Rogier wants to find gold as well as him-

self, just as Ring and the Indian, Twenty-six Horses, are trying to find themselves by other means. Eastlake concludes the
Portrait with a passage which suggests the importance of openness and expansion as well as the temporary aspect of gold:
"They flew lightly and all together up a gaudy-thrown profusion of raging color and the sharp high scent of Indian Country
until they topped out on the end of a day, on a New Mexican
sky infinity of burnished and dying gold." "Flew lightly,"
"up," "high scent," "topped out," and "infinity" all suggest the
expansiveness which is part of a religious experience, even
though Eastlake often treats that experience with humor and
irony. The physical world, especially that part of it which lies
low (in the arroyo, or below the mountains), is the place of
trials and of testing. The picture which Twenty-six Horses has
painted high on a cliff is "a picture of everyone who is at the
mercy of everybody." Nevertheless, these people who are at
the mercy of everyone can ride up, look up, achieve the heights
in a physical way which strongly implies spiritual achievement. In this one instance, at least, the achievement comes in
an atmosphere of "dying gold." The symbolic possibilities are
obvious, especially when seen in relation to Waters's Rogier,
who mixes the search for gold with the search for self and confuses them.

This theory of "out and up" for salvation is fairly consistent
in Eastlake and Waters, although it is not without its complications. Eastlake's "mountains are for dying" must be interpreted
by a later passage: "That's why the ascent of the mountain is so
valuable at the end. Occupied instead of preoccupied. Gaining
ever new heights in spreading splendor, not the visit of fading
visitors between coming-together walls." One thinks of a primary psychological difference between the Indian and the
Anglo, contrasting the Indian practice of burial on outdoor
open scaffolds and the Anglo practice of putting bodies in tight
containers below the surface of the ground. Factually, these
differences will not hold for all groups, but they at least indicate the strong hold which the Indian attitude toward the land
has on many Western writers, particularly in the Southwest.

It is interesting to note that in reading Eastlake's *Portrait* and *The Bronc People* one has the feeling that he is constantly going up and down. This is the basic rhythm, a result of spatial structure and of the thematic search for meaning. "Down" is real world, the physical world, and "up" is the ideal world, the spiritual world. This may seem too easy, too reminiscent of the early Christian concept of heaven as being "up in the air," and yet Eastlake does not jump carelessly from one world to another, nor is he unaware of the ancient earth which has very slowly fostered the growth of man. Out of the earth come his ideas of man. History and landscape do not hang in the background like an elegant tapestry which may be admired apart from the action occurring in front of it—they are there to be used as integral parts of the development of ideas, whether implicit or explicit. In a deceptively simple but brilliant passage in *Bronc People*, Eastlake describes Sant, Alastair Benjamin, and two Indians riding down the mesa:

> The mesa here was eroding away in five giant steps that descended down to the floor of the valley where the abandoned hogan lay. Each of the five steps clearly marked about twenty million years in time. In other words, they had been laid down twenty million years apart, and were so marked by unique coloration and further marked by the different fossil animals found in each. It took the four boys about twenty minutes to descend these one hundred million years but they didn't think that was very good going.

Then the twist of irony: "They went down together and at once, creating a storm, a tornado of ageless dust, a hundred million years in outrage, that followed them all the way down to the level of the Indians." Taken in their several meanings, these passages provide a biting commentary on man and, more specifically, on the Europeanized non-Indian. The important thing is that the meanings of the incident are derived directly from the landscape. The images depend entirely upon the unique characteristics of the Western land. It is in the context of the mountains that "always say things so well, silently," that Alastair Benjamin concludes one phase of his search (high up), passes "beneath a tremulous aspen shattered brilliant with light," walks "beside a mesa brushed in fiery cloud," and then descends into "a long valley that led to another country." But the search never ends; the end of the novel is open; Alastair goes down again into the world of people who are at the mercy of everyone else, and the process will go on.

Whereas Eastlake writes about contemporary New Mexico with an emphasis on Indians as characters, or the white man in Indian country, and is technically concerned with brevity, wit, irony, and occasional fantasy, Frank Waters in his trilogy offers long and solid portrayals of late-nineteenth-century-early-twentieth-century mining in Colorado, with forays into New Mexico and with obvious leanings toward Indian-oriented values. Pike's Peak becomes a symbol in the mining trilogy, both of the spiritual quality of the search and of man's proper relationship to the earth. It is majestic, immense, upthrust, and enduring. Rogier goes into the mountain to unlock its inscrutable will. When the mountain seems to defeat him, he becomes contrite and humble, realizing the insignificance of man and the offensiveness of his folly. This in turn teaches him a lesson which is from the land:

> Like a man dumbfounded by the simplicity of life once everything else has been taken from him, he realized that there might be nothing more sublime than his completest adjustment to that earth and its elements, those intangible forces which had molded him unwittingly in their ceaseless flow.

At the end of *The Wild Earth's Nobility*, Rogier feels that the mountains are a barrier shutting off from his sight "the ever inscrutable vision that rose again before him." The vision is still with him at the end of *Below Grass Roots*, and the mountain still seems to be blocking him from it:

> His square stern face assumed for the moment in the light of the flames a look at once profound, timeless and enigmatic as the face of that immutable Peak which had stood before him and will stand for those to follow, an eternal jest of nature at men

whose folly and salvation is the blind perpetuation of a quest
which has no truth but this—a flashing vision, darkness and
eternal rest.

It is not until Rogier's grandson, March, has acquired additional experience and knowledge of the earth in New Mexico
that the mountain in Colorado ceases to be a barrier and becomes instead a monument of faith. Before that point is
reached, however, Rogier must go through several mystical experiences in which flashes of vision occur to him and spur him
on toward his own ultimate vision. At an Indian dance he feels
the rhythms of blood and earth in the beating of the drums, and
he understands that here is a "place-spirit of the great western
aridity that had made and kept him an exile in the land of his
adoption." As he tries to overcome the place-spirit, or to succumb to it, the rhythm grows in his own blood until the inner-
feeling response to the scene is stronger than the mental recognition of it. Contrary to the arguments of several western
writers and critics who have insisted that only rationalism
can bring Western literature to maturity, Waters insists upon
the validity of the blood, or (better) the intuition which is the
link of man to the earth and to the mystery of creation. The difficulty with Rogier is that he wants to combine knowledge of
the earth's pulse with the acquisition of gold. Later, in the
mine, deep inside the mountain, he wants "to pierce that body
of living rock into the warm flesh that hides its secret heart, to
drain its veins of golden life, to learn at the last that even a stone
may throb to an unseen pulse, may vibrate in unison with all
eternal life." The feeling that the mountain is alive persists in
him for years, but finally he is defeated in his search for gold,
and his son-in-law dies from pneumonia while working in the
mine, so that Rogier never quite reconciles himself to the full
commitment needed to make his earth-feelings complete.

It is the grandson, March, in *The Dust Within the Rock*, who
at last recognizes that everything is of a piece, that a man is his
grandfather and his father, and also the leaf that falls as well as
the leaf that sprouts, the rock that crumbles in time as well as

the dust that is timeless within the rock, and, indeed, everything—"indivisible and intermingled, adobe and granite."
Here, at the end of the trilogy, March sees Pike's Peak, higher
than all the mountains around it. And "like a religious exile
granted the divine concession of a world to be built at his will,
he [walks] humbly but resolutely toward that imperishable
monument of an enduring faith."

Although Eastlake's novels are comparatively short and
episodic, and Waters's are long and as solid as the mountains
themselves, the two men are affected by the land to the same
extent. Man's meaning comes out of the earth, and if his relationship to the earth is a receptive and intuitive one he finds
hope and contentment in the relationship. Eastlake, because of
his somewhat more modern approach through terseness, wit,
and irony, seems to let his theme and his own relationship to
the land come through by implication, although it is fairly
clear. Waters is so fully committed to his theme, and is so Indian-oriented, that he seems obligated to be explicit and quite
detailed—like a man with a mission. He is a genuine product of
the land he writes about. The novels of Waters and Eastlake
alike are liberally sprinkled with the defeats of their characters,
but the defeats are temporary. The open-ended form allows the
Western novel to go beyond a treatment of the land as realistic
antagonist (the end result in the midwestern farm novel) and to
use the land as symbol, metaphor, and the source of metaphy-
sics to suggest a way for man to look beyond himself to a
broader and richer context. The expansive land becomes the
expansive form, forever opening out and looking up.

2

The three novels commonly referred to as the Colorado mining
trilogy (revised and reprinted in one volume as *Pike's Peak* in
1971) show some of the flaws caused by enthusiasm over personal discoveries. Allowing for these impurities of style, and
recognizing that structural difficulties are not uncommon in a
long work (1511 pages in this case), it is possible to say that

Frank Waters has written one of the richest and most detailed stories in Western literature. A family chronicle, the work is also a discussion of history, a repository of ideas, and a journey through the soul of the West. Underlying these concerns is a personal quest, Waters's own search for meaning as revealed through two characters who share the author's identity. Joseph Rogier, the mainstay of the narrative until very near the end, represents Waters's maternal grandfather. Of the six children born to Rogier and his wife Martha, Ona marries a part-Indian, Jonathon Cable, and their son March is the fictional Waters. Perhaps to keep the biographical elements at a safer distance, Waters places his artistic aspirations within another character—Boné—who composes music. However, as with other fiction of this kind (based on family experiences), the narrative rides along on themes and perceptions which are more important than the parallels between fictional family and factual family.

As a portrait of the West, especially in Colorado and New Mexico in the half-century following the Civil War, the trilogy is both objectively detailed and subjectively motivated. Silver and gold discoveries in the Pike's Peak region form the historical basis of the narrative, and the working of the mines provides the realism from which Waters reaches for the primacy of the land, the timelessness and age of the arena in which man strives for new opportunities. The "wrinkled faces of the mountain peaks" and the "dry skin of the prairies" seem to oppose man's efforts to exploit what to him is a new place, a fresh start, a land of riches. Only Rogier's insight is capable of discerning the durability of the land; it will not be molded at will by the peoples who dwell upon it and try to make it their own. Indeed, it is a severe testing ground for man, whether desert, plains, or a mountain pass:

> For like the sea it was a land that slept in solitude promising nothing and giving all—a vast realm of geology alone, raised high above the earth, close under the inscrutable eyes of a Heaven that attested the heroism of man's labor, his greed, his faithfulness or his unfitness to the futile task of its subjection.

Ever changing but forever fixed, the land harbors a sadness that is repeated in the people, especially those who stay. Waters is not precise when he catalogues the many tribes of Indians and insists that the land has done something to all of them. The effect of his suggestion, however, is that of domination, of the power of the land to touch strongly and lastingly all of its creatures. A change may seem to be in the offing as the country is invaded by new hordes of people, more than ever before, representing races and nationalities from all over the world. "But the land remains." Waters's point is that population does not make a people, that the heterogeneity of the invaders will make fusion into a whole more difficult than it was for the Sioux, the Hopi, the Navajo, the Aztecs, and the other older cultures of the ancient continent. Even if new temples should rise, the cost in human hearts would only confirm the greatness of the land.

In time—friendlier to the earth than to its creatures—the humans who have come from England, Italy, Ireland, Sweden, China, Africa like birds migrating mindlessly, might call the land their own. Rogier feels that he has crossed half a continent to discover his soul and that there is a chance that he may be able to call at least a part of the land his own. He worries, however, that he and everyone around him will remain homeless, uprooted from their origins and unable to find a new place of peace. Even the Indian, once rooted in the West, possessing the "unity of form and substance motivated by the spirit of his place," has disappeared. How will the new people find their kinship with the land? For the moment, at least, the question evaporates and in its place rise the Rockies with more than a thousand peaks soaring ten thousand feet and higher.

With Cripple Creek as a hub, the spokes of activity shoot far out onto the plains and into the mountains—gold mining, silver mining, construction of new towns, shipping lines, farms and ranches, and oil wells in Wyoming. As though the expansion into the West could indeed overcome the timeless land, men swarm over the wrinkled skin in their search for wealth. Waters repeatedly affirms the truth of earth's yielding up the riches in the form of gold, silver, and oil, but what he

sees as the tragedy of the people is that they fail to realize a harmony with the earth. There is no sense of unity, and often no
integrity. Speaking of a moment in history, Waters recognizes
the chaos and confusion, the "story without plot," the swiftly
moving panorama of westward expansion as marks of newness,
of unbridled enthusiasm. At some time in the future the people
and places notable in the history of western exploration, conflict, and settlement will presumably take on the quality of
legend and take their place beside the journeys of Ulysses, the
Round Table of King Arthur, and the exploits of Siegfried.

> But today—today their cadence is not yet measured, their tones
> not yet suave and polished. The veil of time has not yet blurred
> their sharp outlines. They stand there, close and untouchable,
> they move truthfully with all their faults and without form.

We might assume that Waters's intention in the trilogy is to
provide the form, but what emerges is a long search rather than
a satisfactory resolution. Pike's Peak, as the center of Rogier's
quest for ultimate meaning, is a point of emphasis; yet the
frame is lacking except for horizon lines, and these are at a great
distance in the West. The history of the period, then, and the
characteristics of the landscape, serve as analogy. Men are
tested as ore is tested. Some assay successfully, and some do
not. The bones of men are hardened by the same iron that
stains the rocks of the mountains, and those who are perceptive
enough to see the intimate relationship between man and land
will sense at least a little of the secret at the center of the
world—the bottom of a mine shaft symbolizing this center.

Until his grandson, March, assumes the search toward the
end of the trilogy, it is Rogier who is most troubled over the
question of alliance with his land of adoption. He reflects upon
the unity of life which had been his on the Carolina plantation
before he moved to the West and wonders whether he can regain it from the new earth. "Unity" has two meanings for Waters. The first is the cohesion and common purpose of a people,
whether they be members of an Indian tribe, a mining community in the hills, or a growing city such as Colorado Springs.

The second meaning is spiritual and primal, its significance lying in an indefinable relationship between man and earth, man and his sources, or man and his God. This union can be accomplished only through intuition. Rogier becomes aware of both meanings, one on the level of social idealism—although it involves insight and the spirit as well—and the other on the higher level of mysticism. What complicates the ultimate understanding of the two levels of unity is that they also should become one in a final and complete unity of all things. This concept, it seems to me, goes far beyond the transcendentalist's notion of oneness. It is more Oriental than American except as it is a major belief of the Indian, that curious mixture of Oriental and First-American.

In his business dealings—primarily in architecture and construction—Rogier subscribes as best he can to the unity of people and place. When he is confronted with the beat of an Indian drum at night, and experiences an intuitive response to the regular and insistent sound, it is not so much a discovery of oneness as it is a recognition of earth power, of timeless dream, of rhythm and mystery—the dance of life. The beating of the drum echoes the elements of the earth and the pounding of the blood stream. Rogier senses that his heart is "trying" to beat in the same time as that of the drums, and as he watches the Indians dance he feels their contact with the earth, as though they are drawing energy directly from the ground upon which their feet stamp. It is a hypnotic scene for Rogier, one which draws him out of himself and makes him aware of the rhythmic connection between man and nature. Believing "with his blood" rather than with his intellect, he has seen intuitively the timeless mystery of creation.

Rogier is not a simple man caught in the normal way by gold fever. As a respected builder in the town, and the patriarch of his family, he is a fairly typical well-to-do member of a growing white society in Colorado Springs. But he experiences, however briefly, the Indians' homage to the mysteries of creation, and Indian blood is introduced into the family line when daughter Ona marries Jonathon Cable. Cable's background is never completely known to the family; some of his behavior suggests that he has been raised within a white society, but his movements and his psychological darkness seem to be those of an Indian. As Rogier develops an obsession for mining—not for the money but to get closer to the secrets of the earth—he resembles a type of man better identified by psychologists in our own time than in Rogier's, the man who has had a successful career but who has not discovered his soul. Rogier's approach to the second phase of life is drastic. Putting almost everything he owns into a mining venture, he insists that Cable work with him even though Jonathon knows the effort is futile and is eventually killed by the mine. In a curious misunderstanding, Rogier convinces himself that mining is "breaking the thin crust" that separates him and perhaps other men also "from complete harmony with the earth" of which he is a part. Not having learned the more important lesson of the holiness of the earth, he cannot see the breaking of the skin of the earth as destructive of the very place with which he wishes to unify himself. To him the rape of virgin earth is somehow logical, balanced, and rhythmical. Breaking through the grass roots of the surface, he will go down to encounter granite, "sterner stuff," and will find the "heart vibrating in unison with all eternal life." Rogier has, in fact, become a hopeless mystic, ironically removed from the earth just as he goes into it to locate the secret.

In dramatic terms, Rogier is clearly the major character of the trilogy. Yet as part of a family chronicle he is important not for his beliefs and his obsessions but for the impact these have on key members of the family, especially Ona, Jonathon, and their son March. It is March who is left with the task of putting together the strands of his heritage, of finding his identity and purpose, in the concluding events of the trilogy. He has seen his grandfather go mad, his father killed by the mine, and his mother turned into a stoic but tragic figure who perceives what is wrong but is powerless to change anything. His inheritance is one of integrity and mystery, courage and passivity, patience and darkness, love and wonder—the union of two races. Subtle characterizations of the parents point up the boy's peculiar position. As he wanders through the West, he becomes acutely aware of the "mystery and dark beauty of his own soul," and of the fusion of bloodstreams on a much wider scale, so that he can characterize America (or at least Western America) as half-breed. His recognition of the American soul is of a spiritual nature and is more profound than the sociological theory of the melting pot. At the end of his quest—which, like all the other endings, is a beginning—March sings of his family:

> "I am the flesh of their flesh, and their flesh is of the flesh of the earth. We are all one flesh! What man can say it is ever dead? Together, undivided and eternal, we echo the pulse which throbs through stone . . . we crumble and wash away, and rise ever again in eternal palingenesis."

At this point individual identity becomes irrelevant. All are one, and it is the earth which endures and holds all together. Waters combines, here, the Indian's communal spirituality with the normally more personal and private belief in the possibility of rebirth into a higher form of being, a belief which is often looked at with skepticism by the white man who wonders at the ease of "rebirth" at frontierlike revival services. It is problems such as this which make it difficult to assess religious experiences and to recognize the true mystic when he appears.

Since the trilogy is autobiographical in part, we may be excused for wondering about the aspirations of Frank Waters as writer. Boné, Martha Rogier's nephew, is a secondary persona who is rarely mentioned in discussions of these novels. He appears early in *The Wild Earth's Nobility*, brought to live with the Rogiers after his father has died. He is slight and dark, with black curly hair, and has exceptionally acute hearing. Obsessed with music, affected by the Indian drums just as Rogier is, he sets high standards for himself as a composer:

> That by thus fulfilling himself complete and without a flaw, he might bridge with ease the unfathomable chasm between mankind's incompleteness and that perfect harmony forever beyond his human reach.

More specifically, the artist's task is to extract meaning from gangue—a word which is important to Waters. In mining, gangue—the nonmetalliferous minerals found in a vein of ore—is considered worthless. Gold itself would seem to represent the unattainable: "Even to the artist the earth remains resistant and enigmatic." Yet one must look toward "that perfect harmony" even though it may be, or seem to be, out of human reach, and even though the materials through which the search is conducted—the materials available to the writer—are impurities. Boné's approach to the problem of communicating his feelings and ideas is not willful but intangible, "an elusive persuasiveness" which describes Waters as a writer quite well. Even more precisely, the problem is to lift out of a racial stream the forms and rhythms that are centuries old and represent or re-create them in the words, structures, and devices. of a mechanical form—literary narrative. It is all the artist can do, Waters says, to take one step toward perfection.

Boné senses that Rogier's life was wrong because it did not blend properly with the intangible whole. The failure lay in the attempt to locate the meaning of life through reason, an attempt which could end only in madness (a process similar to that of Curt in Clark's *Track of the Cat*). Creation and understanding come not from reason but from necessity and an opening up to "the inward flow of life." Speaking again in biographical terms, it is apparent that Waters was deeply affected by his grandfather and learned a great deal from his weaknesses as well as his strengths. To remain open, to be "alertly passive," to rely on the unconscious, and to close the mind to whatever is mean and inferior—these are the requirements of the writer, the artist, and the intuitive man who would discover the dance of life.

The road toward wholeness, oneness, or fusion carries a variety of travelers who undergo hardships and make their own discoveries. And, the completion of the circle requires many images. Just as important, it seems impossible for man to finish the journey or the circle, and the writer's task includes the portrayal of relative failure as well as relative success. *The Yogi of*

Cockroach Court (1947) stands out in Waters's work as an example of the realism which is often forgotten by critics who pounce on the Jungian elements and by relating them to American Indian and oriental beliefs and philosophies are able to call Waters a mystic and let it go at that. The crown of Waters's work may indeed be mysticism, but the body on which the crown rests is a solid realism. At least a part of the realistic base derives from the fact that all of Waters's novels are built upon personal experience, people he has known, or places in which he has lived. The characters and places—and therefore the novels—are contemporary to him. In this respect, at the very least, his work is unlike most of that by Fisher, Guthrie, Manfred, Fergusson, Clark, and other western novelists. In the two instances of precontemporary beginnings (Rogier in the trilogy and Maria in *People of the Valley*, 1941) the major characters live on into the twentieth century and carry the past into the present startlingly and meaningfully.

The cast of *The Yogi of Cockroach Court*, although located in a Mexican seaport just below the California border, reads like the sociological charting of a typical big-city slum area in the present time: Mexicans, Negroes, Chinese, mixed-bloods, Indians, pimps and prostitutes, and beggars and drug addicts. In the border slum of the novel American Yanquis are no better than equal to the other groups. Cockroach Court is indeed the gangue, the impurities, and it is therefore a good testing ground for the yogi precepts which are incorporated lightly into the novel. Tai Ling, the Chinese philosopher of the Court, perceives the many dualities within this coarse and materialistic society and also recognizes the "strange affinity between all of them." He feels that although the people have no meaning, together they are a karma of locality. However, the use of such terms as *duality* and *fusion*, common to Waters's fiction, is here largely restricted to physical contact, as when the half-breed Barby embraces the prostitute Guadalupe:

> For still he hesitated. Always that strange duality which impelled him forward, then jerked him back again. Even now, so close to her utter capitulation, he felt a dim presentiment of ulti-

mate frustration. Thus they lay embraced upon the brink of that profound chasm wherein lay the last fusion and the last dissolution, the final rendezvous and battlefield of their separate selves. It is tempting, certainly, to translate the passage into a symbolic utterance of love, male and female, anima and animus, yang and yin, and the terrible difficulty of bringing all dualities into an alchemic union and an archetypal form. But the force of the passage lies in its humanity, in its delineation of two real people who are not certain of their destinies. Indeed, the force of the entire novel is conveyed through people rather than ideas, through human frustration rather than philosophical questions and probings. The sordidness of the setting, as well as the driven quality of the characters, suggests early twentieth-century naturalism. But where Frank Norris found a mystical experience in the wheat fields, and thus romanticized his naturalistic intentions (which were, of course, not his main intentions after all), Waters seeks the mystical experience in a Chinese philosopher, Tai Ling, who lives in the midst of a sordid and brutal society. Tai Ling remains spiritually apart from his environment (relying on his past for his karma), but is unable to escape the consequences of the smuggling of aliens which goes on around him. Presumably, what he seeks is already in him, but he does not know it until moments before his death and even then hardly recognizes it.

   Because Barby and Tai Ling die of violence and the part-Indian prostitute Guadalupe achieves a measure of success and happiness, the outcome may seem ironic. Yet sadness over the men's deaths does not detract from the curious sense of joy over Guadalupe's somewhat accidental achievement. Barby and Tai Ling, too conscious of what they do and what they want, perhaps fail because they cannot rely on, or make contact with, the unconscious. Guadalupe, with no apparent powers of insight, is nevertheless able to accept herself for what she is—prostitute, dancer, lesbian—an acceptance of which the men are deprived. That is quite enough revelation for this short novel. From the dross, the gangue, Guadalupe emerges as at least one kind of gold nugget, not pure by any means, but worthy in her own terms. Although *The Yogi of Cockroach Court* yields no profound tragedy and no powerful psychic illuminations, it is a very real and vivid narrative. The attention given to Waters's usual themes is slight; yet in characterization, atmosphere, scene, dialogue, and Guadalupe's self-realization it is an exceptional novel. In a way, it is to Waters's work what *To Have and Have Not* (1937) is to Hemingway's—a variation, not always considered seriously by the critics, but well crafted, very real, and containing its own significance.

In contrast to Guadalupe, Maria de la Valle, Waters's most memorable female character *(The People of the Valley)* is completely a woman of the earth. Along with the valley in which she lives—near Mora, New Mexico—and the possibility of a dam being built to flood the valley, Maria is introduced as an old woman of ninety years. When the narrative goes back in time and traces her strange life from the beginning, it does so economically but without sacrificing any of the meaningful details from Maria's long and full life. The conciseness and the imagery of this novel suggest that it is a long poem celebrating the earth and the woman who fuses within herself the sacred and the profane. Lyric intensity combines with ribald honesty in this provocative portrait of an isolated valley and the remarkable woman who spends her entire life there. As a young girl, Maria herds goats in the hills, lives for a time with two philosophical *viejos*, and is left alone when they die in a flood. By the age of fifteen she is known as "queer Maria," still herding goats. From an affair with a soldier on the hillside, a boy is born—Teodosio. The power she will possess in the valley is suggested in a brief physical description of the girl: "Her eyes were quick and bright as a bird's. Her tongue was sharp for she used it not often enough to dull its edge." But she is also covered by the gritty dust common to all the inhabitants of the valley, "the dust to which all would finally return." And so she matures into a wise and strong woman who is also as common as the earth. Her wisdom comes from the earth; she knows this, and she wonders why Jesús had not trusted the earth rather than the heavens, as though this "error" caused all of the superficial fanaticism—and even the hypocrisy—within the organized church. Giving little thought to religion until she lives with a muleteer named Onesimo, and has a daughter by him, she is capable of forgetting the "creed of the spirit" when she enters a splendid church for the first time and is overwhelmed by the ornate beauty. Impressive as the outward form is, it soon proves meaningless. Maria and her man cannot be married by the priest because Onesimo is a member of the Brothers of Light—the Penitentes—outlawed by the church. At this point, in a delightful and almost unnoticeable image (Onesimo, in fact, is not aware of it), Maria sees the priest scratch himself. He is just a man.

In a juxtaposition of scenes, the religions of Onesimo and the priest are brought together in acts of blind faith, but with an important distinction. Chosen for the honor of symbolic crucifixion by his Penitente brothers in their annual rite, Onesimo accidentally dies on the cross. In the purity of the moment he is transformed from a man into "a fact timeless as the earth itself which ever dies to be resurrected again, the only enduring truth." He is a symbol of the earth, and the earth waits to take him back. Nevertheless, death is not the planned literal outcome of the rite, and the announcement of Onesimo's departure is made to Maria only through an empty pair of shoes on her doorstep: "The shoes were old and shapeless, caked with mud and spotted with dried blood." The death seems to accomplish nothing, and Maria breaks her Santo, the cottonwood image representing Onesimo's religion. Shortly, in a bizarre episode, the priest is told that the communion wine he is about to drink is poisoned; asserting that the wine has been blessed and is therefore no longer wine but the blood of Christ, he proclaims his faith and drinks. And dies. Maria ponders the strange faiths of men and returns to the enduring earth.

Her valley, though small in relation to the world, reflects the whole in a mystic strangeness which embodies her own reflection of the earth as well as the creatures which dwell upon it—a roan stallion racing wildly, crows applauding, a rooster losing his fierceness after coupling with a hen. Maria, like the

indomitable hen, remains self-sufficient through her relationships with five men and the births of five children. The impurities of these relationships are translated into purities of mind
and soul. Throughout the novel, its images proclaim the earthy
necessity or reality of the impure in the midst of both false and
true purity (the false purity being that of the church). Maria
stands proudly, yet humbly, as a supreme blending of the pure
and the impure, an archetype of the earth, of the earth-mother.
The narrative itself moves so easily that we are hardly conscious of every detail of Maria's development, and in one sense
she does not develop at all, having been what she is during her
entire lifetime. Poetic images, however, touch the senses and
lead to an awareness of her unique combination of earthiness
and magic, the gross and the ideally beautiful, the body and the
soul. She is caught up in the flow of life, accepting whatever
comes along, presumably with simple faith. The flow is analo-
gous to the free flow of undamned water, and the threat of a
dam in the valley is the only thing that disturbs her greatly. To
the men who wish to build it, the dam represents progress;
Maria believes in fulfillment. Her thought echoes Waters's
philosophy: "Fulfillment is individual evolution. It requires
time and patience." Also the American Indian's way of thinking, traditionally, the emphasis on time and patience grates on
the white American mind and on corporate structure which demands quick results. We must wonder whether the Western
American novel will ever be able to reach deeply enough into
our national culture to make Maria's message convincing:

> We move through time. But the moment comes when each must
> stop and assert that truth of which he is a part. It is not the whole
> truth, for man himself is yet incomplete. But it is the only truth
> he has. It is his integrity.

In a contemporary society which is losing sight of the individual, of wholeness, of integrity, and of the importance of the
spirit, the Western novel may well be the last beacon in the
night, the last warning.

The dam in Maria's valley has no faith behind it, and therefore it has no meaning to the people. As a symbol it represents

both the false idea of progress and the fatal blockage of the flow of water, which is life itself. Maria's faith in the earth as source of being and of meaning is reaffirmed in two images near the end of the novel. The dam will be built, of course, and the people begin to leave the valley. Maria, now ninety years old, remains. The image of her and of the earth is immediately followed by a philosophical pronouncement based upon that image. The image: "Her dirty black rebozo seemed streaked and rusty as the oxidized iron in the rock. She wiggled a bare toe in the green grass. A beetle crawled across her leg. A robin chirped." And the extension of the image: "It was these she really felt and answered. Men pass on, and their shadows follow. But the heaving earth and its blind vitality remains changeless and indestructible." This is, generally speaking, Waters's method throughout the novel, a highly effective method usually associated with poetry. It gives the narrative and the chief character a lyrical quality consistent with the beauties of the earth, and yet it allows for the sharp, detailed, brief images of the duality of man and nature—the pure and the impure. The duality is resolved by implication and for the moment. Meaning is suggested in the images, whether it be the meaning only of the images themselves, or whether these passing meanings accumulate to a larger significance, beyond evanescence, reaching toward broad insights into the place of man in his universe. Waters admits the difficulty of learning the enduring reality behind the images. In the cyclical pattern of life, however, Maria's death (like any other death) will not stop the search. For another of the enduring realities is that "one sunset [is] a prelude to a sunrise brighter still."

People of the Valley, lacking the scope of some of the other novels, may yet be Waters's most artistic novel, concentrated as it is in the images and language of poetry. Nevertheless, *The Man Who Killed the Deer* has received the most critical attention (particularly in Jungian terms, although Waters did not read Jung until later), and deserves its frequently applied label of best novel about the American Indian. Based upon an actual incident in the Taos area, the novel transcends not only history and journalism but also the conflict around which it is built. *The Man Who Killed the Deer* has at least four different concerns which work together: the inner conflict of Martiniano, part Pueblo, part Apache, educated in the white man's world; the social and legal conflict between Martiniano and his own people as well as the whites, because his killing of the deer out of season violates laws of both cultures; an argument for Pueblo ownership of Blue Lake, a sacred place; and an extremely sensitive and perceptive study of Pueblo beliefs and religious practices. These interwoven themes form a complex pattern, and yet what is most remarkable about the novel is that it has functioned successfully as propaganda (helping to bring about an act of Congress, restoring Blue Lake to the Indians in 1970) and also as a source of psychic power (in the manner of the kachina).

The opening pages are rich in texture and in spirit. Palemon and his family lie in a room within the pyramidlike pueblo. The only light in the room fades into darkness as the red coals of a piñon knot in the fireplace cloud over with a gray film "like the eyes of a dead hawk." The images are extended to the mountain of dark pines where Martiniano is killing a deer. The dim whiteness of the adobe walls extends outside to the pale sheets and blankets of Indians singing along the stream. Two interior sounds—the scampering of a rat across the floor and the breathing of Palemon's family—are echoed in a distant drum and in the moaning of the wind outside. The dark cave is like a womb, and outside the shape of the mountain is like a "recumbent woman's great soft breast." Everything in the room has its strange counterpart outside. The man cannot sleep; he hears the throbbing of the mountain, the beat of the drum, the beat of the heart of the world, and his own pulse, each echoing the other, but his is not in tune. This intuitive recognition of a faulty rhythm drives Palemon to the mountain where he finds Martiniano hurt, having killed a deer and struggled with a ranger.

This dramatic beginning marks the capstone of Martiniano's problems. He has already gone to school away from the pueblo, and thus has been deprived of the traditional and secret religious education required of the young men at the pueblo. Making matters worse, he refuses to follow some of the people's customs, such as wearing the blanket, because his white education has made him skeptical of such things. Additionally, he marries outside the pueblo, an Indian girl not of his own tribe. When he kills the deer, however, his sins compound. He has offended his own people by not performing the ceremony or ritual which would have asked the deer's consent to the killing—an attitude toward the earth's creatures shared by other Indian tribes. And, he has broken the white man's law by killing the deer out of season. He is therefore an outcast. Ironically, his people care nothing for the white man's law, and in turn the white law officials are not the least concerned that Martiniano failed to conform to tribal custom when he killed the deer. While Martiniano is attacked from both sides, by two cultures, the tribe and white justice are also at odds with each other. The Pueblo feel that they have been wronged by the presence of a ranger on their holy land.

Caught between two opposing forces, momentarily despised by all, Martiniano is overcome with a sense of guilt which alienates him even more from his people. Unsatisfactory as a husband, he tries peyote, becomes more arrogant, but seems far removed from a satisfactory truce. What he does not realize at the time is that his experiences with the religious group using peyote have given him at least a kind of faith— something he lacked—even though his elders warn of the peyote-induced visions which destroy earthly reality. Nor does he realize that his wife's presence has been working on him quietly. Although she too has attended school away from her people, she is absorbed into the Pueblo view of the world unobtrusively. A more direct influence upon Martiniano is Palemon, his "blanket" friend who speaks encouragingly of the old way of life. Presented in italics in order to provide a tone that is Indian as well as formal, Palemon's discourses reveal the traditional way of approaching Martiniano's problem. At the same time they instruct the troubled man in the beliefs of the Pueblo.

The argument is persuasive. Man is both mortal body and immortal spirit. The two are one. Life on earth is but a small part of existence. While on earth, man is imprisoned in his body and also in the form of his people's life. Yet as the individual body blends into the larger body of the tribe, it expands to encompass all nature and all spirits. The means of expansion—faith—must be applied to the individual body, the corporate body, and the understanding that belief in these will lead to harmony, or oneness, with the flowing stream of life. Martiniano does not lack a form of life; he has three to choose from—the Pueblo ways, the new ways of the white man, or his own way which could be a part of the other two or an extension into a new way. What he lacks is faith in any one of these forms. It is faith that will "free [his] spirit into a formless life without bounds, which will overflow and taste of all life."

To say that faith in a form will lead to a spiritual life which is formless and has no bounds is not unlike saying in Christian terms that discipline and choice must precede freedom. Although Martiniano is impressed by his friend's exhortation, he insists that Palemon has not dealt with the immediate problem—the deer. Referring to the night when he could not sleep, when his pulse was out of tune with the pulse of the mountain, Palemon then admits his ignorance of the power that called him to Martiniano's wounded body: "There is something about this thing that lies beyond words. We do wrong to question it." Again, faith is the only answer. It is not proper to listen only to body and mind—the heart holds all the feelings. And so Palemon talks not only about form expanding into formlessness, or about the discipline of faith, but about the necessity of intuitive response.

Convinced in part, Martiniano's next task is to work his way back to the tribe. He labors on the farms, takes part in a few of the pueblo's ceremonies, and has a son, all the while haunted by the deer. Simultaneously, the pueblo works to regain possession of Blue Lake (Dawn Lake in the novel), and so the individual and the group—perhaps for slightly different reasons—are going in the same direction, toward a restoration of the old ways. The annual religious ceremony at the lake brings them together. Even though Martiniano has not yet been admitted into the ceremony—he needs further training— he is permitted to watch, and he is contented.

As a source book of American Indian belief and ritual (primarily Pueblo), *The Man Who Killed the Deer* is both expository and suggestive. I include the italicized sections under exposition even though they are dramatized and poetic teachings. From the kiva, Martiniano is told, he will emerge as reborn— the kiva being earth-womb. (In the first scene of the novel, already described, the dark cavelike room is itself like a womb from which its occupants are reborn each dawn. It is also like a tomb, because the pueblo building is tiered somewhat like a pyramid, a place of death. By association, then, life, rebirth, and death are one, and the very words giving shape to the idea—room, womb, tomb—are an incantation of the oneness of all life.) Rebirth is at least partly the recognition of the fact that individual life is not self-sufficient; it depends upon all life, and, more important, it is a part of all life. Aside from the history of the people, Martiniano learns of the necessity of being a part of a whole tradition, people, and life-force. Over and over, the kiva teachings say that man cannot live alone. Late in the novel Rodolfo Byers, a trader, speaks openly for the author, summarizing succinctly the basic differences between white and Indian people. This expository device departs from the more imagistic and suggestive techniques of *People of the Valley*, perhaps the wrong thing to do esthetically, but leaving no doubt of Waters's determination to stress the significance of Indian thought (intuitive) as opposed to the rational thought of the white man. To the white man the world of nature consists of rivers providing electric power, mountains containing silver and gold, forests giving up lumber— everything existing for his own purposes, as though he could ultimately "wrest a purpose from eternity." In actuality, he knows nothing of the enduring earth, and he learns nothing as he scratches its surface. For the Indian the whole world is animate; all matter has a spiritual essence; dualities such as Christ and Satan, good and evil, matter and spirit do not exist, because the world is a living whole. All life must be approached with reverence, including animal and plant life. Byers knows that the world is as each man sees it, but his sympathies are with the Indian view.

Two major images (representing intuitive knowledge of Indian ways) govern the ideas as well as the form of *The Man Who Killed the Deer*. The first is the deer kachina, the spirit that is violated by Martiniano in the beginning, is then revived in his wife, Flowers Playing, as she suffuses his spirit with hers, and flourishes at the end of the novel in a constellation of stars as Martiniano begins to feel at peace with himself and the deer. Normally we would simply call the deer a symbol, but in the context of Pueblo belief (and as part of the form of the novel) *kachina* is more proper—subtle and effective. The second image is the circle, or the sacred lake, embodying the waters of life (the Pueblo elders call it the "lake of life") as well as the intuited knowledge of form and formlessness, primal center and expansion of spirit. Martiniano is found, initially, near the lake, but because he has just killed a deer wrongfully he is unaware of the lake. At the end of the novel he lies beside the lake, looking up into the night sky at the pattern of stars resembling a deer, and contemplating: "A man drops but a pebble into the one great lake of life, and the ripples spread to unguessed shores, to congeal into a pattern even in the timeless skies of night." The ripples spread outward in circles, physically confined to the outline of the lakeshore, spiritually limitless. The pattern is there. The form is there, as it is in the novel, nonlinear, organic, grasped by intuitive feeling which also recognizes the ultimate formlessness which is the final freedom of the spirit. Like the novel, the circle of ripples in the water expands even while it is enclosed.

A short distance from Martiniano his people begin to dance, slowly. The dance is not serious this time. "Pure enjoyment." It too is the dance of life.

IX
The Distant Music:
Variations on Western Realism

Timothy Hazard, the semiautobiographical protagonist of Walter Clark's Reno novel, *The City of Trembling Leaves*, expresses distrust of philosophers and historians who change the mutable and the inscrutable into geometry and what they consider fact. He then turns to Henry Adams who left the *Education* unfinished on the grounds that "when blind, dynamic forces move outward in a thousand directions, it is impossible to determine at what point, if any, they will draw together." Multiplicity as a condition of the life-force is evident throughout the novel, and it is largely by implication that the dynamic forces of Tim's own life do indeed draw together and create a circle from the previously scattered pieces of music arising from a collection of diverse people, places, and things. The final unity may not be final, and it may not be obvious to the mind which is limited to rational thought, but the very possibility of it certainly suggests the creative vitality of life, the circular movement of life forces, and the drive toward a fulfillment which is not primarily intellectual. The music which Hazard composes is not discussed in technical, or intellectual, terms but is made to function as the means by which disparate elements may be brought into harmony. Metaphorically, ideas and experiences from Hazard's life (or anyone's life) have the same potential for harmony and, ultimately, for unity. What seems to bother many readers of Clark—and also of Frank Waters—is that the process of achieving unity from multiplicity is not stated, not defined. The mystery is, of course, the crux of the matter, although it is possible to say that answers must spring from the earth, from the unconscious, and from a willingness to learn from sources other than the scientifically factual or the philosophically systematic. Indeed, a sophistication of primitive values may be the major characteristic of the essential Western novel. Waters daringly asks the modern rational mind to accept primitive concepts such as the Hopi kachina—representing the spirits of invisible forces—even though they come from instinct and racial memory rather than from the more visible world of the intellect. His purpose—prophetic rather than presumptuous—is to save the modern world from itself by suggesting a new awareness of world and self, a mode of thought based on the insights of the unconscious rather than on the computerized formulas of technology. Together with Clark he expresses a belief that man's salvation will come only from listening once again to the music and harmonies of the earth, as well as learning from primal sources of human belief and behavior. It is in the American West, with its geological antiquity, its Indian heritage, and its land-based ethos that the nonintellectual links between past and present are most visible and available.

Not all western novelists are as concerned with the unconscious (or the joining together of instinct and intellect for a unified psyche) as are Waters and Clark. Nearly all, however, are reconciled to an investigation of the past, of history, in order to illuminate the present. With differing motives and varied methods, western novelists seek to establish continuity between a past either recent or distant and a present time which cannot be explained properly in its own terms alone. While there is not always a clear-cut distinction between the intentions of one group of novels and another, it may not be entirely amiss to suggest that the highest philosophical calling in the Western novel is the search for unity in multiplicity, and the highest historical calling is the search for continuity. Structurally, the first is circular and the second is linear. The linear can be disguised technically, as in Wallace Stegner's *Angle of Repose* (1971) and *Recapitulation* (1979) with their historical narratives contained within a strong and significant present-time framework. The circular, in turn, often depends upon symbol, metaphor, and archetype to resolve the multiplicities and ambiguities of its historical narrative.

We must keep in mind that the American West is an immense region of apparent contradictions: the fleeting beauty of the wilderness before its wanton destruction by man is still opposed by the eternality or permanence of the earth, including things beautiful; the concept of wilderness is opposed by the concept of development in terms of man's convenience and ambition; the idea that the land influences the people who live on it is opposed by the belief that the people influence and shape the land; and, importantly, place as a determinant of human behavior often conflicts with history, the past, also seen as the major force operating on the destinies of the people. Given these possibilities, it is not at all strange to find a variety of literary treatments of the western experience. Complicating the matter is the ever-present debate over the mythical and the real—the real considered for the moment as historical fact. This issue is confusing. Part of the American myth was the belief in unlimited opportunity and riches to be found in the West. To a certain extent the myth came true, but not for the vast majority who found only hard work, danger, disappointment, futility, and daily obstacles to survival. The historical, or conscious, realist tends to deny the myth, to show the falsity of the dream of gold at the end of the western rainbow. References to the dream are made in titles of novels which then go on to illustrate, ironically, the grim and often tragic truth. In H. L. Davis's 1957 novel, *The Distant Music*, the irony is implicit in the title: the music lies in the brief glimpse of the beauties of the land, but it seems to retreat continually before the struggle to bend the land to man's use. The music, then, is akin to that of the sirens of mythology, luring man toward something he does not foresee and which can be fatal. Similarly, the mythical Seven Golden Cities of Cibola, sought for so long in New Mexico, maintain their distance in Paul Horgan's novel of the hardships of the 1930s, *Far From Cibola* (1936). And the equally mythical "big rock candy mountain" of Stegner's novel by that name is never the one that is reached. For the realists, at least, the music—whatever form it may take—keeps its distance from the people who hear it, or disappears altogether under the strain of survival.

However, the West is home to several kinds of reality, two of which seem to be opposed to each other. From Timothy Hazard's ruminations on Henry Adams and the "blind, dynamic forces" moving "outward in a thousand directions," to "Our life contains a thousand strings," from the Isaac Watts hymn which suggested another H. L. Davis title, *Harp of a Thousand Strings* (1947), may seem but a short step from one kind of multiplicity to another. However, the reality of the first lies in an unconscious recognition of life-forces which are potentially unified both in the world of the spirit and in the psyche of that person who can open his heart and mind to the special kind of awareness that is unavailable to the intellect alone. The reality of the second is historical and cultural, a conscious act of discovery through a search of the multitude of events leading up to a particular culminating event. In this case the issue is not unity or the reconciliation of multiplicity but rather explanation according to verifiable facts, the explanation of a present-time cultural or historical or psychological phenomenon in terms of the various related phenomena which existed in the past and shaped the present. This kind of reality is deterministic and is common in the nonwestern novel. The alternative seen in the most significant Western novels is a reality which springs from the creative unconscious, from that part of the mind whose apprehension of the universe is not limited to objective facts. It should be clear, however, that in fiction the two kinds of reality are not as mutually exclusive as they might be in theory or in a rigid philosophical examination of them. At best, we can suggest that one Western novel might be more pure in its intentions, its mode of apprehension, its theme, and its relation to the natural environment than another novel; yet the West is large enough to encompass several regions and a number of literary styles and attitudes.

2

The belief that the people of a particular time and place can be explained or delineated only through an examination of their backgrounds—earlier times and other places—is not uncommon. In Western American literature, however, influences from another place or culture in the recent past usually give way to the stronger and more immediate pressures of the "new place." The assumption is that the western landscape with its elevation, aridity, and isolation has led to unique experiences for those people who emigrated from the wooded and watered East, and that adjustment to these new experiences and the new land has been necessary for survival. Theoretically, the assumption seems valid, but we must keep in mind that any flexibility of definition of West (for example, expanding beyond the limitations set or suggested by Walter Prescott Webb) exposes a variety of Wests, some of them—like the Far Northwest—characterized by conditions not unlike those of New England and other parts of the East.

Many emigrants who crossed the Interior West, who went beyond the plains and the Rockies, found in Oregon adequate rainfall and a type of soil and landscape no more hostile than that of the wooded East. Indeed, the climate was often better—more temperate and more consistent. It is not strange, then, that the Oregon novelist H. L. Davis should place more emphasis on the cultural and historical backgrounds of his characters than on land-determinism, although he recognizes (in *Honey in the Horn*, 1935) the destructive force of the riches of the land: "Too many things planted in that country grew bigger than you expected them to, and some prospered by it while others destroyed themselves." This is clearly a West different from the one which dominates the fiction of Clark, Fergusson, and Waters. It is a region within the West, but it is set apart from the immense Great Plains–Rocky Mountain area whose environmental forces have played a major part in the American idea of West.

As a regionalist, Davis is a social and cultural historian, fascinated by the facts of his region, by the lore, and by the small and folksy stories that are passed around and that—taken collectively—help to characterize the region. His method is like that of Preston Shively, the self-styled local historian of *Honey in the Horn:*

> Uncle Preston disliked being interrupted when he was telling a story. He had got into the swing of his narrative, which meant that he was through the stages of recollecting middle initials and which bush old man So-and-so had camped under and whether he owned a white mare or a gray gelding, and that he was cracking down on what things had happened and what people they had happened to.

There are many events and many people—a multiplicity which is, however, different from that found in Clark's *City of Trembling Leaves.* In both style and substance, the Davis novel is a piece of folklore; it chronicles the collective life of an Oregon settlement very early in the twentieth century, allowing the facts of this farm-sheep-cattle country to take precedence over plot or interpretation. The style is casual, garrulous, and subtly ironic in the manner of the oral storyteller. In some respects Davis is the Northwest's Mark Twain with his sense of humor, his profusion of details, and his fondness for anecdotes. The result of all this, as it was with Twain, is social history reliant as much on folklore as on actual historical events. Intrigued by the facts of his region, Davis notes at the beginning of *Honey in the Horn* that he "had originally hoped to include in the book a representative of every calling that existed in the State of Oregon during the homesteading period—1906–1908." Perhaps the statement is made with tongue in cheek, reminiscent again of Twain. Yet in Davis, the multiplicity of

things, objects, minor characters, and small incidents is culti-
vated for its own sake, as an act of realism.

One of the dangers of historical realism of this kind is that
significance (or the potential for it) may be lost beneath a welter
of facts. Whatever meaning may be available in the regional details themselves is overshadowed, however, by an overriding
concern for continuity as represented by Davis's belief that
people are not shaped as much by the new land in the West as
they have already been shaped by their previous environments
and customs. The present time, then, merely reveals the past,
or is revealed by the past. This means, simply, that the details
of Davis's fiction must be taken for their own inherent interest—however much that might be—while the underlying importance of the narrative on a larger scale gradually emerges as
a statement about the continuity of generations, of customs,
and of behavior characteristics and patterns. The continuity,
seen in different terms by Waters, Clark, Fergusson, Manfred,
and Fisher, is here short term and linear, and it does not rely on
a sense of place.

Beulah Land (1949) is illustrative of the pitfalls awaiting
Davis's motives and methods. During the Indian Removal,
Ruhama Warne, part Indian, born in 1840 in the Cherokee Nation in North Carolina, leaves for the West with her father and
friends. The entire novel is an odysseylike account of the journey to Oregon, but the narrative becomes so bogged down in
details that it is too easy to lose sight of the overall picture, and
it is difficult to tell whether the incidents of the journey are supposed to shape the two people who finally get to Oregon
(changing them from what they were in North Carolina) or
whether these incidents exist for their own interest. The journey takes Ruhama and Askwani through Tennessee, to
Natchez, up the Mississippi River to Cairo, across Missouri,
into Kansas and Oklahoma in almost aimless wanderings, and
finally into Oregon at the very end of the novel. The past remains thin, the future is a complete mystery, and the intentions of the author seem to be to show one of the meandering

routes to Oregon. The loose plot and the occasional exposition of such things as the danger of malaria in Illinois are indicative of a rambling frontier story, a historical adventure, rather than a study of either character or place. It is only through the fact of the trip itself that we are allowed to assume a theme of continuity (or connection) from one place to another, and in a lesser way from one time to another. The fact that Askwani dies just after reaching Oregon, leaving only Ruhama to enter into a new life in a new place, may suggest that the line of continuity wears thin and almost breaks.

In *The Distant Music* a single place inhabited by three generations of Ransom Mulocks and their women holds the narrative together despite a chaos of minor characters, obscure incidents, and regional folklore. When the first Ransom comes to Columbia River country in 1858, at age forty, he buys a fourteen-year-old white girl from the Indians and marries her. Already pregnant by an Indian, she miscarries. After Ransom has two sons and builds a house, he finds his wife's former lover and kills him. Shortly thereafter he dies from a heart attack at age fifty-six. Briefly, these are the background incidents which serve as the context for the ensuing events surrounding the life of the second Ransom, who is the chief character of the novel, and, to a lesser degree, the third Ransom. By giving the same name to the father, son, and grandson, Davis superficially identifies the theme of historical continuity. More to the point, the three Ransoms have the same characteristics. They are not heroic, not overly ambitious, not farsighted, and not highly intelligent; they are, rather, somewhat crude and rough, careless, unconcerned at times, and often outright wild and unpredictable. Whether these characteristics form any kind of western archetype is debatable, but they undoubtedly represent a part of Davis's attempt at realism. A vague music of the beauty of the land may have attracted settlers to Oregon, including the first Ransom and his wife Medora, but the realities are to be found in weakness of character as well as in the harshness and the struggles which constantly threaten to destroy the

continuity of several generations of a family on the same piece
of land.

The land in question is gradually developed into a small settlement including railroad shops. It is an important part of the
nearby community, and yet Ransom Mulock's son and grandson are reluctant to stay with it. The urge to build is complicated by restlessness, by the desire to get out and go somewhere else. The reasons for this feeling are not clear, but on at
least one occasion they are pushed into the background momentarily by a reference to the past. Medora tells her son of the
lost lives, the tragedies, the difficulties behind the settling of
the land, and of the family's attempt to remain independent of
the town itself. The son then admits that he was thinking of
leaving, but now that he knows "what was back of the land" he
will stay. For Medora, at this point in her life, "it was as if the
land had been in her mind as the meeting-place of trails marked
out by all her dead." We must assume that the statement is serious, and yet the dead have been given the briefest of references
earlier in the novel and are therefore not convincing, and the
land's role is ambiguous, so that what might have been a major
and dramatic theme loses its force. Furthermore, when the
youngest Ransom speaks of leaving, two influences conflict:
the girl he wishes to marry, described as strong and courageous, is perfectly willing to go with him, anywhere; but a lyrical and nostalgic hymn to nature and to "the place" allows the
reader to believe that it will not be possible for young Ransom
to leave. Finally, the father—who had disappeared for a time—
returns, sick, and is given the center of attention. That the people of the community come to visit him seems to prove to Lydia
(whose point of view concludes the novel) that everything the
Ransoms had done was worthwhile.

Davis has a vision, and it concerns the land as well as the
people, but ultimately we must question his kaleidoscopes of
characters, families, and conflicts on the grounds of diffusion
and obscurity, the result of an obsession with scattered details
at the expense of control. Local legends add a regional richness

but refuse to support a major theme which strains to go beyond the limits of the region. Davis as amateur historian, as collector of locally interesting characters and events, is at odds with Davis the artist.

Quite a different objection might be made to the artist who is so intent on his craft or on his technical virtuosity that he allows method to stand in the way of life rather than illuminating it from a half-hidden position within the novel. From *The Big Rock Candy Mountain* through *Angle of Repose* and *Recapitulation* (his three novels which stand in a kind of series), Wallace Stegner has moved from an obvious enthusiasm for his subject and material to an almost coldly academic concern for structure, point of view, and other elements of the craft of writing. The reader who responds to the textural richness and loosely structured vibrancy of the novels of H. L. Davis will probably feel at a distance from the later fiction of Stegner. However, both men are vitally interested in history and in the demythologized facts of the West, although their approaches are different. Stegner's history is more personally familial, taken from those parts of the West in which he lived with parents who wandered about, following the elusive music of success and happiness.

Bo and Elsa Mason of *The Big Rock Candy Mountain*, like the characters of Walter Clark's *Track of the Cat*, seem at first to be typical or representative of some of the kinds of people who (historians as well as novelists have told us) went west even as late as the twentieth century. Bo turns down steady work, acquires a contempt for the law, makes himself likable to "hard-boiled and suspicious men," and has "an ambition to get somewhere where the cream hadn't been skimmed off, get in on the ground floor somewhere and make his pile." As late as 1905 the West can beckon to such a man, and the journey-plot of the novel takes him from the Dakotas to Washington, Saskatchewan, Montana, and Utah where he dies in Salt Lake City, his dream already dead—drowned in gambling, speculations, and shiftlessness. Why Elsa Norgaard, a gentle young woman of Norwegian parentage, should want to marry Bo and accompany him on his futile journey is explained partly by the dismal landscape of eastern Dakota, seen from the train whose rocking has already made Elsa feel sick.

> There were few trees now. Somewhere, while she had been sick, they had come to some sort of dividing line. Farms were more scattered, the buildings unpainted, and either ramshackle or staringly new. There were no hills, only a wide bare green-gold plain, pasture and unthrifty-looking cornfields. Once in a while they came to creeks or rivers flowing turgidly in sandy beds between strips of dusty cottonwoods. Mile after mile, hour after hour, past sod shanties with weeds growing green on their roofs, past unpainted shacks and ragged sheds, past windmills and discouraged plantings of saplings, past fields of wheat still meadow-green in the heat, past flocks of crows that flapped heavily off the wires as the train roared by, past herds of nondescript cattle with cowbirds sitting on their hipbones.

The description is reminiscent of Hamlin Garland's reaction: to the same landscape, and the bleakness of it all is reasor enough for Elsa to want to get away. Although Stegner see: landscape realistically—in Saskatchewan and Utah as well as in Dakota—and is reluctant to make anything symbolic out of it, he allows the land to be a force. It is hardly a coincidence that Elsa's agreement to marry Bo comes shortly after the change of season, after she has sat by the window thinking that autumn is quite different from the end-of-summer season she remembers from a place east of Dakota.

> There weren't any trees to change, for one thing. The land just got brown and then gray, and one night it froze, and then it rained, and froze again so that the roads were ridged with hardened tracks, and every change from summer to winter made the place look more desolate than it had before. And the wind blew interminably, holding you back, hustling you along, sweeping at you from around corners. You weren't free of it even inside, for it whined in the eavespouts and slammed doors and eddied down the chimney and made the stove smoke. It kept you tense all the time.

This is the same prairie-mountain wind that kept the posse tense and edgy in Clark's *Ox-Bow Incident*, and in each case the land and the climate act as an influence—if not a major force—upon the actions of the characters. For Elsa, the dismal place in which she lives causes her to believe in an ambitious and flashy man like Bo Mason, and to think that he might provide something better for her, just as he, in turn, thinks there will be better opportunities farther west. If there is any kind of national idealism (even as manifested in the American Dream) behind the wanderings of Bo and Elsa it is subjugated to the realities of place and character.

For Stegner the future lies in the past, it grows from the past, both from family and from place. History is a sequence of events involving people and land. While Elsa's gentleness and urge toward cultural fulfillment clash with Bo's carelessness and crudities, Stegner is concerned with the son, Bruce, who has inherited more from his mother than from his father and who moves toward a refinement which is seen both as a personal achievement and as a goal for the communities of the West. From a union of opposites—Bo and Elsa—and from such East-West contrasts as community and individualism, culture and backwardness, respect for the law and reliance on physical strength, and a somewhat gentled landscape as opposed to one of difficult extremes, Bruce emerges as his own man. Stegner speculates that it may take several generations to make a man, with combinations of characteristics from the parents and, further back, the grandparents. At the funeral of his father, Bruce is the only surviving member of the family: "He was the only one left to fulfill that contract and try to justify the labor and the harshness and the mistakes of his parents' lives."

The responsibility and the obligation to make sense of his parents' lives continues in the later life of Bruce in *Recapitulation*, a sequel to *The Big Rock Candy Mountain* although it is presented in a series of flashbacks which re-examine that part of his life which Bruce spent in Salt Lake City. The narrative device is a simple one, but it is handled with dexterity and some subtlety. Bruce, now in his sixties, is an ex-ambassador, editor, and expert on Middle Eastern oil. From his California home he returns to Salt Lake City for the first time in forty-five years to attend to his aunt's funeral arrangements. Memories overwhelm him and he is not entirely able to avoid nostalgia although he reminds himself of its dangers. Even as Bruce Mason detects the "fragrance of lost possibility" while wandering around the city he seems to speak for Stegner, saying that perhaps his past is his subject matter, that it is what he really knows. The novel is therefore devoted largely to a series of memories re-created realistically as though acted out in the present. Bruce slips into his memories easily, often in mid-sentence, so that at times it is difficult to divide present from past. We have a choice, then, between viewing Bruce's consciousness as divided into two parts—a disunity—or as a fusion of moments of history into a single reality. Stegner's technical method allows both conclusions.

From the many places in which he lived as a boy and young man (twelve different houses in Salt Lake City alone), Wallace Stegner has always been conscious of movement; and from the places, especially Saskatchewan, he has also been aware of the importance of space. Add to the concept of motion-within-space the elusiveness or relativity of truth, and from Stegner's fiction emerges a search for historical (and family) continuity which is linked to a similar search for personal identity. That identity for Bruce Mason—in *The Big Rock Candy Mountain* as well as in *Recapitulation*—takes on a larger meaning for Stegner when he implies that Bruce may be typical of a certain kind of American, probably a westerner, "born artless and without history into a world of opportunity, who must acquire in a single lifetime the intellectual sophistication and the cultural confidence that luckier ones absorb through their pores from earliest childhood." Bruce both blames his parents (especially his father) for depriving him of cultural advantages and finds it strange, though satisfying, that he has managed nevertheless to bring himself to that stage of refinement which has weeded out of his own person most of the crudities of his father. Yet he is tied to his parents, "who are fate," and is often uneasy about himself. A part of his uneasiness remains misunderstood. At his father's grave he contemplates the fact that Harry Mason's definition can be stated only in terms of the family members resting beside him, that without his relationship to them— without history—he was, and is, nothing. "Without them he would merge with the universal grass." However, he does not recognize an extremely important matter, namely, the Indian point of view that deems it entirely satisfactory—perhaps necessary—that the individual should after death merge with the natural world and with all the spirits that had gone before him. This essentially western view seems totally absent from Bruce's consciousness and, along with his views on cultural deprivation, may identify his personal problem as an inability to see himself either as an intellectual easterner or a spiritual westerner. Indeed, Bruce Mason may well have the same kind of identity crisis that bedeviled Bernard DeVoto (about whom Stegner wrote a biography, *The Uneasy Chair*, 1974). There is irony in the "universal grass."

History and identity merge more clearly, especially through memory. The shift into some of the flashbacks in *Recapitulation* is so smooth and subtle that past and present blend into one experience and continuity becomes an instant. Metaphorically, the Old West and the New are, by way of myth and memory, simultaneously present in the mind, although Stegner is usually reluctant to consider this larger level of meaning, preferring to examine his own experiences realistically. In this respect he is both an antidote to western romanticism and an unwary cousin of the intuitionists. Bruce Mason sees himself as a product of American mobility and as an orphan. Literally, of course, he is without parents; but spiritually he may have been an orphan even while his parents were alive, akin to Vardis Fisher's orphans in Gethsemane. Stegner cannot let the matter rest in that cultural and psychological quagmire. His subject is identity and history, and for the living it is memory that holds history. Stegner plays upon the Cartesian "I think, therefore I am," making memory the factor which explains both existence and its continuity:

> Memory had to be—didn't it?—a series of overlays. I remember, therefore I was. I was, therefore I am. I both contain and commemorate myself. I am both grave and gravestone.

The narrator, whether he be Bruce Mason or Wallace Stegner, is the receptacle of the past, and he is also the marker of it, the sign that it—and therefore he—actually existed.

Stegner is concerned with continuity and community rather than with the self-sufficient individual so often mentioned as an essential part of the western experience but who may be more mythical than historically real. As though to prove the point, while at the same time commenting ironically on it, he establishes a physically disabled and retired professor as narrator of *Angle of Repose* and places him in a modern community for which he has little sympathy. The two conditions force him into the past, into an older West which he refuses to glorify even though it seems to hold more promise than the contemporary West. *Angle of Repose* is a kind of historical detective story, with Lyman Ward using family papers to reconstruct the relationship between his grandparents, Oliver and Susan Ward. Presumably, he does so because his own infirmities and marital problems prevent him from leading a full life of his own. He strives to find his meaning in the life of his grandparents. That meaning is examined in two ways, one in the relationship between East and West (spatial-cultural), the other in the relationship between past and present (temporal-cultural). In a sense, *Angle of Repose* brings together those problems which Stegner has dealt with in most of his fiction and in *Wolf Willow*.

There is no clear solution to the problems. The refinement of the East and the crudity and robustness of the West can live together—as they do in the grandparents' marriage, however uneasily—but the concept of "angle of repose" (a geological term) does not prove satisfactory in the urge toward unity. Nor are we completely convinced that the present is very much like the past except as we understand that the human animal does not change much from one era to another. Within the frame of Lyman Ward's own story, most of the novel goes into the past, into the details of the mining camps in the 1870s and 1880s. At best, on the literal level (and perhaps this is enough), these portraits of western frontier life correct many of the assumptions of romantic writers who depend upon the attraction of the myth. But the major discovery is supposed to belong to Lyman, and while he finds historical continuity a comfort he does not find workable answers to the problems of Susan and Oliver or to his own. It is as though Stegner is telling us that history is not exact, that the realistic attitude must leave it that way, and that we must not resort to myth or to intuition to resolve matters upon which we can only speculate.

Paul Horgan carries the realistic attitude even further in *Far From Cibola*, a short novel which became the center portion of *Mountain Standard Time* (1963) when three of Horgan's novels of contemporary New Mexico were reprinted as a trilogy. Although Horgan's knowledge of the history of New Mexico is evident in his nonfiction *(Great River: The Rio Grande in North American History* and *The Centuries of Santa Fe,* among others), he is less concerned in his fiction with continuity than with specific moments in time. Furthermore, landscape operates less as a force than as a backdrop against which character develops as though on a stage. In the foreword to *Mountain Standard Time* Horgan says: "In those land spaces of the southwest, great as they are, a person stands in relief like an earth feature, small, perhaps, but strongly lighted and as strongly shadowed." And, indeed, Horgan's characters are small, unheroic except as the little people of the earth are heroic in their survival and their occasional small victories over mundane problems; but Horgan's method is to illuminate them, including the shadows of despair, hopelessness, and tragedy, so that they stand etched as in a portrait. Even in Horgan's one historical novel—*A Distant Trumpet* (1960), hailed by his publisher as "romantic" and "heroic"—the emphasis is on characterization, on the ways in which a variety of soldiers will react to a test of character provided by a frontier situation. And while Dr. Peter Rush in *The Common Heart* (1942, later appearing as volume three of the trilogy) professes an interest in the land, the history, the facts and artifacts of New Mexico, collecting books and visiting places where historical incidents have occurred, the land and its heritage hardly rub off on him. In his insistence that he not be called a regionalist, Horgan does not allow himself or his characters to recognize the land as a shaping and compelling force upon either their beliefs or their destinies.

Far From Cibola, therefore, does not reveal man's attachment to the earth except through the practical matter of economics, the problems arising from crop failures during a period of drought. Because the background of the action is the Great Depression of the 1930s, the experience of the Dust Bowl, comparison is invited with Steinbeck's *Grapes of Wrath* and Manfred's *Golden Bowl*, both of which admit of a deeply spiritual relationship between man and earth. While Steinbeck and Manfred are realists in style, they are romantic in concept and vision, so that it is possible for man to experience spiritual insights and growth through his direct contacts with the land. Steinbeck's novel is structured as a journey, and while the destination does not provide the Eden which the migrants seek it is still possible to hold out an optimistic view of the future because of the essential vitality and fertility of all life. Manfred's chief character also embarks upon a journey, across South Dakota and back, the wandering punctuated by three instances of self-revelation in which he first feels reborn out of the earth, then senses his relationship to all former life, and finally recognizes the brotherhood of man. Again, hope persists in the midst of severe economic difficulties and during the testing of faith. Horgan's characters are in sight of "the mountain . . . shining like glass in colour and mystery upon the horizon," but they pay little attention to it; in small groups, and individually, in and near the town, they concentrate on their own problems, some of them psychological, some a matter of economic survival, some rooted in love, and a few rooted in hate. The community is a microcosm of the world at large, with point of view shifting rapidly from one person to another through fourteen mosaiclike chapters. Horgan remains detached from his material, maintaining a limited omniscience but allowing potentially symbolic events to stand on their own and to function structurally rather than metaphorically. The killing of a dangerous snake early in the novel is rendered dramatically in terms of the mother, Ellen Rood, protecting her children, but its full significance is delayed until the tragic death of young Franz, at which time Ellen can feel that in spite of all other problems she has something worthwhile—her own children are still alive because the snake is dead by sundown (according to folklore) even though Franz also dies at sundown. Other acts of violence assist in preparing the stage for the senseless death of Franz. The fragmented portraits come together, as in a mural, and the scattered lives suddenly join, become a mob, protest the lack of help from the federal government, begin to storm the courthouse in communal anger, and then draw back in individual shock as Franz, the young track star, is killed by a stray bullet while perched in a tree to get a better view of the courthouse. In the aftermath, the community breaks down into fragments again, Andrew Lark feeling good about being old after seeing a young man dead, Rolfe and Heart making love in the newspaper office, Fat and two others telling dirty stories in a bordello, and Leo feeling that he must get out of town and seek the "promised land of California" which waited for him with "warmth and money, kindness, a job, security." The portraits are mostly bleak, and the courthouse tragedy can at best offer a catharsis, as in Clark's *Ox-Bow Incident*.

Horgan is aware of the human impulse toward better things, whether they be represented by the mythical Seven Cities of Cibola or by the equally strong myth of California. But Cibola is far from this town, even as symbol, and Leo hardly gets started on his journey to the ocean. Unable to get a ride, he curls up in a wrecked Ford beside the highway to get out of the cold wind. Dreaming of the sea, of warm sand and beautiful women, he dies of exposure. Reality is made up of deep desires as well as stark facts, and Horgan lets it go at that except to suggest that Leo was "in some way a responsibility on all the lives he had ever known." To this extent, then, continuity is important even within a brief moment of history.

3

Considerations of the past may take many forms and attitudes in the Western novel, some of which we have already seen. When the past is dealt with for its own sake, the result in fiction is either an authentic re-creation of a particular time and place, reinforced by material from journals and travel narratives, or it is simply entertaining adventure, romance, and myth concocted by the imagination. When the past is seen as part of the eternal continuum as well as the process of change, it takes on both cultural and emotional significance and, at best, illuminates the present and indicates the future. The West has more than one historical past because of regional and cultural variations within the broad area between Mexico and Canada and between the East-West center of the continent and the Pacific Ocean. Rapid changes, also, during a relatively short period of time have heightened the effects of eras as brief as a few decades. The oldest past is that of the Indian, rarely re-created in fiction but tapped into through those traditions, beliefs, and legends which have persisted into relatively modern times. A middle past is provided by the Spanish in the South, beginning in the sixteenth century, and by the French in the North, beginning a century later. Particularly in the Southwest, through the lingering Spanish traditions, this middle past has overlapped the more recent past, that of the nineteenth century which we tend to refer to—sometimes mistakenly—as "American." And finally, in the twentieth century, there remains in isolated instances a past within the mind, or spirit, as illustrated by Jack Burns, the cowboy in Edward Abbey's novel, *The Brave Cowboy* (1956).

Willa Cather's *Death Comes for the Archbishop* (1927) covers most of the second half of the nineteenth century, but its tone and spirit make the time seem much earlier than that of Conrad

Richter's *The Sea of Grass* (1937) whose historical time is approximately 1885–1910, immediately following that of Cather's novel. The reasons for this condition are explicit. Cather (and/or Bishop Latour) has a brief encounter with the old Indian culture, notably in the cave above a subterranean river, a special place to Jacinto but horrifying to Latour. Yet he comes close to a recognition of the importance of Earth's voices: "He told himself he was listening to one of the oldest voices of the earth." Cather's language here places her on the edge of a vital revelation which, however, is quickly dropped and left veiled. She, like Latour, is not prepared for the full vision of the ancient western earth, so familiar to the Indians. And so it is only the suggestion of antiquity that lingers in the air. A second reason for feeling that we are further back than we really are is that the novel opens just following the Mexican War and the Spanish are still somewhat rebellious against the Anglos, as they had been ever since the first mountain men visited Santa Fe early in the nineteenth century. A third reason is that Cather introduces historical characters such as Kit Carson and Padre Martinez who, although active not much more than one hundred years ago, have become legends and seem, at least, to be from a past more distant than it really is. To complicate matters, the two priests—Latour and Vaillant—are from France, and Cather includes several flashbacks to an earlier time in Europe, the mood being one of nostalgia for the mellower traditions and values of an older white culture. Finally, a quaintness of style, and a measure of sentimentality, both perhaps in keeping with the characteristics of Latour, suggest a method of narrative not to be considered modern even when the novel was published over fifty years ago.

Richter's *Sea of Grass* is not as rich as *Death Comes for the Archbishop* in color, mood, and texture, but it may be more effective in its restraint and in its conception of change under what might be considered tragic circumstances, the dilemma of the large-scale rancher confronted by encroaching farmers. The historical period is an important one in the westward movement, with restless farmers invading what had traditionally been free range, land fought for by the ranchers who displaced the Indian and sometimes the Mexican and then during their own lifetime are displaced in turn by the farmers, by fences, and eventually by communities. This process of historical change lends itself to a more dramatic treatment than does the slower and gentler religious change brought about by the Catholic church. Furthermore, it was Richter's intention to portray the moral and ethical patterns of the turn of the century in such a way that they would, through illumination, suggest answers to more modern problems. Cather's answer to this procedure is only an implication that the church and European culture would be of benefit to the western wilderness. It is the church bells, not the land, that provide the music, and it is not a distant music—it is certain, just as the overall mood of the novel is optimistic. Father Vaillant's death, which might have been viewed in terms of tragedy, is only reported, not rendered, and Archbishop Latour dies contented with his work, knowing that the church will flourish. *The Sea of Grass*, also capable of tragedy, ends quietly on a note of nostalgia, the conflict having been resolved—or removed—by natural forces, in this case a drought which immobilizes the farmers.

While Cather was able to acquire the facts of the region, she was unable to absorb its spirit. The spirit of the novel is to be found in the priests, and it is a spirit of the Catholic church in particular and of the expansion of European enlightenment in general. As a part of the process of refinement and civilization in the American West, *Death Comes for the Archbishop* is a Western novel. But its beauty, charm, and significance—none of which can be overlooked—lie solely in the relationship between the two priests. It is Latour who has the authority and therefore occupies the commanding position; yet his major accomplishment may be the encouragement, assistance, and friendship which he offers his subordinate, Father Vaillant. It is possible that Vaillant is a hero; he is a man of action who almost becomes Americanized, and through his courage, endurance, and mobility he is able to make the dream of Latour come true, giving vitality to the ideas and intellectual projections of an Old World civilization. In the Richter novel, the civilizing force is vague, perhaps understood to be behind the advance of the farmers, eventually to catch up with them through a sense of community, law and order, and the establishment of schools and churches (although a church is already available, it gets little attention). During the change from patriarchal rule to democratic procedures it almost seems as though the progress implicit in the change will destroy the spirit of the land.

Whereas Cather's purpose is to humanize nature (no lasting values are found in the land itself), and Richter's is to lament the passing of a time considered heroic (with the land as battlefield), John Steinbeck, writing at about the same time *(To a God Unknown*, 1933), proposes that the land is the most important thing of all, more than man and more than God. Joseph Wayne, migrating from Vermont to California, becomes obsessed with the land, even to the point of offering sacrifices to an unknown god. His rituals are pagan, and yet he is also seen as a Christ figure. His behavior is called "rot" by his brother Burton, a strict Protestant who has as strong a distaste for the Catholic church as he has for Joseph's paganism, but who blames their father for the madness and, interestingly, insists that Joseph would have been spared his rot if he had remained in Vermont under the influence of a more civilized and Christian society. In the West, however, the mountains are too high, the place is savage, and the people carry the seeds of evil in them. Burton remains the most orthodox Christian in the family, but the others are not especially sympathetic to his ascetic Christ. Thomas, the eldest brother, is primitive, living according to instincts, and feeling a kinship with animals as though he might be one himself. His wife, Rama, functions very much like a high priestess from ancient times, a form of Mother Earth. Joseph is perhaps a pantheist, worshiping nature and finding all things to be holy; he also assumes a patriarchal role in the family and extends this role to the entire valley, feeling responsible for all the people—perhaps an Abraham. The youngest brother, Benjy, rejects all of

the traditions available to him; he is corrupted by civilization
and its signs of decay—a modern man. The pattern of characterization is almost too neatly established, strongly suggesting
archetypal structuring. Symbols abound, some of them sexual, some religious, and some broadly nature-oriented.

For Joseph Wayne the "distant music" is a part of his
blood and is a direct and mystical call from the earth translated into a cry to save the land. His reason seems to have left
him, yet Christianity as an alternative to his paganism seems
no more reasonable:

> Father Angelo got out of his chair and stood over Joseph.
> "You are ill, my son," he said. "Your body is ill and your soul
> is ill. Will you come to the church to make your soul well? Will
> you believe in Christ and pray help for your soul?"
>
> Joseph leaped up and stood furiously before him. "My
> soul? To Hell with my Soul! I tell you the land is dying. Pray
> for the land!"
>
> The priest looked into his glaring eyes and felt the frantic
> fluid of his emotion. "The principal business of God has to do
> with men," he said, "and their progress toward heaven, and
> their punishment in Hell."

Joseph's intensity reaches the priest in a way that the concepts
of heaven and hell can never reach him, and, in a moment of
heresy, or insight, he imagines Joseph becoming "a new
Christ here in the West." Then he goes into the church and
prays for rain, as Indians dance for it and as Joseph sacrifices
himself in pagan ritual for it. Whether the Christian prayers
or the pagan self-sacrifice bring the rain (it does come) is not to
be known. Reason must insist that drought comes in cycles
and the current cycle quite naturally came to an end at this
time.

To a God Unknown is not about reason. It is perhaps an exaggeration of a kind of reality based on instinctual needs and
primal forces; yet it is to the point. If outrageous, it also reflects an old pagan view which once had validity and which
still reaches us through the unconscious, perhaps as a warning

that if twentieth-century man loses touch with the earth his intellectual enlightment, his organized religions, and his technology will not save him. There is, obviously, another kind of reality, based upon collective social concerns such as conformity to what is considered normal behavior and upon the reasonable and traditional attitudes of the American's European heritage. Burton feels that his brother Joseph might have been saved had he remained in Vermont with its stronger European influence; it is the West which has somehow lured Joseph into damnation. Steinbeck writes within the western (and American) tradition of ambivalence toward good and evil as associated with the West. From the plot of *To a God Unknown*, Steinbeck's position seems clear: Joseph has found his own kind of salvation, his own sense of what is right and good, through ultimate self-sacrifice, giving his own life for that of the many lives in the valley. But it is not clear, finally, whether his sacrifice brought the rain, or whether Father Angelo's prayer brought it, or whether the normal wet-dry cycle had run its course and everything else is purely coincidental. What is more important is that Joseph's act dramatizes the distinction between two beliefs, stated in terms of heaven and hell (which are themselves subject to ambivalent reactions since they may be seen as spiritual or as factors in the American idea of wealth as a sign of not only material progress but also salvation—the election of Calvinistic doctrine).

The belief in the holiness of the land appears most strongly in Steinbeck during the 1930s (see also *The Grapes of Wrath* and *In Dubious Battle*, 1936) when western lands were eroding and the topsoil was blowing away, so that a natural occurrence, in addition to political and moral problems concerning the poverty-stricken classes of the West, may well have intensified Steinbeck's feelings about the role of the land. Nevertheless, similar feelings—taking different directions— continue to appear in more recent literature, even in rather unlikely places such as the short stories of an ex-cowboy whose novels are somewhat lighthearted, usually humorous, employing both pathos and pessimism in order to portray the contemporary cowboy exactly as he is. The only heroics to appear in Max Evans's novels are very small and are limited to situations in which courage and endurance can provoke either sadness or wry laughter. What defeats the two cowboys in Evans's best-known novel, *The Rounders* (1960) is simply a homicidal horse named Old Fooler. "The Great Wedding" (in *The One-Eyed Sky*, 1963) is a sequel to *The Rounders*, its plot even less elaborate, its humor more pronounced. Dusty Jones volunteers himself and his friend Wrangler Lewis for all the dirty jobs on Jim Ed Love's ranch so that Wrangler will hate the work enough to accept an alternative—the courting of a wealthy widow. These are homespun narratives in tone and incident, attentive to human nature but not overly profound, aimed at entertainment as much as at revelation. As the saddle-weary cowboy says in "The Great Wedding," "It's pretty hard to think with a numb ass." But the people of this community and the similar one in *The Hi Lo Country* (1961) are affected by the land, the change of seasons, the wind, and the elemental facts of nature, and Evans is sensitive to forces and mysteries both within man and without. The precise and stark novella, "The One-Eyed Sky," pits a cow with her newborn calf against a coyote with four young pups. In this basic conflict within nature survival is the only achievement, and it depends on a death. As the drama runs its course and the cow and coyote face each other for the last time, a man enters the arena, quite by accident. His presence seems strange, almost unwelcome, just as Joe Sam's naked footprint in the snow seemed out of place in Clark's *Track of the Cat*. The creatures have no choice—they must fight. It is the man who is indecisive—it "had always been so." When, at last, he acts, he unaccountably shoots two of the coyote pups, the sound of the shots causing the old coyote to veer slightly in her charge at the cow, exposing herself to one of the splintered horns upon which she is then impaled by the cow's desperate reaction. The man walks away, wondering why he shot the pups, thinking that he knew, at least for an instant, but now cannot remember. Even though the coyote dies in this story (two pups, of course, survive), the coyote of myth and legend is many things, including the creator of man. More realistically—although the concept may seem romantic on first thought—the coyote is the only true survivor. One of Max Evans's most complex stories, "Candles in the Bottom of the Pool" (1973), speaks prophetically of the coyotes: "As long as they howl, people have a chance here on earth. No longer, no less. It is the final cry for freedom. It's home."

This is not nostalgia, nor is it sentimentalism—although Evans is both realist and sentimentalist in his fiction, as the cowboy is in fact. It is a statement of the values of the land, and a prediction that if man destroys his natural world he will also destroy himself. In the process of doing so he may first destroy those fellow men of his who believe in the coyote or in the necessity of wilderness. One such victim is Jack Burns, the tragic hero of Edward Abbey's novel, *The Brave Cowboy.* Unfortunately, because of Abbey's inability to get the most out of his themes and characters, Burns may be taken for a fool rather than a hero, and the implied tragedy may erode away into pathos. Having attempted to free his friend, Paul Bondi, from jail, Burns runs from the law. Magnificent in his elusiveness, he takes to the mountains with horse and rifle and successfully defies a modern police force equipped with helicopters, radios, machine guns, and all the paraphernalia of law enforcement in a technological society. Burns is finally killed when he and his horse try to cross a busy highway.

> From the black arroyo came the scream of the horse, then the sound of the first shot and another scream;—while over the great four-lane highway beside them the traffic roared and whistled and thundered by, steel, rubber, and flesh, dim faces behind glass, beating hearts, cold hands—the fury of men and women immured in engines.

The emotional impact of this concluding passage in the novel is unmistakable, but its meaning must come through a symbolic interpretation lifted out of the melodrama. Relying on conventional patterns of action and characterization in the formula western, even while he aims at something modern, Abbey does not succeed in engaging the past and the present either through the intuition or through the philosophical implications of contemporary problems. When Bondi, jailed because of his refusal to submit to the military draft, also refuses to participate in a jailbreak, Burns can find no solution other than striving to keep his own physical freedom. With both men the major problem is that of the individual conflicting with the institution, the social and political establishment. Bondi prefers a kind of martyrdom in jail, while Burns flees to the hills. The Old West and the New West go their separate ways—wherein the novel fails—and in a disruption of continuity the old provides nothing for the new.

Nevertheless, in Evans and Abbey it is not essentially nostalgia for the past, finally, that prompts them to lament the loss of a nature-oriented way of life; it is, rather, a hard contemporary realization that a nonlanded society which is continually separating itself from the lessons of the past and from intuitive knowledge may soon destroy itself in a welter of mistaken values. As Frank Waters said in *People of the Valley*, it is not progress but fulfillment that man must seek and cherish. The Western novel is rarely didactic—perhaps because it is basically nonintellectual—but its historical or symbolic or intuitive revelation of man's condition is vital to his well-being, both now and in the future. The Western novel, rooted in the past, is prophetic. At its best it achieves a unifying vision of past, present, and future. Such a unity is possible only through a corresponding unity or harmony of man and the earth he walks upon.

Works Cited

Abbey, Edward. *The Brave Cowboy*. New York: Dodd, Mead and Company, 1956.

Adams, Andy. *The Log of a Cowboy*. Boston: Houghton Mifflin, 1903.

Adams, Henry. *The Education of Henry Adams*. Edited by Ernest Samuels. Boston: Houghton Mifflin, 1974.

Applegate, Jesse. "A Day With the Cow Column in 1843." *Overland Monthly* 1 (August 1868): 127–33.

Arnold, Elliott. *Blood Brother*. New York: Duell, Sloan and Pearce, 1947.

Austin, Mary. *The Land of Little Rain*. Boston: Houghton Mifflin, 1903.

———. "Regionalism in American Fiction." *English Journal* 21 (February 1932): 97–107.

Baker, Warren J. "The Stereotyped Western Story, Its Latent Meaning and Psychoeconomic Function." *Psychoanalytic Quarterly* 24 (April 1955): 270–80.

Berry, Don. *Moontrap*. New York: Viking, 1962.

———. *Trask*. New York: Viking, 1960.

Binns, Archie. *The Land Is Bright*. New York: Scribner's, 1939.

Bird, Robert Montgomery. *Nick of the Woods; or, The Jibbenainosay*. Edited by Curtis Dahl. New Haven: College and University Press, 1967.

———. *The Hawks of Hawks-Hollow*. Philadelphia: Carey, Lea, Blanchard, 1835.

Bishop, John Peale. "The Strange Case of Vardis Fisher." *Southern Review* 3 (1937–38): 348–59.

Blake, Forrester. *Johnny Christmas*. New York: Morrow, 1948.

———. *Wilderness Passage*. New York: Random House, 1953.

Bode, Carl. "Henry James and Owen Wister." *American Literature* 26 (May 1954): 251–52. (Includes letter from James to Wister, written in 1902.)

Brand, Max. *Destry Rides Again.* New York: Dodd, Mead, 1930.

———. *The Untamed*. New York: G. P. Putnam's, 1919.

Brown, Harry. *The Stars in Their Courses*. New York: Knopf, 1960.

Burroughs, Edgar Rice. *Tarzan of the Apes*. 1912. Reprint. New York: Ballantine Books, 1963.

Cahill, Holger. *The Shadow of My Hand*. New York: Harcourt, Brace and Company, 1956.

Carver, Jonathan. *Travels Through the Interior Parts of North America*. 1781. Facsimile reprint. Minneapolis: Ross and Haines, 1956.

Cather, Willa. *Death Comes for the Archbishop*. New York: Knopf, 1927.

Cawelti, John G. *The Six-Gun Mystique*. Bowling Green: Bowling Green University Popular Press, 1970.

Clark, Walter Van Tilburg. *The City of Trembling Leaves*. New York: Random House, 1945.

———. *The Ox-Bow Incident*. New York: Random House, 1940.

———. *The Track of the Cat*. New York: Random House, 1949.

———. *The Watchful Gods and Other Stories*. New York: Random House, 1950. (All stories mentioned in text are in this volume.)

———. "Conversation with Walter Van Tilburg Clark." *South Dakota Review* 9 (Spring 1971): 27–38.

———. "Strange Hunting." *South Dakota Review* 11 (Autumn 1973): 7–22.

Cooper, James Fenimore. *The Deerslayer*. New York: Washington Square Press, 1961.

———. *The Last of the Mohicans*. Boston: Houghton Mifflin, 1958.

———. *The Prairie*. New York: Rinehart, 1950.

Corle, Edwin. *Fig Tree John*. New York: Liveright, 1935.

Davis, H. L. *Beulah Land*. New York: Morrow, 1949.

———. *The Distant Music*. New York: Morrow, 1957.

———. *Harp of A Thousand Strings*. New York: Morrow, 1947.

———. *Honey in the Horn*. New York: Harper and Brothers, 1935.

De Voto, Bernard. "Birth of an Art." *Harper's Magazine* 211 (December 1955): 8–9, 12, 14, 16.

————. "Phaëthon on Gunsmoke Trail." *Harper's Magazine* 209 (December 1954): 10–11, 14, 16.

Dos Passos, John. *U.S.A.* New York: Random House, Modern Library, 1937.

Dreiser, Theodore. *An American Tragedy.* 2 vols. New York: Boni and Liveright, 1925.

————. *Sister Carrie.* New York: Doubleday, Page and Company, 1900.

————. *The Financier.* New York and London: Harper, 1912.

Drummond, C. Q. "Nature: Meek Ass or White Whale?" *Sage,* Spring 1966, pp. 71–84.

Durham, Philip. "Riders of the Plains: American Westerns." *Neuphilologische Mitteilungen* 58 (1957): 22–38.

Eastlake, William. *The Bronc People.* New York: Harcourt, Brace and Company, 1958.

————. *Portrait of an Artist with Twenty-six Horses.* New York: Simon and Schuster, 1963.

Ellis, Edward S. *Seth Jones; or, The Captives of the Frontier.* New York: Beadle and Adams, 1860. (No. 8 in the Beadle's Dime Novels.)

Evans, Max. "Candles in the Bottom of the Pool." *South Dakota Review* 11 (Autumn 1973): 110–36.

————. *The Hi Lo Country.* New York: Macmillan, 1961.

————. *The One-Eyed Sky.* Boston: Houghton Mifflin, 1963.

————. *The Rounders.* New York: Macmillan, 1960.

Farrell, James T. *Studs Lonigan.* New York: Random House, Modern Library, 1938.

Faulkner, William. *Sartoris.* New York: Harcourt, Brace, 1929.

————. *The Sound and the Fury.* New York: Cape and Smith, 1929.

Fergusson, Harvey, *The Blood of the Conquerors.* New York: Knopf, 1921.

————. *The Conquest of Don Pedro.* New York: Morrow, 1954.

————. "Conversation with Harvey Fergusson." *South Dakota Review* 9 (Spring 1971): 39–45.

————. *Footloose McGarnigal.* New York: Knopf, 1930.

————. *Grant of Kingdom.* New York: Morrow, 1950.

————. "The Image in Fiction." *South Dakota Review* 11 (Autumn 1973): 85–86.

————. *In Those Days.* New York: Knopf, 1929.

————. Introduction to *Followers of the Sun: A Trilogy of the Santa Fe Trail.* New York: Knopf, 1936.

————. *The Life of Riley.* New York: Knopf, 1936.

————. *Wolf Song.* New York: Knopf, 1927.

Fisher, Vardis. *April: A Fable of Love.* Caldwell, Idaho: Caxton, 1937.

————. *Adam and the Serpent.* New York: Vanguard, 1947.

————. *Children of God.* New York: Harper and Brothers, 1939.

————. *City of Illusion.* New York: Harper and Brothers, 1941.

————. *Dark Bridwell.* Boston: Houghton Mifflin, 1931.

————. *Darkness and the Deep.* New York: Vanguard, 1943.

————. *The Divine Passion.* New York: Vanguard, 1948.

————. *Forgive Us Our Virtues.* Caldwell, Idaho: Caxton, 1938.

————. *A Goat for Azazel.* Denver: Alan Swallow, 1956.

————. *The Golden Rooms.* New York: Vanguard, 1944.

————. *Intimations of Eve.* New York: Vanguard, 1946.

————. *In Tragic Life.* Caldwell, Idaho: Caxton, 1932.

————. *The Island of the Innocent.* New York: Abelard, 1952.

————. *Jesus Came Again.* Denver: Alan Swallow, 1956.

————. *Love and Death.* Garden City, New York: Doubleday, 1959.

————. *Mountain Man.* New York: Morrow, 1965.

————. *The Mothers.* New York: Vanguard, 1943.

————. *My Holy Satan.* Denver: Alan Swallow, 1958.

————. *No Villain Need Be.* Caldwell, Idaho: Caxton; Garden City, New York: Doubleday, 1936.

————. *Orphans in Gethsemane.* Denver: Alan Swallow, 1960.

————. *Passions Spin the Plot.* Caldwell, Idaho: Caxton; Garden City, New York: Doubleday, 1934.

————. *Peace Like a River.* Denver: Alan Swallow, 1957.

————. *Pemmican.* Garden City, New York: Doubleday, 1956.

————. *Tale of Valor.* Garden City, New York: Doubleday, 1958.

————. *Toilers of the Hills.* Boston: Houghton Mifflin, 1928.

————. *The Valley of Vision.* New York: Abelard, 1951.

————. *We Are Betrayed.* Caldwell, Idaho: Caxton; Garden City, New York: Doubleday, 1935.

Fitzgerald, F. Scott. *The Great Gatsby.* New York: Scribner's, 1925.

Garrard, Lewis H. *Wah-to-Yah and the Taos Trail.* Edited by Ralph P. Bieber. Glendale, California: The Arthur H. Clark Company, 1938.

Gastil, Raymond D. *Cultural Regions of the United States*. Seattle: University of Washington Press, 1975.

Gregg, Josiah. *Commerce of the Prairies*. Philadelphia: Lippincott, 1962.

Grey, Zane. *The Heritage of the Desert*. New York: Grosset and Dunlap, 1910.

————. *Riders of the Purple Sage*. New York: Grosset and Dunlap, 1912.

————. *Spirit of the Border*. New York: A. L. Burt Company, 1906.

Gruber, Frank. "The Basic Western Novel Plots." *Writer's Year Book*, 1955, pp. 49–53, 160.

Gulick, Bill. *White Men, Red Men and Mountain Men*. Boston: Houghton Mifflin, 1955.

Guthrie, A. B., Jr. *Arfive*. Boston: Houghton Mifflin, 1971.

————. *The Big Sky*. New York: Sloane, 1947.

————. *The Last Valley*. Boston: Houghton Mifflin, 1975.

————. *These Thousand Hills*. Boston: Houghton Mifflin, 1956.

————. *The Way West*. New York: Sloane, 1949.

Hall, Oakley. *Warlock*. New York: Viking, 1958.

Hart, John Fraser. "The Middle West." *Annals of the Association of American Geographers* 62, no. 2 (June 1972): 258–82.

Harte, Bret. *The Outcasts of Poker Flat and Other Tales*. New York: New American Library, 1961. (Includes stories discussed in text.)

Hawthorne, Nathaniel. *The House of the Seven Gables*. New York: Rinehart, 1957.

Haycox, Ernest. *Bugles in the Afternoon*. Boston: Little, Brown, 1944.

————. *The Earthbreakers*. Boston: Little, Brown, 1952.

————. *The Wild Bunch*. Boston: Little, Brown, 1943.

Hemingway, Ernest. *To Have and Have Not*. New York: Scribner's, 1937.

Horgan, Paul. *The Common Heart*. New York: Harper and Brothers, 1942.

————. *A Distant Trumpet*. New York: Farrar, Straus and Cudahy, 1960.

————. *Far from Cibola*. New York: Farrar, Straus and Giroux, 1936.

Irving, Washington. *A Tour on the Prairies*. Philadelphia: Carey, Lea and Blanchard, 1835.

James, Henry. *The Portrait of a Lady*. Boston: Houghton Mifflin, 1963.

————. *Washington Square.* New York: Dell Publishing Company, 1959.

Jilliffe, Robert A., ed. *Faulkner at Nagano.* Tokyo: Kenhyusha Ltd., 1956.

Johannsen, Albert. *The House of Beadle and Adams.* Vol. 2. Norman: University of Oklahoma Press, 1950.

Jung, C. G. *Memories, Dreams, Reflections.* Rev. Ed. New York: Pantheon Books, 1973.

King, Clarence. *Mountaineering in the Sierra Nevada.* Lincoln, Nebraska: University of Nebraska Press, 1970.

Lawrence, D. H. *Apocalypse.* New York: Viking, Compass Books, 1966.

————. *Studies in Classic American Literature.* Garden City, New York: Doubleday, 1955.

————. *The Woman Who Rode Away.* New York: Knopf, 1928.

Lewis, Meriwether. *The Lewis and Clark Expedition.* Philadelphia: Lippincott, 1961.

MacLeish, Archibald. "Sweet Land of Liberty." *Collier's* 136 (July 8, 1955): 44–55.

McMurtry, Larry. *Horseman, Pass By.* New York: Harper and Row, 1961.

————. *The Last Picture Show.* New York: Dial Press, 1966.

Manfred, Frederick. *Conquering Horse.* New York: McDowell, Obolensky, 1959.

————. *The Golden Bowl.* St. Paul: Webb Publishing Company, 1944. (Published under pen name, Feike Feikema.)

————. *King of Spades.* New York: Trident Press, 1966.

————. *Lord Grizzly.* New York: McGraw-Hill, 1954.

————. *Riders of Judgment.* New York: Random House, 1957.

————. *Scarlet Plume.* New York: Trident Press, 1964.

————. *Wanderlust.* Denver: Alan Swallow, 1962. (A revised one-volume edition of *The Primitive,* 1949, *The Brother,* 1950, and *The Giant,* 1951, all published under the pen name Feike Feikema, by Doubleday, and known by the overall title *World's Wanderer.*)

Meyer, Roy W. *The Middle Western Farm Novel in the Twentieth Century.* Lincoln, Nebraska: University of Nebraska Press, 1965.

Milton, John R., ed. *Conversations with Frank Waters.* Chicago: The Swallow Press, 1971.

Muir, John. *My First Summer in the Sierra.* Boston: Houghton Mifflin, 1911.

Nicollet, Joseph. "From Fort Pierre to Devils Lake." In *Exploring the Northern Plains*, edited by Lloyd McFarling. Caldwell, Idaho: The Caxton Printers, 1955.

Norris, Frank. *The Octopus*. Garden City, New York: Doubleday, 1947.

Parkman, Francis. *The Oregon Trail*. New York: Random House, 1949.

Paulding, James Kirke. *Westward Ho!* New York: J. & J. Harper, 1832.

Richter, Conrad. *The Sea of Grass*. New York: Knopf, 1937.

Russell, Osborne. *Journal of a Trapper*. Edited by Aubrey L. Haines. Portland: Oregon Historical Society, 1955.

Ruxton, George Frederick. *Life in the Far West*. Edited by LeRoy R. Hafen. Norman: University of Oklahoma Press, 1951.

Schaefer, Jack. *Shane*. Boston: Houghton Mifflin, 1949.

Simms, William Gilmore. *The Yemassee*. Edited by Alexander Cowie. New York: American Book Company, 1937.

Siringo, Charles A. *A Texas Cowboy*. New York: William Sloane, 1950.

Smith, Henry Nash. *Virgin Land*. Cambridge: Harvard University Press, 1950.

Stegner, Wallace. *Angle of Repose*. Garden City, New York: Doubleday, 1971.

———. *The Big Rock Candy Mountain*. New York: Duell, Sloan and Pearce, 1943.

———. Foreword to *Conversations with Frederick Manfred*, moderated by John R. Milton. Salt Lake City: The University of Utah Press, 1974.

———. *Recapitulation*. Garden City, New York: Doubleday, 1979.

———. *Wolf Willow: A History, a Story, and a Memory of the Last Plains Frontier*. New York: Viking, 1962.

Steinbeck, John. *In Dubious Battle*. New York: Covici-Friede, 1936.

———. *The Grapes of Wrath*. New York: Viking, 1939.

———. *To a God Unknown*. New York: Robert O. Ballou, 1933.

———. *The Wayward Bus*. New York: Viking, 1947.

Stephens, Ann S. *Malaeska*. New York: Beadle and Adams, 1860. (No. 1 in the Beadle's Dime Novels.)

Straight, Michael. *A Very Small Remnant*. New York: Knopf, 1963.

———. *Carrington*. New York: Knopf, 1960.

Tocqueville, Alexis de. *Democracy in America*. New York: New

American Library, 1956.

Turner, Frederick Jackson. *The Frontier in American History.* New York: Henry Holt and Company, 1920.

Twain, Mark. *Roughing It.* New York: Harper and Brothers, 1913.

Walcutt, Charles Child. *American Literary Naturalism, A Divided Stream.* Minneapolis: University of Minnesota Press, 1956.

"Walter Van Tilburg Clark." *Twentieth Century Authors,* First Supplement, edited by Stanley J. Kunitz. New York: H. W. Wilson, 1955.

Waters, Frank. *Below Grass Roots.* New York: Liveright, 1937.

————. *The Dust Within the Rock.* New York: Liveright, 1940.

————. *The Man Who Killed the Deer.* New York: Farrar and Rinehart, 1942.

————. *People of the Valley.* New York: Farrar and Rinehart, 1941.

————. *Pike's Peak.* Chicago: The Swallow Press, 1971.

————. *The Wild Earth's Nobility.* New York: Liveright, 1935.

————. *The Woman at Otowi Crossing.* Denver: Alan Swallow, 1966.

————. *The Yogi of Cockroach Court.* New York: Rinehart, 1947.

————. In "The Western Novel—A Symposium." *South Dakota Review* 2 (Autumn 1964): 10–16.

Webb, Walter Prescott. *The Great Plains.* Boston: Ginn and Company, 1931.

West, Ray B., ed. *A Country in the Mind.* Sausalito, California: Angel Island Publications, 1962.

Whitman, Walt. *Specimen Days & Collect.* Philadelphia: Rees Walsh and Company, 1882.

Williams, John. *Butcher's Crossing.* New York: Macmillan, 1960.

Winters, Yvor. *Collected Poems.* Denver: Alan Swallow, 1960.

Wister, Owen. *The Virginian.* New York: Macmillan, 1902.

Index

Abbey, Edward, 232; *The Brave Cowboy*, 316, 323–24; the past in, 316, 324
Adam and the Serpent (Fisher), 154–55
Adams, Andy: *The Log of a Cowboy*, 16
Adams, Clifton, 36
Adams, Henry: *The Education of Henry Adams*, 228, 298
Allen, Henry (pseud. Clay Fisher, Will Henry), 35
All the Young Men (La Farge), 68
American Indians. *See* Indians
American Tragedy, An (Dreiser), 90
Angle of Repose (Stegner), 300, 307; continuity in, 312
Anna Karenina (Tolstoy), 66
"Anonymous, The" (Clark), 222
Apocalypse (Lawrence), 272
Applegate, Jesse, 49
Apples of Paradise (Manfred), 68
April (Fisher), 151–52
Arfive (Guthrie), 162, 187
Arnold, Elliott, xiv
Austin, Mary, 18, 68, 213; on the land, 61, 62, 63, 85, 110, 272; *The Land of Little Rain*, 80, 102; on outsiders, 118

Ballard, Todhunter, 36
Barker, Warren J., 24–25
Beadle, Erastus, 9–10
Beadle's Half-Dime Library, 11
Below Grass Roots (Waters), 265, 273, 277–78

Berry, Don: *Moontrap*, 164; *Trash*, 164
Beulah Land (Davis), 304–5
Big It, The (Guthrie), 68
Big Rock Candy Mountain, The (Stegner), 93, 111, 113, 115, 307–9; the dream in, 301
Big Sky, The (Guthrie), 28, 62, 80, 161, 162, 179, 181, 186; form of, 114; journals and, 70–71; mountain man in, 46, 134, 165–69; compared with Fergusson's *Wolf Song*, 234
Binns, Archie: *The Land Is Bright*, 47, 181
Bird, Robert Montgomery: *The Hawks of Hawks-Hollow*, 8; *Nick of the Woods*, 8, 19
Bishop, John Peale, 142
Blacker, Irwin, 248
Blake, Forrester: *Johnny Christmas*, 46, 134, 164; mountain man in, 46; *Wilderness Passage*, 46, 164
Blood of the Conquerors (Fergusson), 117, 234, 243–47
Blood on the Land (Bonham), 33
Bold Passage (Bonham), 33
Bonham, Frank: *Blood on the Land*, 33; *Bold Passage*, 33
Book of the Hopi (Waters), 264
Boone, Daniel, xi, 5
Bower, B. M., 22; *Her Prairie Knight*, 32; *Rowdy of the "Cross L"*, 32. *See also* Sinclair, Bertha
Brand, Max, xiv, 22, 35; *Destry Rides*

333

Again, 23; *The Untamed*, 33; violence in, 23. *See also* Faust, Frederick
Bravados, The (O'Rourke), 33
Brave Cowboy, The (Abbey), 316, 323–24
Bronc People, The (Eastlake), 276–77
Brown, Charles Brockden, 81
Brown, Harry: *The Stars in Their Courses*, 37, 38
"Buck in the Hills, The" (Clark), 209, 224; nature in, 220–21
Buckskin Man Tales (Manfred), 162–63, 187–94; compared with Leatherstocking Tales, 163
Buffalo Bill. *See* Cody, Buffalo Bill
Bullough, Edward, 132, 141
Bunker, Robert: *Crow Killer*, 133
Buntline, Ned. *See* Judson, Edward Z. C.
Burns, Tex, 35. *See also* L'Amour, Louis
Burroughs, Edgar Rice: *Tarzan of the Apes*, 34–35
Butcher's Crossing (Williams), 101
Bynner, Witter, 69

Cahill, Holger: *The Shadow of My Hand*, 20
Caldwell, Erskine, 139, 142
"Candles in the Bottom of the Pool" (Evans), 323
Capps, Benjamin, xiv
Carrington (Straight), 107
Carver, Jonathan, 72
Cather, Willa, xi, xiv; change in, 318–19; *Death Comes for the Archbishop*, 118, 316–17, 318–19; criticized by Fergusson, 118; the land in, 319; the past in, 316–17
Cawelti, John G., 4; *The Six-Gun Mystique*, 26; on violence, 26
Centuries of Santa Fe, The (Horgan), 313
Chadwick, Joseph, 36
Children of God (Fisher), 123–24, 132, 135
City of Illusion (Fisher), 124–26
City of the Living and Other Stories, The (Stegner), 68
City of Trembling Leaves (Clark), 113, 196, 197, 198, 201, 228, 298, 303; analyzed, 211–16; dualities in, 201; unity in, 199, 298–300
Clark, Walter Van Tilburg, xiv, 49, 111; biographical sketch of, 195–96; black and white imagery in, 207–8; non-romantic cowboy in, 202–3; cycles in, 113; duality in, 197–98, 205, 227–28; compared with Fergusson, 197;

Indians in, 221–22; Jungian and Freudian interpretations of, 225–28; the land in, 54, 61–62, 109, 111, 299, 309; nature symbolism in, 126, 206–9 passim, 211, 217, 219–21, 223–24; Nazism and, 201; mobility in, 99–100; the primitive in, 228; unity in, 80, 198–200, 227–28, 298–300; compared with Waters, 200, 267–69; western regionalism in, 204–5; western style of, 197–98, 213–15; wonder in, 212–13. WORKS: "The Anonymous," 222; "The Buck in the Hills," 209, 220–21, 224; *City of Trembling Leaves*, 113, 196, 197, 198, 199, 201, 211–16, 228, 298, 303; "Hook," 224; "The Indian Well," 221, 224; *The Ox-Bow Incident*, 54, 109, 113, 116, 196–211 passim, 217, 254, 268–69, 309, 315; "The Rapids," 228; *The Track of the Cat*, 54, 61–62, 99–100, 101, 125, 196–201 passim, 209, 211, 216–29, 268–69, 286, 307, 322; *The Watchful God and Other Stories*, 68; "The Watchful Gods," 223–24; "Why Don't You Look Where You're Going?", 206

Cody, Buffalo Bill, 10, 12, 15
Colorado mining trilogy (Waters), 265, 270–71, 273–74, 277–86. *See also Below Grass Roots; Dust Within the Rock, The; Wild Earth's Nobility, The*
Colt, Clem, 36. *See also* Nye, Nelson
Commerce of the Prairies (Gregg), 74
Common Heart, The (Horgan), 314
Conquering Horse (Manfred), 163–64, 189, 190–91
Conquest of Don Pedro, The (Fergusson), 199, 247–48, 250, 258–63
Conrad, Joseph: *Heart of Darkness*, 208, 217, 219
Cook, Will (pseud. James Keene), 36
Cooper, James Fenimore: character stereotyping in, 6–8; and the frontier, 5, 204; and Indians, 6–7; inprecise language of, 83–84; compared with Manfred, 163; violence in, 6; influence of on Western novel, 4–5, 81–87, 99; women in, 6. WORKS: *The Deerslayer*, 9, 85–86, 87; *The Last of the Mohicans*, 6, 86; Leatherstocking Tales, 5, 6, 7, 19, 81, 82; *Pioneers*, 5; *The Prairie*, 6, 83–84, 86, 87, 106, 146

Corle, Edwin, 49
Country in the Mind, A (West), 56
Covered Wagon, The (Hough), 181
Cowboy: as hero, 3–4, 15–16, 24–25, 34;
nonromantic in Clark, 202–3; in dime
novels, 11; stereotyping of, 15–17; var-
iations of, 26–28; in Wister, 19–20; and
women, 24–25
Cox, William R., 36
Crane, Stephen, 68, 100
Crow Killer (Thorp and Bunker), 133
Cunningham, Eugene, 22; *Texas Sheriff*,
33
Cushman, Dan, xiv

Dark Bridwell (Fisher), 57, 101, 111, 113–
14, 136, 140–47
Darkness and the Deep (Fisher), 154
Davis, H. L.: continuity in, 304–7; the
dream in, 300–301; the land in, 306;
realism in, 303–4; as a regionalist, 302–
3.
  WORKS: *Beulah Land*, 304–5; *The Distant
  Music*, 300–301, 305–7; *Harp of a
  Thousand Strings*, 301; *Honey in the Horn*,
  302–3
Dawson, Peter, 35. *See also* Faust,
Frederick
Deadwood Dick Library, 11
Death Comes for the Archbishop (Cather),
118, 316–17, 318–19
Deerslayer, The (Cooper), 9, 85–86, 87
Democracy in America (Tocqueville), 90–92
Desert Desperadoes, The (Nye), 33
Desperate Rider (O'Rourke), 33
Destry Rides Again (Brand), 23
De Voto, Bernard, 36–37; *The Uneasy
Chair*, 311
Dickens, Charles: *Great Expectations*, 66
Dime novel, 9–12
Distant Music, The (Davis), 300–301,
305–7
Distant Trumpet, A (Horgan), 313–14
Divine Passion, The (Fisher), 155
Door in the Wall, The (La Farge), 68
Dorson, Richard M., 133
Dos Passos, John, 100
Drago, Harry Sinclair (pseud. Will
Ermine, Bliss Lomax, Joseph Wayne),
35
Dreiser, Theodore, xi, 90, 100–101; *An
American Tragedy*, 90; *Sister Carrie*, 90
Durham, Philip, 24

Dust Within the Rock, The (Waters), 265,
278–79

Early Americana and Other Stories (Rich-
ter), 68
Earthbreakers, The (Haycox), 36
Eastlake, William, 107; the land in, 274,
276–77; compared with Waters, 279.
  WORKS: *The Bronc People*, 276–77; *Por-
  trait of an Artist with Twenty-Six Horses*,
  54, 111, 114, 274–76
Education of Henry Adams, The (Adams),
228
Eggleston, Edward, xi
Ellis, Edward, 5; *Seth Jones*, 10
Elston, Allan Vaughan, 36
Emerson, Ralph Waldo, 127
Ermine, Will, 35. *See also* Drago, Harry
Sinclair
Evans, Evan, 35. *See also* Faust, Frederick
Evans, Max: and the land, 63, 321–23; the
past in, 324.
  WORKS: "Candles in the Bottom of the
  Pool," 323; "The Great Wedding,"
  322; *The Hi Lo Country*, 322; *The One-
  Eyed Sky*, 322; *The Rounders*, 322
Evarts, Hal, 36

Fable, A (Faulkner), 263
Far From Cibola (Horgan), 301, 313,
314–16
Farrell, James T., 100–101
Faulkner, William, 81; contrasted with
Fisher, 135–36, 140–41, 142; on
lyricism, 60.
  WORKS: *A Fable*, 263; *Sartoris*, 135; *The
  Sound and the Fury*, 66, 140–41, 142
Faust, Frederick (pseud. Max Brand,
Peter Dawson, Evan Evans), 22; pro-
ductivity of, 35. *See also* Brand, Max
Fergusson, Harvey, xiii, 49; Anglo-
Spanish relations in, 45, 234, 242–43;
compared with Clark, 197; duality in,
246; as historical novelist, 106, 111,
230–31, 233, 257–58, 262–63; imagery
in, 249–50; Indians in, 237–38,
241–42, 251; the land in, 62, 231–32,
245–46, 255, 261–62; contrasted with
Fisher, 117–19; mountain man in, 46,
234–36; unity in, 80; compared with
Waters, 267; and serious western, 38.
  WORKS: *Blood of the Conquerors*, 117,
  234, 243–47; *The Conquest of Don Pedro*,

199, 247–48, 250, 258–63; *Followers of the Sun*, 234–47; *Footloose McGarnigal*, 247; *Grant of Kingdom*, 247–58; *In Those Days*, 234, 239–43; *The Life of Riley*, 243, 247; *Wolf Song*, 46, 111, 134, 164, 233, 234–39, 248, 250–51
Fighting Man (Gruber), 33
Fisher, Clay, 35. *See also* Allen, Henry
Fisher, Vardis, 49, 111, 199, 311; career summarized, 119–20; cycles in, 113–14; fear and hunger in, 120–21; contrasted with Falkner, 135–36, 140–41, 142; contrasted with Fergusson, 117–19; historical novels of, 119–20, 123, 132, 134–35; Idaho novels of, 119–20, 135–47; the land in, 54, 108, 111; mountain man in, 128–34; nature in, 101, 127–28, 133–34, 138–40; the past in, 94–95, 99; on rationality, 60; realism in, 122–23; time in, 44–45; unity in, 80; women in, 130–31.
WORKS: *Adam and the Serpent*, 154–55; *April*, 151–52; *Children of God*, 123–24, 132, 135; *City of Illusion*, 124–26; *Dark Bridwell*, 57, 101, 111, 113–14, 136, 140–47; *Darkness and the Deep*, 154; *The Divine Passion*, 155; *Forgive Us Our Virtues*, 151, 152; *A Goat for Azazel*, 155; *The Golden Rooms*, 154; *Intimations of Eve*, 154; *In Tragic Life*, 147, 148; *The Island of the Innocent*, 155–56; *Jesus Came Again*, 155; *Love and Death*, 68, 125; *The Mothers*, 123–24; *Mountain Men*, 128, 131, 132–34; *My Holy Satan*, 156–57; *No Villain Need Be*, 136, 147, 150–51; *Orphans in Gethsemane*, 157–59; *Passions Spin the Plot*, 147, 148; *Peace Like a River*, 156; *Pemmican*, 128–31; 132, 156; *Tale of Valor*, 46, 120–23, 126–27, 132, 156; *The Testament of Man*, 60, 94–95, 108, 119, 120, 130, 135, 147, 153–59, 207; *Toilers of the Hills*, 117, 135, 137–40, 147; *The Valley of Vision*, 155; *We Are Betrayed*, 147, 149–50; *The Wild Ones*, 140
Fitzgerald, F. Scott, 98–99; *The Great Gatsby*, 91, 98–99, 141
Flaubert, Gustave: *Madame Bovary*, 66, 141
Flint (L'Amour), 33
Followers of the Sun (Fergusson), 234–47
Footloose McGarnigal (Fergusson), 247
Foreman, L. L.: *The Renegade*, 33

Forgive Us Our Virtues (Fisher), 151, 152
Forster, E. M., 39
Fort Starvation (Gruber), 33
Frazee, Steve: *Lawman's Feud*, 33
Freeman, Mary Wilkins, 83
Freud, Sigmund: in Clark, 225–28

Garrard, Lewis, 71, 74–75; *Wah-to-yah and the Taos Trail*, 74–75
Gastil, Raymond D., xii
Glidden, Frederick (pseud. Luke Short), 22, 35
Goat for Azazel, A (Fisher), 155
Golden Bowl, The (Manfred), 95, 314
Golden Rooms, The (Fisher), 154
Grant of Kingdom (Fergusson), 247–58
Grapes of Wrath, The (Steinbeck), 104, 314 321
Graves, Morris, xiii
Great Expectations (Dickens), 66
Great Gatsby, The (Fitzgerald), 91, 98–99, 141
Great River: The Rio Grande in North American History (Horgan), 313
"Great Wedding, The" (Evans), 322
Gregg, Josiah: *Commerce of the Prairies*, 74
Grey, Zane, xiv, 22, 68; and creation of western novel, 5; fantasy in, 34; and formula western, 36–37; landscape in, 111; productivity of, 35.
WORKS: *Heritage of the Desert*, 22–23; *The Riders of the Purple Sage*, 16, 19, 32, 34; *The Spirit of the Border*, 19
Gruber, Frank: plot notations of, 26–29.
WORKS: *Fighting Man*, 33; *Fort Starvation*, 33; *Town Tamer*, 33
Gulick, Bill: *White Men, Red Men and Mountain Men*, 164
Guthrie, A. B., Jr.: authenticity of, 111; formulas in, 47–48; journalistic style of, 70–71; compared with Manfred, 161, 162–63, 187, 194; mountain man in, 46; openness and cycles in, 114–15; on the past, 160; time in, 45.
WORKS: *Arfive*, 162, 187; *The Big It*, 68; *The Big Sky*, 28, 46, 62, 70–71, 80, 114, 134, 161, 162, 165–69, 179, 181, 186, 234; *The Last Valley*, 162, 187; *These Thousand Hills*, 33, 71, 114, 161, 181, 182–87; *The Way West*, 36, 47, 71, 114, 161, 178–83

Hall, Oakley, xiv; *Warlock*, 37, 38

Halleran, Eugene E., 36
Harper's, 36
Harp of a Thousand Strings (Davis), 301
Hart, John Fraser, xii
Harte, Bret, 68; parallels with Cooper, 82–83; formula of, 12–14; landscape in, 111; and creation of western novel, 5. WORKS: "The Luck of Roaring Camp," 9, 12, 19, 83; "The Outcasts of Poker Flat," 9, 12, 14; "Tennessee's Partner," 83
Hawks of Hawks-Hollow, The (Bird), 8
Hawthorne, Nathaniel, 81; mobility in, 87–89, 92–94; and ties to western novelist, 99. WORKS: *The House of the Seven Gables*, 66, 88–89, 92–93; *Our Old Home*, 88
Haycox, Ernest, 68; and historical western, 36; productivity of, 35. WORKS: *The Earthbreakers*, 36; *The Wild Bunch*, 33
Heart of Darkness (Conrad), 208, 217, 219
Hecklemann, Charles N., 36
Hemingway, Ernest: *The Old Man and the Sea*, 263; *To Have and Have Not*, 289
Henry, Will, 35; *The Last Warpath*, 33; *No Survivors*, 33. See also Allen, Henry
Heritage of the Desert (Grey): violence in, 22–23
Her Prairie Knight (Bower), 32
Hi Lo Country, The (Evans), 322
Hondo (L'Amour), 33
Honey in the Horn (Davis), 302–3
"Hook" (Clark), 224
Hopalong Cassidy (Mulford), 32
Horgan, Paul, xiv; characterization in, 313; the dream in, 301; the land in, 314; reality in, 315–16; compared with Steinbeck and Manfred, 314. WORKS: *The Centuries of Santa Fe*, 313; *The Common Heart*, 314; *A Distant Trumpet*, 313–14; *Far From Cibola*, 301, 313, 314–16; *Great River: The Rio Grande in North American History*, 313; *Mountain Standard Time*, 313; *The Peach Stone*, 68
Horseman, Pass By (McMurtry), 232
Hough, Emerson: *The Covered Wagon*, 181
House of the Seven Gables, The (Hawthorne), 66, 88–89, 92–93
Huckleberry Finn (Twain), 66, 97
Huning, Franz, 231

Indians: in Clark, 221–22; in Cooper, 67, 222; in Fergusson, 237–38, 241–42, 251; in Manfred, 190–91; in Waters, 266–67, 283–84, 285, 292–97; in western novels, 8, 28, 44, 224, 226
"Indian Well, The" (Clark), 221, 224
In Dubious Battle (Steinbeck), 321
Ingraham, Prentiss, 11
In Those Days (Fergusson), 234, 239–43
Intimations of Eve (Fisher), 154
In Tragic Life (Fisher), 147, 148
Irving, Washington, 83; *A Tour on the Prairies*, 73
Island of the Innocent, The (Fisher), 155–56
It Can't Happen Here (Lewis), 201
Ivanhoe (Scott), 5

James, Edwin, 84
James, Henry, 18, 141; and innocence destroyed, 97–98; on mobility, 89–90. WORKS: *Portrait of a Lady*, 97–98; *Washington Square*, 66, 89–90
Jeffers, Robinson, 69; on wilderness, 85
Jesus Came Again (Fisher), 155
Jewett, Sarah Orne, 83
Johnny Christmas (Blake), 164; mountain man in, 46, 134
Johnson, Dorothy, 68
Judson, Edward Z. C. (pseud. Ned Buntline), 11
Jung, Carl Gustav: in Clark, 226–28; in Waters, 265–66

Keene, James, 36. See also Cook, Will
Kelton, Elmer, 36
King, Clarence, 79; *Mountaineering in the Sierra Nevada*, 78
King of Spades (Manfred), 164, 189, 191–92, 193
Knibbs, Henry Herbert, 22; *Partners of Chance*, 33

La Farge, Oliver: *All the Young Men*, 68; *The Door in the Wall*, 68; *A Pause in the Desert*, 68
L'Amour, Louis (pseud. Tex Burns), xiv; productivity of, 35. WORKS: *Flint*, 33; *Hondo*, 33; *Radigan*, 33; *Sackett*, 33; *Shalako*, 33; *Taggart*, 33
Land Is Bright, The (Binns), 47, 181
Land of Little Rain, The (Austin), 80, 102
Last of the Mohicans, The (Cooper), 6, 86
Last Picture Show, The (McMurtry), 232

Last Valley, The (Guthrie), 162, 187
Last Warpath, The (Henry), 33
Lawman's Feud (Frazee), 33
Lawrence, D. H.: *Apocalypse*, 272; *Studies in Classic American Literature*, 188, 193; "The Woman Who Rode Away," 272
Lea, Tom, xiv
Leatherstocking Tales (Cooper), 5, 81; compared with Manfred's *Buckskin Man Tales*, 163; frontier in, 204; pattern of, 82; popularity of, 7, 19; violence in, 6
Leighton, Lee, 35–36. *See also* Overholser, Wayne
Le May, Alan, xiv
Lewis, Sinclair: *It Can't Happen Here*, 201
Lewis and Clark, 49; in Fisher's novels, 120–21; journals of, 70–72
Life of Riley, The (Fergusson), 243, 247
Literary History of the United States, xiv–xv
Log of a Cowboy, The (Adams), 16
Lomax, Bliss, 35. *See also* Drago, Harry Sinclair
London, Jack, 68; naturalism in, 100
Long, Stephen H., 49, 72, 84
Long Valley, The (Steinbeck), 68
Lord Grizzly (Manfred), 113, 141, 164, 188, 199, 207, 263; compared with Fergusson's *Wolf Song*, 234; fresh start in, 91; irony in, 191; mountain man in, 46, 134, 169–78; pattern in, 116
Love and Death (Fisher), 68, 125
"Luck of Roaring Camp, The" (Harte), 9, 12, 19, 83

McGrath, Thomas, 69
MacLeish, Archibald, 41, 56
McMurtry, Larry: *Horseman, Pass By*, 232; *The Last Picture Show*, 232
Madame Bovary (Flaubert), 66, 141
Malaeska (Stephens), 9
Manfred, Frederick, 49, 60; compared with Cooper, 163; cycles in, 113; compared with Guthrie, 161, 162–63, 187, 194; compared with Horgan, 314; Indians in, 190–91; intrusion in, 188–89; irony in, 191–92; the land in, 111, 314; mountain man in, 46, 165, 169–78; nature symbolism in, 126; the past in, 95–96; Stegner on, 189; themes in, 188; time in, 44–45; women in, 192–93. WORKS: *Apples of Paradise*, 68; *Buckskin Man Tales*, 162–63, 187–94; *Conquering*

Horse, 163–64, 189, 190–91; *The Golden Bowl*, 95, 314; *King of Spades*, 164, 189, 191–92, 193; *Lord Grizzly*, 46, 91, 113, 116, 134, 141, 164, 169–78, 188, 191, 199, 207, 234, 263; *Riders of Judgment*, 164, 189, 192, 193–94; *Scarlet Plume*, 164, 191, 192–93; *World's Wanderer*, 95–96
Man in the Gray Flannel Suit, The, 57
Man Who Killed the Deer, The (Waters), 111, 113, 199, 264, 273, 274, 292–97
Masked Gods (Waters), 264
Maugham, Somerset: *Of Human Bondage*, 149
Melville, Herman, 99
Meredith, George: *Modern Love*, 147
Mexico Mystique (Waters), 269, 272
Meyer, Roy W., xiii
Modern Love (Meredith), 147
Moontrap (Berry), 164
Mothers, The (Fisher), 123–24
Mountaineering in the Sierra Nevada (King), 78
Mountain man: in Fergusson, 234–36; in Fisher, 128–34; in Guthrie, 165–69; in Manfred, 169–78; in westerns, 46, 164–66
Mountain Man (Fisher), 128, 131, 132–34
Mountain Standard Time (Horgan), 313
Muir, John, 18, 61, 85; *My First Summer in the Sierra*, 78–79
Mulford, Clarence E., 22; *Hopalong Cassidy*, 32
My First Summer in the Sierra (Muir), 78–79
My Holy Satan (Fisher), 156–57

Nick of the Woods (Bird), 8, 19
Nicollet, Joseph, 49, 72–73
Norris, Frank, 13; mysticism of, 288; naturalism in, 100; *The Octopus*, 101–6
No Survivors (Henry), 33
No Villain Need Be (Fisher), 136, 147, 150–51
Nye, Nelson (pseud. Clem Colt), 36; *The Desert Desperadoes*, 33

Octopus, The (Norris), 101–6
Of Human Bondage (Maugham), 149
Old Man and the Sea, The (Hemingway), 263
One-Eyed Sky, The (Evans), 322
Oregon Trail, The (Parkman), 71, 75–78, 167, 178–79

O'Rourke, Frank: *The Bravados*, 33; *Desperate Rider*, 33; *Warbonnet Law*, 33
Orphans in Gethsemane (Fisher), 157–59
Our Old Home (Hawthorne), 88
"Outcasts of Poker Flat, The" (Harte), 9, 12, 14
Overholser, Wayne (pseud. Lee Leighton; Joseph Wayne), 35; *The Violent Land*, 33
Overland Monthly, 12
Ox-Bow Incident, The (Clark), 109, 113, 196, 197, 217, 254, 268–69, 315; analyzed, 201–11; the land in, 309; nature in, 54; the past in, 200; pattern in, 116; unity in, 198–99

Parkman, Francis, 50, 75, 83, 126; *The Oregon Trail*, 71, 75–78, 167, 178–79
Partners of Chance (Knibbs), 33
Passions Spin the Plot (Fisher), 147, 148
Paulding, James Kirke: *Westward Ho!*, 8
Pause in the Desert, A (La Farge), 68
Peace Like a River (Fisher), 156
Peace Stone, The (Horgan), 68
Pemmican (Fisher), 128–31, 132, 156
People of the Valley, The (Waters), 287, 289–91, 296, 324
Pike, Zebulon, 72
Pike's Peak (Waters), 113, 279. *See also* Colorado mining trilogy
Pioneers (Cooper), 5
Porter, Katherine Anne, 68
Portrait of a Lady (Henry James), 97–98
Portrait of an Artist with Twenty-Six Horses (Eastlake), 54, 111, 114, 274–76
Prairie, The (Cooper), 6, 83–84, 86, 87, 106, 146
Pseudonyms, 24, 35–36
Psychoanalytic Quarterly, 24

Radigan (L'Amour), 33
Raine, William MacLeod, 22; productivity of, 35; *Square-Shooter*, 33
"Rapids, The" (Clark), 228
Recapitulation (Stegner), 300, 307, 309–12
Renegade, The (Foreman), 33
Rhodes, Eugene Manlove, 35, 68
Richter, Conrad: change in, 319; the land in, 319.
    WORKS: *Early Americana and Other Stories*, 68; *The Sea of Grass*, 317–18
Riders of Judgment (Manfred), 164, 189, 192, 193–94

Riders of the Purple Sage, The (Grey), 16, 19, 32; fantasy in, 34
Roethke, Theodore, 69
Roosevelt, Theodore, 17–18
Roughing It (Twain), 14; as journal, 79; compared with *The Virginian*, 18
Rounders, The (Evans), 322
Rousseau, Jean Jacques, 13, 146
Rowdy of the "Cross L" (Bower), 32
Russell, Osborne, 71
Ruxton, George, 71

Sackett (L'Amour), 33
Sartoris (Faulkner), 135
Scarlet Plume (Manfred), 164, 191, 192–93
Schaefer, Jack, xiv, 68; *Shane*, 37–38, 116
Scott, Walter, 3, 7, 19; *Ivanhoe*, 5
Scott, Winfield Townley, 69
Sea of Grass, The (Richter), 317–18
Seltzer, Charles Alden, 22
Seth Jones (Ellis), 10
Shadow of My Hand, The (Cahill), 20
Shalako (L'Amour), 33
Shane (Schaefer), 37–38, 116
Short, Luke, xiv, 22, 35. *See also* Glidden, Frederick
Simms, William Gilmoe: *The Yemassee*, 8
Sinclair, Bertha (pseud. B. M. Bower), 22. *See also* Bower, B. M.
Siringo, Charles A.: *A Texas Cowboy*, 16
Sister Carrie (Dreiser), 90
Six-Gun Mystique, The (Cawelti), 26
Sound and the Fury, The (Faulkner), 66, 140–41, 142
Spirit of the Border, The (Grey), 19
Square-Shooter (Raine), 33
Stafford, William, 69
Stars in Their Courses, The (Harry Brown), 37, 38
Stegner, Wallace, 49; continuity in, 300, 309–12; craft of, 307; cycles in, 113; the dream in, 301; the land in, 62, 308–9; on Manfred, 189.
    WORKS: *Angle of Repose*, 300, 307, 312; *The Big Rock Candy Mountain*, 93, 111, 113, 115, 301, 307–9; *The City of the Living and Other Stories*, 68; *Recapitulation*, 300, 307, 309–12; *Wolf Willow*, 181, 312; *The Women on the Wall*, 68
Steinbeck, John, xiii; modern frontier, 47; compared with Horgan, 314; the land in, 314, 319–21.
    WORKS: *The Grapes of Wrath*, 104, 314,

321; *In Dubious Battle*, 321; *The Long Valley*, 68; *To a God Unknown*, 57, 319–21; *The Wayward Bus*, 47, 261
Stephens, Mrs. S.: *Malaeska*, 9
Straight, Michael, 49; *Carrington*, *107; A Very Small Remnant*, 107
Studies in Classic American Literature (Lawrence), 188, 193
Swallow, Alan, 119, 264

Taggart (L'Amour), 33
Tale of Valor (Fisher), 46, 120–23, 126–27, 132, 156
Tarzan of the Apes (Burroughs), 34–35
"Tennessee's Partner" (Harte), 83
Testament of Man, The (Fisher), 60, 94–95, 108, 119, 120, 128, 135, 147, 153–59, 207
Texas Cowboy, A (Siringo), 16
Texas Sheriff (Cunningham), 33
These Thousand Hills (Guthrie), 33, 71, 114, 161, 181, 182–87
Thorp, Raymond W.: *Crow Killer*, 133
To a God Unknown (Steinbeck), 57; the land in, 319–21
Tocqueville, Alexis de: *Democracy in America*, 90–92
To Have and Have Not (Hemingway), 289
Toilers of the Hills (Fisher), 117, 135, 147; analyzed, 137–40
Tolstoy, Leo: *Anna Karenina*, 66
Tour on the Prairies, A (Irving), 73
Town Tamer (Gruber), 33
Track of the Cat, The (Clark), 99–100, 101, 125, 196, 197, 198, 211, 268–69, 286, 307, 322; analyzed, 216–29; dualities in, 201; dreams in, 209; the land in, 61–62; nature in, 54; unity in, 199–200
Trash (Berry), 164
Turner, Frederick Jackson, xi, 11, 25, 93, 205
Tuttle, W. C., 22
Twain, Mark, 303; mobility in, 97; influence of on Wister, 18–19.
WORKS: *Huckleberry Finn*, 66, 97; *Roughing It*, 14, 18, 79

Uneasy Chair, The (De Voto), 311
Untamed, The (Brand), 33

Valley of Vision, The (Fisher), 155
Very Small Remnant, A (Straight), 107
Violent Land, The (Overholser), 33

Virginian, The (Wister), 16, 37, 102; compared with *Roughing It*, 18; as *the* western novel, 17–22

Wah-to-yah and the Taos Trail (Garrard), 74–75
Walcutt, Charles Child, 56–57
Warbonnet Law (O'Rourke), 33
Warlock (Hall), 37, 38
Washington Square (Henry James), 66, 89–90
Watchful God and Other Stories, The (Clark), 68
"Watchful Gods, The" (Clark), 223–24
Waters, Frank, xiii, 49; compared with Austin, 272; authenticity of, 111; compared with Clark, 200, 267–69; cycles in, 113; duality in, 287–89; compared with Eastlake, 279; compared with Fergusson, 267; form in, 273–74; Indian influence on, 266–67, 283–84, 285; Indians in, 292–97; intuition in, 283–84; Jung in, 265–66; the land in, 111, 274, 279, 280–82, 284, 289, 299; compared with Lawrence, 272; mysticism of, 264, 267, 271–73, 274, 285; nature in, 54, 64; openness in, 114; oriental influence on, 226, 269; realism in, 287; growth in reputation of, 264; scope of work, 269–72; unity in, 80, 283, 299.
WORKS: *Below Grass Roots*, 265, 273, 277–78; *Book of the Hopi*, 264; Colorado mining trilogy, 265, 270–71, 273–74, 277–86; *The Dust Within the Rock*, 265, 278–79; *The Man Who Killed the Deer*, 111, 113, 199, 264, 273, 274, 292–97; *Masked Gods*, 264; *Mexico Mystique*, 269, 272; *The People of the Valley*, 287, 289–92, 296, 324; *Pike's Peak*, 113, 279; *The Wild Earth's Nobility*, 54, 265, 272, 277, 285; *The Woman at Otowi Crossing*, 270–71; *The Yogi of Cockroach Court*, 286–89
Wayne, Joseph, 35, 36. *See also* Drago, Harry Sinclair; Overholser, Wayne
Wayward Bus, The (Steinbeck), 261; modern frontier in, 47
Way West, The (Guthrie), 36, 161, 178–83; form of, 114; formulaic nature of, 47; journals and, 71
We Are Betrayed (Fisher), 147, 149–50
Webb, Walter Prescott, xii, 302
West, Ray B.: *A Country in the Mind*, 56

Western Writers, 28
Westward Ho! (Paulding), 8
Wheeler, Edward, 5, 10
White Men, Red Men and Mountain Men (Gulick), 164
Whitman, Walt, 50
"Why Don't You Look Where You're Going?" (Clark), 206
Wild Bunch, The (Haycox), 33
Wild Earth's Nobility, The (Waters), 265, 272, 277, 285; nature in, 54
Wilderness Passage (Blake), 46, 164
Wild Ones, The (Fisher), 140. *See also Dark Bridwell*
Williams, John: *Butcher's Crossing*, 101
Winters, Yvor, 69
Wister, Owen, 68; cowboy in, 19–20; influenced by Twain, 18–19; *The Virginian*, 16, 17–22, 37, 102; and creation

of western novel, 5
Wolfe, Thomas, 135, 142, 197
Wolf Song (Fergusson), 111, 164, 233, 234, 248, 250–51; analyzed, 234–39; mountain man in, 46, 134
Wolf Willow (Stegner), 181, 312
Woman at Otowi Crossing, The (Waters), 270–71
"Woman Who Rode Away, The" (Lawrence), 272
Women: chivalry toward, 23; in Cooper, 6; cowboy and, 24–25; in Fisher, 130–31; in Manfred, 192–93
Women on the Wall, The (Stegner), 68
World's Wanderer (Manfred), 95–96

Yemassee, The (Simms), 8
Yogi of Cockroach Court, The (Waters), 287–89; realism in, 286–87